THE TIGER IN THE SENATE

THE TIGER IN THE SENATE:

The Biography of

WAYNE MORSE

BY A. ROBERT SMITH

DOUBLEDAY & COMPANY, INC., GARDEN CITY, NEW YORK, 1962

LIBRARY OF CONGRESS CATALOG CARD NUMBER 61–12583
COPYRIGHT © 1962 BY A. ROBERT SMITH
ALL RIGHTS RESERVED
PRINTED IN THE UNITED STATES OF AMERICA
FIRST EDITION

To the one who first offered faith in a journalist's dreams
To one who widens the horizons of the mind and spirit
To one who cares
To Yvonne

CONTENTS

PART TWO: THE LAST SON OF THE WILD JACKASS

PART FOUR: NEW FRONTIERS

PREFACE

"I SOMETIMES wonder if I'm going at this a little too hard," Wayne Morse reflectively told a reporter of the Detroit *Free Press* after bolting the Republican party. "But then I think of all the men and women who wish there were just one politician in Washington who would speak his mind and cast his vote honestly and freely with only his conscience to guide him. Maybe it's a bit brash to assume that I'm that man, but believe me, I'm trying to be."

If this subjective view of his own uniqueness tells us much about Wayne Morse, it also invites many of the questions which I, as Washington correspondent for Oregon newspapers during the past ten years, have been asked: Is Wayne Morse sincere? Did that horse kick in the head really change him? What makes him tick? Is he a figure of historic importance? Now that this Oregon senator has battled his way to positions of authority as chairman of the Senate subcommittees on Latin America and on education, these questions assume more importance. In this biography, designed neither to please its proud principal nor to delight his bitter detractors, I have tried to portray Wayne Morse as he is, and to capture something of the mood and smell of Washington's political jungle.

But a bit more than curiosity about these questions was involved. Walter Lippmann, speaking of the responsibility of the Washington correspondent, has said, "If the country is to be governed with the consent of the governed, then the governed must arrive at opinions about what their governors want them to consent to."

They must, indeed, arrive at opinions about those who govern. The manifest responsibility of a free press in the exercise of this critical democratic function grows heavier. For as the population increases, the number of citizens who never meet, much less converse with, their senators and representatives multiplies. The politicians, seeking to overcome this widening gap, have adopted methods of the advertising world to persuade the voter. All media of mass communication are employed. But what they communicate is designed chiefly to serve the interest of their own political longevity.

How, then, does the sovereign citizen evaluate with any certainty the qualities and the deeds of the men he has sent to Washington? How does he test the product against the claims of the advertising and separate sham from reality? How does he judge where best to place his X on the ballot?

He must increasingly rely upon intelligible reports of events in Washington. The Washington correspondent, giving non-partisan allegiance to these inquiring citizens, makes it his business "to find out what is going on under the surface and beyond the horizon, to infer, to deduce, to imagine and to guess, what is going on inside, and what this meant yesterday, and what it could mean tomorrow," says Mr. Lippmann. "In this we do what every sovereign citizen is supposed to do, but has not the time or the interest to do for himself. This is our job."

To perform this job, I have had countless discussions with Senator Morse, his office staff, other senators and newspapermen, and a battalion of public and private men ranging from Harry S. Truman to Morse's kinfolk in rural Wisconsin. In addition to many candid participants in these recorded events, I am obliged to Mike Forrester and Jerry Uhrhammer and to those careful tenders of the files at the Universities of Oregon, Wisconsin, and Minnesota, the Truman and Roosevelt libraries, the Library of Congress and the Washington *Post*, the Madison *Capital-Times*, the *Oregonian*, and the Chevy Chase, D.C., Public Library. A collection of private letters in the University of Oregon, made available by Martin Schmitt with Senator Morse's sanction, proved exceptionally valuable. So were the senator's scrapbooks, which appeared to contain virtually everything ever published about the man over the past twenty years. I did not have random access to Morse's office files, nor did he review the manuscript in advance of publication. Allowing for the human frailties of fading memories and subjective appraisals, such errors as may persist simply evaded detection.

My debts are many for the helpfulness of others. The understanding aid and fond good wishes of my parents, Inez and Arthur R. Smith, has been a cherished factor of great consequence over the years. So has been the generosity of Johnnie and Layne Rush, the instruction and interest of A. William Engel, Jr., and Wayne Glick, and the constant faith of Gordon Cosby. I am most grateful for the priceless initial professional support of Alton F. Baker, Jr., and Julius Gius; the example of inspiring editorial writing by Charles A. Sprague, William M. Tugman, and J. W. Forrester, Jr., in my formative years as a correspondent; the encouragement and backing of Wendell Webb, Robert C. Notson, Herbert Lundy, and Eric Allen, Jr., in behalf of vigorous political reporting. The confidence of these editors through turbulent events of the past decade has been a treasured experience.

I have been specially favored by the kindness of Bill Tugman, for many years the crusading editor of the Eugene *Register-Guard*. He shared his memories and his voluminous files. Both offered vivid accounts of the thirties and forties, when he and Wayne Morse were frequent allies, as well as events which precipitated a later break. It might be presumptuous of me to challenge Mr. Tugman's assertion that "there are no great men." But Oregon's vigorous intellectual climate, which stimulates dissent, encourages tolerance, shuns mediocrity, and demands excellence in public life, is a monumental tribute to several great editors of recent decades. Bill Tugman is one of them.

I am equally grateful to my friend and excellent history teacher, Dr. Kenneth W. Crosby, of Juniata College, for the vitality of his classes and his many helpful observations upon reading the manuscript.

Completion of this book was immeasurably advanced by the enthusiasm and skillful editorial guidance of Mrs. Evelyn P. Metzger of Doubleday, and by the typing and photographic assistance, the stimulation and prayerful concern of friends at The Potter's House.

Most indispensable was the sacrificial service of my wife, Yvonne, who endured the household agonies imposed by this composition and its single-minded author. More importantly, she offered her excellent judgment, her candid and thoughtful criticism, her typing stamina, and her compassion throughout the long year past.

A. *Robert Smith*
National Press Building
Washington, D.C.

Part One

THE MAN OF LEGEND
AND MYSTERY

1. THE LEGEND

*Everyman's Senator . . . Early Days . . . The Swift Rise
. . . The Great Dissent . . . The Scrapper*

WHEN John Nance Garner descended for the last time from that
oddly remote pedestal in the Senate chamber to which Vice-presi-
dents are relegated, he and Senator Burton K. Wheeler of Montana
retreated to the Texan's private rooms. Squinting through a glass of
spirits, Cactus Jack mused to his companion, "The more I see of the
Senate, the more I am convinced that it is more important for a
senator to have guts than brains."

Wheeler understood instantly; for he had experienced the terrible
pressures that bear upon a United States Senator from every economic group threatened by this or that legislative proposal. If the
pressure is not exerted by a utility lawyer coldly snapping his briefcase
(and figuratively closing off that industry's coffers for the senator's
next election campaign), it is a delegation of aggrieved farmers
observing with gruff candor that if this bill goes through, the farmers
won't forget who was responsible. In this chamber of pressures, brains
are necessary to divine what is right and just and necessary for the
country. But it was Garner's—and it is Wheeler's—view that the
more precious quality is guts, the courage to withstand the pressure.

Sooner or later many a senator makes an accommodation. His
view becomes predictable. He escapes the pressure for a time by
taking refuge from one side within that tenuous security offered by
the other. He is a kept senator.

The Legend of Wayne Morse is that he is nobody's lackey. With
guts *and* brains he resists the pressures of every sort—of political party,
of his home state, of special-interest economic groups—to "exercise
an honest independence of judgment on the facts as I find them."
He remains predictably unpredictable. Moreover, he publicly rebukes all violators of this Morse code, scorning their expediency with
evangelistic moralisms.

Everyman's Senator

Such power and public appeal as have come uniquely to Wayne Morse are the fruits of this Legend. It is a Legend to which many Americans give visceral response. They are readily aroused against corruption in high places and conniving interests. They are frustrated by an awful sense of remoteness from the centers of authority in a nation where they are sovereign. They are cheered when a fresh knight appears to champion their cause, to challenge the power elite.

Wayne Morse, they know, is not one of the power elite. He is, rather, the knight who challenges the forces of evil in their behalf. Wayne Morse, the legendary fighter, is Everyman's senator, fighting Everyman's battles.

The Legend of the incorruptible warrior is important to this essentially puritanical society because the gravest crimes of public life, short of treason, are those varied indecencies which come under the heading of getting caught with a hand in the cooky jar. The hapless government official who takes a gift mink or vicuña must be cast out, for he is demonstrably a weak sentinel among the guardsmen who are sworn to protect justice for the many from the grasping design of the few. The Wayne Morse of Legend is a captain of those guardsmen, leading the charge of the just against giveaways of Everyman's resources, fearless in the face of powerful adversaries.

The legendary Wayne Morse never makes a deal and is no politician, in the unpleasant sense of those terms which exasperate clean-government middle-class America. Nor does he ever yield to the greasy behavior of those who *are* politicians and who *do* deal. Wayne Morse, the Legend, is the Eagle Scout of American politics: trustworthy, loyal, helpful . . . brave, clean, and reverent. He neither drinks, smokes, chews, nor takes snuff. High principle is his only master.

The Legend itself is a fusion of fact and fiction which mysteriously envelops a dynamic public figure. It takes form in the public mind as headlines, pictures, and appealing stories published in newspapers, magazines, and books bombard the reader with the man's vivid characteristics. It gains lasting substance when these storied qualities —he's a fighter; he's as honest as the day is long; he isn't afraid of anybody—become the traits by which he is identified and remembered in the public mind.

For the controversial figure, the Legend is all-important. It is a suit of armor which affords protection from the slings and arrows of his enemies. These opponents say Wayne Morse is an egomaniac, that he will stab anyone in the back who disagrees with him, that he has a flip-flop mind that lacks stability. They seek to create a counterlegend by widely distributing these contentions against him. That they threaten him, there is no question. But so long as the Legend of Wayne Morse is not destroyed or badly damaged, the man behind this knightly breastplate rides on to continued glory.

Wayne Morse is *from* Oregon, but he is *of* Wisconsin. Oregon could send Morse the maverick to Washington in election after election because of its own early romance with agrarian reformers. But only Wisconsin, the fountainhead of modern political unorthodoxy, could have produced and nurtured him. As Mary McGrory, the gifted political writer of the Washington *Star* once put it, "Wisconsin is a portly, Teutonic old lady, full of beer and cheese . . . [with] a weakness for wild men and underdogs."

To those who cherish party loyalty, and even to many a less partisan citizen, Wayne Morse has been a wild man as much as he has been a determined underdog. No one in public life today has successfully ventured to campaign under the banner of both major parties, much less endured a period when he scorned the emblem of either party.

Between those who swear *by* him and those who swear *at* him there is agreement only that he possesses extraordinary ability and remarkable talents. He is positively brilliant in the wide grasp of complex issues and in the art of persuasively communicating to others his point of view. "He can convince the average audience that black is white, and in the same speech put the switch on and make them believe that white is black after all," asserts Palmer Hoyt, editor and publisher of the Denver *Post* and a long-time friend. A deeply conservative Oregon trade-publication editor, the late Carl Crow, called Morse "one of the New Deal's most unconstitutional activities." Refusing to attend a Republican picnic in 1944 at which Morse was to speak, Crow explained, "That S.O.B. has changed my mind twice and I am not going to let him do it again."

This great power of persuasion holds the potential for advancement of the public good in the progressive La Follette tradition, but it also carries with it the danger of perversion to purely personal aggrandizement in the demagogic McCarthy fashion. In a sense both of these ghosts from Wisconsin's wild political past haunt the senator from Oregon, accentuating the mystery of the man as they wrestle for possession of his motive-control panel.

This mysterious internal struggle may explain why one towering liberal senator says of Wayne Morse, "He can be cruel, he is egotistical, but he is a very valuable senator." He has been cruel in personal encounters, behaving like a tiger in a primitive struggle for survival. He has been valuable in public encounters, performing with knightly courage in attacking wrongdoing. In either role he is virtually always pressing the attack, whether it be against the great financial interests, the press, the wire tappers, or his latest personal adversary.

How does a Legend start? When does it begin? Until a man becomes a figure of great consequence to others, he carries no Legend. If he is a colorful figure, he soon acquires one. Those who begin to forge the Legend look into his youth and find the ingredients. Certainly the Legend of Wayne Morse begins in Wisconsin. Here he was born on a homestead, reared to manhood, and educated. Here he drank at the spring of agrarian reform that bubbled up from the prairie and flowed out across the land until it had begun to inundate the old order. Here he learned that the best of all policies is short on party regularity and long on crusading insurgency, in the style of the greatest of the zealous political reformers, Senator Robert M. La Follette.

Early Days

Long before the Legend begins there is a youth. Wayne Morse's grandfather, John W. Morse, came west in a prairie schooner from Pennsylvania to claim his homestead in 1848, stopping in the gently rolling countryside ten miles west of Madison. There three generations of Morses were nourished by the Wisconsin soil. The homestead passed down from grandfather to father Wilbur, who in time handed it on to his eldest sons, Harry and Grant, the identical-twin brothers of Wayne.

More than any of the Morses before him, Wayne personified the American movement of his generation from the farm to the town. His farming was measured in the chores of the stable, the milkhouse, the wood box, until he was old enough to go off to the Madison city schools and, ultimately, to the great universities for the education his mother so yearned for him to have. His father had been to high school and his mother, Jessie White Morse, had been to Downer College at Milwaukee before becoming an eighteen-year-old bride. His brother Grant had managed a year at the University but reverted to farming for a livelihood. Brother Harry later earned his bachelor's degree at Wisconsin, only to return to the rural life of a county agent for the federal Farmers Home Administration. Wayne was the first of his line to make a complete break with the soil.

As a high-school boy, Wayne was regarded by teachers and classmates as bright and talkative. He loved to argue in history classes, but he flunked first-year Latin. "Wayne was better in subjects where ideas counted heavily," recalls a classmate. "Miss Wilson, the Latin teacher, accused him of trying to bluff his way through. Wayne had a great talent for giving the teacher a complete snow job." The trait did not soon vanish. Madison High's yearbook his senior year nicknamed him "Bluff."

A decade and more later, as law dean at the University of Oregon, Morse and a few faculty and town cronies gathered regularly for sociable penny-ante poker. Playing dealer's choice with two wild cards, recalls one of the players, "Wayne was a great bluffer. He liked the long chance. He didn't mind losing four pots if he could win the fifth by bluffing out a good hand with a poor one. He enjoyed that immensely." Where, after all, would be the craft of Legend building without a generous measure of bluffing?

To their pejorative nickname for Morse, the high school yearbook editors added this heroic couplet:

> "Courage, the highest gift, that scorns to bend
> To mean devices of a sordid end."

Whether one called it courage or used Garner's less socially acceptable term for it, here was a force on which a Legend could build. Along the twists and turns of a bold, adventurous career, the quality of courage has been a force of considerable propulsion for Wayne Morse.

At the University of Wisconsin Morse became a "big man on campus" as an orator and political activist. He took a master's in speech before going on to the University of Minnesota for his law degree, and then to Columbia for a doctorate in law with tutelage from Professors John Dewey and Raymond Moley. From Columbia he went directly to the University of Oregon at Eugene to become a professor.

The Swift Rise

Once he was embarked upon his professional career, the Legend began. For Wayne Morse's rise was swift. From an assistant professor of law in 1929 he became dean of the Oregon law school in two years. Specializing in criminal law as a student and professor, Morse helped draft an Oregon crime survey in 1934, and two years later became a special assistant to the Attorney General in Washington to complete work on a five-volume report on a national survey of prison release procedures.

During his deanship at Oregon, Morse became embroiled in the most tumultuous uprising in the state's history of higher education. In a series of brave and brilliant maneuvers, which shall be explored later, he challenged the powers of authority in a style which marked him permanently. Thus he emerged from obscurity in his newly adopted state and became a hero to faculty and students alike, who feared for the very life of the university. Here began the Legend of the knight who jousts with the great and evil dragons.

In 1938 he was appointed by Labor Secretary Frances Perkins as the Pacific Coast arbitrator of maritime disputes. This was a job for a man of strength who could stand his ground between Harry Bridges' Longshoremen and the big steamship lines. Morse had demonstrated earlier ability in labor arbitration work by settling a dispute involving an Oregon lumber company. Applying himself with his characteristic drive, Morse became a labor-law specialist and gained the respect of labor and management alike. In forty successive disputes his arbitration awards won prompt compliance from both sides. The forty-first brought a test of will and purpose between Morse and Bridges.

When the Longshoremen rejected the arbitrator's ruling in that case, Morse abruptly resigned with a flourish and caught the train for Eugene. "The union's failure to live up to its promise to abide by the decision of the arbitrator has destroyed the arbitration agreement and rendered the union's word valueless," declared Morse. "The union must answer to public opinion." Wayne Morse's reputation for fairness was so secure that Harry Bridges, tough guy of the water front, had to back down. He agreed to Morse's terms and the dean resumed the role of arbitrator. Thus began the Legend of the no-nonsense, pull-no-punches public servant.

In the autumn of 1941 President Roosevelt called Wayne Morse to Washington to become chairman of an emergency board assigned to seek a settlement of a labor dispute between the nation's railroads and the brotherhoods of railway employees who were threatening a nationwide transportation tie-up. After hearing both sides, Morse's board recommended a modest wage increase. Management promptly accepted, but labor rejected this as a solution. To underscore its insistence on greater benefits, the brotherhoods set a national rail strike date, Sunday, December 7. When three weeks of conferences at the White House level brought no settlement, Roosevelt reconvened Morse's emergency board, which brought both sides into a downtown Washington hotel and put them through a thirty-six-hour eyeball-to-eyeball confrontation with only a single ninety-minute break after the first twenty-four hours. Whether or not Morse, the indefatigable, wore them down to the point of submission by exhaustion, he did secure a wage formula agreement. The rail strike was averted on the eve of Pearl Harbor. It was an able beginning in the political big leagues. A newspaper, in preparing a human-interest article about this vigorous young law dean from the West, called one of Morse's college professors at Wisconsin to ask what sort of a man he was. "He's absolutely fearless," replied Professor Andrew Weaver. Several others endorsed this view. The Legend of Wayne Morse was growing.

The Great Dissent

The following month President Roosevelt named Dean Morse to the newly created National War Labor Board, a twelve-man agency that was to decide all labor-management disputes so that wartime strikes and lockouts could be averted, as labor and industry leaders had pledged that they would be. Among the four labor members of the board were George Meany of the A.F. of L. and Martin Durkin of the Plumbers, who years later became President Eisenhower's first Labor Secretary—the famous "incredible" appointment, by Senator Robert A. Taft's lights. Among the four management members of the board were Roger D. Lapham of American-Hawaii Steamship

Company, later mayor of San Francisco, Cyrus S. Ching and A. W. Hawkes, former president of the United States Chamber of Commerce. Morse was one of the board's four non-partisan public members. His three associates were William H. Davis, New York patent attorney who became chairman; Dr. Frank P. Graham, president of the University of North Carolina, later a senator; and Dr. George W. Taylor, professor of economics at the University of Pennsylvania.

In the hectic economic conditions on the home front, from gasoline and coffee coupons to price and wage ceilings, the War Labor Board exerted an iron will against massive inflationary pressures.[1] It was a wild, muddling-through period in which anxious citizens with relatives on the world's battlefronts were instantly incensed when anyone seemed to be heaving a wrench into the nation's high-speed production gears. John L. Lewis was such a target for scorn in 1943 during his battle with the government—the periodic strikes in the coal fields, the government seizures of the mines. Interior Secretary Harold Ickes finally brought peace and productivity to the coal fields by giving Lewis a more attractive wage formula than other industries had received. The War Labor Board then rubber-stamped the coal contract, but not by unanimous vote.

Dean Morse, alone, dissented. The board was compromising its own policy of withholding any wage increases from employees who went on strike, protested Morse. It was doing the expedient thing to end the strike in the mines. This was a great public tug of war which lasted for months and injected Morse into the news columns day after day. His dissent marked the beginning of the Legend of the man of principle who rejects all expedient compromises. Conservative columnist David Lawrence put it this way:

> Every now and then someone emerges in public life with the courage of his convictions and refuses to be stampeded into a surrender of principle. Such a man is Wayne L. Morse . . . who has written what is bound to be a historic dissent from the decision of the Board on the matter of yielding to the United Mine Workers under duress. Mr. Morse may be in the minority today, but as time goes on his vigorous protest will become the basis of majority policy.

[1] Wages were much more effectively controlled than war profits or farm income. Nevertheless the cost-of-living index from August 1939 to V-J Day in August 1945 rose from 100 to 133, far less than during World War I, when the index rose from 100 to 162 in but nineteen months. Mitchell and Mitchell's *American Economic History* covers this well.

In his home state the Legend was spreading that Oregon had sent quite a man to Washington. "Wayne Morse takes firm stand for government by law, not by political intimidation," headlined the *Oregon Voter*. Editor Charles A. Sprague, in his front-page column in the *Oregon Statesman*, observed:

> That dissent took real courage. It is safe to assume that the President wanted the agreement ratified and the President may be irritated with this exercise of independent judgment. Morse's courage is the more conspicuous because his name has been prominently mentioned for the position of judge of the ninth circuit court of appeals, and his dissent may jeopardize or even kill his chances for this presidential appointment.
> . . . .
> There is need for more men like Dean Morse, with vision and courage all through the country. Instead the country is too full of John L. Lewises, anxious to "get while the getting is good."

Here was a fork in the highroad to success. When a judge of the federal circuit court of appeals at San Francisco died in September 1943, Morse wanted to be appointed to fill the vacancy. What precise relationship, if any, existed between this desire and the coal dissent five weeks later remains a minor mystery. In any event, his path was blocked. He had had a sulphurous exchange of communiqués with Ickes over the coal crisis, and Richard L. Neuberger later wrote that Ickes went to the White House and got Morse's name scratched from the list of those being considered for that judgeship. John Gunther wrote that Morse's refusal "to kowtow" to Ickes and James F. Byrnes, head of the Office of War Mobilization, was the key to his failure to win the judgeship. Whatever the cause, the effect was this: the Legend of the man who speaks up for what is right, at the sacrifice of his own personal gain, took greater form and substance.

His path to black-robed oblivion blocked, Wayne Morse hustled up the other fork in the highway, and a year later became Oregon's new United States Senator. That sudden advancement into the Senate will receive close attention subsequently. Here it is enough to state categorically that without this growing Legend of the man of fearlessness, integrity, strength of conviction, uncompromising honesty, intellectual vigor, and the willingness to fight—without this public image of Wayne Morse, he would not have become a senator from Oregon in 1944 when he first entered the field. The Legend brought him his first great prize, the seat he has held ever since in the Senate of the United States.

The Scrapper

The magnification of the legend of the fighting liberal during Morse's seventeen years in the Senate has been apparent. Like all highly favorable Legends, it has been self-serving, a glory ladder in the heady days of triumph, a lifesaver in the black whirlpool of defeat and degradation.

"I don't know why he does some of those things, but . . ." With words such as these many a voter has shaken his head over Morse's latest unpopular act. The word *but* usually marks the beginning of some saving concession for Wayne Morse. It might be, as one very liberal Democratic lady in Oregon said to me, "*but* we need a maverick in the Senate." Or it might be, simply, "*but* I like a fighting senator." Wayne Morse is not unconscious of the appeal of this trait. *Inside U.S.A.* published only a year after Morse became a senator, records this comment by him: "You know, people like a scrapper. I always try to be good-natured, but I certainly punch hell out of a lot of people." The Legend, perpetuated by its hero, well and faithfully serves this outer political need of the senator.

It is, however, not simply *self*-serving. It has its undeniable public use as well. One event from his career illustrates the point. One winter night in 1958 an intense trio knocked on Morse's apartment door in Washington. They were Bernard Schwartz, the New York professor who had launched the House investigation of the federal regulatory agencies, Clark Mollenhoff of the Des Moines *Register* and Jack Anderson, Drew Pearson's associate. They were carrying over a hundred pounds of the hottest files on Capitol Hill. Schwartz, acting on the assumption he had been employed to do a thorough investigation of all irregularities, had just been fired for his zeal. Fearful that the evidence of irregularities would vanish once he relinquished the keys to his files, Schwartz relied upon Mollenhoff's quick mind and strong back to haul the files into the night in search of a useful depository.

They were first taken to Senator John J. Williams, Delaware Republican, who gave them a cursory inspection. They then set out for Morse's apartment. Morse willingly took possession of the files. Mollenhoff, the best investigative reporter in Washington, that night wrote a dispatch for the Des Moines *Register* about his midnight exploit to assure wide public knowledge that Wayne Morse had the files. On Speaker Sam Rayburn's request, Morse promptly surrendered them to the House committee, for the desired objective had been achieved: the threat of exposure had been created just in case anyone had in mind burying Schwartz's findings.

Why Morse and Williams? "We wanted a Democrat and a Republican with enough guts to use this information, if necessary, to force the investigation," explains Mollenhoff. "They were the logical senators, and everybody knew they would do it." In his book *The Professor and the Commissions* Schwartz observed: "No one but Mr. Morse himself knows what use he made of the files in the day and a half that they were in his possession. The mere fact that the Senator could have copied every important document has, all the same, been a constant deterrent to the Subcommittee's suppressing of important matters in its files, such as the Adams-Goldfine case." The investigation went forward and provoked the most dramatic episode of White House political anguish during the Eisenhower years—the resignation of Sherman Adams, the President's chief aide, for having interceded with federal agencies in behalf of a friendly textile manufacturer, Bernard Goldfine, whose benevolence toward Adams was symbolized by the gift of a vicuña coat. Senator Morse contributed his legend of incorruptible, unintimidated, outspoken devotion to clean government. But for the Legend of Wayne Morse, there would have been no knock on his door that night—and possibly no subsequent investigation.

In addition to the outer political needs of the Senator from Oregon and the broader public needs of a democratic government, the Legend serves the deep inner needs of Wayne Lyman Morse, the man whom very few persons know. It sustains him in his darkest moments of defeat and rejection. Although part myth, his Legend is very probably the most cherished possession of this unique and mysterious man. More than either of the political parties in which he has served, more than his constituency, more than the Senate itself, he fights to protect the Legend of Wayne Morse. In it there is security for the present, justification for the past, and the hope of glory for tomorrow and posterity.

2. THE ORATORICAL TIGER

Lessons From La Follette . . . Homecoming . . . History Smiles . . . Lady Luce

IN THE cloakrooms of the Senate he is called "Tiger."

The name is used good-naturedly, but it's not without descriptive fitness. For Wayne Morse is a lean, nimble six-footer with enormous stamina and fighting power in the recesses of his wiry frame. He pads softly into the Senate chamber, gazing with steely aloofness at the other beasts in the Senate jungle—the lumbering elephants, the leaping gazelles, the preening peacocks, the aged lions. As he takes up a position of commanding vigilance in the protective tree of high principle, he sits flicking his tail nervously, watching, waiting, set to spring on the first hapless beast to wander into the broad legislative province in which Tiger ranks himself supreme.

No one paces this jungle with a more certain instinct for combat. The tiger's cry in the congressional wilds is chilling to those who press forward with the wicked designs of privilege. No one but Wayne Morse has offered the Lady Luce a ride and returned with the lady inside—and no one but the tiger in the Senate would even have dared try.

Quick, ferocious, eager to test his strength, Morse is unrivaled as an oratorical tiger. His instincts for self-preservation are keen. Recalling that La Follette, the great lion he seeks to emulate, was nearly poisoned during a hot filibuster by an eggnog sent up from the Senate restaurant, Morse had his beverages guarded by two trusted aides during his record-shattering tidelands oration in 1953. As he talked the night through, for twenty-two hours and twenty-six minutes, Morse whispered commands to one of his two assistants, William Berg, Jr., or Merton Bernstein, who took turns at his side supplying the orator's needs for background speech material and liquids. On Morse's firm admonition these two able lawyers that night became all but the monarch's tasters. They fulfilled his orders for tea by brewing it personally and for orange juice by going to the Senate restaurant and examining each orange, the knife that sliced it, the gadget that squeezed it, the glass into which its juice drained. No one was going to slip Wayne Morse a mickey.

There is a minor mystery about how he could physically manage this feat of endurance against the strain placed upon the throat, the legs, the kidneys. It is not solved by noting that his first acts following the end of the speech were, in this sequence, to hold a news conference just off the Senate floor, to return to his office and there to sit down and to discuss the heroic feat, and then to repair casually to his private lavatory. Wayne Morse has a simple explanation: clean living.

The greater mystery is why does Wayne Morse devote so much time and energy to heavy oratory? "His arguments were lost in the excess of verbiage," editorialized the Washington *Post*. "If it is endurance that he wishes to demonstrate, it is a pity that he does not take up pole sitting or marathon dancing." Of course there were many others who shouted, "Hurray for Wayne Morse."

The oration as a tactical weapon of Senate warfare is honored by long and distinguished usage. But the suspicion is not infrequently voiced that Wayne Morse, the Senate's most persistent bombardier, relies upon it as though it were the absolute weapon. Why is his arsenal so sparingly stocked with other tactical devices and more diversified battle plans? Why does he place such heavy reliance on his power to rout the foe with Big Bertha oratory? The answers are suggested by a return to Madison and to Eugene to see the boy and the college professor who became the senator.

Lessons From La Follette

As a college boy, Wayne Morse once met an old fellow in a southern Wisconsin town who well remembered a Fourth of July speech by La Follette. "He was due at the fairgrounds at eleven o'clock," recalled the elder, "but he didn't get there until three. He'd been speaking all along the way. Well, he started talking at three-thirty, and by seven o'clock every cow in the county was bellerin' to be milked. But ol' Bob was still talkin'." To that old-timer, it was a memorable day. To Wayne Morse, it was an impressive feat for an orator to *hold* an audience for four hours. For by this point in his life Morse had become a star collegiate debater and was pursuing a master's degree in speech. The mechanics of this art form were vastly intriguing to him. When he went on to Minnesota to teach argumentation and coach the debate team while taking his law training, Morse made some of the most brilliant and scientific analyses of speechmaking techniques in the long service of his mentor and faculty colleague, Professor Frank Rarig. Had Rarig not rejected his later request for a job, after he finished at Columbia, Morse might have continued as a speech specialist. "He had contributed as much as any man we've ever had on the staff," says Rarig. "He was very stimulating. But I told him I would not consider taking him back because he was now prepared to teach law. He then upbraided me for not showing his letter to the dean. I replied that he ought to go into law and become a law dean. I told Wayne, 'It will be hard for you to work under anybody. You need to be your own boss.'"

Mechanically skillful though he became, deeper compulsions drove him into the arena of verbal conflict. In grade school there were distinguishing traits. "He would interrupt when a slower-thinking student was having trouble reciting," recalls a grade school teacher. "He was a smart student, but he had no respect for the other fellow's viewpoint. I was hard on him. I like teamwork, and when a fellow doesn't play on the team, well, I'm hard on him." Another teacher remembers, "He loved to argue. He could argue on anything." An old school chum says, with faint admiration, that often there was a studied purpose in Wayne's classroom arguments. "If he wasn't prepared to recite on the lesson, Wayne would start an argument on an extraneous issue, and pretty soon the whole class was off the subject."

The yearbook for Madison's Central High School in 1918 states the case in verse:

> There is a young junior named Morse,
>   He can talk 'till you'd think he'd be hoarse.
> He's always in bad.
>   But it ne'er makes him sad.
> For to him that's a matter of course.

He was, presumably, either the most popular student or the best politician in his junior class, for he was its president the second semester. What is more, Wayne brought glory to his alma mater.

"Interscholastic debate in the Madison High School reached the
zenith of its success this year. . . . Alyward, Sharp and Morse righted
matters by a unanimous victory over Stoughton. Not in many years
has Madison won four out of six debates, winning unanimously in
three of them," the yearbook reported.

With a zest for combat, Wayne the teen-ager took on all comers
in debate. When F. O. Leiser, back from missionary work in China,
organized Madison's first Hi-Y club in 1917, Wayne was one of the
first to join. "The purpose of the Hi-Y was to maintain high standards
of Christian living among the high school boys. It was never designed
to become a debating society. Yet that is what it rapidly developed
into," recalls Mr. Leiser. "There was a real reason for this. Wayne
Morse liked to talk. The other members of the club had lots of fun
getting Wayne into an argument, and it was usually a matter of
twenty-nine against one. Wayne seemed the happiest when in the
midst of a hot debate." At one Friday night meeting Wayne brought
one of his older brothers who had never attended a Hi-Y meeting.
When the verbal warfare between Wayne and the others got pretty
hot, protective instincts brought his big brother to his feet. "I've had
enough of this blasting my brother. I'll take you all and throw you
out of this window," he shouted. Wayne shushed his anxious brother,
for he wanted nothing less than to be solicitously "rescued" from such
gratifying circumstances. Wayne never brought his brother to another
Hi-Y meeting.

"He was a pretty good basketball player," recalls a grade school
classmate. "But he wasn't any good as a teamman. He was a grandstand player, believe me." After grade school Wayne concentrated his
most serious efforts on debating. Debating, in a manner of speaking,
is a team activity. But unlike anything in sports, save possibly pole
vaulting, debating allows every member of the team his chance to be
a star. It was a congenial sport for Wayne Morse.

The lessons from La Follette, the consummate orator of his day,
were as impressive as any Wayne Morse was to learn. One of the first
came the time his father took him to hear La Follette give his
favorite reading from the role of Iago in *Othello*.[1] La Follette's
appearance was itself a treat for a young farm boy.

---

[1] La Follette had wanted to be a Shakespearean actor, but Edwin Booth
had advised against it because of his short stature. But for a few inches in
height, La Follette's great zeal might have been channeled entirely into the
Chautauqua circuit instead of political reforms that have left their mark on
twentieth-century America.

"There he was, wearing white shoes—it was the first time I had ever seen a man in white shoes—and white trousers, a light-colored vest, and a light cutaway coat. And he didn't just stand and read Iago. But he would run across the stage——" At this point in reliving that occasion, Senator Morse sprang from behind his Senate desk and demonstrated La Follette's stage technique, chiefly the familiar dramatic pose of actors of that period—the pleading, outstretched-arm gesture, the long stride, and the dramatic stance consisting of the forward leg bent at the knee with the other leg trailing slightly behind. "The dramatics," says Morse, "were wonderful. I'm sure Dad didn't understand most of Iago, but he thought it was magnificent. La Follette was a great platform man." Perhaps this impressive experience helped account for Wayne Morse's membership in the dramatics clubs in high school and college, although there is no record that he ever won a starring role.

"La Follette," says Morse, "originated the empty-chair idea. He would walk onto a stage with a chair, plunk it down hard, and then say to his audience, 'You see that chair. Looks empty, doesn't it? Well, let's see what the occupant of that chair voted for.' Then he would hold up a voting record and read it off, roll-call vote after roll-call vote. La Follette did this to defeat many of the reactionary Republicans of the Senate who opposed his legislative proposals." The lesson of political dramatics, never forgotten, was etched into the consciousness of Wayne Morse long before the issues for which they were employed could be comprehended by even a bright boy.

Although not a flamboyant-mannered man, Morse applied this lesson rather literally on the opening day of the 1953 session of Congress. Entering the Senate chamber for the first time after his bolt of the Republican party, he dragged with him a drab little steel folding chair and explained that he was prepared to place it in the center aisle, which divides the Republican side from the Democratic side of the chamber. As a symbol of his announced independence of either party, that theatrical prop got Morse considerable attention, if also some criticism for lowering the dignity of the august place in which he performed.

A more sophisticated lesson, learned directly from the great insurgent himself, came in Morse's senior year at Wisconsin. He was president of Hesperia, a debating club which was grimly preparing for the annual Joint Debate, an event of great expectation for the university community each year. The rival club this year was Philo-

mathia, whose members were regarded as more conservative than
those of Hesperia. The conservatives got to choose the question for
the debate and selected La Follette's proposal that Congress be
empowered to override a Supreme Court decision by a two-thirds
vote of both houses. "They were clever," recalls Morse, "for on that
issue I thought La Follette was nuts. But I had two radicals on my
team who supported La Follette's proposal. We got to choose whether
we would debate the affirmative or the negative. They wanted to
debate the affirmative. I stalled a decision and finally suggested we
arrange to see the senator about it." Morse and his two colleagues,
Ralph Axley and Karl Karel, secured an interview.

It was an unforgettable scene as they arrived at Maple Bluff, the
great man's lakeshore home. La Follette, then sixty-eight, awaited
them on his front porch, his silver shock of hair glistening in the sun.
After introductions had been concluded, La Follette turned and
said, "Wayne, what did you ever do with Dan?" Dan was Wayne's
stud pony. Every time Dan beat the ponies of his sons at the fair, La
Follette would try to buy him, says Morse. Although flattered, Wilbur
Morse would always reply, "But I can't sell the boy's pony." Wayne
had to tell the senator that Dan had died. Senator Morse said it
showed what "a phenomenal memory La Follette had." Obviously
the incident, etched in Morse's book of fondest memories, indicated
more than that. How flattering to have Wisconsin's most illustrious
figure call to mind with admiration the boy's pet pony. Would this
not turn the head of many a horseman?

If this did not draw Wayne more closely into La Follette's mag-
netic field, perhaps the more serious conversation did. As the college
debaters sat on the porch sipping lemonade and munching cake, their
host made his case for granting Congress authority to override the
Supreme Court. The presidentially appointed justices were really
agents of the powerful financial interests whose legal opinions could
not be expected to protect the public interest, he argued. Only the
Congress, by mandate of the ballot, really represented the people.
Convinced as he was personally, La Follette knew his was not a
popular cause at this time. Harding was in the White House, returning the country to the normalcy the businessmen expected of the
champions of laissez faire. La Follette at length asked his young
admirers, "Do you want to win the debate, or do you want to
educate your audience?" The debaters told him they wanted to do
both. "You can't do both," he counseled them. "You can educate

your audience if you take the affirmative, or you can win by taking the negative."

A year later Bob La Follette demonstrated this very principle in his 1924 third-party presidential campaign, which everyone knew to be hopelessly lost against the two conservative nominees of the major parties, Calvin Coolidge and John W. Davis. He ran on a platform which called for public power, reduced tariffs and railroad rates, child-labor laws, election of all federal judges, popular referendum on any declaration of war, and his Supreme Court idea. La Follette was seeking to educate the people while losing the election to the regular Republican nominee, Coolidge, whose philosophy was that "the business of the United States is business."

As the debaters finished their lemonade, Wayne Morse mused over this new and impressive concept, the idea that sometimes there is more virtue in losing for what is deemed right than winning with what is popular but wrong.

All the way back to the campus the debaters argued which side to take. "I was still convinced that La Follette was wrong on the issue," said Morse, "but my teammates outvoted me, two to one, and so we took the affirmative." What's more, Morse's team won the Joint Debate. The next day Hesperia's victors received a telegram which read: "Congratulations. I heard you did both. La Follette."

As triumphant Hesperia's "closer," as they called the last member of the team who was to clinch the argument, Morse was recognized as the star debater at Wisconsin that year. He won a Vilas medal for his "excellence in forensic endeavor" and represented Wisconsin in the Northern Oratorical League, the annual speech contest of the Big Ten universities. What topic should he select for this crowning occasion? His speech professor urged him to base his oration on his persuasive argument in behalf of La Follette's court bill. "But I don't agree with this point of view," objected Wayne.

"You want to be a lawyer, don't you?" said his mentor. "You must learn to play the role of advocate." Convinced, Morse titled his oration "The Supreme Court and the People." Against five competitors from the universities of Minnesota, Michigan, Iowa, Illinois, and Northwestern, Morse won second place, beaten only by the Northwestern orator, whose topic was "Clean Hands."

If Bob La Follette's admonition about educating the people taught Morse that a politician could justifiably lose for a good cause, these experiences by which he was swept to the heights of oratorical acclaim demonstrated that a skilled speaker could win with a cause in which he didn't believe. The lessons of practical politics were being learned. Wayne Morse was on his way.

Homecoming

A decade later, as an Oregon law professor, Morse was projected from obscurity to heroic acclaim on the powerful thrust of oratory. It was an episode of which it can be said Wayne Morse was marked by his experience.

Beyond Dean Morse's ivy tower a conflict of growing intensity was developing in the early thirties between the university and Oregon State College at Corvallis, forty miles down the Willamette Valley. Oregon State's President, William Jasper Kerr, was master-minding a grand strategy for consolidation of the two state institutions at Corvallis. In the late winter of 1932 some leading citizens of that town deployed a delegation to Eugene with what was taken as an ultimatum. "We told them to go to hell," said William M. Tugman, then the crusading editor of the Eugene *Register-Guard*. The Corvallis delegation instead decided to go to the people. They circulated petitions to put a proposition on the November election ballot which, if favored by a majority of the voters, would make Corvallis the center of a single state-university campus. Some high-spirited Eugene zealots then pilfered the petitions; but, after yelling "foul," the Corvallis crowd gathered new signatures and dramatized their assaulted virtue by delivering the petitions to the state capital in an armored car.

Corvallis had gained the initiative because of the success Kerr had realized in twenty-five years of building up Oregon State College while the university languished under less forceful leadership. After the university got an aggressive new president, Arnold Bennett Hall, in 1926, Eugene set out to redress the balance of power Kerr had gained. The mounting tension culminated in the Corvallis petition drive of 1932. Eight weeks before the voters were to decide the issue, suddenly both Hall and Kerr tendered their resignations to the State Board of Higher Education and the Board then named Kerr to the newly created post of Chancellor of Higher Education with authority over both campuses. All of the melodramatic circumstances underlying these developments have never been, and cannot yet be, recorded, out of deference to those innocents who remain behind.

In any event, Kerr's devious aggrandizement provoked deep bitterness at Eugene. The tempestuous young sophomore editor of the university's daily newspaper, Richard L. Neuberger, burst into editor Tugman's office to ask whether he thought it advisable for Neuberger to organize a mob of students to stone Chancellor Kerr's windows. Tugman disapproved, saying that the important thing was for the university to win the election by defeating the initiative measure on the ballot. Win the election they did, defeating the Zorn-MacPherson initiative by a stunning 6 to 1 margin. Although the battle had been won by Eugene, the war of nerves continued between Kerr and the university faculty, which resented the residence of the "enemy" in its midst.

A year later, when the governor appointed a prominent Portland attorney, Roscoe C. Nelson, as new head of the State Board of Higher Education, Kerr invited him to speak on both campuses. Just before he went to Eugene to address the student assembly, Nelson read an anonymous letter in the university newspaper which criticized the faculty for favoring liberalized immigration laws for Nazi victims. It contained a scurrilous attack upon the Jews and mentioned Nelson, who was partly Jewish. Nelson later said this made him "see red." Dean Morse and Professor Orlando Hollis were among the curious faculty members who crowded into the hall to hear Nelson castigate "a self-appointed few . . . men of boundless ambition and minds tainted by unsated ambition, who even determined that the unified system adopted by the people should not succeed, and who are sabotaging the efforts of W. J. Kerr." Deeply incensed, Morse and Hollis drove to Corvallis to hear what Nelson would say at Oregon State. There he repeated even more severely his charge against the "little coterie" at Eugene for "sabotaging the chancellor's efforts." Hollis recalls that Morse got so angry he could scarcely contain himself. "Orlando," he declared as they drove home, "I'm not going to take this."

Morse didn't say what he would do about it, or what, indeed, he *could* do about it. He was still an obscure professor with no connections politically and no wide acquaintanceship in his newly adopted state. On campus his reputation was growing, thanks in part to young editor Neuberger, who had described him in the

student daily as "a Roscoe Pound of the future" who is "bringing to
the law school a liberal atmosphere and a militant fearlessness."

Two days later, Homecoming Saturday, the alumni gathered gaily
for the pre-game luncheon. At the head table sat Chancellor Kerr,
and two seats away sat Dean Morse. There were the usual rah-rah
speeches of greeting and commendation for the fine alumni spirit
until Dean Morse, rising gravely to address this convivial gathering,
pulled from his coat pocket a carefully prepared speech that was as
lethal as a loaded revolver. Taking quick and sure aim, Morse fired at
Nelson for his "insulting, insinuating, unfair and vicious attack upon
the faculty" and for being a "dupe." Also he implicated Kerr in "a
plot so rotten that it stinks to high heaven." The audacious professor
thereupon demanded Nelson's resignation for plunging the university into the most serious crisis in its history by challenging "certain
fundamenal principles of academic freedom."

Kerr, a man of ramrod military bearing, turned pale and fled from
the hall, recalls Dean James Gilbert, and the faculty and alumni
rose to a thunderous demonstration of applauding, cheering approval.
At long last the university had found a fighting leader. No Homecoming Day heroics on the football field ever outdid the dining-hall
rout of the chancellor by Professor Wayne Morse. His act of derring-
do was a big story on the front pages of the following morning's
Sunday newspapers around the state.

Nelson quickly countered by damning Morse with the faintest of
praise—"a fine chap" who, after all, "is still quite young." But, he
added, Morse's "brutality" and "wholesale condemnation in the role
of prosecutor, judge, and jury, on the strength of a malodorous
whispering campaign" had proved his own point and "disclosed to
the state at large the refinement of cruelty to which the chancellor
is subjected."

Sterling T. Green, Neuberger's successor as editor of the student
daily, said Nelson "absolutely failed to refute a single statement made
by the dean." Rallying to Morse's call to arms, the faculty assembled
the following Monday and voted without audible dissent for a
resolution asking Nelson's resignation and deploring Kerr as chancellor. Two days later Governor Julius L. Meier accepted Nelson's
resignation. Less than a week had elapsed since Dean Morse had
declared, "I'm not going to take this!" With but a single mighty
oratorical charge, the mighty foe had been toppled at the feet of

the brave young cavalier. Was not fearless oratory a swift and powerful sword?

The dean then wheeled to take on the chancellor himself. Kerr had denied Morse's charges of favoritism toward Oregon State in budgeting and failing to consult with the university faculty. But when Nelson resigned, Morse demanded Kerr's resignation as well. Kerr fought back through the State Board of Education to get a charge of insubordination against Morse. An investigation and possible dismissal hung over the dean. Morse's defenders at Eugene took swift countermeasures. The faculty called for the State Board to investigate Kerr; Tugman, in a front-page editorial, said the only issue was Kerr's unfitness to be chancellor; and most importantly, the Association of University Professors entered the case to investigate whether academic freedom and the dean's liberal exercise of it were in grave jeopardy in Oregon. Morse's career teetered on the outcome of these twin investigations.

In this great crisis of Wayne Morse's career we must observe that he was not yet secure in his professional field. He had been trying, without much success, to better himself elsewhere. Before he became dean, Morse had sought a position on the law faculty at Kansas. In the spring of 1933, seven months before he blasted Kerr, he wired his old dean at Minnesota, asking that he write Indiana a letter recommending him for dean of that law school. Two months later he was offered by telephone the deanship at Louisiana, during Huey Long's era, but declined it on his mentor's advice that this might be a "backwater from which emergence would not be likely." Six months after he became embroiled in the Kerr fight he wrote Dean Fraser, seeking his aid in being appointed dean at Missouri. He was not anxious to leave Oregon, he wrote, unless he could better himself materially. "I have been one of the storm centers in the educational row in the state and there are many adherents of Kerr that think that his resignation should be followed by mine," explained Morse. He added that it was not comfortable having to "keep one ear to the ground." He didn't get the job.

Morse's actions were all the more bold considering that he was not in a position of recognized professional security when he made his move. When the State Board informed Morse that he was to be called before it in closed session, the dean refused. He says he informed the acting head of the board, Willard Marks, who was a likely gubernatorial prospect, that if he were fired he would open a law

office in Eugene and "ride your tail." Morse said the case against
Kerr was so damaging the board wouldn't dare investigate them
both. Morse says that at a private dinner at Marks' home he disclosed that he had learned that Kerr was an academic imposter.
Kerr did not hold the proper academic degree to warrant his use
of the title "Doctor." It was an honorary degree of Doctor of
Science and Didactics from a Utah college. How foolish the Board
of Higher Education would look if this became generally known,
suggested the dean. Morse played a daring hand with his ace.

Meanwhile the American Association of University Professors assigned three professors (from the universities of California, Washington, and Stanford) to investigate. After interviewing 100 persons,
including faculty members on both campuses and state officials, the
professors filed their report, calling the elevation of Kerr to chancellor a "stupendous blunder." The A.A.U.P. recommended that
the charge of insubordination and the call for an investigation of
Morse be "expunged from the record." The trial of Wayne Morse
was called off. The dean's position had been secured. Four months
later Kerr filed his resignation. The war of the campuses ended.

If Dean Morse did not singlehandedly "save" the university, he did
stiffen the spines of the faculty and rally them from relative timidity
to outright rebellion. With a different outcome, he and the university
might have been ruined by these events.

The Homecoming Day speech was a Morse masterpiece. The Sunday *Oregonian* the next morning published its full text. To analyze
its composition is to learn something of the orator. Morse began by
pointing the finger of direct accusation at Roscoe Nelson for plunging the university into the most serious crisis in its history, *not*
because Nelson had been critical of a group of individuals, of whom
he was one. What made this a crisis was that Nelson had challenged
a fundamental *principle*, academic freedom. Nelson was quickly
transformed from a carping official into the enemy of all that was
academically sacrosanct. Next, Morse skillfully alluded to Nelson's
glancing blows at the student newspaper and the Eugene *Register-
Guard*, but said he would not dwell upon this because the free
press needed no defense, as any fair-minded man knows. Then he
declared:

> But I shall dwell upon Mr. Nelson's insulting, insinuating, unfair
> and vicious attack upon the faculty. May I assure you that my emphasis
> does not mean that I am angry. As a member of the faculty my feelings

are too greatly hurt, my sense of right and fair play too completely crushed to allow me to be angry. I should like to disbelieve what I know to be true, that Roscoe Nelson, brilliant lawyer, lovable personality, a man for whom I can sincerely say I have a deep affection, stands today before the people of Oregon as a man who has been duped.

Speak not in anger but in love, sayeth the Lord. And when rhetorically quartering an antagonist, always speak kindly of him as a person—lovable and often righteous. Love the sinner but hate his sin. Justice must be served.

In his address on this campus which was surpassed in awfulness only by his address on the Corvallis campus, he charged that there exists on your faculty a little coterie of faculty men whose opposition to the administration rests in disappointed ambitions and frustrated desires. Time and time again he referred to these men of mystery as Catilines. As a little boy, I learned from my mother a lesson that Mr. Nelson needs to learn; that calling a proposition or its advocates names proves nothing against the proposition or its advocates.

Yes, Mother warned us about men like this. After invoking the Bible and motherhood and going on to demand that Nelson prove his case or quit, the orator added the ingredient of intrigue:

Mr. Nelson referred to Catilines: I shall not call anybody any names, but I shall call attention to what you know is a fact—that a group of men in Eugene have been unjustifiably purporting to speak for this faculty. Some of these are [Morse then named five prominent Eugene citizens]. For too long a time this faculty, with a fine charitable spirit, has suffered encroachments upon its rights. But now Mr. Nelson has declared war on this faculty and the faculty will respond fearlessly. We have stood by and witnessed the selection of a chancellor by a plot so rotten that it stinks to high heaven. In my Dad's Day speech I said that politics, with all its nefarious practices, must be kicked out of higher education. I repeat that warning, and I believe that the people of this state will be with me!

Not just one man or two, but a ring of traitors within the community itself was part of this. Don't reveal the nature or details of the plot. With cavalier boldness, assert it as a fact. Then strike a sharp blow at "politics," that shabby business of furtive shadows in the back alleys of democracy. And close with a ringing declaration that the people will stand with our righteous cause.

It was all there. And it worked. Small matter that he was dead wrong about several of the Eugene citizens who had, in fact, disposed of a craven threat which could have scandalized and possibly destroyed the university community in its hour of vulnerability. Morse did not know, and could not have known, of their true role. Although he had no sure grounds for his allegation, he displayed no hesitancy in suggesting *they* were the Catilines.[2]

His oration had a righteous, brass-knuckle brilliance worthy of one possessing a master's degree in speech, a driving compulsion toward rhetorical combat, and a puritanical hatred of oppression. Others might have quailed at the prospect of so dangerous a course, or at least sought the advance support of those about him. Morse did neither. His closest colleagues had no intimation of what he planned to say. To his student assistant Morse said, in the manner of an eager gladiator anxious to close with his opponent, "Get a seat up front, Steve; the fur is going to fly."

Wayne Morse, in this deeply molding experience, had discovered a recurring rhythm of public affairs. Up from the multitude there stood a man righteous with indignation, courageous in damnation of evil, calling his listeners to join in a noble crusade, arousing them with assurances of the ultimate triumph of goodness. And what were the results? His first bold entrance upon the public stage wearing the toga of Cicero was an astounding triumph.

With sheer forensic force Wayne Morse had toppled Nelson and so weakened Kerr that he was soon forced into retirement. The foe had been put to rout. At thirty-three, to have gained this objective *in this way* must surely have brought experiential inner assurance to Wayne Morse that skillful oratory was more than a way of winning collegiate medals. It was obviously a reliable way of altering, even reversing, the course of onrushing events. For Wayne Morse, this reliance became a way of public life.

[2] Catiline was a rival of Cicero for one of the consulships of Rome in 63 B.C. Earlier, as governor of Africa, he had been impeached for extortion. Thus disqualified for the consulship, he unsuccessfully plotted, possibly with Caesar, to murder the consuls. Through bribery, Catiline was acquitted of extortion; but Cicero defeated him for consul and escaped a Catiline attempt upon his life. After Cicero aroused the people through powerful oratory in the Roman Senate, Catiline was declared a public enemy against whom Rome's second consul, Antonius, was dispatched with an army. Catiline fell in battle and the Catiline conspirators were arrested and put to death in Rome's underground dungeons.

History Smiles

After he became a senator, Wayne Morse's oratorical talent came into wide demand outside the Senate. He is sought as an after-dinner speaker from coast to coast by a heterogeneous assortment of organizations which have in common only their interest in getting out a good crowd with the promise of a rousing speaker. Wayne Morse is all of that. His audience may be a local labor group, for whom he will urgently press his charge against the crushing business interests; or a fund-raising dinner for Israel, for which he will speak fervently of the dangers of foreign events; or a public-power gathering for which he will blister the oppressive utility interests; or an altogether non-partisan audience, a university student assembly or a civic club, for whom he will deliver a sophisticated lecture on, say, the peril of the assaults upon the integrity of the Supreme Court. His repertoire is broad. Morse is well compensated for his speaking services. He says five hundred dollars is his standard speaking fee, but he will triple this when the traffic will bear it. But his greatest compensation apparently comes from the emotional experience, the forceful speech and its visible effect upon an audience. The whistling, foot-stomping crowd of responsive partisans in a labor temple, a Grange hall, or a party rally is a reward of inestimable value to Wayne Morse. Small wonder that he makes, by his own count, more speeches in most election campaigns than anyone else.

The world's greatest deliberative body wisely outlaws responsiveness. Senators do not normally encourage one another with physical demonstrations of approval, albeit a word of approval for what the distinguished senator has just said is accepted practice. In the galleries above, those citizens who come to watch the Senate are admonished by the attendants that a breach of silence is grounds for expulsion from the galleries. There are, even so, rare occasions of high feeling when a senator's words will bring his cohorts to their feet with applause, an act of intimidating the opposition perhaps as much as honoring the speaker. And there are occasions when a crowded gallery is carried away with enthusiasm and must be gaveled into silence by the presiding officer, who dutifully manages a stern-voiced announcement that he has authority to clear the galleries, if he must, to maintain order. To some senators, the lack of audience responsiveness makes for dreary, mechanical mouthing of words (words often written by someone else). Their colleagues are usually too busy to squander time in the chamber listening to one another's speeches, unless they are of preannounced significance. Often a senator, after plowing through the first page or so, gives up and asks that the balance of his remarks be printed in the daily *Congressional Record* as though they had been spoken aloud.

To Wayne Morse, lack of an audience is no deterrent. There are days when his voice of alarm, rising to a strident crescendo, echoes through an all but empty chamber, his convictions going as unheard as his flailing gestures go unseen. There throbs within his being a compulsion to speak and a conviction that while his colleagues go about mundane tasks elsewhere, *history* smiles down upon him and catches every golden word. "Scholars will read this record," he will frequently say, as though to fortify himself to go on. And so when he talked through the night against the tidelands oil bill, Morse was no cookbook-reading Huey Long, conducting a clowning filibuster. Scholars would frown upon such behavior. Morse attacks the issue with the thoroughness of a biologist, dissecting it laboriously at every joint, exploring every fiber, and writes a treatise on the subject as he proceeds. Other senators might conceivably not take time to read it all in the next day's *Congressional Record*, and the press might overlook the true significance of it all, if not the dramatics. But surely one could rely upon the scholars of tomorrow, who would recognize these ingredients of history.

If his colleagues in the Senate are not always impressed by this skill, one reason is that he has seldom practiced the art of substituting a phrase for a paragraph. He can jump into a debate with quick, lucid contentions on a key point, but more often his rising to seek recognition is the signal for an intolerably protracted exposition from which most colleagues quickly seek refuge. Not insensitive to his behavior, Morse nevertheless makes only one accommodating concession. Instead of shortening his orations, he often delivers them at the conclusion of the day's business so his colleagues can safely leave for the day. The chamber is never completely empty, in any event, for the listener who matters most is there with his big shorthand pad, taking it all down for publication in the *Congressional Record*.

Morse can speak, and usually does, on every significant issue

which confronts the Senate. He does his homework, as senators put
it, and is seldom less prepared than his colleagues to discuss complex
issues and the implications of alternatives. His retention of detail is
staggering. He defies the accepted practice of deferring to senators who
make a specialty of certain problems. He rejects advice to become
a specialist himself in one or two areas—say, labor law and international affairs, leaving monetary policy, farm legislation, and all
the rest to others whose eminence is recognized. "A true liberal
can't limit himself to a few areas," he replies. "He must be on guard
everywhere, ready to pounce on evil wherever it raises its ugly
head." The only senator of the past decade who could take on
Morse in head-to-head debate and appear as disdainful of him as
Morse is of lesser opponents was the Ohio patrician, Robert A.
Taft. With mere hapless opponents, Morse employs belittling ridicule.
"If a freshman law student ever used such a fallacious argument,
I'd run him out of my class," he may snort. Or he will turn to fury—
not the calculated anger of those other occasions when he flays the
big interests with studied indignation, but the uncontrolled fury of
a man suddenly possessed. His face becomes a contorted study of
flaming scarlet, accentuated by those bristling black brows, as he
scourges those who fail to agree with him—a gentle liberal such as
Herbert Lehman of New York just as unsparingly as a bumptious
conservative such as Homer Capehart of Indiana.

More than the fearless challenger of Chancellor Kerr, more than
the forceful orator of the banquet circuit and the campaign trail,
more than the lucid or long-winded speaker of the Senate, Wayne
Morse is a visceral combatant with what the jargon of the Senate
knows as an instinct for the jugular.

"You've got to realize," says a man who has known Morse since
boyhood, "Wayne loves a cockfight." When he was just a lad whose
folks had moved into town (Madison), he and "Wienie" Stamm,
the butcher's son, were the promoters of the best cockfights any boy
could find in their end of town. Wayne's entry would be a bantam
cock from the small flock of pet poultry he had brought from the
farm to the city. Master Stamm's challenger would be any rooster
he could pirate from the fattening pens of his father's shop. Later,
when Morse's university studies and campus exploits failed to fulfill
his zest for conflict, he would steal away to attend Madison's clandestine cockfights. Today Wayne Morse continues to raise prize bantams,

but none of his cockfights are clandestine. They take place on the
floor of the United States Senate, as Clare Boothe Luce learned in the
spring of 1959.

Lady Luce

Mrs. Luce made her famous wisecrack about Morse's being kicked
in the head by a horse right after the Senate voted 79 to 11 to
approve her nomination as ambassador to Brazil. Morse had been
the only outspoken dissenter. After an Associated Press reporter
called to convey the news of her confirmation, her comment was
flashed on the news wires, and it came in on the chattering Associated Press news printer which stands in the Senate cloakroom
as a link with the outer world. There Morse snipped off the news
bulletin and rushed back to the cockpit for one final assault. The
previous day he had talked for three and a half hours against the
Luce appointment, but the lopsided vote in her favor suggested
the ineffectiveness of that forceful oration. But now, in no more than
three and a half minutes, Wayne Morse clawed back with effective
ferocity. The similarity of these circumstances and those from which
he had made his famous Homecoming denunciation of Nelson
and Kerr over twenty-five years before is unavoidable.

In both instances an outsider had dared to speak with unvarnished
disrepsect. In both instances Morse rose up to defend what he called
right and holy with the noble savagery ready at his command. His
Luce speech merits close examination as a collection of oratorical
devices which were spontaneously drawn up from the deep well of
his combat experience. They reveal more about the oratorical
tiger than any hundred other orations in his repertoire.

"Mr. President, I rise to a point of personal privilege."

This is the stock opening phrase for a senator who feels aggrieved
and seeks a moment of the Senate's time to make a personal rebuttal.

"I have in my hand a very interesting news release. I happen to be
one of those politicians who can take it as well as dish it out. Whenever a politician reaches the point where he cannot laugh at himself,
then he ought to get out of politics."

This introspective opening probably was less disarming than amusing to the Senate, where Morse is least of all noted for the ability to laugh at himself.

"I hope my colleagues who voted against me a few minutes ago will pardon my chuckle at their expense in view of their votes (on the Luce nomination). I say that because not so soon did I expect that those of us who voted against the nomination of Clare Boothe Luce would be proved so right. We had pointed out in the debate her complete lack of tact and diplomacy, and we have been proven right by this very interesting bit of news on the wires. It reads:

"Mrs. Luce said in New York: 'I am grateful for the overwhelming vote of confirmation in the Senate. We must not wait until the dirt settles. My difficulties, of course, go some years back and began when Senator Wayne Morse was kicked in the head by a horse.' "

The *Congressional Record* shows that at this point there was laughter in the chamber. But Wayne Morse was not there to entertain his colleagues by reciting Luce witticisms.

"Mr. President, I was confronted with that Republican smear all through my 1956 campaign. It came out by the reams. It was a whispering campaign with such a windy blow to it that it not only rustled the leaves of Oregon but, in some parts of the state, almost tore the sagebrush up by its roots. The people of Oregon answered that smear by a large majority of votes for me against the hand-picked candidate of the President of the United States, who was taken right out of his cabinet to 'get me.' They thought that this smear was one of the devices they could use."

You see, gentlemen, Morse was saying, this is not just the wise-crack of a New York sophisticate whose repartee we might laugh at if it were an innocent thing. This is part of a vast conspiracy by the Republican party which goes all the way up to the White House, and this is just the latest insidious attack.

"But, Mr. President, the people of Oregon passed upon my mental judgment."

Morse was re-elected in 1956 and, he was saying, this cleared *him* of any suspicions. The people are sovereign. They *know*. So whose mental health should be questioned now?

"I am not surprised that this slanderer, whose nomination the Senate confirmed only a few minutes ago, would make this kind of statement, because yesterday, for three and one-half hours, I documented her record. This is an old, old pattern of emotional instability on the part of this slanderer; the same pattern which caused her to put on a scene in the Roman Parliament after her candidate for President of Italy was defeated. We read the newspaper statement about her conduct, and the widespread comment at the time that if she had been a male ambassador, she would have been recalled."

It is unfortunate, gentlemen, that you couldn't see this danger as did some of us, Morse was saying, but now surely you can see that the whispered rumors are true.

"But the issue is settled. I simply happen to be one of those persons, whether before the final bar of the court when the decision is rendered, or before the final bar of the United States Senate when a decision is rendered, who believes in government by law. I take the decision.

"As chairman of the subcommittee on American Republics Affairs of the Committee on Foreign Relations, I am much concerned about Mrs. Luce's relations with all the Latin American countries, including Brazil.

"The nomination of Mrs. Luce has been confirmed. I wish her well. So far as my subcommittee is concerned, on a strictly impersonal, professional relationship, she will have the full co-operation of my committee.

"I promise to the nation that each night in my prayers, I will pray for God's guidance to this lady, so that for the welfare of our nation she will be more stable in her ambassadorial duties than she was when she issued this press release this afternoon."

For posterity, the *Congressional Record* shows that this socko peroration brought applause from other senators, their number and names unrecorded. In quick succession Senators Lausche of Ohio, Yarborough of Texas, McGee of Wyoming, and Chavez of New Mexico rose to side with Wayne Morse against the statements of this outsider. There was an immediate scurrying about in the cloakrooms which one official observer likened to a bunch of small boys, notably among the small legion of presidential contenders who were noticeably solicitous for the welfare of the wife of the nation's most powerful and possibly most influential magazine publisher.

"Get her to withdraw the statement," declared John F. Kennedy of Massachusetts in a voice of some urgency, says a State Department official. But the State Department characteristically was pinned down by the cross fire, unable to contain the sudden onset of inflamed passion on either side.

Senator Stephen M. Young, Democrat of Ohio, brought the episode to its literary peak the next afternoon by reciting the following lines of poetry:

> She is not old, she is not young,
> The woman with the serpent's tongue,
> The haggard cheek, the hungering eye,
> The poisoned words, the fevered hand,
> Who slights the worthiest in the land,
> Sneers at the just, condemns the brave,
> And blackens goodness in the grave.
>
> In truthful numbers be she sung,
> The woman with the serpent's tongue,
> Ambitious from her natal hour,
> And scheming all her life for power,
> With little left of seemly pride;
> With venomed fangs she cannot hide;
> Burnt up within by that strange soul,
> She cannot shake or yet control;
> Malignant-lipped, unkind, unsweet;
> Past all example indiscreet;
>
> Hectic, and always overstrung—
> The woman with the serpent's tongue.
> To think that such as she can mar
> Names that among the noblest are.
> That hands like hers can touch the strings
> That move who knows what men and things?
> That on her will their fates have hung.
> The woman with the serpent's tongue.

"Very apropos," said Morse when Young had finished. The Luce episode from the start had been so disconcerting as to cause even the mellifluent Republican leader, Everett McKinley Dirksen of Illinois, to stumble in an idiomatic plea for mercy: "Why thrash old hay or beat an old bag of political bones?" As other senators chuckled, Hubert Humphrey jumped to his feet to quip, "I must rise to the defense of the lady."

Three days later a tremulous Clare Luce emerged from the White House to announce her resignation because "the climate of good will was poisoned by thousands of words of extraordinarily ugly charges against my person" by a senator whose "natural course" would be "a continuing harassment of my mission, with a view to making his own charges stick." She explained to James Reston that she became frightened of Morse when she learned that he had telephoned her doctor in New York in an effort to learn whether or not she had been under psychiatric care. "If he would go that far to defeat her, she reasoned, he would not hesitate to use the $150,000 fund he has as chairman of the Latin American subcommittee of the Foreign Relations Committee to investigate, harass, and embarrass her after she got to Rio," wrote Reston in the New York *Times*.

The backing for the rumor was a collection of reports of her behavior as ambassador at Rome, chiefly the excusive *Time* magazine story that she was forced to leave that post due to illness caused by "a deadly fallout" of tiny dust and flakes from the ceiling of her bedroom in Rome into her breakfast coffee cup. The particles, so the *Time* story went, contained arsenic of lead poison. Much doubt was cast upon the authenticity of this story, notably by the architect who had decorated Mrs. Luce's villa, who said the ceiling hadn't been painted in forty or fifty years. But the point here is that Wayne Morse had no proof of the rumor he had heard, and the statement of her doctor tended to contradict it. He did not ask Mrs. Luce for permission to consult her physician further about her health. He watched her reactions through a two-hour question-and-answer period before the Foreign Relations Committee and drew his own conclusions. And when she suggested a horse's kick had unbalanced *him*, Wayne Morse made his conclusion about her retroactive—"an old, old pattern of emotional instability on the part of this slanderer."

The weird episode evoked little sympathy for the diplomatic nominee and less for her senatorial challenger. The Washington *Post* said, "It is time she learned that the kind of acid which is funny in *The Women* sears when it is sprayed in public," and that Morse's "consummate gall" in calling her doctor constituted "an invasion of privacy which, we should think, would have sent the Senate liberals into a tizzy."

When her resignation was announced, Morse issued one of those I-hated-to-have-to-do-it-but-duty-called statements and expressed gratitude for the "large number" of senators who he said had privately expressed their approval of his good deed.[3] If this climax was not ample gratification, during that same week at a large banquet held in Washington to celebrate the tenth anniversary of the Point Four program and attended by Mr. Truman, many members of Congress, and hundreds of other Democrats, the heaviest ovation accorded any man in the house went to Wayne Morse. The only tizzy into which these liberals were thrown was a spasm of joy over the thrashing this man had given that Republican woman with the serpent's tongue who had used it so unsparingly on their demigods, Roosevelt and Truman, during her partisan days in Congress.[4] Wayne Morse, their hero of this hour, had done what most of them, in their moments of deepest partisanship, would have liked to do.

That night, in that wide sector of Washington's dense political jungle, this lionized tiger ranked supreme.

[3] Mrs. Luce got off the final wisecrack after her resignation. In a letter to a Brazilian editor who shares her love of skin diving she said, "After what happened in the Senate sessions I am anxious to look an honest shark in the face." An Oregon citizen, W. D. Nickelson of Portland, objected to the original crack because it shifted the blame for Morse's behavior onto a horse. "It's time for us horse lovers to stand up and assert ourselves. I am sure that none will believe one horse *could* do all this."

[4] The remark most cited was her contention that Roosevelt "lied us into war."

3. MAN OF LETTERS

*Too Much Horse Liniment . . . The Curmudgeon . . .
Brotherly Critics*

INTERIOR Secretary Harold Ickes blustered into the White House one sultry day in 1943 and demanded that President Roosevelt fire that Trojan Horse professor on the War Labor Board who was causing the Interior Department so much anguish. Did the President know that Wayne Morse was a *Republican* troublemaker? F.D.R. replied that Dean Morse's party affiliation surely shouldn't bother an old Bull Mooser like Ickes.

Ickes finally got to the real source of his ire. As Roosevelt knew, Ickes and Morse had become vinegary pen pals because of differences over government policy during the coal strike of that year. "What's the matter, Harold," asked Roosevelt, grinning, "have you finally found someone who can write a nastier letter than you?"

Wayne Morse delights in telling this tale. Being portrayed as a nasty letter writer is a matter of honor to him. Dean Morse, the newcomer to bureaucratic throat-cutting, was actually outclassed by the Old Curmudgeon; but he sharpened his literary blade over the years. By the time he went after his brother senator, Richard Neuberger, the edge had been honed to razor sharpness.

Dictating a tough letter is almost as much fun for Wayne Morse as making a fighting speech. And it is as hard for him to write a brief letter as it is to make a brief speech.

A compulsion to get things off his chest and onto paper dates at least from his faculty days at the University of Oregon. A colleague recalls Morse frequently delighted in reading aloud his most vivid letters. The gratification he realizes in this exercise must be counted as a clue to his contemporary behavior. As recently as the spring of 1960 he used the letter-writing device to brighten a gloomy day. At his breakfast table the morning after the presidential primary election in the District of Columbia in which he lost to Hubert Humphrey, Morse read an editorial that criticized his campaigning in churches the Sunday before the election. His first act at the office was to dicate a testy reply. "I twisted that guy's tail. It set me up for the whole day," he explained to me that afternoon, after reading me his letter to the Washington *Post*.

Too Much Horse Liniment

This inner need to get his gripes onto paper helps explain a curious letter Morse wrote in 1943 to the supervisor of a large chain of retail drugstores operating in Washington, D.C. Its full text follows:

April 17, 1943

Mr. Louis Chrisman,
Supervisor Peoples' Drug Stores,
77 P Street, N. E.,
Washington, D.C.

Dear Mr. Chrisman:

This letter is written to bring your attention to a complaint which I wish to make against the Manager of the Peoples' Drug Store on Pennsylvania Avenue, two doors from the Raleigh Hotel. Although the incident is not a matter of great concern, it nevertheless constitutes a type of service which I have not assumed in the past was consonant, at least with the public representations, of Peoples' Drug Stores. I particularly object to the insolence and discourtesy of your manager in the beforesaid drug store.

The facts are as follows:

On Thursday, April 15, I sought to purchase in this particular drug store a bottle of Savoss Horse Liniment. I was told by the lady clerk that the store did not have any on hand, but would be glad to order a bottle for me and that I could call for it on Friday, April 16, after five P.M. I told her to order two bottles.

On Friday, April 16, I called at 7:30 P.M., but the liniment had not arrived and the manager of the store told me that it was on the way. After the liniment arrived, one of the clerks brought me one bottle, but I told him that I had ordered two, and although one would probably be enough, I would take both bottles. He went back to the prescription room and brought the other bottle, although it was perfectly evident that at the time he did not consider I was under any obligation to take more than one. However, I took both bottles and when I got home last night and read the directions it became perfectly clear to me that one bottle would last me for a long time.

This morning, I returned to the drug store and asked to exchange one of the bottles for a bottle of absorbine. One would think from the reaction of your manager that I was attempting to commit a crime because he, most impolitely and accusingly, said that I had ordered both bottles and that it was impossible for him to send one bottle back. I endeavored to explain the situation and point out to him that his own clerk offered to sell me but one bottle last night. My comments only accentuated his ire; whereby I told him if he felt that way about it, I would keep the bottle, but I would purchase my absorbine and all my other drug supplies elsewhere.

I fully appreciate the fact that my business is of no consequence to your concern, but as a member of the consuming public, I want you to know that I do not appreciate such discourtesy as I received in this particular store. There is no justification for your manager's refusing to take the liniment back, especially in view of the fact that I was not asking for a cash refund, but only an exchange for other goods. I say there is no justification because the liniment itself is sold under a refund guarantee and for your manager to argue that he could not return the liniment is obviously false.

I think it is also interesting that he would refuse to take back into stock for resale the liniment, because his refusal would seem to imply that the liniment is not saleable. If that is the case, it should not have seen sold to me in the first instance, but of course we know that it is good liniment and there is a sale for it.

I think his position is untenable in another respect; namely, when I ordered the liniment, I did not even leave my name and had I not come back for the liniment, your manager would have had on hand the two bottles.

The truth of the matter is, I have no objections to keeping the liniment, although I need only one bottle, in view of what I have discovered concerning its use since the purchase. However, what I do object to is the insolence of your manager and his refusal to live up to the reputation of service and accommodation which your concern professes. The extra bottle of liniment will remain in my office for a period of days in case you wish to send someone to get it in accordance with common business decency.

Yours very truly,
Wayne L. Morse

WLM:mbl

The Curmudgeon

In June, 1943, Morse became verbally entangled with Ickes. Provoked by that most common cause of bureaucratic ill will, a jurisdictional dispute, in which the War Labor Board and the Interior Department vied for authority in settling the spring coal strike of 1943, the participants debated their conflicting legal views before Roosevelt on June 2, 1943. Ickes and his undersecretary, Abe Fortas, argued that a precedent had been set in the Toledo, Peoria and Western Railroad case, in which the Director of Defense Transportation, Joseph Eastman, had been authorized to make new employment agreements to benefit the workers during government operation of that railroad. On this ground Ickes and Fortas maintained their right to dicker with John L. Lewis and to placate him with wage increases, after the government seized the mines and Ickes' department was given the responsibility for operating them.

Morse and his War Labor Board colleagues maintained that only the board had authority to set new wage agreements, that Eastman had acted in the railroad case only after close consultation with the board. To empower Ickes to deal with Lewis, Morse contended, would amount to special, and unfair, procedures for Lewis that were not avaliable to disputants in other cases.

After this White House conference, Fortas dispatched a memo to Roosevelt reiterating and expanding his point. The next day Morse answered the Fortas memo with a letter to FDR, written on behalf of the entire board. The language in both missives was most proper. The following day Fortas wrote to Morse to take issue with the dean's letter to Roosevelt. Respect began to deteriorate in this communiqué. A few excerpts suffice:

> I had not expected a simple quotation from an executive order to cause you or the National War Labor Board so much concern. After all, I considered your erroneous statement at the White House to be merely a lapse of memory.
>
> . . . .
>
> You doubtless have already had an opportunity to re-examine your charge that I wrote the language of the American Railroad of Porto Rico order with a prescient eye on future difficulties with the handling of the coal dispute. Apart from a rather startling implication that I make

unscrupulous use of occult powers, you will note that the operative language is identical with the Toledo order of March 21, 1942.

. . . .

To your triumphant discovery that I would like to have the Secretary of the Interior fix wages during the period of government operation, I care to make only one answer: I would like to have this coal controversy handled so that it will be terminated as soon as possible, and stable conditions restored to the mines. You might think about that awhile.

Sincerely yours,
Abe Fortas

P.S. I am not bothering the President with a copy of this comment upon your trivial letter, nor am I discussing it with the press.

On June 7 Morse answered Fortas and dispatched copies of their exchange to the White House with a brief note to Marvin H. McIntyre, Roosevelt's secretary, saying, "As far as I am concerned, this correspondence will end the incident because after I am convinced that a person is not acting in good faith and I have told him so, further communications are useless." To Fortas, who is now a prominent Washington attorney, Dean Morse wrote:

June 7, 1943

CONFIDENTIAL

Mr. Abe Fortas
Under Secretary of the Interior
Department of the Interior
Washington, D.C.

Dear Mr. Fortas:

I doubt if any further exchange of correspondence will change our views of each other. Such differences of opinion as have arisen between us are entirely understandable when it is realized that our conceptions as to the responsibility of Government in holding steadfast to basic principles of judicial processes in meeting such challenges to Government as are presented by the Coal Case are diametrically opposed to each other.

I think that you and the Secretary of the Interior have written a disgraceful page of American Industrial History by adopting the methods which you have followed in handling the Coal Case. The first truce which you arranged with Mr. Lewis scuttled the President's speech, and thereafter it became clear that you also were willing to scuttle the

War Labor Board. To my way of thinking, expediency is never a justification for sacrificing basic principles. Even though you may be entitled to the benefit of the assumption that throughout the Coal Case you have been motivated by a desire "to have this Coal Controversy handled so that it will be terminated as soon as possible and stable conditions restored to the mines," nevertheless you have adopted techniques which in my judgment have compromised your government.

As to the Toledo, Peoria and Western Railroad matter, my view has not changed. Without knowing the history of the case and without being at all familiar with the procedures which were followed or with the understanding which existed at the time the President signed the Executive Order, you seized upon certain language in that order in an endeavor to justify what you and the Secretary of the Interior would like to have done in the Coal Case. However, not only the War Labor Board but the President also knew exactly what the understanding was in the Toledo Case. It was only because the War Labor Board considered your tactics to be of the trickster type that it decided to authorize me to file an answer to your memorandum with the President. Hence it unanimously approved the letter which I sent to the President.

Very truly yours,
Wayne L. Morse
Public Representative

Fortas hastened to reply that very day:

My dear Mr. Morse:

Your letter of June 7 is as intemperate as has been your entire conduct in the handling of the coal case. After reading it, no one can doubt that you are completely unsuited for any position which required the exercise of judgment and balance.

If the statement of the unmistakable and indisputable meaning of a provision in an Executive Order, which is somewhat embarrassing to you, is trickster tactics, I am sure that you will never be guilty of that offense. But I believe that it is completely useless to argue with a man who conducts himself as if he were bereft of his senses. My only remaining hope for the War Labor Board is that your splendid colleagues will be able to restrain your unscrupulous, undignified, and irrational conduct. If and when Secretary Ickes and I feel that we need guidance as to our responsibilities to the President or to the Government we certainly will not consult a person who is so obviously irresponsible as yourself.

Sincerely yours,
Abe Fortas
Under Secretary

Morse replied with relatively respectful language and uncharacteristic brevity:

June 8, 1943

CONFIDENTIAL

Honorable Abe Fortas
Under Secretary of the Interior
Department of the Interior
Washington, D.C.

My dear Mr. Fortas:

I note from your letter of June 7 that you have not learned that calling a proposition or its advocate names proves nothing against the proposition or its advocate. Your letter is most amusing, and it displays your own weaknesses in an unmistakable manner.

I am perfectly willing to stand on my record of public service, and I am particularly glad to stand on the record which I have made in defending the position of the National War Labor Board in the coal case against your "fixing" tactics.

Sincerely yours,
Wayne L. Morse
Public Representative

Fortas that same day sent back to Morse another letter which read:

June 8, 1943

CONFIDENTIAL

Mr. Wayne L. Morse,
Public Representative,
War Labor Board,
Washington, D.C.

My dear Mr. Morse:

I have not opened your letter of today and I do not propose to do so. I am sure that if I opened it, I would find that you had excoriated me, my motives, intelligence, character, and habits of life. Perhaps there are a few additional categories that would have occurred to you; and I am willing to concede that you would have done just as thorough a job of excoriation and vituperation as I did in my last letter to you. Perhaps you would have done a better one.

In any event, I am sure that if I read your letter, I would feel it necessary to reply and to attempt to match, if not excel your own effort.

I am sure that neither of us, try as we might, could convince the other that he is a worthless thus and so, absolutely lacking in essential decency and unworthy of the position that he holds or any other. So I propose to let the matter stand.

> Sincerely yours,
> Abe Fortas
> Under Secretary

It was then that Ickes nonchalantly entered the brawl and demonstrated his superior professional form in the following letter to Morse on June 11, 1943:

> The Secretary of the Interior
> Washington
> June 11, 1943

PERSONAL

My dear Mr. Morse:

Knowing my keen pleasure in the bizarre, Mr. Fortas has given me an opportunity to read the passages-at-arms between him and you in your recent correspondence and I cannot resist my incorrigible habit of commenting when I am involved, even if only indirectly.

My first, as my last, reaction to the sticking out of tongue in which you have indulged is an image in my mind of a street urchin of not particularly good manners who tauntingly assures his disputant that "my dad can lick your dad." I am sorry that recent events have not only given me an opportunity, but have made it necessary for me to form an appraisal of you. Before you came to Washington, on the basis of apparently authentic information, you stood high in my regard.

There was a time when I was seriously considering making you a proposition. That was before I heard you in the President's office argue that the Puerto Rican and the TPW orders did not give Mr. Eastman the power to make new contracts with the workers. You had made the same untrustworthy statement publicly previously. Now if I read aright the copy of your letter of June 4 to the President you admit, which is all that Mr. Fortas argued, that "technically, literally and legalistically," Mr. Fortas' interpretation of the executive orders in the two cases was correct. But you didn't admit this before the President. You argued flatly to the contrary.

There is a name that we of the legal fraternity have for lawyers who sally boldly forth on thin ice and cite an authority in point while "cleverly" omitting important language, the honest incorporation of which would turn the "precedent for" into a precedent against. You stand on pretty weak ground when you try to justify your attempted deception of the President at a critical time in an important matter by the defense "that neither Mr. Eastman nor the War Labor Board adopted technical, literal, or legalistic interpretations of the Executive Order in the Toledo, Peoria and Western case, such as Mr. Fortas has sought to apply throughout the handling of the coal case."

I may add, as final comment upon this extraordinary situation, that I know of no circumstance in which a subordinate is justified in undertaking to deceive his superior officer, especially when his superior officer happens to be the President of the United States, when he is considering the taking of an important step which might be a serious misstep.

After all it isn't a question of whether Mr. Eastman exercised his powers technically or not. The question is whether he had such powers, and it was on this point that you deliberately undertook to deceive the President.

I note with amusement the minatory finger that you wiggle-waggle in my direction in your letter of June 7 to Mr. Fortas. Time will show whether Mr. Fortas and I "have written a disgraceful page of American industrial history." At any rate, we will not be found to have written a comic strip.

> Very truly yours,
> Harold L. Ickes
> Secretary of the Interior

Mr. Wayne L. Morse
National War Labor Board
Department of Labor Building
Washington, D.C.

Morse's reply to Ickes—presumably the letter which provoked Ickes to demand his dismissal—was as follows:

June 14, 1943

Honorable Harold L. Ickes
Secretary of Interior
Washington, D.C.

Dear Mr. Secretary:

Thank you very much for your letter of June 11, 1943. It is in keeping with and supports my low esteem of you. The attempt of you and Mr. Fortas to try to convict me, without justification, of deceiving the President in order to divert attention from your gross mishandling of the Coal case should be beneath you as a Cabinet officer.

The facts in regard to the Toledo, Peoria and Western Railroad case are just exactly as I represented them in our conference with the President. What I said then and say now is that it was definitely understood by all concerned when the Government took over the Toledo, Peoria and Western Railroad that the War Labor Board would be consulted in connection with fixing wages and working conditions. It was consulted.

At the time the executive order in the Toledo case was signed it was not contemplated, as you proposed to the President in connection with the Coal case, that Mr. Eastman would fix wages and working conditions independently of the War Labor Board's obligations in connection with the wage dispute. The President understood that and told you so at the conference. I did not argue concerning the literal contents of the executive order in the Toledo case, but I did point out to the President the understanding which existed and which he also recalled to be the fact. At no time have I said that the executive order did not contain the literal language which Mr. Fortas referred to. What I did argue was that the order read in its entirety and in light of the understandings existing at the time it was signed did not mean what Mr. Fortas said it meant. I still say so.

I surmise that because of the very marked differences of opinion which developed between you and the War Labor Board at the conference with the President, you have found it easy to imagine the existence of motives on my part which were, in fact, not present. However, in view of the fact that you have seen fit to write me such a letter, I welcome the opportunity to tell you that I consider your conduct in the Coal case, plus the contents of your autobiography, all the evidence I need as to your emotional instability.

I deeply resented the "off the record" statements which you made at your press conference at the time you announced your scuttling truce with Lewis. Whether you know it or not, those comments to the effect that you did not even listen to the President's speech on the Coal crisis had the effect of holding the President up to ridicule.

I am perfectly aware of the fact that for one in my subordinate position to express his complete lack of respect for and confidence in men in such high positions as you and Mr. Fortas is not in accordance with Government protocol, but I could not have done less and kept faith with myself respect.

Very truly yours,
Wayne L. Morse
Public Member

There the matter concluded. Whoever was the more right in the labor case at issue, it is little wonder that Ickes was reported to have exerted his influence against the appointment of Dean Morse to a vacancy on the Federal Court of Appeals at San Francisco a few months later. No official verification is available for this account of Ickes' revenge, for presidential papers dealing with appointments are held confidential until after the death of the individuals involved. If Ickes was not to blame, then perhaps Attorney General Francis Biddle, as Morse suspected, blocked his path to the bench. Morse had earned Biddle's enmity the year before by writing to an official of Harry Bridges' Longshoremen's Union to declare that Biddle's decision on the Bridges deportation case "appears to be pregnant with the twins of twisted logic and unsound public policy." Probably neither Biddle nor Ickes would have sanctioned a Judge Morse. The point here is that Wayne Morse very probably lost his chance for a judgeship that he very much wanted, and thereby gained his later opportunity to become a senator, because of his style and persistence as a man of letters.

Running through all Morse's correspondence like a bold red line of continuity is an outer positiveness. If there were inner doubts, they were kept well out of sight. Morse himself described this personal condition in a letter to his faculty colleague, Orlando Hollis, in 1943:

> Last week I wrote a 14-page dissent in the Allis-Chalmers case, and it so shook the majority that the Chairman of the Board on the record has made the statement that the dissenting opinion is unanswerable and that he feels the case must be reconsidered. Although I am glad to have the case reconsidered because I am satisfied that the reconsideration will result in the majority of the Board coming over to my point of view, nevertheless, I am disappointed that the dissenting opinion will never see the light of publication because it is a honey so far as taking the boys for a ride is concerned. I am going to have some copies of it run off, and I will send you one because I think you will enjoy it.

Besides asserting his confidence in being right in the Allis-Chalmers dissent, it is valuable to note that the prospect of the other Board members' coming over to his side caused Morse to betray a certain melancholy mood at this turn of events. This tends to bolster the conviction that Morse is happier in righteous dissent as a lonely minority of one than he is when successful in converting others to his point of view.

The adamant conviction of personal rightness and the propensity for letter writing have figured in the bitter termination of some long and useful friendships, notably with editor William M. Tugman in 1952. Tugman had backed Morse in his most difficult battles—his university fight, his bid for the Senate, and his re-election campaign in 1950; but when Tugman advised his readers that Morse was the better man or had the better of the cause at the moment, he did not deceive them with the notion that Morse was faultless, as editorial writers are often prone to do when recommending their favorite candidates to the voters. "The Senator could never believe that Bill Tugman really liked him," a close associate recalls. Nevertheless, Morse retained a good working relationship with his hometown editor for two decades. In 1952 Tugman climbed on him editorially for supporting Truman's seizure of the steel plants. His editorials were amply documented from Morse's speeches in the *Congressional Record* and the text of the Supreme Court opinions which ruled the seizure unconstitutional. Morse replied with a long letter, and Tugman retorted with another editorial. Back and forth it went for some weeks, with the newspaper publishing Morse's letters on the front page. Finally, Morse wrote:

> At the beginning of your editorial you refer to the risk of marring a friendship. Let me assure you that no friendship of mine is ever marred by lapses of good judgment on the part of friends. One soon learns on this job that differences over issues frequently cause friends to strike out in unfair criticism of one holding public office. That is one of the prices one must pay in politics if he is willing to say what he thinks ought to be said even though it may involve a criticism of the press. As far as I am concerned you haven't marred a friendship, you have only provided me with a disappointment because of your failure to be fair to your readers.

For all this noble philosophizing, the friendship waned. Morse was used to fighting with members of the press, but Tugman had done more for him than most editors or reporters. He had helped him win many a battle. The degeneration of this alliance, along with similar episodes, has led to the wide belief that Morse cannot abide criticism from anyone, that the only way to gain and maintain Morse's favor is to pat him on the back, and that one word of stern advice, however constructive or merited it may be, is the signal for Wayne Morse to turn on his adviser. There is, it appears, much truth in this; but there is evidence that Morse can take criticism without blowing up, if it is given by the right person in the right manner.

Brotherly Critics

Two illustrations have come to my attention, both involving men who were law students of Morse's at Oregon. Neither of these men, so far as I know, ever feuded with Morse, and yet both were free with criticism. One told me, "When Wayne would stop by for a visit during a trip to Oregon, he loved to talk about his adventures in the Senate. I used to tell him in dead seriousness some of his most serious shortcomings—that he had a messiah complex, that he had a wonderful mind but no heart, that he insulated himself from emotional tolerance and understanding of the individual persons involved in causes and issues, that he did not know how to be a friend. Wayne would always pass off such comments, even though repeated, as so much ribbing. He never got mad, he never appeared to take them seriously and never discussed the comments."

The other friend was the late Jim Landye, who practiced labor law in Portland when Morse served on the War Labor Board. It is said by some who knew them both that Morse had a closer relationship with Landye than with anyone else in Oregon. In August 1942 Landye wrote Morse to say:

I noticed a very good article by John Chamberlain in the Sunday *Journal* editorial page in which he accuses you of using 'lecture methods' for yelling at the poor workers! Them's my sentiments exactly! If you have not read the article, I suggest you do so. It stated, if I remember correctly: 'Even a judicial mind such as Dean Morse has, stooped to the lecture methods!' I think the words are well chosen and well merited. If you cannot get the column, let me know, and I will be only too glad to send it with underlining. . ."

The following week Morse replied:

Nuts to you! However, send the *Oregon Journal* to me because I haven't seen it. I hope to shout I have been doing some lecturing, but I can assure you that my lectures to labor have had more educational effect than any of my lectures to you. I may be in dutch in certain labor quarters where the facts are not known, but the labor members of the War Labor Board highly approve of what I have been doing even though as a matter of policy they have to vote against me on some cases.

Morse, in this reply, then went on to urge Landye not to feel that he must volunteer for military service, that it was important for him to remain on the home front and help "labor fight its battles." Later, in February 1943, Morse wrote to Landye in a most fatherly fashion to urge that he ease up on his work after hearing that Landye had passed out several times recently:

> . . . in many respects we are peas out of the same pod. However, take it from me, I have learned how to let down, and I am sure that had I not learned that lesson I would have been a physical wreck long before this. One of the chief reasons for my taking to horseback riding was because I found in it a relaxation outlet, and I also have learned to relax in other ways as a pressure outlet. You have got to do the same thing. You, too, have got to learn to laugh at the things that bother you, particularly the cases that you try. Why in hell you let yourself be so disturbed personally over cases is beyond me. It doesn't help you solve the cases; it isn't necessary in order to protect the interests of your clients; and it isn't going to help you but will play havoc with your health.

Morse concluded with a series of instructions on getting regular exercise, more sleep, spending more time with his family, and finally by offering assurances that Landye was doing work that was outstanding war service for which he need not apologize to anyone.

A month later Landye wrote to complain that a recent lumber decision was "a mess" because workers were leaving the Northwest pine industry in droves. Said Landye to his old professor:

> I still say the War Labor Board is going on a lot of damned theory, and are doing about as good a job of holding back production as any group I know. . . . It seems to me the Board should make up its mind if it wants to win the war or if it wants to sustain some classic theory of economics.

Did Morse blow his top at the audacity of this former pupil? Quite the contrary. He replied by saying he hoped to get Landye to come to Washington to "present some of the points of view that only you would present to this Board." Added Morse:

> I warn you in advance that when you get through you probably will be told that you sound like Wayne Morse, because Jim, I think we are the only two fools in existence that are willing to say just exactly what we think about these labor matters. . . . I am enclosing copies of an exchange of letters between Mr. Ickes and myself which I am sure will provide you with a laugh or two.

Morse could take criticism from these two friendly attorneys, it appears, because of the way they offered it and because of the sort of men they were. Full of brotherly love for Morse, they criticized only in private. Criticism aired in public—the scolding editorial, the remark of another public figure quoted in the press, the challenge in debate—predictably invites invective from Morse. One can't comprehend Morse's most bitter letter-writing feud—with another former student, Richard Neuberger (Chapter 18)—unless he first recognizes this distinction between Morse's reaction to private, kindly criticism and to public criticism, however kindly it too might be.

Today Wayne Morse has no Jim Landye to offer him tough, kindly private criticism. His capacity for breaking off friendships outruns his desire to make new ones. The world has grown more heavily populated with his enemies, who by definition are public critics of the senator. If he is the loneliest man in Washington, as Sam Grafton once termed him, this would appear to be a significant reason for his isolation.

The widow of Harold Ickes, however, is confident that not all of Morse's past adversaries have retained their hostility. As the Kennedy administration took power, she told me, "If Harold was looking down on the last eight years, I'm sure he was saying, ''Atta boy, Wayne. Give them a kick for me!'"

4. THE DRIVING FORCE

The Conflict . . . To Be King . . . The Mystery

IF Wayne Morse's fights with Harold Ickes and countless others appear in harsh contrast with his frequent declarations in behalf of high moral principles, they illustrate a basic conflict which has confronted the man since boyhood. It is the eternal conflict between Christ's commandment to us to turn the other cheek and the natural instinct to fight for self-preservation. In the family in which Wayne Morse was reared, this philosophical conflict confronted the boy in the most personal way. His mother and his father stood on opposite sides of the issue, and the conflict was perhaps intensified for young Wayne because he was the baby of the family until he reached his teens, when sister Caryl was born.

The Conflict

The first-born child of Jessie and Wilbur Morse on their Wisconsin homestead was a girl, Mabel, followed by twin boys, Harry and Grant. A fourth child died in infancy. Wayne was born in 1900, the year of his parents' tenth wedding anniversary. His mother was twenty-eight his father forty-one.

Jessie and Wilbur Morse were different in a number of obvious ways. His father was six feet tall and heavy-set, a man of powerful build, quiet-spoken but readily aroused. His mother was short and slight, a woman of limitless energy, talkative, always working and eager to advance her children.

One wintry day when Wayne was nine or ten, two neighborhood boys began abusing some of his toys. His father, who was loading firewood into the basement, finally said to his youngest son, "Wayne, why don't you stand up for your rights?" Brother Harry, six years his senior, says Wayne pitched in, arms flailing, and "cleaned up on both of them." His mother, who kept a switch close at hand but never used it, strongly opposed violence. "Mother was mad at all of us for the rest of that day," recalls Harry vividly. "She didn't think that was proper."

This conflict was neither casual nor temporary. Their mother was a deeply religious woman who played the organ successively at the First Baptists and the Trousdale Methodist churches in Madison. Every Sunday morning she shepherded her youngsters to church school, there to absorb the Biblical teachings which were the rock of her moral code. Sunday afternoons were often spent visiting other families from the church.

Father was not opposed to this, as long as it was not carried too far. He had been an amateur boxer and he believed that a man, outside the ring as well as in, must stand up for his rights. Wilbur Morse meant to see that his sons learned this manly principle.

The boys loved the story of conflict their father told upon returning from a St. Louis livestock show. The great John L. Sullivan had come barnstorming into that city, offering $200 to anyone who could last two rounds with him in the boxing ring. Wilbur Morse resisted the importunings of his companions, who wanted to see a good match. Sullivan at length persuaded Morse to enter the ring, assuring him an easy time of it. Wilbur Morse, however, landed the first good punch and sent the startled champion to the canvas. Sullivan sportingly gave Morse not only the $200, but the boxing mitts as a souvenir of his wondrous feat.

As a boy, Wayne resolved the conflict as best he could. "Wayne wasn't a fighting boy," says Harry. "He never picked a fight. He wrestled some, but too often he would break a bone." In grade school he played a scrappy game of basketball, but in high school he shunned football, the sport in which his older brothers vigorously engaged. Wayne, instead, took up debating. To turn from the bruising physical-contact sports and to channel his aggressiveness into intellectual lines represented a triumph for his mother's point of view.

A few years later, however, Wayne asked his father for a gun. He was planning to go to the Dakotas to work on a wheat-harvesting gang with other university students during the summer vacation. Not knowing what dangers he might encounter in the Wild West, Wayne wanted a dependable means of protection. Wilbur Morse shook his head and took down his old boxing mitts to instruct his son in the less dangerous art of self-defense.

In his rough-and-tumble career, Wayne Morse has not been known to smite any man in the chops, though his fists have occasionally been cocked in anger. If his mother would be pleased that he never resorted to fisticuffs, his father might be proud that Wayne never failed to stand up for his rights in political combat. Indeed, his son's public career is a monument to the success of bruising verbal force. His father might also be gratified that Wayne Morse seemed to remember the strategy he taught him that day with the boxing mitts—the strategy that floored the great John L.—"Always get in the first punch."

Today Wayne Morse visualizes himself as one who fights only of necessity, one who never throws undeserved punches, only standing up for his rights and the rights of the public. "You know, I just hate to be mean," he told me. When this remark drew a friendly retort of disbelief, Morse told of an unpleasant encounter the night before at Washington National Airport. A man came upon him suddenly and snarled, "Who are you working for now, [Roy] Chalk?" Puzzled at first, Morse soon recognized him as an attorney who had once appeared before his Senate committee representing a business group which unsuccessfully sought control of Washington's transit facilities. "No," the senator retorted, "and let me tell you, I'm not working for you either. I'm working only for the best interests of all the people." Morse allowed as how his mother would not have approved of even this relatively mild rebuke, but "the fellow obviously needed to be taken down a peg."

In the battle of public issues Morse is more inclined to take his father's advice and land the first blow, but even then he maintains that he starts punching only because the other side is telegraphing the punches it hopes to land. For example, only twenty-four days after President Eisenhower entered the White House Wayne Morse rose in the Senate and began the battle against resource giveaways. He then and there branded the new regime as "an Administration which, in my judgment, unless it is checked, will exploit our natural resources for selfish interests." Morse urged his liberal cohorts to "stop talking about a honeymoon" with the new G.O.P. regime and "fight them in the streets, in the alleys, and on the housetops and not let them get their guns of exploitation entrenched to mow down, as they will if we do not stop them, the public interest."

Paul Douglas of Illinois replied, "I do not wish to have as close relationships with the incoming adminstration as might be indicated by the phrase 'honeymoon,' but I do wish to preserve friendly relationships with the adminstration." Morse insisted "this is the hour to start the battle." Douglas said if Morse was convinced of that, then "he should begin the battle. But I do not wish to start indiscriminate firing until I see precisely what is under way." Not many weeks later Douglas and other liberals had joined Morse in the assault.

Wayne Morse has been a fighter throughout his career. But always, he contends, he has fought for a great moral principle. Apparently he has resolved his philosophical conflict by using Father's methods to serve Mother's ideals.

Although this is a neat solution, it has led to a major source of resentment against Morse within the Senate. There he is widely regarded as self-righteous. A liberal cohort, with whom he has never feuded and who admires his superior intellectual qualities, shook his head as he mentioned this trait and said, "He'll stand up and say, 'Whatever others may do, the Senator from Oregon will never compromise with principle or take the path of expediency.' It's as though everyone but Wayne in the Senate abandons his principles." Apparently Wayne Morse, in the role of the Senate's most eager fighter, must remove any philosophical taint by also raising himself up as the senator most dedicated to principle.

To Be King

Morse's greatest difficulty has come from yet another force within him. He is the knight who wants to become King Arthur, and quickly. Perhaps every knight wants to be king as much as he wishes to serve a great cause. Certainly nearly every political knight, and quite a few knaves, in Washington are driven by the compulsive force of ambition. This is the powerful thrust which drives them through the storms of controversy, fortifies them to endure the attacks that are a commonplace in public life, which, hopefully, will take them to the top.

Ambition, as such, is a useful and necessary ingredient in the American politician. Public office does not seek the man, whatever idealists may advocate to the contrary. The highest office, least of all, seeks its occupant. Ambition, the driving force of men in public life, propelled Abraham Lincoln to the White House just as surely as it did John F. Kennedy.

It is not amibiton that faults a public man, but the measures it can drive him to take. Ambition, wisely served, can take him to the top; unwisely served, it can plummet him to the depths.

As a boy, Wayne Morse was taught the value of advancing himself by means of a sound education. His mother, dissatisfied with the one-room country school down the road from the farm, insisted that her children go the ten miles to the Madison schools. Until the family moved to town subsequently, Harry and Grant hiked that ten miles to and fro each day. Wayne rode a horse. Jessie Morse visited the teachers periodically to see how her children were doing, showing anxiety about their need to progress, one teacher recalls. Wayne did well. Before he had laid aside his texts, Wayne had acquired four academic degrees, overcoming financial obstacles by hard work and sacrifice.

When he arrived in Eugene, Oregon, to begin his law-teaching career as an assistant professor, Morse could not have been overly impressed with the little law school at the University of Oregon, its six teachers and tiny band of barristers relegated to the top floor of one building. Fresh from a great citadel of higher education in Manhattan, the bright doctor of laws had an understandable desire to advance. Anyone in his position might expect to rise to associate professor, then to full professor, and possibly one day become dean of the law school, but all in good time. Dr. Morse was not that patient. In April, 1930, eight months after he began teaching at Oregon, he hit upon an idea for speeding up the normal processes. The dean of the Oregon law school was Charles E. Carpenter, who had been promoted to this post from the law faculty only three years before. Wouldn't it be fine, thought Morse, if Dean Carpenter advanced to a larger institution? Being new to his profession, he wrote to Dean Fraser at the University of Minnesota and asked his advice on how they might promote the appointment of Carpenter as dean of the Wisconsin law school. Dean Fraser nipped the plan quickly by advising his former law student that this would be an unwise endeavor.

If Assistant Professor Morse's eagerness for the advancement of his superior was mixed with impatience to advance to Carpenter's position, Morse had not much longer to wait. A year later Carpenter moved on to the University of Southern California, and Wayne

Morse, at thirty years of age, ranking fourth in seniority on the law faculty, became a candidate for dean. In his favor was at least one circumstance. The president of the University of Oregon, Arnold Bennett Hall, had been his professor of government at Wisconsin during Morse's undergraduate years. Hall, an able orator, undoubtedly appreciated Morse's rhetorical talent. "Wayne had a flair that some of his colleagues didn't have," a faculty veteran recalled. "Hall probably felt that he was up-and-coming." If his youthfulness was an issue, Morse sought to make it a virtue rather than a handicap. "Naturally, I think my age is my greatest asset, provided the president believes I possess a maturity of judgment," he wrote to a friend. He added that he had obtained Carpenter's support.

This, his first effort in professional advancement, was successful. Professor Morse became the youngest dean of law in the country.

Two years later, with his brilliant and daring Homecoming speech, Dean Morse became a public figure. Here he risked his deanship, indeed his professional career, by his attacks on the chancellor and the head of the State Board of Higher Education. As we have observed, he not only survived this episode, but became a heroic figure who was marked by the success of his first great oratorical onslaught. Having survived personally, Morse was not content simply to have saved the university. As editor Bill Tugman put it, Morse "soared into front-page orbit, and he has never quite been able to make his re-entry into the atmosphere in which most of us live and breathe." What justifies such a critical observation?

Tugman cited a most revealing chapter in the turbulent life of Wayne Morse, an episode which makes his subsequent political behavior more understandable. It occurred at the university after the Board of Higher Education decided to restore the office of president of the university, which had been abolished upon Hall's resignation in 1932. The Board selected as president the dean of the college of arts and sciences, Val Boyer, a quiet, altogether non-controversial professor of literature.

Until Boyer's appointment, Tugman had figured Dean Morse "for the daredevil champion of the university, the superb horseman and horse lover, the talented poker player, the bold exponent of a liberal philosophy in the law." But now a new aspect of the man emerged. Riding home from a meeting one night with Morse and some of his faculty cronies, Tugman says "they told me a long and circumstantial story of how meek little Val Boyer had plotted with Chancellor Kerr to obtain the presidency of the university."

"That can't be true," Tugman retorted. "I attended every single meeting of the board during that period. Many people were suggested—you, Wayne, and Jim Gilbert—but the problem was to find somebody acceptable to both Kerr and to the faculty. Poor Val was *it*." But now Dean Morse and his faculty rebels threatened President Boyer.

Tugman recalled having had breakfast with Boyer the morning after he was chosen. "Bill, I'd rather teach English literature, but I may be able to take care of myself. Did you know I once wrote a book about Machiavelli?" Tugman then warned Boyer that "writing a book about Machiavelli and meeting him in the arena might prove to be two very different tasks."

This prophecy was soon fulfilled. Boyer was caught between those who wished to compromise with Chancellor Kerr and Morse's faculty group, which advocated continued hostilities. Unsuited for this role, "the frustrated little scholar slowly took to drink," said Tugman. It became only a question of how long he would survive.

In the spring of 1937 Tugman received a telephone call from Dean Morse in Washington, where he had gone for a temporary assignment with the Justice Department. As Tugman recalled it, the conversation began with Morse asking whether Boyer had resigned yet. Tugman replied, "No, but it won't be long." The editor said, "Wayne launched into an extended discussion of the presidency and the kind of man who ought to be selected for the job—a man in the prime of life, aggressive, farsighted, courageous, a man of intellectual integrity, devoted to the highest educational principles, a skillful speaker, a man at home with people of every station in society."

"Look, Wayne, knowing how the board feels, you haven't got much chance for this job," interjected Tugman, "but keep your head down. Don't talk to anybody. Do nothing. We'll let you know when and if Boyer quits. Then it will be time to think up strategy."

When Boyer at length resigned, Tugman wired Morse in Washington, repeating his advice to keep low. By return wire came a lengthy telegram describing in detail the qualifications of the next president of the university. "No human being could have fitted this description but Morse himself," recalled Tugman. "Wayne, of course, denied that he would be a candidate.

"There followed an amazing chapter in the history of the university. Morse bombarded graduates of the law school and friends throughout Oregon with wordy letters similar to his original telegram outlining the specifications for president, always concluding with a denial of any personal ambitions. In the faculty council, which is usually consulted by the state board on presidential nominations, it became impossible to get an agreement, because Wayne's friends controlled the faculty council."

Tugman said a faculty friend of Morse's at length came to him with a compromise candidate "that even Wayne will accept." He named a prominent person who had been instrumental in getting Morse his first job in Washington. Tugman said the choice sounded good. The faculty member had scarcely left when a telegram for Tugman arrived from Washington: "Nomination of —— —— must be stopped at all cost. Airmail letter follows. Wayne L. Morse." The letter, said Tugman, was marked confidential and contained "an infinitely detailed report on stenographer scuttlebutt in Washington about —— ——'s personal morals. I was dumfounded." Tugman permitted the faculty member to read Morse's letter, and the prospective presidential candidate was that afternoon discarded.

Soon thereafter Tugman's newspaper, the Eugene *Register-Guard*, began to receive a cascade of press releases from Morse's office in Washington. First Morse revealed he was dickering to buy a new thoroughbred horse in Illinois. Then he announced he would ride his new mount in Eugene's Pioneer Parade and Oregon Trail Pageant later in the summer, official duties permitting, of course. Tugman continued:

"Some time later, in late July, we received a bulletin that Wayne was leaving Washington with a horse trailer. That was followed by a series of daily bulletins—he had arrived in Illinois and had met the horse; he had bought the new horse and was starting westward; that Morse and horse had crossed the Mississippi; that they were nearing the Platte; that they had passed Cheyenne and were nearing the Great Divide; that they were following the historic Oregon Trail down the Snake; that they had crossed into Oregon. It was a race against time, and my little staff was quick to appreciate the dramatic as well as the humorous elements. On the morning of the great Pioneer Parade, Wayne and his family and the new horse arrived at the Lane County Fairgrounds just about ten minutes before starting time for the procession. Wayne left Midge and the girls to find their way home, saddled up his new mount, and rode in the parade, bowing right and left and doffing his ten-gallon hat in sweeping gestures to the applauding multitudes who lined the way.

"The next morning Wayne was one of my first visitors. As he entered my office, he said humbly, 'Bill, what have I done wrong?'

" 'Writing all those jackass letters was bad enough, Wayne, but you've done one thing a grown man does not do. You wrote that letter bitching —— ——, the man who was your benefactor in Washington.'

" 'Oh, but I did that to save the university.'

" 'In a pig's eye, Wayne. There are plenty of us to save the university when it comes to that.' "

When Morse asked Tugman what he should do next, the editor advised him to get on that horse and "ride so far back in the Spencer Hills that nobody will see you the rest of the summer. Whatever chance you may have had to be president is probably gone now, but if you'll keep that big mouth shut, maybe there's some salvage. But the Board and a lot of other people are pretty disgusted." Morse was quiescent for about two weeks, and soon Tugman began hearing reports that Morse was telling friends that the editor had "betrayed his confidence."

Later in the summer the Morses gave a large reception for a member of the university faculty who had taken a bride. Tugman said more than 500 invitations were sent to prominent persons throughout the state. Recalled Tugman:

"It was a fabulous affair. The bride and groom were scarcely noticeable in the long receiving line. As one approached the end of the handshakers, he was mobilized for a personally conducted tour of the Morse stables. In the paddock he was introduced personally to each horse, and in the tack room he was shown 'the little saddle which the Dean's father gave him when he was only six, and upstairs, ladies and gentlemen, is a genuine Minnesota snow sleigh, which may interest some of you people who are not used to seeing snow in the winter.' "

Steeped in the professional skepticism of the journalistic trade, Tugman surmised that quite possibly the ambitious dean had more in mind than honoring the newlyweds. In the newspaper's city room, the affair was long remembered as the "horse-and-bride show."

Two weeks later Tugman was asked to the home of the late Professor John Ganoe, who advised the editor sternly, "Mr. Tugman,

I represent two thirds of the university faculty, and we are determined to have Dean Morse for our next president." He paused for effect, then resumed, "I have been authorized to serve warning on you, Mr. Tugman, that if you do not stop obstructing our candidate, we will be compelled to make it very tough for you and the *Register-Guard*." Dr. Ganoe went on at length to explain why his faculty group felt that only Morse could "save the university," speaking all the while in the manner of "a patient uncle explaining the dangerous character of fire to a venturesome child," noted Tugman. The editor, who had earlier been a police reporter on the Cleveland *Plain Dealer* in the twenties, at length said:

"Okay, John, now I'll tell you a little bedtime story. In a locked file at my office I have a bundle of letters as thick as your unabridged dictionary. Every one of those letters was written and signed by Wayne L. Morse. I have never published a line out of those letters; indeed, I cannot think of any way in which I have privately or publicly opposed the candidacy of Morse, although I have said a few blunt things to his face. However, if you and your friends want to play rough, I will start publishing those letters in the *Register-Guard* on page one. And John, I assure you, I do not want to do this, because I like Wayne personally; I like Midge and the children, and I do not want to hurt them. But let me warn you, if I am forced to publish those letters, Wayne L. Morse not only will never be president of this or any other university, it will be difficult for him to get a job in any self-respecting institution. Naturally, I do not want to do this."

It was Dr. Ganoe's turn to ponder. At last he asked to see the letters. The next day Tugman handed the file to the professor, asking only that he return them. When Ganoe returned them, Tugman said he shook his head sadly and whispered, "Incredible."

"Then the war is over?" asked Tugman.

"As far as I'm concerned, yes," replied the disheartened professor.

The courageous champion of academic freedom, the bold defender of the faculty against the wicked chancellor, the man who wanted only to "save the university," the unannounced candidate for president had faulted himself. His candidacy became unacceptable even to his staunchest admirers. Morse's controversial part in past campus battles perhaps precluded all chances of his becoming the university president. As Tugman put it, Morse was admired for his talents and his courage, but deplored for his lack of discretion and his tendency to "grandstand." Morse's letters outlined the qualifications the new university president must have, explained Tugman, and "only one human being in the world would fulfill all those specifications— Wayne L. Morse." And in the end the driving force of compulsive ambition drove him to take measures which brought the utter collapse of his support.

The Mystery

In these early adventures of Wayne Morse we have seen his Legend grow and thrive upon fearlessness, daring, advocacy of principle, rhetorical and intellectual vigor. Also we have pried beneath this carapace to take a long glimpse at the fundamental man, his reliance upon oratory, his own inner conflicts, his compulsive driving force.

Public life constantly suffers a shortage of men with such extraordinary raw material as Wayne Morse possesses. "The Lord has given him a great deal of ability," Senator Wiley of Wisconsin once put it. "The Lord has given him opportunity to perform a great service. . . . He should rise with the occasion, not fall with it." Why does Wayne Morse rise with some occasions, fall with others?

At the heart of Everyman, there is an inherent mystery of purpose, a struggle between warring attributes, the noble and the ignoble. As each new adventure challenges him, there begins a period of grand suspense as the internal struggle mounts. Vanity threatens modesty. Opportunism strikes against integrity. Fearful deceit vies with fearless candor. The expansive ego menaces selfless creativity. Intellectual arrogance intimidates kindly forbearance. Bitterness undermines tolerance, and ambition drives him ever onward, upward or downward as the struggle is decided.

Everyman's struggle becomes greatly magnified by the pressures and opportunities of public life. It becomes all the more dramatic as a public man nears the pinnacle. In Everyman's senator, the outcome is altogether unpredictable. This is the mystery of Wayne Morse.

Part Two

THE LAST SON OF THE
WILD JACKASS

5. THE CONSERVATIVE HOUR

What Kind of Republican? . . . Muted Liberal . . .
Middle of the Roader . . . Anti-New Dealer

THE POLITICAL feat for which Wayne Morse is wholly unique, his complete and successful transition from one party to the other in mid-career, has been the cause of no small discomfort to a substantial segment of the party which gave birth to his senatorial life. Sired and reared to national stature by the Republicans, he left home, became estranged from his parentage, and grew to give succor to the despised Democrats, a cruel ingratitude from any father's point of view. To Wayne Morse, admittedly a son of the Grand Old Party, leaving home was the only honorable course for a good boy whose father grew more heartless as the years passed.

More significant than determining who was more beastly to whom when Wayne Morse fled to the foster home of the Democratic party, important as that is, there is the heavier charge that Wayne Morse has been a traitor. When he made his bolt from the Republicans at the height of the Eisenhower-Stevenson presidential campaign in 1952, he and his family suffered for weeks from abusive remarks hurled by outraged partisans. The mail was choked with venomous messages; the telephone jangled at their home incessantly from callers with vituperative declarations; there were unpleasant encounters in public places, even in the White House. Long after the passions of that election campaign had been spent, few Republicans would defend those indecencies, but many Republicans would stand relentless upon their charge that Wayne Morse was a traitor to their party.

But the matter of switching parties is not a heinous crime in the minds of many American citizens, whose own political party affiliations are often tenuously held. For those who said consistent party attachment is required of political leaders, Richard L. Neuberger cited in Morse's defense the example of Lincoln, the Whig congressman who became the Republicans' greatest President, or Willkie, the ex-Democrat who became a Republican presidential nominee.

When Morse bolted the G.O.P., the Oregon *Journal*, Portland's afternoon newspaper, sympathetically observed that Wayne Morse was following the tradition of the Sons of the Wild Jackass. These political reformers of yesteryear—Bob La Follette, George Norris, William E. Borah, Hiram Johnson, Burton K. Wheeler, et al.—gave little heed to the stalwart code of party regularity. Marching to the Senate from the American prairie and mountain states, they were the scourge of party leaders. Was not Wayne Morse, true to this heritage, simply the last Son of the Wild Jackass? There was historical substance and perspective to this appraisal of Wayne Morse's maverick behavior.

Why, then, did Republicans become so incensed when he left their party? Why did they elect him in the first place?

What Kind of Republican?

To a little group of Eugene friends whom he consulted in January 1944 about the wisdom of entering the lists for the Senate, Morse described himself as a La Follette Republican—a liberal, but nonetheless a genuine Republican. The group happily accepted this, recalled editor Tugman, for "most of us agreed that the Republican party in Oregon and throughout the nation needed a transfusion of new blood."

What did it mean to be a La Follette Republican and a liberal in 1944? The La Follette Republicans were isolationists and the liberals were internationalist. Morse had differed with La Follette on this as early as his school days in Madison. He traces it to the chance circumstances that sent him to the Longfellow Grade School which served the "Bush," the ghettolike area of early twentieth-century Madison where the Negroes, Jews, Italians, Greeks, and other new immigrants found their place. He might just as readily have gone to Randall School, which served the children of greater privilege, including those of the university faculty. Miss Lorena Reichert, for forty-six years a teacher and the long-time principal of Longfellow, was one of the most influential persons in Morse's life, he feels, because she planned school programs to accentuate the rich culture from which her immigrant students came. Foreign customs, native costumes and folk dances were presented so agreeably that young Wayne, fresh from the farm where the taproot of American isolationism burrowed deep, became acquainted with foreigners as friendly school chums.

During World War I Morse was a high school boy, too young for military service, but old enough to discern the political turmoil that embroiled Madison. The popularity of Fighting Bob La Follette was jeopardized as waves of war sentiment crashed about the aging isolationist and all but engulfed his political career. Outspokenly against American involvement in the Allied fight against the Kaiser, he led the successful filibuster of 1917 against the bill to arm United States merchant ships, and was denounced by President Wilson as one of the "little group of willful men representing no opinion but their own." The editor of the *Wisconsin State Journal* had no difficulty filling a long petition with the names of university professors demanding La Follette's expulsion from the Senate.

Although not expelled, he was hanged in effigy on the Wisconsin campus—an act of impulsive passion, no doubt, but one nevertheless which occurred in a center of intellectual and progressive ferment concerning a man who was the leader of that school of thought and who was forty years later named by the Senate itself one of its five greatest members. Philip F. La Follette, the senator's son who was a schoolboy contemporary of Wayne Morse, recalls, "During, before, and after World War I there was intense feeling abroad in the university and in Madison—and in the state. Lines of demarcation were sharply drawn. Those on our side who were or could be vocal were few enough to be lastingly remembered. And Wayne was not among them."

To be a La Follette Republican, then, Wayne Morse necessarily had to be faithful to the spirit of domestic reform, if not to all its letters, which the great Progressive leader championed. John D. Hicks, the Midwestern historian, synthesized the spirit and the goals of this reform movement in his essay on the political heritage of the Middle West as follows:

> The Progressive movement had its roots in both the country and the city . . . and it based its protests on the same resentment against the efforts of a greedy few to monopolize for themselves the principal profits of the new industrialism. . . .

The Progressives won some notable victories. They made a substantial beginning in the reform of city government, they instituted primary elections and other procedures that changed the whole character of state government, they invaded the national field under Roosevelt and Wilson, and they kept their banner aloft under La Follette, even during the reactionary decade of the 1920s. They improved, too, on the Populistic formula for the use of the powers of government. They saw less and less virtue in the attempt to restore competition by an attack on big business as such, more and more in the extension of governmental regulation. Big business had come to stay; what the people needed was a fair-minded government that would lay down rules for its behavior, protect the interests of the public, and, to quote Jefferson again, restrain those who would 'take from labor the break it has earned.' But, as a matter of fact, the working class as a whole did not participate extensively in the Progressive movement. From beginning to end it was primarily a middle-class affair, seeking only incidentally to better the interests of labor and often interesting the labor leaders, but with its eye fixed firmly on the goal of keeping business subordinate to government and middle-class opportunity alive.

This side of Progressivism appealed to young Morse. Recalling the senator's periodic visits to the Wisconsin campus, Morse says, "There is no question but what La Follette had a terrific influence over young people. He filled them with crusading spirit." Yet there was a discernible ambivalence here caused by the tug of strong opposites— the sentiment *against* La Follette on the war, which Morse shared, and the sentiment *for* La Follette's domestic reforms, which had become a veritable way of life in Wisconsin.

This ambivalence is signified by the contradiction of views on whether Wayne Morse campaigned for La Follette. As Morse tells it, he and Ralph Axley and other students stumped through southern Wisconsin towns on Saturday afternoons with a bass drum in a model T. "The town squares would be full of farmers," he says. "We'd beat the drum awhile, and then one of us would make our speech for La Follette." Axley, now a prominent Madison attorney, has no recollection of Morse's ever joining his four-student team of La Follette campaigners in either the 1922 or 1924 campaign. Axley does recall Morse used to rib him about his devotion to the controversial Progressive leader. Philip La Follette, too, has no recollection of Morse's helping in his father's election efforts. If Morse did go electioneering for Fighting Bob, obviously it was not of memorable duration. Yet a fraternity brother attests that Morse "was a liberal and a great admirer of the elder La Follette" during his student days.

The circumstances of Morse's life helped make La Follette's program appealing. Born neither to privilege nor to poverty, Wayne Morse is a product of the middle class, from which comes the basic strength of the G.O.P. and whence came the Progressive movement. He shares the odd trait of successful American males who enjoy reflecting on the underprivileged moments of their youth. Wayne and his elder twin brother Harry, who for twenty years has been the agent for the Farmers' Home Administration in Barron County, Wisconsin, sat in the senator's office one wintry night reminiscing for my benefit. Harry remembered their father's stomping into their frame farmhouse one snowy day, crowding close to the steaming wood stove to crack icicles from his beard. "Jess, Jess," Wilbur exclaimed to his young wife, "they might as well take the place. I paid $39.68 in taxes today." McKinley was President and a recession had hit the plains. Wayne recalled later seeing his father sell a winter hay supply to raise the taxes, and then feed the livestock a mixture of molasses-watered straw and shredded cornstalks. One of his boyhood chums, Eugene Sinaiko, was the son of a Madison feed dealer who "carried my father through many a winter when times were tough." As a young boy, Wayne had the job of churning the butter and putting it into the cool cellar. "Mother spent Friday nights packing the butter jars. We had one-, two- or five-pound jars for our regular orders. On Saturday we served a regular route of customers in Madison. We served the millionaire section of the city. It was a very fancy route. Every once in a while I got tipped a nickel. Sometimes on Sundays our customers would drive out from town in their fine carriages to inspect our farm. We always had it spick-and-span for inspection."

But tough as times seemed to impressionable boys, there was none of the grinding poverty which other Americans in other places experienced eking out an existence from the land. Wilbur Morse had a fine barn, a plain but respectable two-story house, 160 acres, a modest herd of twenty-five to thirty dairy cows which the boys milked by hand, hogs, poultry, riding horses, and Devon beef cattle. Wilbur gained local fame as the first Wisconsin cattleman ever to win the grand sweepstakes at the Chicago International Livestock Exposition with his Devons.

In the family division of labor on the farm, young Wayne gravitated to the horse stalls while his older brothers slopped the hogs and milked the cows.

Grade school was a miniature class struggle, to hear Morse tell of it. He will pull up a trouser leg to reveal a shin scar as a badge of honor from the fierce rivalry between Longfellow and Randall schools. "We thought the Randall kids were snobs," he says, because many were the children of the university's professors and Longfellow was on the wrong side of the tracks, serving the children of the Bush. Rivalry was expressed in rough-and-tumble basketball games in the tiny Longfellow gym, where a hapless player might suddenly find himself shoved against a coarse plastered wall. Wayne's teachers from these days at Longfellow find it astonishing to think there was any class consciousness between the two schools. Contrary to being *the* school for the underprivileged, Longfellow served not only the racial-nationality section but also some very substantial families and a large group of middle-class families such as the Morses, notes Miss Reichert. Longfellow's hard-working P.T.A. raised six hundred dollars to give the school the first lantern in town to show educational pictures.

Wayne Morse's identification with the underdogs of society is illustrated by his recollection that his closest boyhood buddies at Longfellow were "Ellis Tipple, freckled-faced son of an Irish immigrant; Teddy Washington, son of the Negro janitor of the Trousdale Methodist Church where I attended Sunday school; and Eugene Sinaiko, son of a Jewish feed dealer." To a contemporary politician with one eye on appealing to urban minority voters, the story carries great appeal. To Ellis Tipple, still a friend of Morse's and a deputy sheriff of Dane County, the story provoked a good chuckle. Tipple is neither Irish nor the son of an immigrant. His father was born on a Wisconsin farm and came from New England forebears with roots in Wales. He and Morse were classmates and buddies from the third grade until they finished high school. Tipple recalled Teddy Washington as a good basketball player at Longfellow Grade School, but not as a buddy of theirs, inasmuch as he was several years younger. A warmhearted man with a fraternal attitude toward Morse, Tipple passed off the inaccuracies as "Wayne's way of making a good story."

The Morses didn't live in the Bush. In addition to the homestead ten miles west of town, they had a modestly attractive two-story frame house on Mound Street, three blocks west of the school. The Bush (formally it is Greenbush, and it is now giving way to an urban-renewal project) lay east of the school. The journey "across the tracks" came easily when Wayne went off to the university after he finished high school. Throughout his college years "Wayne never had any class consciousness," stated his friend Axley categorically. His campus peers were farm and small-town boys come to the land-grant college with the beautiful lakeshore campus in Madison, then a city of 25,000.

Muted Liberal

After he left Wisconsin, a strange silence which suggested indifference to politics settled over Wayne Morse for fifteen years. Faculty colleagues at Minnesota and Oregon have no recollection of his ever talking politics. At Minnesota, engrossed in his law studies during the complacent Coolidge years, Morse's apparent indifference would not be strange but for the fact that La Follette ran against Coolidge for the presidency in 1924, the autumn Morse began at Minnesota. At Oregon during the most revolutionary period of the century, from the stock-market crash to the war in Europe, when few remained indifferent to what FDR was doing, political silence was most curious. The available evidence is that he was more discreet than indifferent. Some associates of that period believe that Morse felt certain a closemouthed law professor would go farther in the state university of conservative Oregon than would an outspoken liberal. Even in the private seclusion of his penny-ante poker club, the dean never let down his hair politically, possibly because among the players were a banker and a town doctor whose sympathies probably were anti-New Deal. But with a liberal student assistant, the dean on several occasions emerged from his shell of silence in the safety of privacy. "He used to love to talk about Wisconsin politics," says Stephen B. Kahn of their chats in the dean's office. "I got the impression that he was a strong follower of La Follette. He had a strong feeling for the underdog."

This feeling was conveyed to his students in the law school. "He not only taught us what the law was, but what he thought it ought to be," recalls Kahn, now a wealthy liberal of Carmel, California. "In the field of domestic relations, for example, he thought the laws were too rigid and didn't adequately protect the rights of women." There

was a strong mixture of social consciousness—liberalism, if you will—
in Morse's law-class observations. "He pointed out that juries could
be stacked against a defendant of a minority race because some
methods of selecting jurymen preclude all but property owners, and
in many areas Indians and other minorities didn't own property. He
thought a jury should be composed of one's peers," says Kahn. From
his earliest teaching days Morse stressed a theme which has carried
over into his senatorial insistence on adhering to proper procedures.
"One's substantive rights are only as good as the procedural rights
which protect them," he has declared time and again in Senate debate
on civil rights and related legal issues. "He would tell us that the
rights of a man were only as secure as the procedures available to
him," says Kahn, "that unless you had money for a lawyer, civil
liberties didn't mean much. In the Loeb-Leopold case, Morse thought
that if they hadn't had the money to employ Clarence Darrow, the
defendants would have been electrocuted." In a word, Morse gave
his students a strong dose of liberal social philosophy with their law.

Morse's muted liberalism was expressed on at least one other
significant occasion. In 1934 Oregon had a three-way gubernatorial
race in which the only liberal candidate was Peter Zimmerman, an
Independent with Socialist backing. Kahn and his roommate, Richard
L. Neuberger, in the midst of making campaign sorties in Zimmerman's behalf, ordered 100,000 campaign pamphlets and had to raise
one hundred dollars to pay the printers. "I told Dean Morse about
it," Kahn recalls. "He dug down into his pocket and threw twenty
dollars on the table and said, 'You don't know where this came from.'
That was a lot of money in 1934." Zimmerman ran second to
General Charles H. (Iron Pants) Martin, a non-liberal Democrat
whose election signified the mood of Morse's relatively conservative
adopted state.

In the late thirties, when some faculty liberals were attracted to a
farmer-labor reform movement, the Commonwealth Federation,
Morse kept his distance. "I thought it was too leftish," he explains.
"I've never had anything to do with leftish groups." It is a noteworthy
irony that Morse years later readily accepted membership in Americans for Democratic Action, which was far more leftish for the placid
fifties, when Morse joined, than was Commonwealth Federation for
the turbulent thirties.

In 1940, finally, Morse spoke out on politics. Invited to make a

Middle of the Roader

Lincoln Day dinner speech before the Republicans assembled in the southern Oregon logging town of Klamath Falls, the forceful and dynamic orator left no one that night in doubt about where he stood:

> We should recognize that public opinion generally favors the broad international views of the present [Roosevelt] Administration. We should not oppose views simply because they are held by the Administration. That would be only to put party above country. We must cease to be a party dominated by an outworn theory of isolationism. There is no room within our party for blind nationalism.

This was pretty strong medicine for a partisan Republican gathering in February, 1940, for even though Europe was in flames and American aid to Britain was going forward, G.O.P. party leaders Taft and Vandenberg remained staunchly isolationist or nationalistic right up to Pearl Harbor. But what did Dean Morse say of the domestic liberal reforms of the New Deal?

> The New Deal, by its program of confiscating savings through taxes and of stifling private enterprise, has in a real sense created a general financial panic. We cannot confiscate the private wealth of our country and preserve at the same time the economic opportunity of our people through individual initiative to create wealth under our profit-motive economy.
>
> . . . .
>
> Legislation such as the Wagner Act, which is totally one-sided and discriminatory against the employer, carries with it its liabilities as well as its assets. Although labor is opposed to the suggestion, I have no hesitancy in saying that the Wagner Act cannot prove of lasting benefit to labor unless it is modified and amended in a manner which will give to the employer the same protection against unfair labor practices as it gives to labor against unfair practices by employers. The claim of labor that such amendments would scuttle the act are without merit. . . .
>
> . . . .
>
> The New Dealers are trying to convince us that the more taxes we pay the higher our incomes will be; the fewer pigs we raise the more food we will have to eat; the more wheat we burn the more bread we will have to eat. You make sense out of it; I can't.

This was the choice red meat the conservative Republicans expected. Dean Morse served it up to them bloody rare that night, broiling it over the pit of fiery damnation. Unsparing, he roasted the New Deal further for:

> The nostrums of an economy of scarcity, a regimentation of our economic life, a centralization in Washington of government functions which can be administered best by the people on a local basis . . .
>
> The idea of being paid for not producing, of working for the government when private industry was failing to produce work, of building up alphabetical pressure blocs in the interest of perpetuating the regime of the party in office . . .
>
> Superficial remedies . . . cleverly devised and plausibly presented by master politicians . . .

Even Fighting Bob La Follette didn't escape the pit that night. Recounting his debating success at Wisconsin, Morse allowed that he had argued in behalf of La Follette's proposal for allowing Congress to override the Supreme Court, but later he realized, he declared, this had "dangerous implications to constitutional government as we know it." As a student, Morse went on, he had "refused to align myself with the very active La Follette club on the . . . campus. La Follette's opposition to the war made it impossible for me to accept him as a party leader. Although critical of the more radical features of La Follette-ism, nevertheless I feel that we are indebted to the Progressive movement within our party because it has done much to challenge and test the tenets of Republicanism since 1900. Disagree as we do with the state socialism aspects of some of the La Follette philosophy, it nevertheless has influenced the liberal trends of our party in recent years."

If this speech had come in the emotional peak of a hot election campaign, Wayne Morse's righteous damnation of the Roosevelt administration might be classed with Willkie's "campaign oratory," if not altogether excused. But that year's election campaign was many months distant and Wayne Morse wasn't running for any office. Or was he? Neuberger, developing into an outstanding writer on Northwest politics, observed later in a magazine article that Morse's speech "told Oregon's cautious Republican party officials, reliant on lumber and utility financing, that the spectacular young dean hankered for their endorsement. They expected Morse to enter the lists for public office at once. . . ." Neuberger thought the most revealing aspect of the speech, in this respect, was that "he waxed autobiographical and talked more about himself than about Abe Lincoln, topic of the occasion."

Morse went back to his teens to reassure the G.O.P. that night about the sort of family political discussions within the Morse household:

> I was not of voting age, but in the family arguments, sometimes for the sake of argument but to a large measure out of youthful conviction, I would contend that a more acceptable political program lay somewhat halfway between the reaction of the Stalwarts and the ultra-liberalism of the Progressives. Thus I suppose it may be said that I have always been a middle of the roader in Republican politics.

Nothing is so safe and ideologically pliable as a middle of the roader, for it is his special privilege to denote *where* the middle is, which is to say, where *he wishes to stand*. Small wonder that Oregon Republicans expected Wayne Morse to enter the lists. He looked attractive, forceful, intelligent, and safe.[1]

But Wayne Morse did not enter the lists that year. The Legend, indeed, refutes all suspicions that this man was the self-seeker and opportunist this speech tends to make him. It never occurred to him to run for the Senate, he says, until nearly four years later, after he had issued his courageous dissent in the Lewis coal dispute, and had quit in disagreement over a matter of principle. Only after these events, when he was beseeched by many admirers, did Wayne Morse turn his thoughts toward seeking elective office, or so goes the Legend along one of its fictional byways.

Wayne Morse *is* ambitious for himself but, unlike some others, he would rather die than admit it. To him, those who appear to hold or admit to political ambitions are the unwashed, the unprincipled, and it is the special calling of Wayne Morse, a hell-fire and damnation political missionary, to preach the gospel of unwavering high principle to these lost souls.

In March 1942 Morse wrote from Washington to a law-faculty colleague at Oregon, Kenneth O'Connell, urging that he start a

[1] This self-portrait of a safe middle of the roader in 1940 is an interesting contrast to the self-portrait Morse painted for an Associated Press reporter in 1947 after his election to the Senate. After his interview, the reporter wrote about the political discussions in the Morse household which went like this: "Wayne's father and elder brothers were 'regulars' but he was inclined to take the La Follette 'Progressive' side in family discussions."

movement in behalf of Orlando Hollis, the acting law dean, to run for a new congressional seat given Oregon after the 1940 census. Referring to a Eugene printer who aspired to that seat, Morse wrote: "What we need is [sic] some congressmen with guts. Hollis has an ample supply." O'Connell, now an Oregon Supreme Court Justice, replied that Hollis wasn't very enthusiastic but there was some sentiment for Morse to run for the Senate. From Washington, two years after his Klamath Falls speech and two years before he quit the War Labor Board to run, Morse wrote:

> What you say about my political future is kind of you although I do not have any illusions about it. I never talked to you about it, but you will probably enjoy a chuckle with me when I tell you there was a very strong undercover movement in certain quarters of the state to have me run against McNary this year. However, I told my friends who were interested in it, and they represented some powerful forces in the state, that I thought it would be a mistake to try to beat McNary this time. Furthermore, I felt I needed just the experience I am getting on this Board and the knowledge which I am obtaining about Washington and its methods. I can still say honestly that I do not have any political ambitions, but if in 1944 or 1948 there are enough people in the state who seriously would like to have me make a run for the Senate, I might consider it.

Most wisely, Wayne Morse knew that his time had not yet come. To challenge Charles L. McNary, Oregon's senior senator, the Republican leader of the Senate and Willkie's vice-presidential running mate in the 1940 campaign, would, indeed, have been a "mistake." Better to go to Washington, get some experience, and bide his time. Besides, coming up for re-election in 1944 would be the much less formidable, in many ways hapless, Rufus Holman, Oregon's junior senator, a much easier mark than McNary.

While in Washington, Morse corresponded with Oregon's G.O.P. state chairman, Niel R. Allen of Grants Pass, and made a point to refresh this Republican leader's memory about what Morse thought of New Dealers. On September 25, 1942, for example, he wrote Allen:

> I am not at all fearful about the President's exercising what I consider to be his inherent war powers during the war period. What I am fearful of is that his successor, or at least his party, will get it into their heads that after the war is over they can continue to exercise such

power by decreeing one emergency after another. I tell you in confidence and with all sincerity that I am very fearful of what is going to happen to our check-and-balance system of government after this war if we do not succeed in developing a more effective opposition party. Why, Niel, some of these New Deal administrators back here seem to take it for granted that they have a vested interest in their jobs and that the thought that they may be turned out of their jobs by a change in administration is absurd.

In the hundreds of other letters Morse wrote to friends, associates, and former students during his tenure as a wartime official in the Roosevelt administration, his comments on the New Deal were fragmentary. To most of those with whom he corresponded, Morse discussed his labor-board decisions at length, the difficult living conditions in wartime Washington, his horses, his family's ups and downs, occasionally something about the progress of the war, but not politics.

The Republicans weren't alone in visualizing Wayne Morse as a candidate. Monroe Sweetland, an ardent New Dealer who had been executive secretary of the "leftish" Commonwealth Federation, says, "I was one of those who went to him in Washington to persuade him that he should file for the Republican nomination against Holman. We really wanted him to change his registration and become a Democratic candidate, but this seemed impractical and unlikely of success." Sweetland, a principal organizer of Oregon's presently revitalized Democratic party, knew that much work needed doing at the Oregon grass roots before a Democratic liberal could expect to hold state-wide office.

Wayne Morse's opportunity came when Oregon Republican leaders in late 1943 began casting about for a fresh replacement for the aging Holman. When the quest narrowed to Palmer Hoyt, publisher of the *Oregonian*, State Senator Merle Chessman of Astoria, and the vigorous law dean, Morse wasted no time letting the Washington press corps know that he was seriously considering the race "as a result of a tremendous amount of support wired to me from Oregon during the last forty-eight hours." Both the other men declined to run. Hoyt, then serving as National Affairs Director, Office of War Information, urged Morse to run. When Morse let it be known to the Administration that he was considering quitting, War Secretary Robert Patterson offered him a commission as an army colonel. But Morse said he was thinking of running for the Senate, and he says Patterson agreed the defeat of Holman, a confirmed isolationist, would be a high public service. Patterson promised that if he lost, a job would await him. When he told the President his plans, he recalls Roosevelt told him, "That's fine. You go out and run." So it was that Wayne Morse went back to Oregon in January 1944 to declare his availability.

Editor Bill Tugman, his influential ally in the university battle, recalled testing Morse's determination to run by relating some of the melancholy experiences of others who had ventured into the cockpit, battled loyally, only to be left bleeding and unnoticed by the crowd when its attention later shifted to a fresh contender. It could be a cruel life. Was he certain this is what he wanted? Wayne Morse was certain. Tugman and his friends thereupon suggested that he take a trip around the state to sound out key men in every county. Morse returned aglow with reports of enthusiastic response. Businessmen, labor officials, professional men all greeted Morse with promises of support, with but one exception, Tugman recalled. Morse said E. B. McNaughton, president of the First National Bank of Portland, transfixed him with a cold eye and said, "Wayne, you've been listening to the usual lot of cheap flattery. If the election were held tomorrow, Holman would skin you three to one. I wouldn't put a nickel back of you until you get some organization built up." Tugman said one of his group remarked, "There's the first real friend you've met on this trip, Wayne. He's the only S.O.B. that has told you the truth. Okay, let's start with that."

On January 27 Morse wrote a letter of resignation to Roosevelt, noting he had written 118 of the formal opinions of the War Labor Board, including ten dissents, and expressing regret for leaving such important work. Morse advised FDR that he had decided to run for the Senate "only after a large number of friends and groups in my home state urged that I could perform a much-needed public service if elected, especially in view of the fact that the issues which undoubtedly will be decided by the Congress in the next six years will greatly affect the destiny of our nation for many years to come." A memo written by James F. Byrnes to FDR, attached to the letter of resignation, provided this intelligence for the Chief Executive: "Wayne Morse handed me the attached letter. He intends to announce his resignation on Sunday and is exceedingly anxious to have you accept the resignation on Saturday. From his statements and my conversations with some well informed persons from Oregon, he stands an excellent chance of winning. Of course, he will have a

Democratic opponent but we do not seem to have in sight anyone who would make a very strong candidate."

In one sense Wayne Morse's decision to seek elective office was an audacious gamble. His credentials were more suitable to the peculiar needs of a British Member of Parliament seeking a vote of confidence from a district with which he had little in common and no history of residence. Morse did have his voting residence in Oregon and he owned property there. But his period of residence—ten years—was incredibly brief for a would-be United States Senator. A third of the fifteen years since his arrival in Eugene had been spent in sojourns for the government at Washington. Little wonder his opponent quickly branded him a carpetbagger. Nor was his profession a discernible asset in a state in which many voters had subdued the range and mountain forests for a livelihood which demanded more sweat than book learning. His opponent tried to belittle Dean Morse as the "perfessor."

Had Wayne Morse been nothing more than an absentee professor, and had incumbent Holman been more formidable, this venture into the arena would have been a very bad gamble for the favor of the multitude. But Rufus Holman was a splendid target in 1944. He was past his prime (sixty-six), dull of intellect, a large, bumbling politician, a bigot, an isolationist, and a labor baiter. Wayne Morse, with his youth (forty-three) and vigor, quick mind, persuasive speaking skill, righteous combat experience with John L. Lewis, his popularity with labor, and international-mindedness, offered an attractive contrast. He was so attractive that even the Democrats approached him. "I made some effort to get Wayne to run as a Democrat," says Marvin Warlick, then the Lane County Democratic Chairman. "He said he had voted for President Roosevelt but he was a lifelong Republican." The practical problems of campaign funds were also discussed. Warlick recalls Morse said, "I'm a poor man, and whichever party I ran in would have to put up the money. If I were a Democrat, I don't think there would be enough money to win." Many have speculated that had the strength and weakness of the two parties been reversed in Oregon at the time, Wayne Morse would have started his career as a Democrat.

Morse, following advice to form his own organization, recruited former law students all over Oregon to work for his candidacy. Young men never before active in politics responded and began spreading the Legend of Wayne Morse through Oregon's sawmills, fruit orchards, small shops, and vast wheatlands. One tale has it that his advisers told him to emphasize his boyhood on a farm, but that Morse recalled to them once when his father took him to a political meeting at which one candidate presented himself as a farmer. "A good day's work on our farm would kill that buzzard," Morse said his father muttered to him. The campaign advisers agreed that this would be risky for Morse, the candidate with the slender, urbane appearance of, as one student is said to have called him, an academic Simon Legree. But, to their delight, when Morse reached the rural areas he recited this entire internal discussion among his campaign strategists, thus cleverly identifying himself as a farm boy who was too honest to try to exploit his background as the politicians had recommended. Later, during the fall campaign, Morse rode his horse at Oregon's famous Pendleton Round-Up to win over the dubious ranchers.

Hoyt's *Oregonian* editorial page opened up on Holman as "assertedly an officer of the Ku Klux Klan in the old days" with a "record for racial and religious prejudice." To which Rufus issued his classic rebuttal, quoted all the way to London in the *Economist*: "Anti-Semitic? Now why should I be anti-Semitic? My own father was an Englishman. I have relatives in England." Holman's campaign manager, perhaps realizing there would be many anti votes cast against his man, hoped a third candidate would enter the race so as to split the anti-Holman vote and assure the incumbent's renomination. But the third entry, Earl E. Fisher, a Beaverton horseradish grower, had as one of his slogans, "Relocate all Japs back to Japan." Fisher sounded the isolationist theme so much that he doubtless siphoned votes away from Holman instead of Morse. A statistician could make a plausible case that Fisher actually beat Holman for Morse, inasmuch as Fisher received 12,241 votes and Morse's margin over Holman was only 10,280 votes. Although he failed to secure a majority of the votes in the Republican primary, Wayne Morse was the victor and the choice of 70,716 Republican voters.

Anti-New Dealer

No one can say with perfect assurance why the electorate makes its choice in any election, but through this very close Oregon primary contest one issue outlasted all the others and evoked the strongest declarations of faith from Wayne Morse. That issue was whether or not he was a New Dealer. "It is inconceivable that the Republicans of Oregon will be gullible enough to allow the New Deal to slip one of its outstanding field men onto the ticket to run for Senator . . . and to send Professor Morse back to Washington would make the Republicans in this state the laughing stock of the Nation," declared a conservative trade publication, *Crow's Lumber Digest*. Morse fired right back: "I fought the New Deal in the clinches whenever they attempted to settle labor cases in a manner not in accordance with law. Mudslingers like Mr. Crow are making votes for me. I wish to thank him."

This postscript of magnanimity was sheer bravado. The New Deal coloration was tough to erase and threatened to make Morse stand out like a flaming bush against the conservative blue skies of Oregon. His defenders dug up that Klamath Falls speech and recited Morse's damnation of the New Deal *before* (they bore down hard on the word *before*) he ever ran for office. This, they argued, proved he was sincerely opposed to the New Deal long before it became politically expedient for him to be so. Up and down the state Wayne Morse found new ways to lambast the Roosevelt administration, whose New Deal had brought to fruition for the first time some of the reforms Fighting Bob La Follette had cried out for in the political wilderness of the twenties. "Roosevelt's hand-picked Supreme Court has rendered another decision that shatters completely basic guarantees of the Constitution to protect individuals from autocratic government," he told Portland Republicans a month before the primary election. "Private enterprise cannot survive if the growing trend toward socialization and nationalization of industry, agriculture, and the professions continues. Those in the present Administration who show very clearly by their program that they favor industry by government will take advantage of every opportunity to blame industry for existing social and economic problems, most of which have been created by the New Deal's fallacious economic theories," he told the applauding faithful at Silverton. "No matter how soothing the New Deal economic syrup may be represented by the quacks who concoct it, analysis shows it is doped with the ingredients of totalitarianism," he assured the Kiwanis Club of Albany.

The crisis on this issue came, by chance of timing, when the government seized Montgomery Ward that spring and soldiers carried its president, obstinate Sewell Avery, bodily from his office for one of the memorable scenes of the battle of the home front. Conservative businessmen railed against a government that would go that far. Since this was an action growing out of the War Labor Board, Morse was peculiarly vulnerable. He lost not a moment in disassociating himself and his philosophy from this latest New Deal sin by roasting the White House and the War Labor Board for "highhanded, arbitrary use of power to send in troops instead of following the American way, government by law and court orders."

This was a close call for Morse, closer than most Oregonians had any idea, for during his tenure on the board, Morse had advocated a tough line against Avery. He was prepared, he had written to a friend, to recommend to Roosevelt that any defiance by Avery of a government wage compliance order should be met by denying Montgomery Ward the use of the mails for the duration of the war, thus effectively closing down the big mail-order house. The reason he thought it important to be tough with Avery, explained Morse in a letter to the president of the University of Oregon, Don Erb, was that "there is no doubt about the fact many anti-union employers were waiting to see whether or not Montgomery Ward could get by with its defiance."

But now the demands of the moment, from Morse's vantage point, were excruciatingly different. The government hadn't gone so far as to deny the company the mails; but upon a court order it had seized the company to keep it in operation, just as the government, acting on compliance orders drafted by Morse, had previously seized numerous war plants during labor disputes. To candidate Morse, this became another reason why he should be elected to go back to Washington and do battle with the New Deal. He went on the radio and said:

> The exercise of such arbitrary power not passed upon by court review is the stock-in-trade of those palace guarders in our national capital who, in my judgment, are bent upon setting up an economic order in America in which all major industry will be controlled, operated and regimented by government.
>
> It can happen here. It is happening here. By that I mean we are traveling rapidly down the road of government by men instead of government by law in America. For two years, as your public representative of the National War Labor Board, I fought in the battle of Washington in defense of principles of government by law, in defense of preserving the legitimate interests and rights of both employers and labor under the national no-strike no-lockout agreement and in accordance with constitutional guarantees of fair judicial process.

The editor of the Salem *Capital Journal*, refusing to accept Morse's professions on this issue, cited chapter and verse from the War Labor reports to contradict him, without knowing of Morse's privately expressed proposal for denying the firm the mails. "Running for office with CIO endorsement, it has been convenient to shed his New Deal proclivities at the hustings for votes," wrote editor George Putnam. "It was Thomas Jefferson who said, 'Whenever a man has cast a longing eye on office, a rottenness begins in his conduct.'"

Like most campaign crises, this one passed quickly. But probably many Oregonians had their fingers crossed about Morse. Editor Tugman, whose editorial endorsement of political candidates always had the distinctive merit of being candid about the man's weaknesses as well as boasting of his strengths, was probably typical of many citizens who thought the state could not in good conscience return Rufus Holman to the Senate. As for Morse, he advised his readers that he had served ably and fairly on the War Labor Board and he "has great talents to offer." Tugman added:

> In preferring Morse we are not blind to his shortcomings. He is not any superman, just another very human being. His chief fault is his tendency, now and then, to see himself as a "knight on a white horse" and when he gets into his role of "St. George" he is not always a good judge of "dragons." When he sits down with 95 other senators (always a high percentage of prima donnas) for the give and take of building laws, he will need to control his oratorical flights as to facts and timing.

In the end more Republicans decided to take their chances with the young newcomer than the frankly embarrassing incumbent. With his liberalism completely submerged throughout the contest, Wayne Morse had successfully navigated the most narrow political estuary of his life. Cruising into what looked like the calmer seas of the general election against a weak Democratic contender from the sparsely populated region east of the Cascades, Edgar W. Smith of Pendleton, Morse stuck up the periscope of his liberalism to have a look around at this uncharted area. To his astonishment, he was almost blown out of the water—by his own Republican forces. Like Holman, Smith disparaged the New Deal and organized labor. So Morse boldly put in an appearance in July at a union convention and commended the CIO Political Action Committee, then a favorite whipping boy of conservatives. Some leading G.O.P. conservatives became so indignant they talked of finding a "partisan of un-questioned regularity" to finance and enter against Morse in the general election as a Independent; and a group of Republican county chairmen threatened rebellion, until Morse pledged his allegiance so convincingly in a hotel-room meeting that they laid down their arms.

When the CIO-PAC later embraced Morse's candidacy, the nomi-nee of the Grand Old Party turned blushingly to his conservative backers and exclaimed in anguish, "I have refused their money; I have refused their help." He is said to have declined $4100 which the CIO had offered for his campaign budget. Caught between the danger of being repudiated by conservatives and disappointing his labor-liberal admirers when, in fact, he wanted the support of both elements, Morse enunciated the credo which has endured through the years:

> I will exercise an independence of judgment on the basis of facts and evidence as I find them on each issue. I will weigh the views of my constituents and my party, but cast my vote free of political pressures and unmoved by threats of loss of political support if I do not do the bidding of some pressure group.

Morse took to excoriating the New Deal once again, kept his liberal periscope out of sight, and a heavy calm fell over the scene. By the end of the campaign he had collected such glittering editorial accolades as "a man of courage and intellect," one who is "inde-pendent and fearless," "dynamic," and "the real spokesman for virile republicanism which today is the hope of America." On election day every one of Oregon's thirty-six counties went for Wayne Morse. He became the popular choice for senator by a handsome 95,000-vote margin.

If Wayne Morse today is a knee-jerk liberal, as some not-so-liberal commentators have classified him, in this first campaign of 1944 he won on the votes of many knee-jerk conservatives. All he had to do was kick the shins of the New Deal and the hands of countless Oregonians automatically thumped together in applause and their heads nodded in approval. This is not to say that he had no genuine misgivings about the destiny of the country as things had been moving. In a private letter written from his wartime post in Washing-ton, Morse revealed these thoughts:

I really think Avery of Montgomery Ward is a fanatic, and the thing that worries me is there are too many of his type in the country. I am not an alarmist, but I tell you Bill that I am very much afraid about what is going to happen in this country after the war. Those of us that believe in seeing liberalism are going to be in danger from three forces as I see it—communists, fascists and reactionaries. It is going to take some pretty clearheaded thinking and lots of courage to stand up and be counted when that struggle comes to a head.

This letter to a former student was written in December 1942, midway between his "damn the New Deal" speech at Klamath Falls in 1940 and his anti-New Deal campaign of 1944. In another 1942 letter, to a New York lawyer who expressed criticism of labor, he replied:

. . . I think strong organized labor is not only essential to the winning of the war but is essential to maintaining the stability of our democratic form of government. I fear very much that as an aftermath of this war we shall be in danger of both Fascism and Communism, and I am satisfied that organized labor, which is basically conservative in spite of some of its wild-eyed leaders, is one of the best safeguards we have against either a Fascist or Communist movement.

Where was the fear of the New Deal's socialistic trend, its depressing effect upon business, its favoritism for labor, which he expressed in public political meetings?

A favorite epigram of Morse's is, "Here is one senator who is not afraid to be defeated," a self-designated mark of distinction which cannot be made retroactive to that 1944 campaign. If Morse ever relived during that campaign his visit with La Follette on his Maple Bluff porch and heard the great leader ask, "Do you want to win the debate or educate the people?" the answer this time was unequivocally "win the debate." Roosevelt, a fox among politicians, understood expediency and excused it. A leading Oregon Democrat of that period, Willis Mahoney, reports that FDR that summer told him that he hoped Morse would win but that he realized Morse would have to campaign against his administration to get elected. "Tell him to make it on the New Deal, though, and not against me personally," Roosevelt is reported as saying.

Had Wayne Morse not been a young advocate of La Follette Progressivism, and had he not subsequently endorsed much of the

Truman Fair Deal and shifted over to the liberal ranks of the Democratic party, this expediently unliberal campaign by which he convinced thousands of Oregon Republicans that he was safely conservative might be explainable in other terms. This senatorial campaign was no high school snow job or wild-card poker game, but a supreme act in the democratic process to which Wayne Morse applied his considerable talent for bluffing. To reach the Senate, Wayne Morse turned his back on La Follette and Progressivism, damned his liberal reform program, and castigated the New Deal, in which Progressivism had come to considerable fruition.

This is not to suggest that this, the conservative hour of Wayne Morse, was *uniquely* barren of intellectual honesty, considering the dismal spectrum of American political campaigns. It is simply to enter a quiet objection to one of the unwavering demands that Wayne Morse and the Legend he perpetuates make upon the Senate and the outer world for recognition as the *one* senator who places his liberal principles above all other considerations. There was the occasion in 1948 when he handed the press a list of Republican colleagues—Aiken, Flanders, Tobey, Young, Langer, Baldwin, Smith (of New Jersey), Lodge, Saltonstall, Knowland, Cordon, Vandenberg, and Cooper—and belittled them one and all as merely "sometime" liberals who too often "talked liberal but voted reactionary." Then, after his switch to the Democratic party, there was the occasion following Langer's funeral when he put an arm around Hubert Humphrey's shoulders and solemnly mourned the passing of their friend. "Now, Hubert, you and I are the only *true* liberals left in the Senate," said Morse. Before the week was out, Morse had resumed his curious bid for the presidential nomination by denouncing Humphrey, in Humphrey's own state of Minnesota, as a "phony liberal."

Few progressive Democrats have escaped Morse's sermonizing on the evils of "half-a-loaf liberalism" in the past few years. To them it is a mystery why their colleague, whose liberalism no senator has challenged, is so impelled to take this more-liberal-than-thou attitude and to protest his innocence of the sin of compromising for which he frequently blames them. It is perhaps a pardonable conclusion that Wayne Morse doth protest too much.

6. THE SENATOR AND THE LEADERS

Following Vandenberg . . . Defying Taft . . . Taft-Hartley
. . . Deadwood Dave

THE SENATE, like a small town or an exclusive club, is a place in which the pressures to conform are strongly felt. If one wishes to rise in the esteem of his peers in this place, then gentlemanly behavior and a display of proper respect for the leaders are unwritten but essential imperatives, especially for those newly arrived.

When Wayne Morse walked up the center aisle to take his oath in January, 1945, appearing as orthodox as any newcomer in his properly conservative suit with the Rotary pin in the lapel, who was there so perceptive as to think before long he would be described by columnist Marquis Childs as "a kind of Peck's bad boy, lighting firecrackers with great glee under those of his colleagues whom he finds overly smug or overly cautious," acceptable neither to the surviving New Dealers, who held him in contempt, nor the old-guard Republicans, who regarded him "with all the cordiality they would greet a gila monster found in the midst of a cosy picnic ground."

Plainly Wayne Morse came not in awe to the citadel of high legislative authority. "In the few short months he has been here, [he] has laid about him with a broadsword," observed a Washington *Post* writer in August. "He has bearded the formidable Senator Kenneth McKellar, president pro tem of the Senate; baited the venerable Senator Tom Connally, touchy chairman of the Senate Foreign Relations Committee; and made Majority Leader Alben Barkley fighting mad. He has lambasted the leadership of his own Republican party, crossed swords with Senator Robert A. Taft and ignored the counsels of Minority Leader Wallace H. White of Maine." At the conclusion of one such early episode, Morse recalls that Senator Robert M. La Follette, Jr., son of Fighting Bob, came to his desk to say, "The leaders now know they can't control you. So you'd better learn the rules of the Senate because you are going to need them to protect yourself." As his subsequent one-man insurrections show, Morse took this counsel seriously. "That's the best advice I've ever had in the Senate," he now says.

Implicitly, the image Wayne Morse holds of himself is that of the lone tiger, depending on no one but himself for protection against the threats of the jungle. Or, to return to the metaphor of the small town, he resists the social pressure to conform and holds himself apart from—often above—the group, scorning its habits, violating its customs, frequently with useful results.

Following Vandenberg

After taking his seat on the Republican side of the aisle in 1945, the company in which Wayne Morse moved was dominated by two towering men who might, either of them, be the next President. This impressive political circumstance, the cause of noticeable deference in others, did not overpower Morse's belief that both of them, Bob Taft and Arthur Vandenberg, were basically wrongheaded on the most vital question which faced the country as it moved toward triumph on the world's stained battlefronts: would the United States once more go it alone, isolating itself behind its seacoasts?

Consistently internationalist, Morse had two years before written Niel Allen, Oregon's G.O.P. chairman: "I regret that the Taft-Vandenberg crowd appears to be so bent on 'getting' Willkie, but the fact remains that he is the one man in the Republican party today [1942] of national stature who seems to have the imagination, the perseverance, the fight and the social consciousness necessary to keep the party before the people." But Willkie and another internationalist Republican, Thomas E. Dewey, had lost the elections of 1940 and 1944. Now what was to prevent the isolationists from gaining power and killing any visions of world peace organizations? Had not Henry Cabot Lodge and his isolationist cohorts inflicted their will upon the country against the League of Nations?

This great struggle between opposite views of America's future task never embroiled the Senate at the close of the World War II. For it was waged and won for internationalism in the mind of Vandenberg months before the war ended. In the Senate, the week after Wayne Morse arrived, the Michigan orator made his now famous

"speech heard round the world." This may lead historians to rank
Vandenberg near Webster and Clay, for it was the most significant
and effectual oration in the Senate in decades. Calling for "the most
courageous thinking of which we are capable," Vandenberg said:

> A global conflict which uproots the earth is not calculated to sub-
> mit itself to the dominion of any finite mind. . . . The United
> Nations, in even greater unity of military action than heretofore, must
> never, for any cause, permit this military unity to fall apart. . . .
> We not only have two wars to win, we also have yet to achieve such
> a peace as will justify this appalling cost. Here again an even more
> difficult unity is indispensable. Otherwise, we shall look back upon
> a futile, sanguinary shambles and—God save the mark—we shall
> be able to look forward only to the curse of World War III. . . .

A long-time newspaper editor with an artist's touch with words,
Vandenberg shaped his ideas with the care of a potter—turning a
lumpy notion into an exquisitely turned idea. Speaking of the need
to preserve the freedoms pledged in the Atlantic Charter, Vandenberg
declared:

> These basic pledges cannot now be dismissed as a mere nautical
> nimbus. They march with our armies. They sail with our fleets. They
> fly with our eagles. They sleep with our martyred dead.

The events that followed were dominated by this single Republican senator carrying his party for the first time into willing involvement in world affairs of a long-term peaceful design. That year the
Senate ratified the Bretton Woods agreement, authorizing American
participation in the International Bank and Stabilization Fund, by
a 61–16 vote; extended the Reciprocal Trade Act, 54–21; and ratified
the charter of the United Nations by the astonishing vote of 89 to 2.
In a letter to his wife Vandenberg candidly said, "Everybody now
seems to agree that I could have beaten the Charter if I had taken
the opposition tack. . . . Heaven only knows whether the Charter
will 'work.' I think it will. If not, nothing would. Everything in the
final analysis depends on Russia (and whether we have guts enough
to make her behave)."

Vandenberg's historic conversion made him a leader in the highest
national sense, and one whom Wayne Morse admiringly followed
through this period of crossroad decisions. Upon the UN charter's

ratification, Morse introduced a resolution in July, 1945, to implement its provision for American adherence to the authority of the new International Court of Justice, or World Court. Referred to the Foreign Relations Committee, there the resolution lay for months until Morse asked why prompt action on this meritorious proposal was not forthcoming. The answer, in the mossy traditions of the place, was that whatever the merit of this proposal, it bore the handicap of having only a freshman senator for its sponsor. Bowing this time to the custom, Morse secured an influential corps of co-sponsors, Taft among them, and the World Court resolution was called up for a hearing. Morse and Dean Acheson were the leading witnesses. Even here, however, Morse displayed some spirit. Vandenberg, who had been attending meetings of the foreign ministers in Europe in that spring of 1946, asked Morse not to press his resolution at one point for fear it would make matters more ticklish for Secretary of State Byrnes at these continuing meetings. Morse, having wisely sought Byrnes' advice, proudly produced a cable of endorsement. "The leaders, Vandenberg and Barkley, thereupon changed their position and backed my resolution," says Morse. "Taft was a great World Court man from the beginning."

Called up for debate, the resolution encountered no difficulty until Tom Connally arose to offer a six-word alteration. Morse's resolution provided "that the Senate advise and consent to . . . the jurisdiction of the International Court of Justice in all legal disputes hereafter arising concerning—1. the interpretation of a treaty; 2. any question of international law; 3. the existence of any fact which, if established, would constitute a breach of an international obligation; 4. the nature or extent of the reparation to be made for the breach of an international obligation. Provided, that such declaration shall not apply to—a) disputes the solution of which the parties shall entrust to other tribunals by virtue of agreements already in existence or which may be concluded in the future; b) disputes with regard to matters which are essentially within the domestic jurisdiction of the United States——" When the clerk reached this point, in reading the resolution aloud for amendments, Connally proposed to add the words "as determined by the United States."

By this innocent-sounding phrase, the Connally amendment attached a critical qualification to Morse's resolution. It meant, in plain language, that the United States would abide by the authority of a world court only when it wished to do so.

Morse, joined by Claude Pepper of Florida, sharply contested the Connally amendment, but in vain. For this time the leaders were backing Connally, not Morse. Only eleven others voted with Morse. Connally won by a 51 to 12 vote, thus providing the basis for the contemporary controversy concerning this amendment, which some reputable groups have urged the Senate to repeal.

In this amended form, the Morse resolution was adopted by a 60 to 2 vote, with only Langer and Shipstead opposing it, as they had the UN charter. Heavily hedged though it was, the Senate made a commitment it had rejected a decade earlier when the World Court proposal had previously been advanced.[1]

This, Wayne Morse's first legislative effort, demonstrated the power of the party leaders to influence, if not absolutely to control, the legislative outcome. By sanctioning Morse's resolution initially, the leaders allowed it to emerge from a committee pigeonhole; but then by shifting their weight behind Connally, they carried with them the strength of numbers to alter its wording and weaken its intended purpose over the protests of its sponsor. Any man as bright as Wayne Morse would see instantly the force of that old saying that persists on Capitol Hill, "To get along, go along."

If Wayne Morse had been willing to go along with his party's leaders, surely he would have fared better in his early and persistent quest for a seat on the Foreign Relations Committee. When the Republicans gained control of the Eightieth Congress by their 1946 election victories, Vandenberg became chairman of that committee. Morse, in his own behalf, complained that the west coast was not represented on the committee. This was a weak point, in the face of the Senate's adherence to the seniority system for appointment of committee members without regard to a senator's geographic origins.

---

[1] In the fifteen years since adoption of the World Court resolution, the United States has exercised the Connally reservation only once, on a minor point in the Interhandel case, involving ownership of assets in the United States claimed by both Germany and Switzerland. But under the international law of reciprocity, other nations may exercise the Connally reservation against the United States. This has happened once. When the United States filed suit against Bulgaria for shooting down an American plane, Bulgaria cited the Connally reservation to claim this was a matter of its own domestic jurisdiction. Other U.S. suits against Russia, Hungary, and Czechoslovakia over plane incidents have been fruitless because these countries have never accepted jurisdiction of the court over any affairs involving them. No major international disputes have gone to the court, although several boundary cases have been settled. Settlement of one of them, between Honduras and Nicaragua, may have averted war, in the opinion of the State Department.

Sympathizing with his faithful internationalist colleague, Vandenberg pledged his support to Morse for the next vacancy.

After Morse was re-elected in 1950, he made public a letter from the ailing Vandenberg which stated that "the path is now clear for you to cash your I.O.U. on a seat on the Foreign Relations Committee." Obliquely daring the party leaders who privately assign senators to committees, Morse told reporters, "I'd be surprised if any Republican colleague of mine does not take it for granted that I will be offered the appointment." If Morse was daring them to deny him the seat, they did not hesitate to accept. The appointment went to William F. Knowland of California, thereby destroying Morse's argument that the committee lacked a west-coast member. If there was any doubt that Morse was deliberately passed over in this selection of Knowland, whom Morse outranked in seniority, it vanished a few months later upon Vandenberg's death, when his seat was given to Owen Brewster of Maine, another more conservative and more agreeably orthodox member of the party faithful.

Had Vandenberg lived on instead of falling to cancer in 1951, it is conceivable that Morse's subsequent career might have taken a quite different course. Vandenberg's attitude toward Morse was revealed during the struggle of 1949 over the greatly debated issue of implementing the North Atlantic Treaty by sending arms to western European allies, a proposal which at last divided Vandenberg and Taft. The day he saw the arms bill safely through the Senate by a 55 to 24 vote, Vandenberg wrote to his wife that it had been "tough going. The Republicans ran out on my right and left—only nine of 'em standing by to help beat the chief amendment with which we had to contend. . . . The old dependables were Dulles and Ives, Morse (who came down on a stretcher to vote), Thye (who never left me), Margaret Smith and Wiley. . . ." Obviously it was a cause of admiration as well as gratitude that Morse should leave a hospital, where he was recuperating from a bad spill taken while racing his horse at the Oregon State Fair, to be carried to the chamber for the critical votes that were to come.

Defying Taft

Vandenberg's death opened a power void into which Taft and Knowland swiftly moved to commence a major offensive against the Truman administration's policies in the Far East. The period of constructive bipartisanship in foreign affairs following the war now ended. The agonizing, frustrating war in Korea was in progress, and the Communists, who had swept all of China before them, were spilling into Korea with "volunteers" to the military despair of General Douglas MacArthur, whose orders prohibited counterattacking China itself. As Taft's biographer, William S. White, observes, an Asian politico-military cult which developed around MacArthur came "to dominate the whole Taft wing of the Republican party."

Against this cult Wayne Morse, already twice denied a committee role in foreign relations, opened his own harassing operation from the Senate floor. He applauded the dismissal of MacArthur from the Korean command as a member of the joint committee which investigated this passionate episode. He contended that an insidious China lobby was functioning in Washington to arouse sympathy for the fading Nationalist regime and to create a climate of congressional opinion favorable to a war against the Chinese mainland with American military support.

Morse's resolution calling for a congressional investigation of the China lobby, applauded in many editorial columns, was ignored by the party leaders. Nonetheless Morse was a constant burr under the Taft-Knowland saddle right up to the time of the 1952 Republican convention, when the Dewey forces wrested control once more, in the name of Dwight D. Eisenhower. By his harassment of the Asian cult in his own party, Wayne Morse played a significant part in the massive political struggle of that period—a struggle not for or against some legislative proposal, nor even his own resolution to probe the China lobby. This was "a grim struggle for political power, a war for the American mind . . . a contest for the power the American people are able to bestow."[2]

The power soon to be bestowed was the presidency, toward which Taft drove with indiscriminate zeal in his onslaught against the waning administration. In a struggle of this great range, ideas vocalized in the Senate, faithfully reported by the news media, were spread out across the land to work their unseen magic in the American mind. No one can see the shifting tides of a battle for the mind in order to say with certainty *why* it was concluded as it was. What is certain is that the leaders cannot stop a senator of Morse's disposition from becoming his own field general. They

2 *The General and the President*, Rovere and Schlesinger, 1951, Farrar, Strauss and Young.

might blockade him from the commanding heights of the Foreign Relations Committee, but none can deny him the power which flows to all articulate senators, the right to speak from the floor of the Senate.

If this period, marked also by the rise of McCarthy with Taft's encouragement, showed Bob Taft at his worst, as biographer White maintains, it also affords a strong case for maintaining that it showed Wayne Morse at his best. Early in 1952, at the height of this struggle, members of the American Political Science Association chose Morse as the best of the Republican senators, behind only Paul Douglas and Estes Kefauver as the best of all the senators of that period. Morse also rated near the top of the list of best senators in magazine polls of Washington correspondents in 1949 and 1951.

Morse's outspoken and consistent internationalism caused him no major political problems in his home state, for his position in the Senate was consistent with his election promises as against the isolationism of Rufus Holman.

But on domestic affairs Wayne Morse encountered immediate difficulty. The first sin, in the view of his conservative backers, was his vote in favor of Henry Wallace as Roosevelt's Secretary of Commerce. From a candidate who had said on the campaign trail, "The New Dealers are trying to convince us that . . . the fewer pigs we raise, the more food we will have to eat," Wayne Morse became a senator who voted to give the cabinet post usually reserved for a businessman to the very author of the New Deal pig plan. Morse's justification was scholarly and persuasive. He explained that he had boiled down the entire history of Senate debate on appointments. Four tests had become standard: 1. Is he a man of good character? 2. Is he one who believes in our form of government? 3. Is he free of any disqualifying factors caused by professional, personal or financial interest in the office so that he cannot render impartial, honest service? 4. Is he mentally sound?

In all of American history, nearly 400 cabinet nominations had come before the Senate and all but seven had been confirmed. Only Presidents Jackson, Tyler, Johnson, and Coolidge had sent up nominations to which the Senate refused to consent. Wallace passed all four historic tests, said Morse, so he felt constrained to vote for his confirmation.

Morse became the darling of New Deal critics once more when he rose at a critical point near the Senate's vote on a war manpower-control bill and, in his maiden speech, offered such trenchant criticism that the bill was ultimately abandoned. Morse observed that in this bill, granting authority to an administrator appointed by the President with power to freeze workers in their jobs or direct them to take other jobs, the only right of appeal from the manpower administrator's decisions was to a board appointed by him. "There is growing up in this country a trend toward . . . administration of law by the executive branch of government through administrative officers who, in my judgment, do not have their opinions and views sufficiently checked by other branches of government," Morse told the Senate. "I think it is a dangerous trend. . . . The citizen should have protection from the arbitrary exercise of power. . . . If we pass a law to conscript labor then we will have lost the peace at home even though we have won the war abroad."

Conservative columnist Mark Sullivan praised Morse as "a liberal in the true sense—the sense which says the main objective of real liberalism is protection of the individual citizen from arbitrary acts of government." The Baltimore *Sun* said, in an editorial widely reprinted in Oregon newspapers, that "Senator Morse put his finger on one of the less dramatic but more important public issues of the time. As the government tries to do more and more things, what happens to the older notions of individual rights?" The defeat of this manpower bill, a humiliation to Roosevelt at the outset of his fourth term, served to elevate Morse's national prestige and reassure his Oregon constituency that the trust imposed in their new senator had not been misplaced.

In the long pull of his career, this achievement was more characteristic than was the World Court victory; for it is the special place of the maverick to resist bad legislation, to stop it or change it if he can. To undertake this task, as Morse has, requires that he sit loose from the subtle intimidation the party leaders exercise in pressing for a favorable vote from every man in their ranks.

The pressure from the party leaders to conform is not the only, nor often the most severe, force which bears upon a senator. The exhortations from the lobbyists for the major pressure groups—business, labor, agriculture, et al.—create an added or a counter force. In his defiance of the Senate's leaders, Wayne Morse has been a maverick from the first days he entered the chamber and voted for Wallace; but whether by coincidence or design, his course more often than not has paralleled that of a major pressure group, organized labor. The

CIO was strong for placing Wallace in the Commerce Department. When Morse torpedoed that war manpower bill, he delighted labor as greatly as conservative businessmen. Better than any other pressure group's officials, Morse had become acquainted with the labor chieftains during his War Labor Board days; and they displayed confidence that, with his considerable labor experience, Morse would be receptive to their point of view. For his part, Morse had repeatedly said the Republican party must not allow itself to become an anti-labor party. Although political circumstances impelled him to keep labor at arm's length during his first election campaign, his good relations with labor officials resumed when he arrived in the Senate. It has been to labor leaders that he looked in some of his most severe political crises, and they to him.

Beyond the great national pressure groups and their smaller companions in the art of buttonholing senators in the lobbies of the Capitol, the home-state interests exert a powerful thrust by which they seek to lead their congressional representatives. Their diversity ranges from the wheatgrowers who want a better government program for their product to the shipyard operators who would benefit by more shipbuilding contracts from the navy, to the mail carriers who know how to employ the mails to bombard Congress for a pay increase. To these groups a senator will look with hope of support in his re-election campaigns, and to him they seek redress of wrongs during the years between elections.

Out of these crosscurrents of individual interests, the senator's included, the broad public interest must somehow be determined. It is the happy politician who can on occasion manage to align a number of these interests. Morse's attack on the war manpower bill was one of those rare occasions. Not only did it please his anti-Roosevelt constituents and his national labor admirers, but it had its application to a problem in Morse's state. "There are 10,000 war workers out of jobs today in Portland, Oregon, because of the cancellation of shipbuilding contracts," Morse said in his speech against the bill. "Don't tell me that this Administration proposed to meet unemployment by passing a bill to put workers in jail if they don't take the jobs the Administration wants them to." Defeat of the manpower-control bill did not solve the unemployment of the Portland workers, but Wayne Morse conveyed the idea that their senator was in there battling in their behalf, saving them from incarceration by the bureaucrats.

Since that episode, Morse has responded to many of Oregon's problems by presenting himself as a fighter against all who have brought on his state's difficulties. His fight, quite often, is solely a quick succession of verbal haymakers from the Senate floor, published in the daily *Congressional Record*, clipped by a clerk in his office, and mailed back home to the group or persons seeking relief. Whatever the outcome, there in black and white is the evidence that they have been fought for. Nowhere, not even in the lovelorn columns, are more problems of local citizens aired in a public way, and solved not one whit in the airing, than on the floor of the Senate of the United States.

There are those gratifying times when a "fight for the people of my state" is won. Wayne Morse had this experience in his first year when he heard from Oregon sheepmen about a problem of marketing soft lambs created by meat rationing regulations of the Office of Price Administration. Taking the Senate floor to blister the OPA and its director, Chester Bowles, Morse pounded away with daily recitals about his wronged constituents. In deference to his colleagues' desire to go home, he waited until the end of the afternoon, gaining thereby the nickname "the five o'clock shadow." Oregon's more reserved Senator Cordon was also endeavoring to solve the problem, but in a quiet way. In the end the OPA took Oregon's milk-fed lambs off the ration list. Who is to say which senator's method was the more responsible for the favorable result? In the public mind, however, there was little doubt that Wayne Morse had carried his fight to the bureaucrats and had won.

Taft-Hartley

Not until the Taft-Hartley labor fight of 1947 was Wayne Morse at last unmasked as anything but the anti-New Dealer his Oregon backers had expected him to be. For many conservatives this was the only test of a public man's soundness. Behind this supreme effort was American conservatism's pent-up emotional and rational opposition to the social changes which the New Deal had brought upon America. Taft marshaled the strength of this sentiment and channeled it entirely into a single assault upon the New Deal's Wagner Labor Act. Had Taft suspected that Morse might be unsympathetic to his endeavor, it is unlikely that Morse would have been assigned as a freshman senator to the Labor Committee. So

when the struggle commenced, Taft had to contend not only with
Morse's maverick spirit and considerable knowledge of labor law, he
had to reckon with Morse as an adversary within the committee
that drafted the bill.

Unintimidated by Taft, Morse's attitude toward the high-domed
Ohioan was rather more like that of David's toward Goliath. He
had, as a War Labor Board member, once appeared before the
Senate Labor Committee, advancing more with slingshot than with
hat in hand. He proudly related the incident to a labor-attorney
friend, the late James Landye of Portland: "It was lots of fun. I
took Senator Taft on and it just happened to be one of my good
days or one of his most stupid ones, I don't know which. Anyway,
it was obvious that the Committee did not share his views after I
got through explaining the decisions of the board to which he took
exception. . . . Tom Kennedy [of the CIO] expressed the view to
me that my testimony before the Committee had undoubtedly
checked some pretty bad legislation."

When the 1947 duel between Taft and Morse ended within the
Senate Labor Committee, Morse must have felt equally elated. A
coalition of liberal Republicans—Morse, Ives, and Aiken—and New
Deal Democrats—Murray, Pepper, Hill, and Thomas—had beaten
Taft in a series of seven to six votes on critical features of the bill.
Hence the labor bill which went to the Senate floor was much
milder than Taft desired. Yet it did call for changing the Wagner
Act, certainly enough to fulfill Morse's 1944 campaign pledges to
do so.

The bill provided for: expansion of the National Labor Relations
Board from three to seven members; a new independent mediation
agency; court injunctions to make unlawful any acts which threatened
the national health or safety; definitions of unfair labor practices
of employees as well as employers; the NLRB could get injunctions
against secondary boycotts or jurisdictional strikes while it was determining whether such acts were unfair labor practices; prohibition
against strikers voting in collective bargaining elections unless they
struck against an unfair labor practice by the employer; permission
for employees under a union shop to campaign for a rival union
during a sixty-day period prior to termination of a union contract
without risking discharge from their jobs; procedures for handling
national emergency strikes by which the Attorney General could
appoint a board of inquiry, petition a court for a sixty-day injunction

against the strike, after which the NLRB could poll the workers to determine whether they wanted to strike or accept the final settlement offer.

"If the Senate wants to pass constructive legislation that the President cannot justify vetoing, and which I think he, as a fair-minded man, will recognize as good legislation, it will pass the bill reported out of committee without change," Morse declared that day in April 1947.

On the surface it appeared that Taft had lost control of his own committee. He vented his frustration in a Republican caucus, giving Morse and his allies a proper scolding. Taft, however, had won what turned out to be the major tactical point. Taft insisted on a single omnibus labor bill, which Truman would have either to accept or veto. Morse wanted four separate bills. The committee upheld Taft.

When the floor fight began, Taft advanced with four amendments designed to toughen the labor bill. "These amendments," countered Morse, "will bring forth a veto. I think that is really playing politics with the people's interest, and I won't be a party to it." Morse moved to split the labor measure into four bills. In this act, reported William S. White in the New York *Times,* "Senator Morse crossed the last line in rebellion against his party's leaders on domestic affairs."

In Oregon there was mixed reaction to Morse's break on so emotional a fight against the New Deal, but the Portland *Oregonian* viewed Morse's strategy as "eminently reasonable" and thought Taft was "playing for high stakes, and dangerously so." Whoever had righteousness on his side, it was Taft who had the votes. Morse's motion to compel splitting the bill into four bills was defeated by a vote of 59 to 35.

This was the key to Taft's ultimate triumph. Had Morse succeeded in splitting the bill, Truman could have signed the mildest of the lot and vetoed the others, as the labor unions had hoped would be the outcome. After retaining the package bill intact, Taft pressed ahead with his first amendment to outlaw union coercion in organizing campaigns. Morse contended this would forbid all organizing strikes and subject unions to harassing actions before the NLRB. Taft won, 60 to 28. Next day Morse made a strong comeback to defeat Taft's second amendment curbing industry-wide bargaining. The vote was 44 to 43. The third day Taft won, 48 to 40, to ban automatic payroll deductions for union dues without the workers' consent, and to curb union control of health and welfare funds by requiring that employers be equally represented in their management. Taft toned down his final amendment and marched on to ultimate victory, receiving a 68 to 24 vote on the final version of the labor bill as it passed the Senate, six votes more than needed to override a veto.

Morse's crossing of the "last outer line in rebellion" against the G.O.P. leaders was plainly visible to conservative Republicans in Oregon. It mattered little to them that Morse had favored and fought hard for some changes in the Wagner Act; it mattered immensely that he had fought against Taft in this one great breach of the New Deal.

Deadwood Dave

Before Morse had completed his first term, the most conservative Republicans in the state were searching for a "good Republican" to challenge him in 1950. The hottest political issue in the Pacific Northwest at the moment was the proposed Columbia Valley Authority, a regional river-development scheme similar to TVA. The champions of CVA were the liberal Democrats—Magnuson, Jackson, and Hugh Mitchell in Washington State, and Neuberger, Monroe Sweetland, and Jebby Davidson in Oregon. The utilities and other conservative business interests were strongly opposed to CVA.

Wayne Morse was in a strategic position. If he supported CVA, it would have prominent bipartisan backing for its tough going in Congress. If he opposed it, solidifying the opposition of Oregon's congressional delegation, it was surely doomed. Morse had indicated early sympathies for public power, so the liberals had their hopes up.

In the fall of 1949, when Morse was bedridden due to that racing accident at the Oregon State Fair, reporter Marian Lowery Fisher, an old friend, visited him in the Salem hospital. He gave her a statement on the hot issue:

> I am going to let the politicians play politics with the CVA issue if they want to, but I intend to keep my eyes on the economic facts of the river-development program and not become embroiled in a partisan controversy. . . .
>
> I have delayed and shall continue to delay any final commitment on the CVA issue until we have all the facts. I believe in handling first

PLATE 1. Wayne Morse, born on a Wisconsin homestead, learned to ride early. At age nine he proudly rode his white pony, Queen, at the head of a big Fourth of July parade in Madison, never flinching as horseflies nipped his legs *(top photo)*. During undergraduate days at the University of Wisconsin he lived at home in Madison with baby sister Caryl and his parents, Wilbur and Jessie Morse. Before leaving for law school, Wayne proposed to his high school sweetheart, Mildred Downie, shown here three months before their June 1924 marriage.

PLATE 2   Dean Morse reads *Little Women* to his three daughters, Nancy, Judith, and Amy, as Mrs. Morse listens and knits in their Eugene, Oregon, hillside residence *(above)*. Now the girls are mothers on their own *(below)*. Seated before smiling grandparents, they are Judith and Wade Eaton holding sons Nicholas and Peter, Nancy Campbell holding her daughter Melanie, and Amy and John Bilich holding daughter Patricia.

PLATE 3   From a strong-willed law dean (*above*) who forced Harry Bridges to back down in Pacific Coast maritime arbitration disputes, Wayne Morse entered the national stage on the eve of Pearl Harbor as successful chairman of a board appointed by President Roosevelt to avert a threatened nationwide rail tie-up. Carrying the bundle of facts his board gathered, Morse is flanked (*below*) by Thomas R. Powell and Huston Thompson to his right and Joseph H. Willite and James C. Benbright to his left.

International Newsphoto

PLATE 4   From the back of a train with GOP presidential candidate Thomas E. Dewey, from a tiny smoky meeting hall, or from a giant billboard in Oregon's green countryside, the candidate on the trail seeks the voters' support.

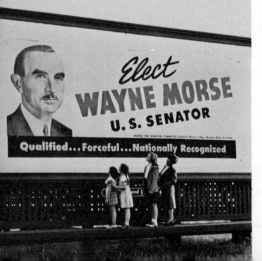

© 1947 by the Chicago *Tribune*

© 1951 *The Washington Post Co.*

© 1953 *The Washington Post Co.*

© 1956 *The St. Louis* Post-Dispatch

PLATE 5   Carey Orr in the Chicago *Tribune* came near repeating the famous "Iron Cross" cartoon about LaFollette during World War I, for Vandenberg and Morse, Aiken and Tobey, internationalist Republicans, were too radical for Colonel McCormick in their support of new treaty commitments with Europe. Herblock in the Washington *Post* encouraged the Oregon maverick and Fitzpatrick in the St. Louis *Post-Dispatch* gave him monumental standing against Douglas McKay on the Hells Canyon question.

PLATE 6 Wayne Morse in three contrasting moods with his horses. Above right, he is informally attired to mingle with the cowpokes and cattlemen at the famous Pendleton Round-Up during his first Senate campaign. Above left, he is formally suited for the fashionable horseshows he entered in the Washington area. Below, he is a hard-driving racing driver at the Oregon State Fair in 1958.

J. F. Maloney, Seattle, Washington

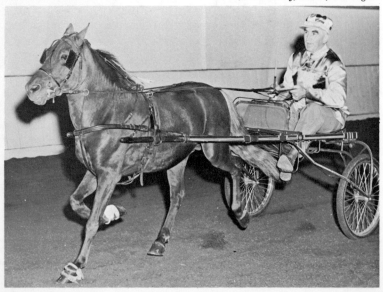

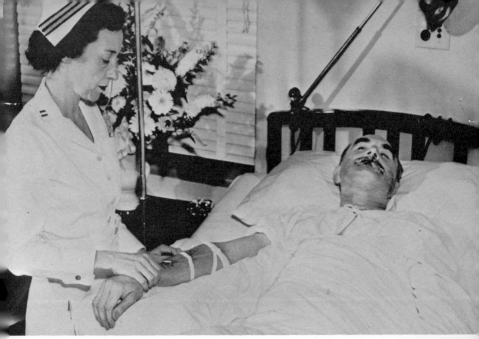

PLATE 7   The famous horse kick in 1951 sent the Senator to the hospital. After his recovery, his attention shifted from spirited stallions to docile Devons, which he raises on a farm at Poolesville, Maryland.

PLATE 8 Jim Berryman in the Washington *Star* wryly portrayed Morse and his actions as many have observed them. The Senator, incidentally, has the originals of these and other unflattering cartoons, which he requested from the cartoonist, hanging on his office wall alongside many favorable ones.

things first—and the first thing we need is completion of the blue-
prints for the construction of these Northwest river-development
projects. . . .

My position on CVA will be determined after the congressional
hearings have been held in the Pacific Northwest and I have had time
to study thoroughly all economic angles of the issue.

Three days later, Oregon newspapers indicated that State Senator
William Walsh of Coos Bay might challenge Morse in the G.O.P.
primary. Walsh, an outspoken opponent of CVA, would say only
that he was waiting to see what position Morse took on this
delicate question.

Walsh didn't have long to wait. Eight days later Wayne Morse,
back in Washington, called the CVA bill an "administrative strait
jacket." Two days later, as though to erase any lingering questions
about his position, Morse declared:

No CVA law of any kind, type or description should ever be passed
by the Congress. . . . I do not propose to swallow the line that liberalism requires the advocacy of the pending CVA bill.

Writer Neuberger cited this sequence of events to show that Morse
has "a slippery quality when issues get red-hot." Neuberger was then
a state senator who never compromised on such liberal doctrines,
but this was possible for him because he represented an urban district
in which liberalism was more acceptable than it was across the entire
state, which Morse represented. Neuberger recognized Morse's practical problem when he wrote:

Trying to be a Republican with a perfect CIO voting record in the
West's most conservative state is like crossing Niagara Falls on a
piano wire with a man-eating tiger trying to chew its way out of a kit-
bag on your back.

Years later, after Morse had become a Democrat, a Northwest
liberal asked Morse why he came out against CVA at that critical
time in 1949. In a moment of quiet candor, Morse explained that
Eddie Sammons, a Portland banker who was the finance chairman
of his forthcoming re-election campaign, advised that he take a
strong stand against CVA. Morse probably needed no coaching to
detect the trouble he would encounter if he straddled the fence

any longer or endorsed this Fair Deal proposal. In any event Walsh did not run against him—and the CVA proposal died a sudden death, never to be revived.

But conservative Republicans were not distracted from seeking a safer candidate. At length a volunteer came forward, an anonymous but not inarticulate dirt farmer from the community of Deadwood. Dave Hoover's only public service theretofore was as a member of the Los Angeles constabulary. Aside from a heavy file of letters to the editor of the Eugene *Register-Guard* against Morse and the Fair Deal, Deadwood Dave's one prior act of public notice was that he had once crated a hog and sent it to the White House to protest against OPA restrictions which ruined the hog market. All he could do, he said, was give them away. He was plunged into gloom upon later reading that Eleanor Roosevelt had served the roast pig at a dinner party and explained that it came from an Oregon farmer who couldn't afford to keep it. "That," moaned Hoover, "wasn't the point at all."

Preposterous as his candidacy was, Hoover attracted attention and financial backing as a "real Republican" who was not soft on the Truman Fair Deal and who promised to be very hard on Wayne Morse. "Never in the history of the direct primary in Oregon has so much money been contributed to defeat or nominate an Oregon candidate as was put up to defeat Wayne Morse," said the Oregon *Voter*, reporting that Hoover received $51,473 for his campaign. Considerable sums came from C. F. Swigart, Jr., A Portland manufacturer; Howard W. Irwin, a Coos Bay lumberman; and seventy-three Oregon doctors who were solicited for funds by the president of the Oregon State Medical Association. Morse himself had a few large benefactors, mostly out-of-state internationalist Republicans such as John Hay Whitney and the Duke family, as well as labor unions. He reported spending $30,662.

Robert Sawyer, widely respected and deeply conservative editor of the Bend *Bulletin*, spoke the sentiments of many who backed Hoover:

> . . . [Morse] appeared to be a Republican, but as time went on our regard for him began to erode. Over and over he voted far away from his party line. . . . In recent months he has tried to overcome the feelings that have so justifiably grown up against him . . . We supported him six years ago, but cannot do so now.

Morse sought to placate conservatives with stern attacks on "socialized medicine," the Brannan farm plan, a "soak-the-rich tax policy, and CVA." His abuse of Fair Deal programs provoked an incisive rejoinder from Monroe Sweetland, Democratic National Committeeman, who wrote in the *Oregon Democrat*:

> Morse is 100 per cent liberal when the issue is far away . . . But at home in 1950, with a G.O.P. primary at stake, Morse cuddles up to the Oregon bankers and power trust, lumber barons and investment boys. At the liberal cocktail parties on the Eastern seaboard, Oregon's Morse is the darling of free-lance radicalism. How different is the mood when he is campaigning at home, amongst his stalwart supporters . . . (the) minions of privilege and exploitation who head his 1950 re-election campaign. Someone is being badly fooled. We hope it is the reactionaries.

For Oregon Republicans, Morse did not this time deny his liberalism, but sought to make it palatably Republican in origin. "His liberalism is the same liberalism of Lincoln," said the Morse statement in the official voters' pamphlet.

The choice for Oregon Republicans, of course, was not between their Republican senator and a more admirable model of conservatism —say, a Taft; but the alternatives were were either Wayne Morse or Deadwood Dave Hoover, who offered a return to the isolationism of Rufus Holman along with his blunt reactionary views of domestic affairs. The surprise was not that Morse won by 56,678 votes, but that Hoover gained as many votes as he did. Hoover and a second unknown, John McBride, together collected 40 per cent of the total vote in that primary, indicating the strength of anti-Morse feeling in G.O.P. ranks. Nevertheless it served as no noticeable brake on his liberalism once he returned to the Senate for his second term. The liberal issues he had selected for condemnation in Oregon never came up for votes in the Senate, saving Wayne Morse the acute embarrassment of having then either to disappoint his eastern liberal admirers or utterly destroy his acceptability to those Republicans who had again taken him at his word and returned him to the Senate.

Having survived his first re-election test in 1950, Morse showed even less deference for his Senate elders during his second term. Ultimately he bolted the G.O.P. and became an Independent. Then, for the first time, he came suddenly into a period of exquisite power. As a result of the 1954 elections, the Senate was so evenly divided between Republicans and Democrats that the Independent senator acquired the momentary power to decide which party should take control of the Senate, elect the committee chairmen, and hold a majority of seats on each committee.

By siding with the Democrats, Wayne Morse gave Lyndon B. Johnson the chance to become the Senate's majority leader for the first time. Johnson, in turn, gave Morse the grand prize which Taft had always withheld, a seat on the Foreign Relations Committee. Taft, to be sure, never needed Morse; but Johnson did.

7. THE SENATOR AND THE PRESIDENTS

*FDR . . . HST . . . Salem Rebuff . . . The Crossroad . . .
Bolting the G.O.P. . . . Ike*

ONE SUNDAY morning in July, 1949, Wayne Morse climbed into
the front seat of a Lincoln convertible, its top down in readiness for
a promised drive through pastoral northern Virginia. In the rear sat
two Secret Service men. Behind the wheel as the car rolled out
from the White House grounds was the President of the United
States. Their destination was the Leesburg home of George Catlett
Marshall. On a previous visit there, Harry S. Truman had become
intrigued by a marker he and General Marshall had stumbled upon
in the weeds of the nearby Ball's Bluff battlefield. The marker indicated the place where Colonel Edward D. Baker, in command
of the seventy-first Pennsylvania Volunteers, had fallen in a battle
with Confederate forces. As a Senate man himself, Truman thought
it a grievous oversight that Baker, a former Senator from Oregon,
should have only this entangled marker to memorialize his final
act of glory and to mark his remains.

When Truman's invitation had arrived, Morse placed a request
with the Library of Congress for a background memorandum on
Colonel Baker. This hero, the library advised Morse, was buried at
San Francisco, not at Ball's Bluff. As they sped down the Leesburg
Pike, Morse at length shared this intelligence with his driver. A
published account of the trip says that at this point:

> The Presidential car nearly swerved off the road. Recovering, Mr.
> Truman said that General Marshall would feel bad about bringing
> them all the way to Leesburg for nothing. "We mustn't hurt his feel-
> ings." he added. "You leave this to me." So after lunch, as General
> Marshall escorted the party three miles away to the supposed grave of
> Senator Baker, Mr. Truman broke the news that he wasn't buried

there after all. . . . General Marshall felt bad about bringing the President and Senator Morse down to Leesburg on a wild-goose chase, but they didn't feel that way at all. They were delighted to have the excuse to get away from Washington, and they arranged to have a gardener tidy up the spot where Colonel Baker fell. No new monument, they agreed, was necessary.

Why would President Truman, never noted for extending the hand of friendship to Republicans, be so generous as to take the Republican Senator from Oregon on this idyllic jaunt to Leesburg? More than a history buff's enthusiasm was involved here, otherwise Oregon's *senior* senator, Guy Cordon, would have been the more likely one to be consulted. Wayne Morse was not only Oregon's *junior* senator, but the one who had impetuously belittled Truman for "ham acting" a few years earlier. In his memoirs Truman recalls that slur, but adds that he always thought well of Morse for later making a public apology.

Harry Truman and Wayne Morse, different in many ways, had a rapport which perhaps only two political gamecocks could have. Truman liked Morse because the senator battled Taft frequently to support the President's Fair Deal program, and Morse liked the flattering attention he got from the President. Correspondence between Morse and Truman shortly before their trip to Leesburg reveals much of this. Morse wrote to Truman as follows in June:

I would be less than human if I didn't say that I am deeply moved by your statement [in a previous letter]: "The only reason I am writing you on this subject is because I like you and I want you to have the facts." In response to your expression of friendship, it seems to me I can best assure you of my very affectionate regard for you, both as an individual and as President of the United States, by saying I have always welcomed every opportunity to support you both personally and as to your policies in the Senate whenever it has been possible for me to do so. In fact, I have done this so frequently that my political enemies in Oregon often charge me with being a better Democrat than most of my colleagues on the Democrat side of the aisle!

Be that as it may, I intend to continue to support you as a person on all occasions and to support your political policies in the Senate when they coincide with my general liberal views—which to date has been true of a good majority of the issues you have advocated during your Administration. As I said in a press conference just a few days ago, "The leadership of the Republican Party makes a serious mistake in seeking to create the false impression that Harry Truman is automatically wrong on every proposal he makes to the Congress and to the country. I intend to continue to support him whenever I think he is right, and to date he has been right according to my sights much more often than have been the leaders of the Republican Party in the 80th and 81st Congresses." I understand that those comments to the press have added fuel to the fires of determination of ultraconservative Republicans in Oregon to run a candidate against me in next year's Republican primary, but I shall welcome such a fight.

A few days later Truman replied, saying, "I think you and I understand each other. We are both working for the public interest and while we sometimes may not agree on the methods, the objective is just the same." He then added the invitation to visit Ball's Bluff. After their return from that Sunday drive, Morse wrote: "Dear Mr. President: I want you to know that the highlight of my service in the Senate was the rare privilege and great pleasure I had last Sunday in being your guest on the trip to Ball's Bluff."

Here are threads to the solution of one of the major mysteries about Wayne Morse. "Wayne," says a senator who feels close to Morse, "is a very sensitive person. He likes to be appreciated. He's more sensitive to lack of appreciation than some. He likes to have his back scratched, so I scratch it once in a while. That's why we get along so well, I think." This insight from a fellow senator offers an explanation for the curious paradox of Morse's attitude toward the Presidents of his time. The paradox is this: though elected as an anti-New Deal Republican, Morse never abused Roosevelt, took only a few cracks at Truman, and went on to support much of Truman's Fair Deal; though an early apostle of Eisenhower for the presidency, Morse jumped off the Republican bandwagon in 1952 as it rolled toward the White House and went on to abuse Eisenhower personally, holding him responsible for the wrongs he alleged against his Administration. The short explanation is that Roosevelt and Truman scratched Wayne Morse's back, and Eisenhower never did.

FDR

Take a look, first, at his relations with Franklin Roosevelt. Morse was so greatly appreciated in his first six months in Washington following Pearl Harbor that the White House had to settle a conflict of demand for his services by different agencies. Roosevelt had appointed Morse to the War Labor Board, following his success in settling the national rail labor dispute just before war broke out. But Admiral Emory S. Land, War Shipping Adminstrator, wanted Morse to do a job for him as chairman of the West Coast Maritime Industry Board. A White House aide, Wayne Coy, advised Roosevelt in a memo: "I believe Jerry Land is writing you about sending Wayne Morse to the Pacific Coast to coordinate ship loading and unloading operations. Morse is an excellent choice for this job because of his knowledge of the situation and because of his prestige on the West Coast. This matter is vitally important . . . his appointment would show that vigorous action was being taken to make full use of our equipment. This would be a great boon to West Coast morale." The President wrote "O.K., F.D.R." on the memo.

Labor Secretary Perkins, however, interceded against the assignment because it would be "most unwise to disturb Mr. Morse in the work which he is now doing." The chairman of the WLB agreed. Roosevelt then sent a memo to Land saying: "I understand you and Eddie Macauley still want Wayne Morse as coordinator of the *East* Coast, and that he did a splendid job on the West Coast. I wish you would talk with Miss Perkins about this. It seems to me that this is even more important than the work he is doing now. F.D.R." In the end, Morse did extra work on the Pacific coast, happily handling a large workload for those who reposed confidence in him.

A high point in his relations with the New Deal President came later that summer after the WLB had issued its famous "Little Steel" decision, fixing a formula for settling wage disputes by allowing for a 15 per cent increase in wages to compensate for the increase in prices. In his written opinion in this case, Morse revealed that he favored strong wartime powers for the President. But the New York *Times* rapped his knuckles for threatening the application of treason laws against unions which call jurisdictional strikes in wartime. "I shall be glad to stand before the Supreme Court any time and defend the proposition that a deliberate overt act resulting in the closing down of an arsenal or munition plant over a jurisdictional issue amounts to giving aid and comfort to the enemy in time of war," averred Morse.

A few weeks later Morse was summoned to the White House. "I called you over here because I want to discuss with you your views as to my war powers," said Roosevelt. "We have a very difficult situation, as you know, and it is a question as to what my powers are, and you know how we lawyers are. I get all sorts of advice. I get one group telling me I can get something and another group telling me I can't. . . . I am familiar with what you said in the Little Steel decision and I agree with what you said. I don't want to exercise my powers to the fullest extent and I think you take the view that there is no limit to my powers."

To the man who still described himself in letters to friends in Oregon as "a country boy in the big city," this must have been an exhilarating experience. That he gave Roosevelt assurance on this point is manifest from the memo which showed these exchanges of view:

The President: Do you think my war powers extend to these two matters? Can I say to the American farmers, "You will be guaranteed 100 cents in 110" and the government will give it to them and the government will take their supplies?

Mr. Morse: The government is the purchaser and then the government can distribute those supplies in accordance with the stabilization program we worked out. There is no doubt about it. You can confiscate property in time of war to protect the country. If you can take tangible property, you can take intangible property in the sense that there is intangible property there. . . .

The President: The second matter in regard to exercise of war power on this farm matter is whether I can do that in the face of the Price Act. There is a section in the Price Act (3a) which says that farm parity must be maintained in accordance with the Act and cannot be changed by any other power of government. Do you think that stops me?

Mr. Morse: No. Congress can pass all the laws it wants to, but if you decide that a certain course of action is esssential as a war measure, it supersedes congressional action. It is a drastic thing to do. I don't think this is a question of superseding. I think Congress was talking about freezing. You aren't freezing. Price is not the controlling thing in the exercise of your function here. It is not a question of your being interested in prices. It is a question of your getting those supplies so we may win the war. As Commander-in-Chief you have the right to go out and get it.

The President: That is what I think. But I wish you would talk to Sam [Presumably Sam is Judge Rosenman, who that day drove Morse to the White House and was one of Roosevelt's closest advisers.]

Roosevelt then turned to the pending problem of "Big Steel."
Philip Murray's Steelworkers in the "Little Steel" case had received
their 15 per cent wage increase in July. Murray hadn't been happy
about the size of this award, but Roosevelt had placated him with
a written memo of assurance that this wage increase would be
granted to the "Big Steel" company Steelworkers without a hitch.
But now there was a hitch. Murray had failed to serve notice
simultaneously on "Big Steel," and the law didn't permit the board
to award a retroactive pay increase that would make the wage
increase effective industry-wide simultaneously. The memo continues:

> *Mr. Morse:* That is our problem. We feel all the equities are with
> Murray but that the law is not with him.
> *The President:* Well, I don't think these are times in which the law
> should prevail above equities. You have to fight a war on moral
> grounds, and I think that moral obligations have to prevail and I
> think Phil has a right to feel that he was to get the same total for
> his men in "Big Steel" as in "Little Steel." He talks of a difficult
> time in selling it to his men, and I had a difficult time selling it to him.

Morse went on to tell Roosevelt that Murray had threatened to
make public the memo the President had given him if he didn't
get what he was promised. "That makes me very angry," said Morse,
"and I don't think we should have to act on the basis of threats."
Roosevelt said he thought the steel companies knew they ought
to pay the higher wage. Four days later the board awarded the
Steelworkers a retroactive 15 per cent increase over the protests
of the industry representatives. The majority opinion, written by
Dean Morse, said: "It would be highly unrealistic to expect
maximum production from workers who, in all equity, were entitled
to a back-pay adjustment which was denied to them on purely
legalistic grounds of form and not of substance."

Upon Roosevelt's death in April, 1945, shortly after Morse took
his seat in the Senate, the Oregon senator said the life of Roosevelt
is "a symbol to me of the new spirit brought into the world which
insists that institutions must recognize the dignity of man and the
spiritual value of human life." Six months behind him was the
necessity for expedient damnation of the New Deal. Wayne Morse,
the liberal, spoke that day from the heart about the President who
respected his legal judgment, his ability, and encouraged him to run
for the Senate.

HST

President Truman thought, if anything, even more highly of Morse, despite an episode in which Truman admitted that "my feelings were somewhat ruffled." This was in June 1946 when the President appeared before a joint session of Congress to request drastic legislation for breaking a national rail strike by drafting workers into the army. During the course of his address, Truman was interrupted when Senate Secretary Leslie Biffle handed him a slip of paper. The President read it, then announced to a relieved Congress that he had just been informed that his aides had achieved a settlement at the White House. "That was one of the cheapest exhibitions of ham acting I have ever seen," declared Wayne Morse to the Senate later.

Morse charged that Truman and his aides had known before the President ever mounted the rostrum to address Congress that the railroad brotherhoods were prepared to make a settlement, that union leaders were kept at arm's length by the White House until the crucial afternoon hour when Truman went to Capitol Hill, and that they were then admitted to the White House for a signing which the President then dramatically announced. Senator Barkley, the majority leader, rose to defend Truman against a charge he said was "utterly without foundation," and to recite a chronology of events which refuted Morse's contention. Morse widely repeated his assertions nevertheless. The Washington *Star* made an independent investigation which satisfied it that Morse had overreached himself. Whatever the internal verity of the matter, nine months later Wayne Morse publicly repented. "I want to say I was unkind in the language I used in expressing my disapproval. For that unkindness I regret," he said in the Senate.

A few days later the President, during a trip, took pen in hand and scrawled this message on "The Flying White House" stationery:

Dear Wayne:
    I have just read your remarks in the *Record* of March 12. I appreciate what you said very much. I'll admit that my feelings were somewhat ruffled by your comment on the Rail Strike Speech. I've always been an admirer of yours. Honest men may differ but they may still be friends. With kindest regards, I am, Sincerely, Harry Truman.

The President's words of tribute and forgiveness appear to mark a turning point in Morses' attitude and spoken words concerning Truman. In the previous election, 1946, when Morse stumped the country for every Republican no matter how reactionery, his standard pitch was that any Republican looked good compared to the leader of the Democratic party, whom he characterized as the "head of one of the most corrupt political machines int his country." But after Truman wrote him that note, Morse more often than not found in Truman a statesman.

Years later Mr. Truman told me in an interview at Independence, "I always liked Wayne Morse." The Truman Library holds much additional evidence of this sentiment. There was the telegram to Morse when he was in a Salem, Oregon, hospital after his accident at the State Fair in 1949: "I hope you are not seriously hurt and that you will be able to win the prizes before the show is over. Harry S. Truman"; and the paragraph in a subsequent letter written to Morse after he had been transferred to a hospital in Washington: "I hope you are fully recovered. I have been trying to get to the hospital to see you, but as you know, I have been covered up with work, working almost from daylight to dark every day. I am still getting letters on Senator Baker [of Ball's Bluff fame], and some of them are most interesting. I had one a day or two ago from his niece, evidently a good maiden lady out in Illinois. She wrote me a most interesting letter, and I sent her a reply on it. . . . Harry S. Truman." Or there is the picture which hangs in the Truman Library museum which shows that Morse that spring was among the notables with the President at Griffith Stadium for the opening of the baseball season.

These tokens of affectionate regard from the highly partisan Democratic President for a Republican maverick were doubtless based on gratitude for Morse's frequent defense of Truman's embattled legislative program, from his Fair Employment Practices Commission proposal to his veto of the Taft-Hartley Act, especially in the President's struggle with the Republican-controlled Eightieth Congress. Many conservative Democrats weren't giving Truman the support Morse offered. "Whenever I could have Wayne in my corner, I always wanted him there," Truman told me.

In the worse domestic political crisis which confronted his Administration—the discovery of wrongdoing within the Internal Revenue Service and the Justice Department—Harry Truman turned to

Wayne Morse for help. As disclosures of tax tinkering mounted, Truman in November 1951 was considering appointing a commission headed by a New York judge to clean up the trouble. Morse, in a speech at the University of Southern California, said this would be a mistake, that the proper action would be to get a new Attorney General to clean up internal corruption. Later Morse debated this point with three other senators on a radio program from Washington. A few nights later Morse received a telephone call at his home. President Truman came on the line to ask if the senator could come down to his office the next afternoon at three o'clock. Morse said that of course he would be there. Truman instructed him to come into the White House grounds via the southwest gate so the newsmen, who intercept visitors coming through the west gate, would not know of his arrival. When Morse arrived for his appointment with the President, Truman got right to the point by telling Morse he was absolutely right about the weakness of establishing a cleanup commission. As the senator recalls it, Truman then said:

"I've called you down here to offer you the Attorney Generalship of the United States."

(Years later, Truman told me he offered the job to Morse because: "I thought he would clean things up. I thought he would do the job, do the work, as it should be done. People don't understand. They think there is a deep, dark, under-the-table reason. It isn't true with me.")

Morse says he thought at first that the President was kidding. But he says Truman added, "I mean it. Howard McGrath is a fine fellow but he can't do the job. You can write your own ticket. It isn't often that a President gives anyone an offer like this. I'm satisfied that 99.9 per cent of our people are fine public servants. Apparently I've got a few rotten apples in the barrel. I want you to clean them out."

Morse says he immediately advised Truman that "you couldn't make a worse mistake because you must do this with a Democrat." Truman replied, "You're no Republican. You're an Independent, and that's what I want." Morse says he observed that he would have to appoint a lot of people if he replaced McGrath and this would cause "every Democrat on the Hill to be on my neck. I can be of greater service to you in the Senate."

A further consideration was that this offer came in December 1951, less than a year before the next presidential election. Morse says he remarked that time was so short that he would just be able to get the indictments ready and not be able to complete the cases by the time a new President was elected in November 1952. Morse says he will never forget Truman's reply: "I don't know whether or not I'm going to run again—that's up to my doctor. But I feel fine, and if I run I will be re-elected—and you will still be the Attorney General."

To Wayne Morse, this meant that Truman would surely run again in 1952. Neither of them could then know that Truman three months later would announce that he would not run again or that ten months later Wayne Morse would bolt the Republican party. Morse says after they discussed the matter for two and a half hours, Truman asked him to sleep on it. He went home that night, he says, and discussed it most of the night with Mrs. Morse. He telephoned three close political friends who had helped him in his Senate campaigns: Ralph Cake, Oregon's Republican National Committeeman; Eddie Sammons, Portland banker and his campaign finance chairman in 1950; and Palmer Hoyt, who had moved from the *Oregonian* to the Denver *Post*. As Morse recalls it, Cake and Hoyt were against his accepting the cabinet offer and Sammons thought it was tough to turn it down. The next day Morse wrote Truman a letter declining the offer.

It would have been a hazardous assignment for anyone, but particularly for a Republican when it was apparent that the G.O.P. planned to run against Democratic corruption in the next election. Morse, also, had five years more to go on his second Senate term, but a cabinet post in an administration that might be voted out within a year was anything but secure.

Moreover, Morse was struck by the glittering possibility that General Eisenhower might lead the G.O.P. to victory and toward progressive international policies that would thwart the "Fortress America" approach then being championed by Taft. As far back as October 1947 Morse had spoken of Eisenhower as a presidential possibility, after both senators from the general's home state of Kansas had led the way. "I think he would sweep the country because the people have a great confidence in his fairness, they honor his great war record, and they believe he would function on a plane high above the level of partisan politics," prophesied Morse accurately.

By early 1952, when the Dewey forces were organizing effectively to extricate Eisenhower from his NATO command at Paris, Morse was drawn into some of their strategy talks, especially respecting the upcoming Oregon primary in the spring. A conference in the office of Senator Henry Cabot Lodge, attended by Morse and other liberal Republican senators, decided the question of putting Ike into the Oregon primary. A slate of pro-Eisenhower delegates, to be identified as such, was to be the vehicle. Such other leading Oregon Republicans as Governor Douglas McKay and Ralph Cake favored Eisenhower and were confident they could carry the state for him against the Taft forces. Political strategy talks in Morse's office occasionally focused on the possibility of Wayne Morse's being Eisenhower's running mate. An exciting, possibly highly rewarding, year lay ahead.

Salem Rebuff

The Eisenhower forces swept the field in the Oregon primary and Morse, McKay, and a corps of other top Republicans were elected as delegates to the Republican convention. A few weeks later, Morse suffered a rough jolt. The elected delegates met at Salem to elect officers and assign delegates to the various convention committees. With Congress in session, Morse stayed in Washington and gave his proxy to his alternate, Clay Myers, Jr. The chairmanship, traditionally going to the person who gained the greatest number of votes, was expected to go to Governor McKay, who had edged Morse in popular votes. Morse's desire was to serve on the platform committee.

Mark Hatfield, then a twenty-nine-year-old political science instructor at Willamette University in Salem, recalls going to see Governor McKay to discuss plans for the meeting. He says he told McKay he assumed Morse would be put on the platform committee. "Oh, I don't know about that," McKay replied. He went on to reveal to Hatfield that some of the delegates were displeased with Morse's behavior in the Senate and were determined to deny him any recognition because "he gives Oregon a black eye."

What was then enraging Oregon Republicans was Morse's defense of Truman's springtime seizure of the steel mills, an episode which in itself bears later examination. Cake, particularly incensed over this position of Morse's, did "considerable work behind the scenes before the meeting," recalls Lamarr Tooze, prominent Portland attorney who was a delegate.

When Hatfield asked McKay which delegate was likely to be put on the platform committee, the governor named Tooze. But Tooze wanted to be placed on the credentials committee in order to participate in the fight with the Taft delegates from the southern states. As the delegates filed into Salem's Senator Hotel for the meeting, Tooze took Hatfield aside and suggested Hatfield ought to go on the platform committee and that he would see that a nomination was offered. At the meeting both Hatfield and Tooze were nominated for the platform committee. Tooze withdrew. Then a staunch Morse man, Howard Dent, a blind lawyer from The Dalles, nominated the senator. The discussion grew warm and intense. When the vote was taken, Morse lost badly to Hatfield by a 13 to 5 vote. Tooze, also denied the committee of his choice, was given a sop, the rules committee. There was no sop for Wayne Morse. Widely and properly regarded as a slap in the face for Morse from his party's leaders in Oregon, this rebuff was explained by delegate Gordon Orputt: "He's a controversial hot potato because of his New Dealish attitude."

This episode made it painfully clear to Wayne Morse that the law of diminishing returns was running agianst him in the G.O.P. "The Salem meeting disclosed for the first time to the state that the McKay-Gard-Cake-Cordon element of the party—the reactionary machine—didn't want me in the party, or, if they wanted me in the party, they wanted me only to use me. They didn't want to give me any position of leadership," Morse said subsequently in *U. S. News and World Report*. (Jess Gard, Portland businessman, had succeeded Cake as Oregon's Republican National Committeeman.)

There is no doubt that the G.O.P. had used Morse to advantage for some years, sending him out to campaign for conservative candidates such as Senator Dworshak of Idaho in 1946, for one thing. Years after Morse had left the party, Governor Hatfield told me he lamented Morse's withdrawal because the senator had always given the party a valuable entree with labor.

On the other hand, Morse used the Republican party to gain his immediate political ends. To him the party was an instrument of power which could be cast aside when its utility had been expended. To many party leaders, Morse was equally expendable. Morse says: "I have always felt that at the Salem meeting the

Republican machine kicked me out of the party in Oregon, at least out of the inner councils of the party. For the first time it clearly dawned on me that the Republican powers of the state were planning to destroy me politically if they could. I then and there resolved to give them a good, hard fight and carry that fight to all the people of the state."

Shortly before going to the convention, Morse told Alice Frein Johnson, correspondent for the Seattle *Times*, and me of his expectation that Taft was going to get the nomination. What would he do under those circumstances? we asked. "Issue a call for a new party," declared Morse. We reporters inferred that Morse was then psychologically prepared to launch a third-party movement in the event Taft gained control of the G.O.P. (Morse subsequently denied ever making this remark, saying any thoughts he might have expressed along this line referred to possible realignment of the two major parties, with conservatives in one and liberals in the other.)

In any event Morse was not confronted with this dilemma. The night the Eisenhower forces defeated the Taft forces, Morse and Hatfield, Phil Hitchcock, Clay Myers, all still wearing the sporty straw hats which symbolized the Ike men, and I shared a car from convention hall to the downtown hotel district. Listening to Wayne Morse lecture on the historic importance of that night's great victory, we were all convinced that the Grand Old Party had been reborn— and that the maverick senator from Oregon, ebullient in this hour of Eisenhower's triumph, at last felt very much at home in the Republican party.

Three months later Wayne Morse resigned from the Republican party, took the stump with vigorous cricitism of General Eisenhower, and began his transition from one major party to the other. What could possibly have caused such a drastic and sudden shift of allegiance? Why did Wayne Morse do what the successful American politician almost never does—cut the last tie with the party which gave him birth?

The Crossroad

It is a conviction of some that Wayne Morse soured on Eisenhower because he was not chosen to be the general's running mate. Morse flatly denies having held any ambition to be, or any illusions of being, the vice-presidential candidate. "I was at work with a group that had become very interested in Lev Saltonstall for the vice-presidency," says Morse. Cake says he told Morse before the convention that he had no chance because of Morse's past fights with other senators.

Senator Saltonstall recalls that Morse advised him during the convention preliminaries that he had told newspapermen he favored Saltonstall; but he says he knew of no group action on his behalf. Saltonstall says he was never a possibility for that position for plain geographic reasons, for his state of Massachusetts was too close to New York State, which Eisenhower, as president of Columbia University, had claimed as his residence.

The depth of Morse's commitment to Saltonstall's candidacy was indicated by a close friend of Morse's who recalls the senator's telling him before the convention that "Saltonstall had ruined his chances of becoming Ike's running mate by appearing to be ambitious for the job, which lost him prestige in the Senate. Nevertheless Wayne said he supported Saltonstall." This friend asked Morse, what about himself? "Wayne said he didn't think he had any chance to be the running mate because he had stepped on too many toes," says the friend. He inferred from their conversation that Morse "wouldn't have wanted that position because it would have silenced him in the Senate," inasmuch as the Vice-president is not permitted to enter into debates when he presides over the Senate.

During the convention preliminaries, Hatfield says he passed a note to Governor Dewey suggesting Morse for Vice-president. He says he either showed the note to Morse or told him its message. "He was tongue-tied," recalls Hatfield. "He sort of grinned and shrugged his shoulders in helpless delight. But Dewey sent back word that they had to concentrate on getting Eisenhower nominated first and not worry about the vice-presidential nomination for any individual." Hatfield and Morse got along well at the convention, sharing a car to ride back and forth between the hotel and the convention hall. Hatfield says Morse never mentioned any endeavors in behalf of Saltonstall, nor did he observe any.

After the Eisenhower nomination was secured, the general's top strategists—Dewey, Lodge, Saltonstall, Fred Seaton, and about thirty-five others—met in a hotel room to select a suitable running mate. Dewey, running the meeting, wanted Senator Nixon. So did Lodge. Saltonstall suggested Dan Thornton, Colorado's governor. Other names were mentioned and dismissed. In less than an hour Nixon was the agreed choice. No one mentioned Wayne Morse. What was perhaps more galling, no one asked his advice or invited him into the inner councils where the decisions were made. No one scratched his back. Hard as it was to be slapped in the face by his own delegation, it was harder still on Wayne Morse to be utterly ignored. He was lost in a sweaty mob of elbowing sign carriers who whooped it up for Ike and Dick.

Morse says he wanted an open convention to determine the vice-presidential nomination, with at least three candidates placed in nomination. He was prepared to make a nominating speech for Saltonstall, he says, when he got the word from Cake that it was nobody but Nixon. "What do you expect me to do in the campaign if you nominate Nixon?" he says he asked. "He's a red flag in every labor hall in America." Later he grumbled to an Oregon delegate, "There goes the election." "Why?" asked Jess Gard. "Nixon's stand on labor," replied Morse. After the Nixon nomination was whooped through, a correspondent stopped by Morse's hotel room for an interview. "He was prostrate," the reporter recalls. "He kept talking about the *way* Nixon was nominated." Far from being unique, the *way* Nixon was selected is the traditional way. Candidates have to run for the presidential nomination; they are normally hand-picked for second place by the winner of first place. Morse says he was horrified at this method, because the main argument of the Ike forces against Taft was that "we were going to eliminate the smoke-filled hotel-room technique by making our decisions in the open out on the floor of the convention."

If it had been thrown open to the convention, would a powerfully delivered speech for Saltonstall have overcome the geographical handicap Saltonstall himself said ruled him out—or would its effect have been to project to the convention delegates the oratorical skill of Wayne Morse? For a man who had talked his way from the campus to the Senate, whose reliance upon oratorical power plays is nearly absolute, is it so preposterous that such a man might entertain the vision of thunderous acclaim, of a convention's being swept off its feet to add a fighting liberal to the ticket headed by a popular general? In these giddy moments of hope, exuberance, and anxiety at Chicago, only the secretive inner Wayne Morse could identify these uncertain shadows.

Whatever motivated the man, when he left that convention hall he was on his way out of the Republican party. Never again did he make a move in behalf of the G.O.P. If the party leaders had

wanted to keep Morse on the reservation, they could probably have
done so by some wisely generous efforts to counteract the effect
of the rebuffs given Morse at Salem and Chicago. But Wayne Morse
was not wanted—and the senator was quick to realize this. Palmer
Hoyt, Morse's publisher friend, recalls that when the Eisenhower
strategists met at Denver following the convention, the general's
"hunch was to send for Morse, pat him on the head, and get him
to make some labor speeches." Hoyt strongly supported this idea,
but he says Senator Duff of Pennsylvania, Governor Thornton of
Colorado, and Ralph Cake "vetoed this idea." Ironically the President, who received the roughest treatment from Morse, had the
right instincts for winning him over—a little back-scratching of
the sort that goes a long way with the senator. Here, as in so many
subsequent political events, Eisenhower accepted dubious advice
and ran into trouble.

Upon returning to Washington, Morse dashed off an article for
the *New Republic* that was highly critical of the Republican platform. In private conversation he was hardly less critical of the G.O.P.
candidate. "Eisenhower isn't the man for the job; he's not big enough;
he hasn't the mind for it," Morse told Roulhac Hamilton, correspondent for the *Oregon Journal*. He added that he feared Ike was
"a man of compromise rather than a man of determined principle."
He told me on August 4 he expected Adlai Stevenson to "make
mincemeat" of Eisenhower when the campaign got under way.

In an effort to placate Morse sufficiently to subdue his mutinous
spirit, the Republican leaders at Denver did all of the wrong things.
They assigned a number of minor luminaries at headquarters to fly
to Washington or to telephone the wounded warrior. After one of
these emissaries had called on him, Morse said he sent him away
"not with his tail between his legs but without any tail." The senator
was waiting to hear from the general, not from his flunkies. That
call never came.

The most Eisenhower headquarters got from Wayne Morse was a
public statement (issued the same day Morse privately told me
Adlai would "make mincemeat" of Ike) which concluded on this
promising note:

> As an independent Republican, I shall not in any way compromise my
> views in respect to those issues concerning which I think the Republi-
> can party should change its course of policy. However, I am sure that

voters generally will understand and appreciate the fact that a liberal Republican can disagree with his party on certain issues and still work hard for the election of such a great leader of its party as Eisenhower because of his deep conviction that a change of administration in November, 1952, under our two-party system is essential for a strong America both domestically and internationally."

Next day, August 5, Morse and Senator Russell Long of Louisiana left for an inspection tour of NATO installations. When they arrived in London, Morse found a letter awaiting him, signed Dwight D. Eisenhower. The general wanted to see him as soon as he returned, said the letter. To this first communiqué he had received from Eisenhower, Morse sent back an ecstatic reply on August 19:

Dear General:

I deeply appreciate receiving your letter of July 26th, which has been forwarded to me here in London. You may be sure that upon my return to the United States on or about September 15th, I shall throw myself into your campaign with all my vigor, and do whatever I can to help you and Nixon. It will be a matter of great pride to me to campaign for you, because I was the first Republican in the Senate by about a year to publicly urge your nomination.

It is unimportant that I disagree with you on certain specific issues, because as to those issues, only time will tell what is the correct solution. What is important is that our people have as a President a man such as you, in whom they can place their complete confidence and know that you will exercise an honest independence of judgment on the merits of each issue.

As a liberal Republican I am proud to support you and after your election I shall be happy to cooperate with you and Nixon in trying to develop a legislative program which always will place the welfare of our people, and thereby the security of our country, in a position of first consideration.

I have advised Walter Williams and Mrs. Mary Lord to arrange any speaking engagements for me they care to in connection with their campaign program.

With best wishes always,

Sincerely,
Wayne Morse

P.S. Whenever I go abroad I hear enthusiastic reports about the great work you have done over here for our country and for Peace and Security.

When Morse returned from Europe September 9, another letter from Eisenhower awaited him. It thanked the senator for "your warm assurance of wholehearted support" and said Morse's "vigorous and articulate assistance will be of great help in the tough fight we are facing." But now Wayne Morse was not so choked up with superlatives about the general. Senator Long says that Morse noticeably cooled toward Eisenhower as they proceeded out from London to the Far Eastern terminus of the alliance in Turkey. Morse and Long subsequently submitted a report to the Armed Services Committee criticizing waste in the NATO program.

In a post-election article in the *New Republic*, Morse said he returned from Europe still planning to campaign for Eisenhower. "But I began listening to Stevenson, whom I had never met. As I listened to his speeches and compared them with the demogoguery of Eisenhower's speeches, I realized that a dramatic and historic thing was taking place in the United States—a brilliant statesman was running for the presidency for the Democrats, and a demogogue, who was obviously willing to commit any expedient act for support, was running for the Republicans. Every speech of Eisenhower's keenly disappointed me. I soon found myself in the midst of a terrible conflict of conscience."

Upon his return, the Republicans made their worst mistake in trying to use the prickly Oregonian. They asked Morse to go to the AF of L convention at Atlantic City in mid-September when Eisenhower was to deliver his labor speech. What was he to do? Make a ringing speech? No. Wayne Morse was not to say a word. He was just to sit on the stage in a mute symbolic endorsement of the general's remarks. Well, what was Eisenhower going to say? asked Morse. They didn't know.

Morse was furious. "I'm no whore," he snorted as he told me these events over lunch the day they occurred. The one enjoyable facet to Morse was that the man assigned to "deliver" him to Atlantic City was Ralph Cake, the Oregon party leader who apparently had influenced Morse's rebuff at Salem and his isolation from the Eisenhower high command at Chicago and Denver. Morse was now going to show them that Cake couldn't deliver. "What made them think they could get along without me?" growled the tiger.

Perhaps I contributed a bit to Morse's determination that day by telling him that while he was in Europe I had seen Cake and had asked about the reaction at Denver to Morse's criticism of the platform. Cake had replied, "Well, you know what that was—anything to get the biggest headline." It infuriates Morse when anyone regards his outspokenness as crass headline-hunting.

During this September 12 luncheon, Morse praised Stevenson as "a scholar" and said he didn't see how he could campaign against him and maintain his integrity. "I have a lot of things I want to do before I die, but I won't sit in the Senate unless I can do it with honor. I couldn't go out and campaign for Eisenhower without ruining the record I've made." He cited two episodes which up to that day had upset him about Eisenhower. The Indianapolis speech, which he mentioned to Cake, was that awkward occasion on which Eisenhower found himself arm in arm with Senator William Jenner, who had called General George Marshall a "front man for traitors." Jack Bell relates the event in *The Spendid Misery:*

> The hall was packed as Eisenhower marched triumphantly on stage, his arms upraised in response to the thunderous applause of the crowd. As the photographers began to pop their flashlight bulbs, Jenner skipped quickly across the stage, wrestled briefly for possession of the general's left arm, and then raised his own with it in a pictorial token of friendship and comradeship. After an expression of disgust had flitted briefly across his face, Eisenhower smiled. The deed was done when the presidential nominee endorsed all Indiana Republicans, including Jenner, in his speech.

The other incident Morse cited to me was Eisenhower's appearance in Milwaukee, Wisconsin, where General Marshall's other venomous critic was running for re-election. Richard Rovere describes this episode in *Senator Joe McCarthy:*

> He (Eisenhower) had from the start looked upon McCarthy as a cad, a guttersnipe, and he had planned a small gesture of defiance and dissociation. He would go into McCarthy's Wisconsin and speak a few warm and affectionate words about his old chief and patron, General Marshall, whom McCarthy had all but called a traitor. . . . Learning of Eisenhower's plans to dispute this view of Marshall—and trem-

bling at what they were certain was the prospect of McCarthy's fury—
the party leaders in Wisconsin and half a dozen other Republican
politicians pleaded with him to omit that part of his speech, which
he did. (In fairness, the President did, on other occasions, stoutly
defend General Marshall.)

In citing this episode, Morse told me he thought Eisenhower would
win the election on demogoguery because the nation was in a
trough of reaction.

This same day, September 12, was the occasion of the famous
meeting at Morningside Heights between Eisenhower and Taft,
for what Jack Bell termed "the great surrender." The terms of
agreement between these two former rivals for the nomination
were spelled out in a long statement which Taft had written and
brought to the meeting in his coat pocket. As White states it in
The Taft Story, "it was a proud manifesto and an apologia for
nearly all that Taft and the other orthodox Republicans had stood."

To Wayne Morse, this proved that Eisenhower had indeed surrendered or been captured by the Taft wing. If there had been any
chance at all of Morse's being brought into the Eisenhower campaign, it vanished that day as Morse read the afternoon newspaper accounts of the Taft triumph. Cake came down for dinner
that evening and, according to Morse, tried to dismiss the import
of the Taft meeting. "He said the whole Morningside Heights business was in the interests of party unity, and didn't mean anything in
terms of long-term commitments. And I said I just wanted an
answer to one question: "Have you told that to Bob Taft yet?"
Cake's mission failed.

The day that Eisenhower met with Bob Taft, Wayne Morse
saw President Truman at the White House. Morse has a "Truman
file" locked in his office safe which contains memos on his visits
with Truman which he is saving for his own memoirs. Whether
anything significant occurred during that White House meeting is
not known. Before he went to see Truman, however, Morse told
one of his aides in Oregon, "Something dramatic is going to happen
tomorrow." He refused to say what it was. "I have to see the
President first. I can't announce it until then."

Bolting the G.O.P.

Wayne Morse had decided to hop off the Republican bandwagon. The only thing that remained was the method of getting the most political mileage from his leap. Better to hang by his finger tips from the trailing edge for a time than to leap off suddenly and be lost in the dust.

So the day after the Morningside Heights surrender Morse hinted to reporters that he would probably spend the lovely autumn months showing his cattle at various fairs instead of campaigning for the G.O.P ticket. This move had the virtue of inciting a bit of suspense —will he or won't he?—while affording him the opportunity of climbing back on top of the bandwagon if he later should decide to do so. In any event his strange vow of oratorical abstinence for the remainder of the campaign was a major political story on the front pages of Oregon's weekend newspapers, as this veteran politician knew that it would be.

Harold Stassen was then dispatched to Washington to see the man who had once been his professor of argumentation at the University of Minnesota. As Morse tells the story of their visit, Stassen argued that this was a time to be practical. That was why Eisenhower had skipped nimbly over any praise of General Marshall at Milwaukee, even though in private Ike exploded with epithets about McCarthy. This was no time for an idealist to make impractical demands on the Republican candidates. Morse says he replied:

Harold, this is one of the saddest moments of my life. It is very clear that I did a poor job of teaching when you were in my class, for I never got across to you one of the principles I have always tried to get across to my students, and that is the only practicality they will ever experience is an ideal put to work. Now you sit there and tell me that to be practical I have to be expedient. In effect, what you say is that I have to compromise my principles.

Harold Stassen, too, went back empty-handed. By this time Morse's displeasure with the G.O.P. ticket had gained him another invitation to go to the AF of L convention—but this one came from the union, which wanted him to address the delegates. Wayne Morse accepted in an instant. The quiet cattle shows could wait.

Speaking at the labor convention, Morse could well have taken the reaction of the 800 delegates as an indicator of the national mood. When he poured it on Taft and the "fantastic document of political compromise" adopted at Morningside Heights, he drew the most effusive demonstration of approval given any speaker during the four-day convention, A. H. Raskin observed in the New York *Times*. When he made a few polite and uncritical references to General Eisenhower's labor speech of the previous day, the delegates sat on their hands. From Oregon there came additional enthusiasm in a telegram of approval from the state CIO convention. Both unions then endorsed Stevenson.

A short time later Wayne Morse's friend in the White House offered his verdict of the senator's maverick behavior. Speaking from his campaign train as it swung through Oregon, President Truman said of Morse:

> He is one of the finest men and best liberals I have known. Up to this summer, he had hopes the Republican party could be reformed. He worked for the man who is now the Republican candidate for president, thinking he was a liberal. And then what happened: Just a few weeks after the Republican convention, the candidate surrendered to Senator Taft—and gave in to the Old Guard on every issue from public power to national defense. He didn't stand up for a single liberal principle when the going got tough.
>
> So Senator Morse has refused to work for him—and I respect Senator Morse for that. Wayne Morse can see through the five-star glitter to the sad fact underneath, that the Republican candidate is the captive of the Old Guard.

On October 18 Wayne Morse called in reporters and photographers, pulled out an absentee ballot, and voted for Adlai Stevenson. Once again he had timed his dramatic move to hit the Sunday editions. He said:

> The demogoguery, double-talk and dangerous desertion by Eisenhower in this campaign of his once-professed political principles leaves me with no honorable course of action but to disassociate myself completely from his candidacy. The Eisenhower I supported for the nomination is not the Eisenhower who is dangling and dancing from campaign platforms at the end of political puppet strings being jerked by some of the most evil and reactionary forces in American politics.

A week later Morse announced his resignation from the Republican party. Repeating much of what he had earlier said in criticism, Morse quoted Woodrow Wilson as saying, "The man who adheres to any party after it has ceased to avow the principles which to him are dear and in his eyes are vital; the man who follows the leading of a party which seems to him to be going wrong, is acting a lie, and has lost either his wit or his virtue." Said Morse, "My decision to repudiate Eisenhower has not been an easy one to make because I was the first Republican senator to declare publicly for Eisenhower."

As a matter of fact this statement was not accurate. Morse was the third Republican to come out for Eisenhower. Robert C. Albright reported in the Washington *Post* that he was preceded by two Kansas senators in 1947. But this assertion showed something of Morse's scale of values. It was more difficult for him to cast away the fancied virtue of the carefully built up legend of being Ike's *first* booster than to tear up his repeated pledges to support Eisenhower and the Grand Old Party. On this latter point he concluded:

> The profound statement of Woodrow Wilson directly applies to the situation in which I find myself. With my party going so wrong in the campaign, I would be acting a lie if I supported Eisenhower. I would be letting down the independent voters who have confidence in me. Henceforth, I shall stand in American politics as an independent Republican and let the people be the judge of my brand of Republicanism.

Adlai Stevenson and the Democratic party at large expressed elation over Morse's withdrawal from the Republican party. Oregon party chairman Howard Morgan likened Morse to George Norris, Gifford Pinchot, and Fiorella La Guardia. Republicans were equally vivid with comparison. An interesting disclosure came from a Republican editor, the late Robert W. Sawyer of the Bend *Bulletin*, who dug out a letter Morse had written him in the fall of 1946 when the senator was busily campaigning for right-wing Republican Senators Cain, Dworshak, and others. Said Morse then:

> Many of the so-called liberal Republicans have shown themselves to be political prima donnas with the result that they have no great influence within the party itself. I recognize that it is important that liberal Republicans hold their support among independent voters, but

I am convinced that the independent voters, once they stop to think about it, will have much more respect for a liberal Republican who is loyal to his party convictions at election time than they would have if he adopted renegade and bolting tactics at election time—which is too frequently the case among liberals.

Oregon editors had mixed reactions. Editor Frank Jenkins, a personal friend of Morse's from his university days, said in the Klamath Falls *Herald* that he had taken a lot of ribbing over the years for backing Morse, but he had done so cheerfully "because I've believed that under your exhibitionist exterior you were sincere." He added, "But now I know how Robert Browning felt when he penned these lines of *The Lost Leader*:

> *Just for a handful of silver he left us,*
> *Just for a riband to stick in his coat."*

Jenkins said the "riband" was Taft's scalp. Robert W. Ruhl in the Medford *Mail Tribune* said, "There is no more reason to condemn Morse or to accuse him of dishonesty . . . than to accuse Senator Byrd of Virginia of dishonesty or disloyalty for bolting the Democratic party under Stevenson." George Putnam in the Salem *Capital Journal* wrote, "Morse has a prima donna complex and has talked more than any member of the party. He plays the role of an egomaniac and has been a blatant double crosser, publicity seeker and opportunist." Robert Ingalls in the Corvallis *Gazette-Times* declared, "Most of us common folk have been so awed by the junior senator's bushy eyebrows and his fabulous opinion of himself that we haven't taken a good look at the real Morse. Now that he has shown his real colors, such a look is no longer important or necessary . . . we are well rid of him."

Tugman in the Eugene *Register-Guard* wrote, "The importance of this event for either Stevenson or Eisenhower is probably greatly overrated—because the senator is not the shining knight he once appeared to be. He has contradicted himself too many times and in too many different situations. . . . The man has dissipated gorgeous talents in his pursuit of headlines." The *Oregonian* found Morse's explanation for his apostasy glib. "Our faith in Wayne Morse's 'constitutional liberalism' was sadly shaken when he supported President Truman's unconstitutional seizure of the steel mills.

We find his lastest political gyration equally inconsistent with his public utterances of the last eight years." J. W. Forrester, Jr., wrote in the *East Oregonian*, "The Democrats love it and the Republicans are ready to banish Wayne to Siberia. . . . The Republicans greeted the pronouncement of Messrs. Byrnes, Byrd and Shivers [in support of Ike] with great joy and the conclusion that they were 'men of principle.' It's all a matter of whose ox is getting gored."

Charles A. Sprague, then serving as a United Nations delegate but still writing his daily editorial column in the *Oregon Statesman*, wrote, "When a man makes a decision on principle I am not inclined to condemn him. Morse has acted from conviction, though personal slights from party regulars may have made his conscience more sensitive."

Did Wayne Morse believe that his switch to Stevenson in the home stretch of the campaign would bring victory for the Democratic candidate? "I never expected Stevenson to win," says Morse. "One of the smears is that I bet on the wrong horse. My enemies charge that I thought Stevenson was going to win. The contrary is true. I said right along that I didn't think he had a chance of winning."

There is ground for hearty skepticism about this postelection assertion. The senator has enormous confidence in the power of his own oratory to sway voters. But beyond this faculty, Morse believed that he had the confidence of *millions* of independent voters. He revealed this personal conviction accidentally early in the campaign when he dictated a telegram to Oregon's Young Republicans which contained these words:

> The greatest contribution I can make to the Republican party is to maintain and retain the confidence which millions of independent voters in our country have in my determination to place what I consider to be sound political principles above partisan politics.

On the carbon copies of this telegram which were given to newspapermen, a few alterations had been made before the wire was sent. In place of *millions of* independent voters, the senator had modestly substituted *many*.

Given Wayne Morse's self-confidence as an orator, his penchant for playing the long shot, his self-image as the leader of millions of independent voters, and his powerful, driving ambition, it would

have been altogether out of character for Wayne Morse to concede
or to believe that Adlai Stevenson had no chance of becoming the
next President—once he had gone vigorously to Stevenson's aid.

Ike

In any event the senator went after Eisenhower with a broadsword in the last days of the election drive. He called Ike's "I will
go to Korea" declaration "a cheap, grandstand political play." The
day Morse bolted the G.O.P., Eisenhower made a speech at Detroit
that was critical of the Truman administration for events leading
up to the Korean War. "I knew as a member of the Armed Services
Committee that Eisenhower was one of the key leaders in the drive
to take the troops out of South Korea. So I called President Truman
the next morning," said Morse in *U. S. News and World Report*.
"The Eisenhower speech was given on Friday night, I called
Truman about nine o'clock Saturday morning, and I said, 'Mr.
President, are you aware of the fact that Eisenhower misrepresented
the facts time and time again in his Detroit speech last night?' Mr.
Truman said that he knew it and that they were at work on preparing
an answer to it. I said, 'I called you to make a suggestion. You will
find down in the Pentagon Building a document, I don't know
the date, it was late in 1947, in which the Joint Chiefs of Staff,
acting through the Secretary of Defense, recommended that the
troops be taken out of South Korea as a matter of military policy
and military strategy.' Eisenhower was chief of staff of the Army at
the time. The military felt that Korea was no place to have our
troops. In fact, the document used the language to the effect that
the troops should be taken out as a matter of 'military policy and
strategy.' I said, 'Also you will recall, when he was your chief
civilian adviser, after he became president of Columbia University,
he urged and urged and urged that the troops be taken out of
South Korea.' The President said, 'Yes, I recall it very well.' I said,
'Mr. President, if you will get me that document and authorize me
to use it in my speech in Minneapolis Monday I'll prove to this
nation the kind of campaign misrepresentation this man's making.'
Truman said, 'I'll have it up to you in an hour.' He had it up to
me in less than forty-five minutes."

In his Minneapolis speech, Morse charged Eisenhower with telling
a falsehood when he blamed the State Department for placing

South Korea outside the defense perimeter in the Far East. He gave newsmen copies of a memorandum labeled "top secret" but declined to say who had authorized him to make it public. Dated September 26, 1947, the memo was signed by James Forrestal and directed to the Secretary of State. It read:

The Joint Chiefs of Staff consider that from a standpoint of military security, the United States has little strategic interest in maintaining the present troops and bases in Korea for the reasons hereafter stated.

In the event of hostilities in the Far East, our present forces in Korea would be a military liability and could not be maintained there without substantial reinforcements prior to the initiation of hostilities. Moreover any offensive operation the United States might wish to conduct on the Asiatic continent most probably would bypass the Korean peninsula.

If, on the other hand, an enemy were able to establish and maintain strong air and naval bases in the Korean peninsula, he might be able to interfere with United States communications and operations in East China, Manchuria, the Yellow Sea, the Sea of Japan and adjacent islands. Such interference would require an enemy to maintain substantial air and naval forces in that area where they would be subject to neutralization by air action. Neutralization by air action would be more feasible and less costly than large-scale ground operation.

In light of the present severe shortage of military manpower, the corps of two divisions totaling some 45,000 men now maintained in South Korea could well be used elsewhere. The withdrawal of these forces from Korea would not impair the military of the Far East command unless, in consequence, the Soviet established military strength in South Korea capable of mounting an assault in Japan.

At the present time, the occupation of Korea is requiring very large expenditures for the primary purpose of preventing disease and disorder which might endanger our occupation, with little, if any, lasting benefits to the security of the United States.

Authoritative reports from Korea indicate that continued lack of progress toward a free and independent Korea, unless offset by an elaborate program of economic, political and cultural rehabilitation, in all probability will result in such conditions, including violent disorder, as to make the position of the United States occupation forces untenable. A precipitant withdrawal of our forces under such circumstances would lower the military prestige of the United States, quite possibly to the extent of adversely affecting cooperation in other areas more vital to the security of the United States.

General Eisenhower two nights later on a radio-TV broadcast questioned how this top-secret memorandum had got out. "Wouldn't you like to know?" he asked his audience. "Many Americans would." Morse cracked back, "The trouble with Eisenhower on this matter is that he's whining because I took the American people to the record. The top brass have concealed for too long the facts that are vital to a clear understanding by the people of the danger of military politics in our country."

A week after Morse first revealed this memo, President Truman officially made it public, perhaps because Senator Knowland of California was calling for an investigation by the Justice Department of Morse's disclosure of top-secret material. The import of the memo's disclosure was difficult to grasp in the passion of the closing days of the campaign, but the Washington *Post* analyzed it as follows:

> President Truman's last-minute "declassification" of the top-secret documents made public earlier by Senator Morse is a thoroughly unedifying example of the use of security information for partisan purposes. . . . What the President has made no effort to explain . . . is that the opinion of the Joint Chiefs was sought *after* he and his advisers had decided upon a drastic cut in the military budget. The Joint Chiefs were saying, in effect, that if this country's forces abroad had to be reduced, they could be reduced in Korea with the least damage to American security.
>
> In other words, these particular documents standing alone and out of context mean little. Their release at this time served only to distort further an already distorted issue—and possibly to take Senator Morse off the hook for a deliberate violation of security. . . .
>
> It is apparent that the blame, such as it is, for the troop withdrawal is widespread; it is questionable in any event whether the United States could have flouted the UN request for the removal of occupation forces. The Republicans, to be sure, have made some loose charges concerning Korea. What is reprehensible is that the President, pretending to set the record straight, has made use of selected parts of the record available only to him. He has attempted to shift the responsibility for what was in the last analysis his own decision.

The New York *Times* said editorially, "we find this incident shocking . . . for this is a matter of delving into Defense Department files for campaign material." But Morse went to Town Hall in New York, to Chicago, to Cleveland and elsewhere in the East in the last days of the campaign repeating the charge and saying he was "frightened" because he was certain Eisenhower harbored a "psychology" that war is inevitable. The Washington *Post* deplored this attack and the efforts of both sides to "frighten the people for all they are worth."

As election day neared, Morse predicted a "landslide" for Stevenson because "the people of this country are becoming aware of the true nature of Eisenhower and Nixon." But on election night, as the Republican victory margin mounted, as Stevenson made his graceful concession to the winners, Wayne Morse declared sourly, "Eisenhower and Nixon fooled the people and won the election. The people allowed themselves to be fooled and lost the election."

Whether Wayne Morse, too, was fooled into believing the force of his own oratory would turn the tide is a matter for speculation. Certainly he failed in the most daring political performance of his career to this date. He had performed an extraordinary political strip tease, first dropping his intent to campaign for Eisenhower, later discarding his pledge to vote for the general, and finally throwing off the last veil of Republicanism to go into a spirited dance as a naked Independent. For all of the considerable attention his act received, it did not distract the bulk of the voters from being quite dazzled by the hero with the big smile and the sincere manner. Millions of independent voters helped elect Eisenhower, shunning the harsh indictment of the senator who fancied himself as the independents' Independent.

The icy condition that developed between Morse and the Eisenhower command thawed not a particle during the general's eight years as President. In this long, bleak period of utter isolation from the pinnacle of power, Morse had but two occasions to enter those big iron gates through which he had earlier passed for many gratifying experiences. The sole reason for the first visit was that Eisenhower had opened his first term by seeking the good will of Congress through a series of luncheons, to which every last senator and representative was at length invited. Seated directly across the table from one another, the President and Morse talked about their cattle. The senator smilingly declined a cigar, still gaily wrapped in a red-white-and-blue "Ike and Dick" band, an apparent leftover from the campaign or the inaugural festivities.

But there was little good will in Wayne Morse for this first Republican administration in twenty years. This became evident on

Inauguration Day. After the new President was duly sworn to his duty in ceremonies on the Capitol steps, he asked the Senate that day to confirm eight members of his cabinet. The Senate committees had earlier completed their hearings on all of these men, encountering no difficulty recommending their confirmation. Against the wish of the Senate to be accommodating on Inauguration Day, Wayne Morse set his will that the nominations be delayed. As is often his way, Morse exploited the power which occasionally falls to a single senator, for he cited the Senate rule which states that nominations can be acted upon the same day they are reported from committees only if no objection is raised by any senator. Morse objected, causing, no doubt, much frowning at his pesky behavior that night as the new cabinet members-to-be waltzed with their ladies at the inaugural ball and waited for another day. No greater issue was here at stake than Morse's insistence that he, and all other senators, have a day to read the committee reports and printed transcipts of their hearings before voting to confirm.

Five years later, when the Adams-Goldfine case had captured national attention, Morse revised history a mite to upgrade his Inauguration Day peskiness into support of a moral principle. He told the Senate:

> Let the *Congressional Record* speak for itself. I blocked the cabinet on Inauguration Day, when many of my friends on the Democratic side were pleading with me to go along with Eisenhower on a honeymoon. I wanted no part of that political wedding party. . . . I stated then that we needed time to examine the cabinet nominations from the standpoint of conflict of interest; and of all the various political immoralities of the Eisenhower administration since, the stenchiest one is the matter of conflict of interest, whether we are dealing with Wenzell, Adams, or anyone else. There has been a betrayal of an ethical responsibility to a democratic people.

The *Congressional Record*, speaking for itself, records no mention from Wayne Morse on Inauguration Day of possible conflict of interest involving the eight cabinet nominations he that day blocked; nor on the day following, when the Senate without further objection from Morse confirmed Secretary of State Dulles, Secretary of the Treasury Humphrey, Attorney General Brownell, Postmaster General Summerfield, Secretary of Interior McKay, Secretary of Agriculture

Benson, Secretary of Commerce Weeks, and Secretary of Labor Durkin.

The conflict-of-interest issue was raised later in the ensuing debate over Eisenhower's belated nomination of Charles E. Wilson, head of General Motors, as the Secretary of Defense. Wilson had, in his appearance for a hearing before the Senate Armed Services Committee, prejudiced himself with his senatorial judges by a "breezy and unconscious patronage," as observed by William S. White. It was on this occasion that he unwisely remarked that what was good for our country was good for General Motors, and vice versa, an epigram which underwent much tortured interpretation. The conflict lay in Wilson's ownership of some 38,000 shares of stock in General Motors, a corporation then engaged in filling defense contracts amounting to some three to four billion dollars. When Wilson saw no reason to give up his corporate interest, Chairman Saltonstall gently informed him that he would either divest himself of his securities or the President would be obliged to find another man for the Pentagon post. Wilson tried for a week to avoid the inevitable, thus contributing to the conclusion that, as Walter Lippmann put it, "his conscience in this field was not sufficiently instructed."

Upon these circumstances Wayne Morse quickly seized. His attack was strengthened in persuasiveness by the stern commandments of the legal code. "We do not allow a juror to sit in judgment on a case if he has the slightest financial interest in it," said Morse. "In fact if we find that he has the kind of indirect interest that grows out of a feeling of affinity for one of the litigants, he is excused from the jury. In the administration of justice we guard our legal procedure against the possibility of bias on the part of jury or judge. We should do as much in this instance." Morse noted that Wilson was retaining his substantial holdings in oil and gas, and that his wife retained heavy interests in General Motors. Senator Lehman joined Morse in arguing against the Wilson nomination. Wilson was confirmed, 77 to 6.

Harold E. Talbott, designated as Air Force Secretary under Wilson ran the same gauntlet and promised to sell his Chrysler stock. In his case an Armed Services Committee member, Kefauver of Tennessee, had led the opposition because of Talbott's "equivocal attitude" concerning the proprieties of certain past business dealings with the government by Talbott family enterprises. Morse thought Talbott as insensitive as Wilson to the spirit of the law which forbids conflicts of interest. The vote again was heavily against the dissenters,

76 to 6. When Talbott was later forced to resign because of an impropriety in which he blandly promoted a business enterprise in which he was interested, the six senators who were in a position to say "I told you so" were Fulbright, Gore, Kefauver, Kilgore, Murray, and Morse.

Quite apart from his Inauguration Day stunt, Morse's opposition to Wilson and Talbott must be viewed in the La Follette context of "educating the people." He knew that he was destined not to win the debate. But in the curious opaqueness of these cases there was need for some penetrating clarity. What columnists Lippmann and Krock were saying in measured, but nonetheless stern, language outside the Senate about the need for ethical sensitivity in high public office, Wayne Morse was impelled to say with characteristic bluntness in the Senate where a heavy mood of unhappy silence otherwise prevailed. Wilson and Talbott were confirmed, but not without wide attention's being focused on the hard realities of making and keeping a government as clean as a hound's tooth. Wilson himself was doubtless made more sensitive by his experience, if Talbott was not.

When Eisenhower later nominated Admiral Lewis Strauss to be his second Commerce Secretary in 1959, Strauss was placed upon the rack for his prior conduct as chairman of the Atomic Energy Commission—chiefly for involvement in the Dixon-Yates case and for what senators regarded as a tendency to deal uncandidly, even deceitfully, with them. Morse was a leading warrior in this intense fight, which ended in a 49 to 46 vote against confirmation of Strauss. No senator would claim that he dealt more harshly with Strauss than did Morse. To him, the admiral was not simply disqualified by one of the four customary standards; Strauss was "an enemy of the people." One need not defend Strauss to question an arraignment which suggested that the nominee was very high in the FBI index of public enemies. Why does Wayne Morse go so far as frequently to cause like-minded but more moderate men to wince or even exclaim in protest?

In the most general sense, there is a discernible competitive factor which works like yeast within the man, causing him to expand his arguments beyond the dimensions of all others. If the fight is in behalf of civil rights or federal aid to education, Morse rarely will let another senator get beyond him in advocating a *more liberal* approach. If the fight is against what he and others deem to be bad legislation, no one can outdo Morse in condemning it.

In the most specific sense, there was an evident drive within Morse to take on the Eisenhower administration, to be the one senator absolutely unafraid to tangle fist and fang with the popular general who confounded the Democrats by somehow remaining safely above the din and blood of political warfare and beyond blame for short-comings. For their part, the Democrats uncomplainingly accepted Wayne Morse on these terms, as any party frequently makes use of a hatchet man who knows his assignment and executes it with daring but dubious acts of aggression.

Eisenhower's second term brought him relatively more criticism than his first, partly due to outer events such as the Little Rock school disturbance and the Soviets' initial success in launching space rockets, but also because of the President's delayed reaction to these events, his dispatch of federal troops to Central High School, and his pooh-poohing the Russian lead in rocketry. But Eisenhower's conduct in office belied Morse's frightening campaign charge about harboring a psychology that war is inevitable. Indeed, he personified America's peaceful intentions, notably in his courageous opposition to the British-Israeli invasion of Suez.

Except for the partisan organ the *Democratic Digest*, and for a few liberal cartoonists and journalists, most critics were kind to Eisenhower. Even garrulous Senator Kerr of Oklahoma, who had defended Truman's firing of General MacArthur with more persistence than any other senator, felt obliged to tone down his remarks in the Senate about Eisenhower. Having said the President had "no brains," Kerr modified the published version in the *Congressional Record* so that his critical observation was limited to the President's intelligence respecting fiscal affairs.

Was it any wonder, then, that a tremor was noted on the Senate seismograph when Wayne Morse discharged a bomb instead of waving a feather duster in the direction of the White House? In a Jefferson-Jackson Day dinner speech at Detroit in May 1957, Morse bracketed Eisenhower with the discredited Teamster boss, Dave Beck. To the President's defense quickly came the Republican shock troops. Senator Bridges of New Hampshire, who had voted against censuring McCarthy, said Morse had gone too far. Capehart of Indiana suggested censure action was in order for Morse. Schoeppel of Kansas thought Morse had "transcended the bounds of decency and fair

play." Goldwater recalled earlier days when Morse had admirably
opposed smear attacks, and Dirksen quoted a couplet from his youth
to ennoble the President in this hour of degrading attack.

The irony of *these* Republicans, the remnants of the Taft Old
Guard who resisted features of the President's more liberalized international program, rushing to Eisenhower's personal defense was no
less amusing than the indignant defense of Morse by the conservative
Lausche of Ohio in the Luce affair. The Democrats never joined
Morse in questioning Eisenhower's morality. Wayne Morse was on
his own. The only Democrat who came to his rescue at all was his
Oregon colleague, Neuberger, who offered no defense of Morse's
remark but made diversionary thrusts at the Republicans for not
supporting their President's foreign programs with equal vigor.

After fifteen Republicans had risen to deplore Morse's attack,
Morse at length invited any others to pay him "their disrespects."
The more the merrier, the greater the feat of one against many.
Giving no ground, he said:

> I cannot see any distinction between Dave Beck reaching his hands
> into the pockets of the Teamsters of his union and taking out of those
> pockets what amounts to an interest-free loan, and in doing so, em-
> bezzling or stealing from the individual Teamsters what amounts to
> interest money which would accumulate into great value; and an
> Administration headed by Dwight D. Eisenhower putting its hands
> into the pockets of the taxpayers and taking out of those pockets
> an interest-free loan, involving millions of dollars, over the years,
> belonging to the taxpayers, and giving that interest saving to the
> Idaho Power Company.

Beck had fallen into disrepute for financial deals exposed only
shortly before by the McClellan Committee's intensive investigation
into labor-management racketeering. Among the prerogatives Beck
assumed with his office as head of the Teamsters was the privilege of
quietly dipping into the treasury. When this was disclosed, Beck said
it was a loan which he intended to repay. Only an imaginatively
aggressive politician would think to bracket Beck's peccancy with the
Administration's grant to Idaho Power of a rapid tax-amortization
certificate.

This attack was double-edged. Morse was making one more attempt
to pass his Hells Canyon bill, which the year before had been
defeated in the Senate. The Hells Canyon story demands detailed

attention in a later chapter. The point here is that Morse held
Eisenhower *personally* responsible for what he regarded as the wrongdoing of his administration. This he never did with Truman for the
wrongdoing of his administration. In a letter to Tugman in 1951
Morse wrote:

> I think everything must be done that can possibly be done to defeat
> the Democratic Administration in 1952, because I am convinced that
> it is thoroughly corrupt. I am satisfied that Truman is not a party to
> the corruption as an individual, but he certainly has failed to do the
> housecleaning in his party that I think he should have started several
> years ago.

In his speech about Eisenhower and Beck, Morse said:

> . . . look at the latest act of political immorality on the part of this
> Administration, and I put it where it belongs, squarely on the shoulders
> of one man, the President himself. I do not join with Democrats
> that try to put the blame for the immorality of this Administration
> upon underlings.
> . . . history will record that this President made an honest admin-
> istration out of Harding and a statesman out of Grant.

For the President who scratched his back, there was mercy. For the
President who sought him not, there was naught but condemnation
from Wayne Morse.

8. THE INNER CIRCLE

Protecting His Cubs . . . Midge . . . The Horse Trader . . .
Devoted Women . . . The Poor Working Girls

WHEN the Senior Senator from Oregon received an invitation from President and Mrs. Eisenhower for a reception for members of the new Congress during the general's first year in office, Wayne Morse had no desire to R.S.V.P. But his daughter, Judy, then a college student, wanted very much to dance with Daddy at the White House. The defiance of Wayne Morse melted under the warmth of her plea.

The Morses went to the Executive Mansion for this gay evening, stood circumspectly in the long line of VIPs who filed past the Eisenhowers, shook hands with a nod of courteous recognition when they reached the host and hostess, and then edged their way past the red-jacketed Marine Corps musicians who serenaded the guests from the front hallway.

As the Morses picked their way through the throng toward the ballroom, a Republican senator and his wife intercepted the maverick from Oregon. As Morse relates the encounter, he bowed slightly in the direction of the lady, but she drew back a threatening arm with the apparent intention of clouting the senator. But for the strategic footwork of her husband and Mrs. Morse, who gracefully stepped into the line of fire, an incident was averted which might have caused the Marines to put down their violins to restore peace and order to the assembly. Wayne Morse refuses to identify his would-be assailant; he charitably observes that she had been bending her elbow a bit before she raised it in anger toward him.

After a fox trot or two in the ballroom, the Morses returned early to the security of their Washington home. It was the last time Morse went to the White House while the Republicans held power. But avoiding Republican social affairs did not protect the Morse family from strong emotions which showed in many incidents.

Even in faraway Eugene, Oregon, his eldest daughter, Nancy, a student at the University of Oregon, telephoned her father one day to tell him that at church she was getting the cold shoulder from folks who despised his attacks on Eisenhower. When she said she wasn't going to attend church any longer for this reason, the senator is said to have all but shouted into the phone, "You are going to church. We don't surrender like that by retreating into hiding."

Morse is proud of having quit the Republican party to back Stevenson, rather than following the example of those Southern Democrats, such as Senator Byrd of Virginia, who supported Eisenhower without leaving the Democratic party. "They had their cake and ate it too," he says somewhat disdainfully. Once his decision was announced and he turned on Eisenhower, the emotional reaction against him mounted.

"For weeks," he recalls, "it was a favorite device of strangers, especially intoxicated women, to impress their friends by accosting me in airports and other public places. For months my mail consisted of thousands of denunciatory letters, ranging from indignation to vile pornography, charges of treason and insanity, and threats of violence against me or my family. Telephone calls brought similar messages. Being hung in effigy was a common occurrence. Many lifelong Republican friends wrote to advise that they never wanted to see or hear from me again."

Protecting His Cubs

As the circle of associates narrowed, Morse turned instinctively for sustenance to the inner circle of his immediate family. The inner circle is composed of his wife, Mildred, his three lovely daughters, and his "kid sister" Caryl and her family. In this circle Wayne Morse is fortified for his battles with the hostile forces of the outer world. Here he is braced with loyalty untainted with the slightest doubt of the righteousness of his ends and means. Here he need not be a tiger. For in the inner circle Wayne Morse is the benign lion, paternally watching over his cubs and his mate, receiving the constant adoration his eminence commands.

Morse's strong paternal concern and keen insight into his daughters' developmental progress was conveyed in the following letter which he took time to write during his hectic early days in Washington on the War Labor Board:

June 29, 1943

Mrs. Hoffman
Camp Strawderman
Columbia Furnace, Virginia

Dear Mrs. Hoffman:

Mrs. Morse and I are very pleased to send the girls back to Camp Strawderman this summer. We were well satisfied with the camp last year and I am sure that it will be very good for them again this year. There are several things in regard to the girls that I should appreciate your calling to the attention of the counselors in charge of them.

First, as to Judy. She is not particularly anxious to go to camp this summer, apparently because she finds it difficult to meet the competition of other children her own age. We have noticed that rather than stand up to competition, she withdraws from a group of children, goes off by herself, and tends to live in a dream world in which she is successful. During this past year in school, she evidently was unsuccessful in winning recognition from her associates, although her work was satisfactory and she passed into the fourth grade. Her teacher made this comment on her final report: "It was a pleasure to have Judy in the third grade this year. She is a very affectionate and imaginative child."

She did not make the psychological and social adjustments, however, that Mrs. Morse and I wanted her to make. I think that part of her difficulty is that she over compensates for a sense of inferiority that we just have not figured out. She seems to be sensitive about the fact that she is inclined to be quite chubby and I have noticed that when her playmates really want to upset her or when they quarrel with her, all they have to do is call her "fatty" to make her burst into tears.

There is no way of protecting her from that and hence I hope you will call the problem to the attention of her counselor, who can probably help her make a more objective adjustment to her physical characteristics. I am sure that if her counselor can win her confidence, it can be done. Judy is a very trusting little girl and develops strong affections, almost of the teacher's pet type. As a result, she is inclined to have strong child jealousies and she is easily hurt. She must be led to see that she has ability and that she can do things successfully. All of the psychological tests given to her at school show that she is a superior child mentally, but at the same time a sensitive one emotionally.

Her teacher also reports that she apparently has no sense of responsibility for her belongings. She leaves them all over the school and, during the past year, has lost rubbers, books, gloves, sweaters, etc. We feel that we are making some progress with her on this point and hope that she will be required to check her belongings at camp period- ically and keep them in order.

I am particularly anxious to give Judy, as well as the other girls, a full program of horseback riding. They cannot ride too often to suit me and hence I should like to stress the point that I want them to ride and ride and ride. In fact, I should like to have them ride practically every day that they are in camp. It will be very good for all of them and particularly good for Judy.

I keep a horse here in Washington and this spring, I have had all the girls ride quite frequently. Judy has learned to post very well, although Amy has just started to post. I can see that Judy's horseback riding is beginning to develop a type of self confidence in her that offers us a medium through which to help her with her problems. My horse is a five-gaited stallion, with lots of animation, but at the same time a very gentle horse, especially when one of the girls gets on his back. I think the fact that they have been riding the stallion has been a matter of pride with them as you will probably discover when you have a chance to talk to them about "riding Daddy's horse."

All three of them are ready to ride in the ring and Nancy is ready to go out on the road. She has developed into a very fine rider this year and I hope you will allow her as much liberty in riding as the camp rules permit. Amy is fearful that you will only let her ride on the path as she calls it. She is ready for riding in the ring and I hope you will tell her riding master to push her along as rapidly as possible. Judy should be kept in ring riding for the first part of the camp, but I hope that after two or three weeks you will let her take one of the evening or morning rides out on the road because that will help build up her ego and give her a sense of accomplishment.

The other girls, Nancy and Amy, will fit into the group without any difficulty, I am sure. They both made fine progress in school this year and both seem to be well adjusted. There is a certain amount of con- flict between Nancy and Judy, but not as much as there used to be.

The conflict between them will not create any problem in view of the fact that the girls will live in separate cabins. I am eager that you keep the girls separate as far as living in cabins is concerned because they need to be away from each other. There is a deep sense of loyalty between and among them, they will battle for each other, but at the same time, I think they need to live apart for a while. It has been neces- sary for the three girls to use one bedroom this past year because we could not find a larger house and after having spent a year in such close relationship, I think it would be a good thing for them to get away from each other for a few months.

Nancy needs to be watched for sportsmanship too, although I think she has gone a long way during the past year in learning how to take it. The best way to approach Nancy's character building problems, in my judgment, is through horsemanship because she loves it and in my opinion is a very fine rider and knows a great deal about horses. I am sure she will not talk about them unless she is asked, although she has had many interesting experiences with me at horse shows that she might describe if you could persuade her to talk when the girls gather in the evenings to discuss their experiences.

I trust that you will pardon this unduly long letter from a parent who, I suppose, is over concerned about his children. I felt that it would be helpful in handling the girls for you to know what I think some of their problems are. I hope you will write to me whenever any problem develops with the girls that you think I should know about or could help out with. If there is anything the girls need during the summer, please go ahead and get it for them and put it on my bill. Whatever you do, don't economize on their horseback riding. I think that encouraging them to ride is one of the best ways in which we can help them with their character building.

With best wishes for a very successful camp season,

Sincerely yours,
Wayne L. Morse

Wayne Morse obviously agreed that his father's prescription, "the outside of a horse is good for the inside of a boy," was equally applicable to girls.

It was perhaps inevitable that a man with such strong paternal instincts would have difficulty relinquishing his daughters to eligible suitors. Daddy Morse did not want to let them go. One daughter threatened to elope if he attempted to break up another romance. The senator kept one suitor waiting for hours in his outer office until it was plain that the persistent young man was not to be discouraged. Until the eve of the wedding of one daughter, the senator adamantly refused to prepare to attend the ceremony—but a firm Mrs. Morse brought him into line at the last moment. Today Nancy, Judy, and Amy are married and Wayne Morse is happily thriving on grandparenthood.

Midge

The mother of these three girls is a thoroughly domesticated woman whom the senator frequently calls "Mama" when he telephones from the office. Most everyone calls Mildred Downie Morse by her girlhood nickname, Midge. A pert, diminutive lady with sparkling blue eyes, Mrs. Morse is highly intelligent and fervently loyal to the complex man who has been her husband through thirty-seven years of unceasing adventure.

Midge and Wayne grew up in the same section of Madison, Wisconsin, near—but not in—the Bush. Mildred Downie's father was a railroad conductor and a strong labor man. In high school Midge became a student leader with Wayne. He was president and she vice-president of their junior class during its second semester. Their high school yearbook poetically saluted another aspect of their relationship with this gem:

> The parlor sofa holds the twain
> Mildred and her lovesick Wayne
> He and she.
> But hark! A step upon the stair
> And Papa finds them sitting there
> He———and———she.

The yearbook editors spoofed Wayne Morse even then for enunciating a strong principle which was honored in the breach: "by these words ye shall know them: Wayne Morse—'I don't believe in going steady with a girl.'"

Midge played the lead in the high school rendition of Snow White, won the annual reading contest with a passage from Trojan Woman, and bested Wayne in the realm of scholarship. Mildred Downie was the class valedictorian.

At the University of Wisconsin Wayne continued his pursuit of pert Miss Downie, and both continued to excel. Wayne became a student senator and provoked a senate investigation of the commerce department of the university. As chairman of a three-student investigative committee, Morse interrogated the business-department professors (an heroic feat in itself to the students) about the great number of students who were flunked out of accounting. A fellow investigator, Ralph Axley, forty years later could not recall what, if any, results the senatorial probe had brought, but Morse very positively asserts that it produced a beneficial effect on the "tyrannical" head of that department.

In their senior year Wayne and Midge ran on an independent ticket for class officers. The students split their votes. Midge was elected vice-president, but a football star became president. Wayne Morse lost his first big election by twelve votes. Midge, with a truer instinct for domesticity than politics, is proudest of having won the University's annual Glicksman award for excellence in scholarship, leadership and womanliness.

In 1924, after Morse had stayed on for a master's degree in speech and Midge was graduated in home economics, they were married in June and set out to brave life with much confidence and little money. Upon their arrival in Minneapolis in September, the bridegroom found that their assets had dwindled to twelve cents. He rented a room on credit from an old Swedish lady and took his bride out on the town—to a nickelodian movie. They blew their last pennies on chewing gum. The following Monday morning one of the first customers in the Hennepin County Bank was the young man with the earnest, persuasive manner who had need of money. His only evidence of being a creditable risk was a letter identifying him as the newest instructor in the speech department of the University of Minnesota. The banker sized up the young man favorably, and Wayne Morse walked out with a two-hundred-dollar cash loan.

While Morse went to law school at Minnesota, he carried a heavy teaching load and Midge taught "home ec" in a nearby public school. In 1928, with a law degree in hand and a fifteen-hundred-dollar teaching scholarship promised by Columbia University, the Morses went to New York for a final year of academic training. That winter Midge worked for a women's magazine to keep the household budget balanced. John Gunther observed in *Inside U.S.A.* that they typified the "familiar American pattern, that of the brilliant-but-poor student, ably assisted by a young woman with her own job as well as the job of raising a family and washing dishes."

Toward the end of his year at Columbia Morse wrote his old law dean at Minnesota that he was developing "a case of anxiety neurosis looking for a job." He had been recommended unsuccessfully by Professor Moley to the law faculty at North Carolina. He had been interviewed by George Washington University, but that position had gone to another man. He had applied at the University of Oregon, but understood that opening had been filled. His chances of becoming a professor appeared so gloomy to Wayne Morse that he considered returning to Minneapolis to "look for an opening in some good law office." But a few weeks later there arrived a letter of acceptance from the state university located in a country college town named Eugene in the heart of the most tranquil and conservative state on the far Pacific coast. The wheel of fortune, which spins for every college man as he makes his first play in the world, had stopped for Wayne Morse on the University of Oregon.

Once launched upon his teaching career, Professor Morse followed his father's horse prescription in rearing the three little girls who came along during the Depression years. Three weeks after arriving in Eugene, he bought a horse and boarded it near by. In 1932 he purchased a 29-acre hillside tract of heavily overgrown land overlooking the town. When he put 105 goats on his property, they "cleared the place as if it were a park," he recalls with satisfaction, and the first year's fleece paid for the goats. In 1936 he built a handsome, spacious frame house and stable. Near the house he built a circular training track with a heavy sawdust base to avoid muddy riding conditions during Oregon's soft but steady winter rains. Through the trees below the house he developed a sloping riding path to teach his horses to shuffle, a single-gaited step used in horse shows.

When wartime duties took the family to Washington, Morse brought along his prize stallion, Spice of Life, despite the high stable rent. For a stall at the Meadowbrook stable in Rock Creek Park, he paid forty-five dollars a month, when he was getting only sixty-five dollars a month rent for his handsome home in Eugene. But the big stallion partly earned his keep by bringing fifty-dollar stud fees, especially after Morse began winning trophies in Washington's fashionable horse shows. One year Spice won eleven prizes.

In Morse's early years in the Senate, his horsemanship and fine horseflesh brought much favorable comment, many ribbons and trophies. The senator's ring behavior did not escape attention either. Rosemarie Goldsmith, who covered Oregon congressional offices for the United Press, once went to a Maryland horse show to learn more about the colorful new senator on horseback. She noticed that each entry, in passing the judges' stand, saluted the judges ever so slightly with a tip of the cap or a discreet gesture with the hand. Wayne

Morse passed in review, however, with eyes dead ahead, hands on reins, cap untipped, head unbowed. "He was the one rider," she recalls, "who wasn't going to toady to the judges."

Even as a school lad, Wayne Morse revealed something of his inner make-up when he mounted his pony to lead the Fourth of July parade through the streets of Madison. It was a steamy, hot July day. Wayne was dressed in a Little Lord Fauntleroy suit. As the parade meandered through town, the pony drew a swarm of horse-flies. By the time the proud little leader was well along the parade route, his long white stockings were red with blood from the bites of the attacking flies—but Wayne Morse rode bravely on, never flinching or surrendering his place at the head of the big parade.

When he first campaigned for the Senate, Professor Morse entered the cattle country of eastern Oregon astride a horse—to visit the famous Pendleton Round-Up. Instead of yielding to his normal compulsion to orate, the professor wisely remained silent in the saddle, apparently winning over many dubious cattlemen. One of them reportedly remarked, "Any fellow who can ride like that can't be the S.O.B. I thought he was."

While their daughters were growing up in Washington, the Morses owned a modest home in a quiet residential section, attended Cleveland Park Congregational Church, and sent the children to the public schools. The senator took time to be president of the Alice Deal Junior High School Home and School Association in 1948. For a while the family's horses and chickens were kept on nearby farms owned by friends. Later they rented a farm near Poolsville, Maryland, thirty miles from Washington; and after the girls had made homes of their own, the Morses sold their Washington house, bought the farm, and moved to an apartment on the edge of the city. This arrangement suits the unpretentious private life of the Senator and Mrs. Morse, who do little entertaining, never on a large scale. On weekends, while other political leaders socialize, Wayne Morse fraternizes contentedly with his animals. "Wayne just isn't happy without a farm operation," Mrs. Morse told me, "and it's wonderful for him."

Morse's life on the farm reveals a private aspect of the man which his public life obscures. Here he is the personification of kindness and solicitation, sitting up all night with a sick animal or mourning over the barbed-wire wounds of a young colt. Here he engages quietly in husbandry, crossbreeding in hopes of developing poled

Devon cattle, experimenting with a diet of stale baked goods and bituminous coal for hogs. Here there are no fights to be waged— not even cockfights—only herds and flocks to be improved and multiplied.

The Horse Trader

If there is any spice in this life, it comes from his David Harum traits. Morse searches for bargains at county sales. Better, he loves horse trading, to improve his estate and to outsmart the other fellow. As a matter of strict principle, Morse refuses to engage in legislative horse trading within the Senate. But outside the Senate he will dicker over horseflesh with any politician who strikes him as an easy mark.

One night in 1960 Oscar Chapman, formerly Truman's Interior Secretary, picked up the telephone at his Washington residence and heard a friendly but insistent voice say, "Oscar, I've got just the horse for you—one of the finest palomino stallions you will find anywhere in the country."

"What do I want with a horse?" asked the puzzled Chapman.

"Why, you're managing Lyndon Johnson's presidential campaign, aren't you? How do you expect Lyndon to win if he isn't riding a good horse?" asked Wayne Morse.

"Well, I, er . . ."

"Tell you what you do, Oscar. You get hold of some of those rich oil men down in Texas, and tell them Johnson needs a horse. I'll do you a favor. I'll reserve this stallion for you for twenty-four hours. I'm only going to charge you $2500. This palomino is worth twice that. But you have the check up to my office by tomorrow and you can have him for that price."

As Wayne Morse bargained, mischief played across his face. As the idea of selling a horse to Chapman had come to him in a flash as we sat talking one day about his farm, he spun around in his swivel chair, picked up the phone, and instructed a secretary to track Chapman down immediately, no matter where he happened to be. It was a matter of great urgency. After finishing with Chapman, Morse returned to trying to sell me a twelve-year-old Cadillac—a steal at $500! It would make a comfortable journey across country to Oregon, he assured me, waving aside my recollections of having ridden in that vehicle all over his farm where he used it as a carryall. Morse habitually drives a Ford on the streets.

In neither effort did Wayne Morse make a sale. He enjoyed the effort nonetheless. Later he clinched a deal for the horse with Senator Cannon of Nevada for $2250.

When Clare Luce wisecracked about the senator's trouble, she was articulating what others had said privately—and what some still believe. But those who know him well know that Wayne Morse's difficulties have come not from any horse, not even the one that kicked him in the head.

That accident occurred in the summer of 1951 after Morse had won the championship at a two-day horse show at Orkney Springs, Virginia. Morse was walking behind a mare named Missy, owned by the daughter of a Sears, Roebuck executive, when Missy suddenly kicked up her heels and hit him square on the chin. The senator was seriously hurt. He suffered a compound fracture of the jaw, his chin and mouth were slashed, and he lost thirteen teeth. An ambulance was summoned and a doctor attending the show administered morphine to reduce the pain. Instead of having a sedative effect, the morphine so stimulated Morse that the ambulance attendants had to sit on him all the way to the hospital in Harrisonburg to keep him prone. Morse had previously had a violent reaction to this drug when he was hospitalized in Eugene in 1946 for an ear infection. After receiving a shot of morphine, the wiry patient leaped from his bed and slugged a nurse before he was overpowered and restrained until the drug wore off.

Morse says an eyewitness to the horse-show accident visited him in the hospital the next day and told him that although dazed by the shattering blow, Morse staggered to a pile of hay, lay down, started spitting out his teeth and instructing the bystanders. "The way you took that blow, you should have gone into the prize ring instead of politics," the friend said. Morse replied, "The only difference between politics and the boxing ring is that in the ring there is a referee to call the low blows."

Morse was taken to Bethesda Naval Hospital outside Washington to mend.

When I visited him there, his lower jaw was wired into a fixed position, but the senator conducted an animated discussion, assuring me the doctor said he needed vocalizing exercise. A few weeks later he returned to the Senate to speak his mind, his jaws still wired tight together, the space left by the lost teeth affording a passageway for his muted rhetoric.

The senator says his doctor was certain that his torn face would require plastic surgery, but it healed so well this was unnecessary. The only scar is hidden beneath his mustache. "The doctor told me later that the reason for this unexpected result was that I was in perfect physical condition; and that if I had even indulged in social cocktails, this would not have been possible because alcohol first breaks down the capillaries of the face. My face would not have healed as readily, he said, if I had been a drinker," says the teetotaling senator.

Morse endured without public whimpering the long, painful oral surgery needed to restore his mouth with artificial teeth. His ordeal came to public notice when he passed out in the Senate cloakroom one afternoon. He explained later that a jaw infection had necessitated a painful scraping operation that morning. When he returned to the Senate that afternoon, he disregarded instructions and took too many pain-killing pills during a speech and an hour later suffered a "codeine blackout."

The postscript to the horse story that Wayne Morse usually neglects to tell, but does not deny, is that Missy used to be his horse. When he sold this mare, says an associate of that period, "he knew Missy was a kicker."

Whether the painful kickback from this horse trade had anything to do with it or not, Morse soon after shifted his interest from spirited show horses to docile beef cattle. Now instead of making the rounds of the horse shows, he goes to fairs and livestock shows with his Devons. He became president of the American Devon Breeders Association, and in August 1959 issued a typical press release about this activity:

> Senator Wayne Morse jocularly announced today that he played hooky from the Senate for three hours this morning to show his Devon beef cattle out in Maryland at the Montgomery County Fair at Gaithersburg. He said, "Although I was back in the Senate by 11:30, I am sure that the relaxation I enjoyed in the cattle-showing ring put me in good fettle to wind up the debate on the Labor Bill."
>
> When asked if his cattle won any prizes, Senator Morse stated, "The judge seemed to like my Devon cattle, as was shown by the awards." The fact of the matter is that Senator Morse's herd of Devons was the

top winning herd, as it has been the past three years at the Gaithersburg, Maryland, fair. His Champion cow, Potheridge Countess V, won the silver trophy for the best Devon of the show. His herd won Champion and Reserve Champion Bull, Champion and Reserve Champion Female and blue ribbons in the majority of the other classes. . . .

"This place helps me forget there's a Capitol," he told me one day as we toured his 74-acre Poolsville farm. Beyond his own fields he rents additional acreage on which to graze his chunky, red-brown Devon cattle and grow feed crops. His stock includes sheep, hogs, chickens, ponies, donkeys, in addition to his horses and cattle. Morse has converted a small milkhouse into a cozy apartment for overnights at the farm.

Devoted Women

The little political entertaining the Morses do is usually in informal picnic style at the farm. The senator especially likes to take visiting Oregon farmers out to Poolsville. "Those who say I've never met a payroll ought to see this operation," he says. A farmer and his family live on the place to execute Morse's meticulous instructions.

Mrs. Morse is equally content outside of Washington's high social whirl. In fact, in her determined way, Midge deliberately avoids it. When she was new to the capital, she met the embittered wife of a senator who had just been defeated. The attitude of the lady made a deep impression. "I decided then and there never to become emotionally involved with this social life. I tried to stiff-arm it, to hold it away from me and never let it become so important that I would become bitter if the time ever came that Wayne would be defeated." This attitude may explain the experience of one perplexed senator and his wife who took the initiative in hopes of drawing the Morses into a social friendship: "They seemed eager for companionship when we invited them to our house," he recalled, "but they never reciprocated." Midge's closest friends are former college classmates who are not in politics.

Mrs. Morse's socializing with other senatorial wives has been chiefly through the sterile auspices of the Senate Ladies' Club, whose members meet each Tuesday during the cool months of the year, garb themselves in the costume of the "Gray Ladies," and spend a few hours rolling bandages for the Red Cross. Midge was secretary of the

club for two years and once served as chairman for a luncheon the
ladies gave for Bess Truman, the first lady.

Although she stays out of politics almost completely, Mrs. Morse
encounters persons who wish to argue about her controversial husband. She has disciplined herself not to rise to the bait. "Wayne can
get into enough trouble by himself without me opening my mouth.
I don't feel that I know enough about it, because most of these
matters are so very complicated."

If Midge Morse ever contradicts or differs with her outspoken
husband, she has kept it a secret. Friends believe that she usually
assures Wayne Morse that he is right. Indeed, instead of moderating
his volatile nature, some old friends think she hastens or intensifies
his explosive outbursts. Through all his ups and downs, Midge has
been unfailing in the loyalty and admiration which Wayne Morse
demands in his associations. Her attitude toward his ups and downs
is this: "When you have been through as many of Wayne's vicissi-
tudes as I have, you know when he is riding the crest and when he is
in a trough. And I sometimes think the trough is easier. That's when
you find out who your friends really are." The depth of some of the
troughs has perhaps made Midge more fiercely defensive and protective of her husband's dogged positiveness.

Even in good times, Morse's ego demands were apparent. When
he won his first election in 1944, Dean Morse heard the returns at
his home in Eugene. His triumph secure, he headed for Portland
in the family auto with Midge and a secretary. As the effusive
senator-elect drove down the Willamette Valley, he spotted one of
his huge "Vote for Morse" billboards. "Who is that?" he asked his
companions with triumphant zest. "Why, you, Wayne," his faithful
wife replied. Some miles closer to Portland another Morse signboard
appeared. The driver called out, "Who won this election?" His
secretary gave a reassuring reply, "Why, you, Senator, you won the
election." And so it went, billboard after billboard, the ladies becoming progressively more uncomfortable after the initial fun in the
game vanished. As they approached their destination, and Wayne
Morse once more called for the name of the people's hero, one of
the ladies blurted out, "Roosevelt!" This perfect squelch, which
ended the game, did not come from Mrs. Morse.

A liberal Democrat tells a story of more recent vintage which
suggests the degree of Midge's commitment to her husband and his
Legend. At a Washington dinner party a few years ago, someone

mentioned the name of the then senator from Minnesota, Edward Thye, a Republican. Morse is said to have launched into an exposition on Thye's shortcomings as a liberal. Another dinner guest then spoke up in behalf of some good works by Thye. Mrs. Morse, perhaps feeling that her husband had been rebuked, drew herself up and, according to this story, said a trifle too loudly that in all her years in Washington, she had known only one statesman. As she looked admiringly at the proud statesman in her life, an uneasy quiet settled over the group, until someone found words on another subject to break the barrier of collective astonishment. "She idolizes him," says a long-time friend.

In some of the small, practical details of a busy senator's life, Midge has learned proficiency, to be useful in a semiprofessional way since her daughters have made homes of their own. "Until then I was like any other housewife and mother, giving teen-age parties, chauffeuring the kids to the dentist, making ends meet," she noted. She completed a shorthand course offered at an early morning hour by a Washington television station. "Wayne will sometimes dictate memos to me at home," she explained. "It's great fun. I love it." Also she brushed up her Spanish in order to help translate when she accompanied him on trips to Latin America for the Foreign Relations Committee. She has a desk in his Senate office where she works periodically, making corrections in the huge list of names and addresses of voters who receive the senator's monthy newsletter. But she is not on the government payroll.

Her maternal instincts overpower any career attractions. She takes turns visiting her daughters and going "from one borning to another," as she put it. The senator usually prefers for the children and grandchildren to visit him.

The other member of the inner circle is Caryl Morse Kline, the senator's sister, who was born when he was fifteen years old. Like Wayne and Midge, Caryl was a student leader at Wisconsin. She is a slim, attractive, highly intelligent, vivacious woman, now the mother of two boys. Her husband, Dr. Hibbard Kline, is a college professor. When he taught at Syracuse a few years ago, Caryl got into politics as a Democrat in upstate New York where Republicans enjoy a comfortable numerical superiority. When she ran for president of the Syracuse City Council, she lost but led the Democratic ticket. The next year she was nominated for Congress, but again lost while conducting a strong campaign.

Caryl made such an impact in this conservative area that the New York *Times Magazine* did an article on her entitled "The Woman from Syracuse." Since then, the Klines have moved to Pittsburgh.

Though he campaigned for her—just as she campaigned for him in Oregon—Wayne Morse says he tried to dissuade his sister from running for office. "I didn't want her to go through all of the character assassination I've been through," he said. "It is one thing for me to take these attacks and it is another thing to recommend that someone else do it." To the senator, she is still "the baby sister in the family," a member of his inner circle whom he seeks to protect. Caryl's feeling for her brother is suggested by the name of her second son, Wayne Morse Kline.

Between these women devoted to Wayne Morse there has been an occasional rivalry. When Caryl went to Oregon during one of the senator's re-election campaigns, the senator and his campaign managers were confronted with a ticklish family problem. Midge was given few speeches to make for fear of committing a political *faux pas*. Consequently Caryl's speechmaking, in which she excels, also had to be limited, to avoid ill feeling by the senator's wife.

Though Wayne Morse enjoys unflagging attention and admiration within the intimate family circle, he becomes a figure of controversy only a few paces outside this circle, within the bounds of kinship. When I asked one of his uncles in Madison to tell me about his famous nephew, this emphatic gentleman, a former police officer, snapped, "I've got nothing to say." Gently pressed for some elaborating remarks, the uncle blurted out, "If I can't say anything good about a man, I don't have anything to say about him." Another uncle said, "Just say he was a damn good kid."

The Poor Working Girls

Outside his immediate family, Morse's close associates diminished drastically when he bolted the Republican party. Even his office was riddled with secretarial resignations, sometimes due to the senator's temperamental flare-ups, sometimes simply from their fatigue. As one faithful secretary from his Republican period put it, "He is, of course, brilliant, dynamic, forceful. Working for him can be stimulating and challenging if one can endure the drive, the constant pressure, the temperament, and the long, long hours of hard, hard work. Not many secretaries who worked for him in earlier years had the stamina for the job."

The longest link of continuity in the staff of a dozen or so is William Berg, Jr., the senator's administrative assistant. Berg was one of his law students. He has worked for him for more than fifteen years, off and on since the thirties, first in the Justice Department, again on the War Labor Board, and for the past decade in his Senate office. Between these stints with Morse, Berg has been a law professor at the University of South Dakota and the University of Colorado.

Berg is a capable, overworked aide who has learned to ride with Morse's moods, faithfully following the senator's instructions, handling the day-to-day managerial stresses and strains of the office. Although completely loyal to his boss (Berg made the same political transition from Republican to Democratic party), Berg is not the senator's alter ego. Conversely, he often gives the impression of walking on eggs. He does not venture to challenge Morse's ideas or actions. Apparently because of his own self-assurance, Wayne Morse employs no one on whom to test his ideas before voicing them publicly. Unfortunately he apparently has no one who is brave enough to tell him candidly when he has blundered.

Morse's irregular habits impose an added burden upon his staff and reduce its effectiveness. Time after time a secretary has said to me, well into the working day, "We haven't seen him yet today." Morse may have gone straight to a committee meeting then to a luncheon date, then to the Senate floor. He may have delivered a hot speech, not only extemporaneously but without the knowledge of his staff. When he arrives at his office later, stimulated by the day's battles, he may tend to a few must items, see a few visitors, or catch a plane for a distant city for a scheduled speech; or he may settle down to a long evening's work to reduce the pile of correspondence on his desk.

For years I have threatened facetiously to expose the labor conditions of the poor working girls in this (and many another) liberal's sweatshop. Once, in passing the Senate Office Building after midnight and observing the lights in Morse's fourth-floor suite, I ventured in and found the senator pacing the floor with the tireless step of a caged tiger. He was dictating a speech to be delivered the coming day. As stenographers wilted in faltering relays, Wayne Morse carried on, his necktie and collar neatly in place, with never a care for the energy tomorrow would demand. Of *that* there is never a shortage. Morse, in earlier days, might work straight through the night, preparing a speech, or, in the War Labor Board days, drafting a decision.

Little wonder that his office has been called a "hardship post" on Capitol Hill. Those who survive or stay longest are blessed with the most passive or phlegmatic natures. From these faithful, unquestioning members of his staff and family, Wayne Morse draws support to battle the forces ranged against him.

9.   A MAJORITY OF ONE

Bumped from Committees . . . Smoking Mad at the Press

THE OUTCOME of the 1952 elections brought grave trouble for Wayne Morse. Outwardly he appeared to have attained an altogether appropriate status, given his temperament, for now he called himself an Independent, the only one in the Senate. When the leaders of the two established parties in the Senate mused about the headaches of holding their forces in line, Morse announced proudly that he had no such problems as the leader of the Independent party.

The Senate that convened in January 1953 comprised forty-eight Republicans, forty-seven Democrats, and Wayne Morse. Had Morse voted with the Democrats on the matter of organizing the Senate, they would still have lacked the strength to control the Senate that year because incoming Vice-president Nixon, as presiding officer of the Senate, could have broken the ensuing tie vote to guarantee the Republicans control. Morse, in any event, had promised after the election to vote with the Republicans because of the G.O.P. election mandate.

But where should the Independent senator sit? The Senate is divided by a center aisle, Republicans to the right and Democrats to the left as they face the Vice-president's rostrum. Morse on opening day arrived carrying a metal folding chair which he said he was prepared to place in the center aisle, apart from either party's side. He was encouraged to forget such crude improvisations and resume his old seat on the Republican side of the aisle. But before the session was very old he petitioned for a change to the Democratic side for unexplained "personal reasons." Columnist George Dixon, the court jester of the Washington press corps, reported that Morse wished to move because Republican Senators Ives and Welker had been conducting a war of nerves against him by whispering insults

whenever he arose to lambast the Eisenhower regime. Dixon reported
that Ives, sitting next to Morse, even practiced not moving his lips
when he hissed at Morse, "You silly jackass! Just listen to that
asinine drivel you're spilling! Why don't you shut your silly mouth
and go out and drop dead!" Then Welker would meander up and
down the aisle, apparently aimlessly, Dixon reported, but every time
he got abreast of Morse while the Oregon senator was talking he'd
whisper: "You stupid ass. Everybody knows you're a dope. Do you
have even the faintest idea what you're yapping about?" Morse
promptly denied that he was retreating under fire, and to prove it
canceled his request to change sides.

The more serious circumstance for Morse was not where he sat
in the Senate chamber but the unexpected dumping he got from his
two highly prized committees, Labor and Armed Services. He had
expected that he would be dropped to the foot of these committees
as far as seniority rights are concerned, a matter of no vast importance
to anyone but the most senior senator, who serves as chairman; but
he expected no less than to remain on these committees. By virtue of
his seats on these committees, Morse had been in the thick of the
Taft-Hartley labor fight, which began in the Labor Committee, and
he had been on the panel which had investigated the dismissal of
General MacArthur. To be on a powerful committee is to stand at
what the elder La Follette called "the gateways of legislation." "A
powerful committee in secret session has almost autocratic power in
deciding what laws shall or shall not be passed; and it is in the
committees that the great financial interests of the country have
found their securest entrenchment," observed La Follette.

The committee system of breaking down the huge congressional
work load into fragments assigned to committees is even more necessary today than in the less busy time of La Follette. Through it great
power is invested in a handful of men in each field. A President may
urge upon Congress certain legislation affecting labor-management
relations, say; but it is the Labor Committee members much more
than the Senate at large who will shape the character of that legislation—or determine, indeed, whether there shall be *any* legislation in
response to the President's request.

In his vain effort to retain his committee posts, Wayne Morse discovered that his insistence upon being strictly independent placed
him in the unhappy circumstances of Edward Everett Hale's man
without a country, eternally sailing to and fro, denied the privilege of

disembarking on either party's shore. To declare himself independent of either party very much suited the temperament of Wayne Morse. But for him to insist on the literal and ultimate application of the notion that he was a third political party was most unsuitable to the Senate.

In the selection of committee members, each party takes care of its own by established practice of the Senate. As the Senate chamber is split by a center aisle to group senators of the two parties on opposite sides, each committee room is constructed to divide the Republicans from the Democrats. There are no triangular committee tables to take care of third-party members. The physical plant as well as the customs of the place have been based upon the presumed endurance of the two-party system. Young Bob La Follette, twice elected as a Progressive, had always accommodated himself to this system by accepting the committee assignments given him by the Republicans, with whom he joined only for these necessary purposes of organizing the Senate. Norris of Nebraska did the same after his re-election in 1935 as an Independent Republican. Lundeen of Minnesota, elected on the Farmer-Labor ticket in 1936, turned to the Democrats to receive his committee assignments.

Wayne Morse, not unaware of these lessons from the past, was determined neither to seek nor accept any proffered committee assignments from either party's leaders. He insisted that the Senate at large give him his committee assignments as a member of a minority party, according to Senate Rule XXIV, which states: "In the appointment of the standing committees, the Senate, unless otherwise ordered, shall proceed by ballot to appoint severally the chairman of each committee, and then, by one ballot, the other members necessary to complete the same." When Morse asked that this rule be literally implemented so that he would be appointed by ballot, he knew there was no precedent for this precise procedure. By custom, each party leader presented the list of his party's committee assignments, to which the Senate would simply agree. No ballot as such was ever employed, although the lists offered by the party leaders constituted something of a ballot.

This year the Republicans had appointed a special committee, headed by Case of South Dakota, to propose G.O.P. committee-seating arrangements. When on January 7 Case's group publicly suggested that Morse be retained on the Armed Services Committee, but dropped from the more ideologically sensitive Labor Committee,

Morse took the Senate floor to make it clear he wanted no such assignments from his old party. Taking Morse at his word, the Republicans in caucus January 13 approved a list on which Morse's name did not appear. The Democrats did likewise.

On that same day, the Senate then moved awkwardly to implement Rule XXIV, as Morse had requested. Taft started by offering his list of eight Republican senators for assignments to the Armed Services Committee. Democratic Leader Johnson followed with his list of seven Democratic senators entitled to seats on that committee. A third list contained the "Independent party's" nomination of one senator. Morse's nomination of himself meant that there were sixteen senators nominated for the fifteen seats on the committee. The critical question was how would the Senate determine which one of these senators was to be eliminated?

Taft suggested that the clerk call the roll to allow each senator to announce his choices for the fifteen seats. This could most simply be done, Taft offered, by each senator's saying he accepted the two major-party lists or, if he wished to vote for Morse, to state which party regular he was voting to scratch from the lists.

Realizing this procedure was bound to work to his disfavor, Morse countered with the suggestion that the Senate first vote simply on whether he should or should not be seated on this committee. If he were approved for membership, then the party leaders could later work out the seating arrangements for the other senators to assure Republican control, he said. Taft objected. Morse then proposed that a ballot be taken in such fashion that each senator should write out on a slip of paper the names of the fifteen senators he wished elected to the committee. Only by such a secret ballot could Morse hope to pick up support; for if forced to state their choices openly, few if any party regulars would oppose one of their own men in favor of Morse. In secret, they might.

Taft agreed to Morse's secret-ballot proposal. But Russell of Georgia interceded against it, for this would set a precedent which might "plague the Senate and cause unspeakable confusion in the committee assignments in the days to come." Taft was won over, noting that the Senate never employs secret balloting on legislation; and Morse could do nothing but acquiesce. By common consent, the procedure adopted was for each senator, as his name was called, to submit his selections, which were then read aloud. Predictably, the nominee of the "Independent party" was snowed under by the regulars. He received but seven votes. "I accept with good grace the decision which has just been rendered," said Morse. "The members of the Senate will have to live with the precedent they have established with respect to the status of minority parties in the Senate in the future."

But on this graceful note, unhappily Wayne Morse could not let his defeat rest. Before long he was bitterly blaming everyone for the position of weakness into which he had backed himself. The Republicans were to blame for disciplining him; the liberal Democrats for not protecting minority rights; and the press for misrepresenting his position.

To keep the issue alive, Morse introduced a resolution by which he and an extra Republican, to assure G.O.P. control, would be placed on the Armed Services and the Labor Committees. Pending action on this resolution, he secured Senate permission not to take the seats left vacant for him by that ballot procedure on two lesser committees, the District of Columbia and the Public Works committees. He had no objection to serving on these committees, he explained, but he objected to receiving them by a "garbage-can disposal" method in which he was required "to take the leavings." When two months had elapsed without any action on his resolution, Morse loudly threatened to enter every state to tell voters what their senators had done to him, especially the liberal Democrats who, he charged, had "walked out on their responsibilities to minority rights in the Senate" by substituting "political expediency for political principle, as they well know."

Herbert Lehman, probably the most gentle liberal of all, scolded Morse for blaming his frustrating predicament on senators no less liberal than he. He disclosed that he had offered Morse his own seat on the Labor Committee in good faith because he thought Morse "an extremely valuable member" to have on the committee. And then Lehman gave Morse what probably was the most severe rebuke the Oregon senator has ever received in the Senate, not in terms of the bitter invective others would employ, but in the manner which befits a guileless gentleman:

Let me say in all kindness that although the Senator from Oregon has been in the Senate for many more years than I have, he has not been in public life longer than I have, or longer than some of my colleagues, nor has he served the people of the Nation longer, nor has he served liberal causes longer. I cannot help remark that the Senator from Oregon has no monopoly on liberalism, on liberal leadership, or on liberal action, and that some of the Senators he has attacked, both on the Republican and on the Democratic sides of the aisle, have records on liberalism which I believe would not suffer by comparison with his record, much as I admire and respect him.

He has no monopoly on liberalism, on liberal leadership, or on the support of liberal causes which extend over a great many years. Others too have principles and convictions. I am sorry that I had to engage in this colloquy with my friend from Oregon. It has not been bitter on my side, and certainly I did not want it to be, because in spite of statements and remarks which have been made by him on the floor of of the Senate and on the outside, I still have a great affection for the Senator from Oregon, and I have great confidence in him. He is a real liberal, but I do not think he is the only liberal in the United States.

Morse shot back that Lehman was "getting pretty close to the belt line" by suggesting Morse thought he had a monopoly on liberalism. "I make no such profession," said Morse. "I do say that when it has been pointed out that a principle of liberalism was at stake, I never knowingly walked out on it." Morse was literally correct. In his Oregon primary-election campaigns, Morse did not walk out on liberalism—he ran in horror from it.

Morse kept up a steady fire against the liberals, even to holding them responsible for "vicious editorials" against him which observed that not even the liberal Democrats will stand by him. When his resolution finally came up for floor action, organized labor put on a telegraphic pressure campaign in hopes of getting Morse back on the Labor Committee. And, without the reprisals against Morse which his invective invited, the liberals spoke in his behalf. Pleading with Democrats to support Morse, Paul Douglas asked his colleagues, "Should we drive him, at the point of the bayonet, back to the Republican party and say, 'You are an Ishmael; you can find refuge nowhere?'" What would happen if the Democrats fell to disciplining their wayward brethren, asked Douglas, plainly referring to those Southern Democrats who failed to support Truman and Stevenson in 1948 and 1952?

Two Democratic patriarchs drove home the points which were Morse's undoing. Walter F. George of Georgia said he could not support the request of the Independent party representative because "we would then be inviting splinter parties in the United States, and coalitions between factions of both parties, and, in a very short period of time, we would have all the ills of the coalition governments which have afflicted practically all of Europe." Carl Hayden of Arizona, a member of Congress since his state was admitted to the Union in 1912, echoed this theme against tampering with the two-party method for assuring government stability.

Unable to dent this argument, try as he would, Morse claimed Oregon would have been denied equal representation as guaranteed under the Constitution if he were rejected in his committee quest. George, a lawyer of some considerable acquaintance with the Constitution and its origin, said that in the Constitutional Convention there had been talk of allowing each state to have a senator on each committee, but then only a few committees were contemplated and there were but thirteen states. Subsequently, he noted, the equal-representation clause of the Constitution ("No state, without its consent, shall be deprived of its equal suffrage in the Senate.") was adopted and thereafter "agitation for representation on each committee in the Senate lost much of its force and effect." Obviously a Union grown to fifty states could not effectively grant representation to each state on each Senate committee.

George granted only that when a senator "is not given a committee which will enable him to do his best work . . . there is a limitation upon that member, and it is to that extent a limitation upon the State he represents in connection with his effectiveness to serve his state or his section." But this limitation is suffered by every senator until he gains the seniority through which desirable committee posts can be secured. While expressing the "keenest sympathy" for him, George noted that Morse had cast away his precious seniority when he broke with the G.O.P. and refused to accept that party's committee offering.

Even in Oregon this claim of Morse's was rejected. Editor Charles A. Sprague was sympathetic to the senator's desire to retain his committee posts, but he put the blame where it evidently belonged. "Oregon's lack of representation on these committees is due to his own manuvering," wrote Sprague. "Morse refused to let Republicans or Democrats give him assignments, so he simply fell between two stools. Oregon has no claim to committee representation. Morse, as senator, has; but he muffed his claim by his antics. Basing his demand on ground that he constitutes an independent 'party' is a transparent fiction."

Considering the mythical nature of the Independent party, in which Wayne Morse was a majority of one, the Senate displayed magnificent forbearance in three times voting on various Morse proposals for rectifying his sad tumble into the oblivion of District of Columbia affairs. Had he wanted his committee positions more than he wanted a political issue with which to thrash the Senate, Morse could have accepted what he spurned as Lehman's "charity" in offering his own seat to Morse on the Labor Committee; and he could have taken the original offer of the Republicans to be kept on Armed Services.

Worse than losing his seats, Morse was denied what he seemed most to want: a show of public indignation over his being horse-whipped by the party regulars for his "act of conscience" in bolting the G.O.P. during the election campaign. The Senate was being very much itself, firmly committed to its established ways. It gave Wayne Morse his day in court, refrained even from asking why he called himself an Independent but failed to change his official Republican registration at the Lane County Courthouse; and yet the Senate refused to be browbeaten by charges of expediency, declined to deal with Morse on his own unprecedented terms when they fell outside the two-party structure.

In his humiliating defeat, Morse had served a useful purpose. He had for the first time challenged the two-party structure with all his energy and resourceful ferocity. His failure to open a breach had proved it suprisingly taut. Columnist Doris Fleeson interpreted the result as a notification by the Senate that "there is no place for independents in Congress. Independent Republicans, yes. Independent Democrats, yes. But the 48 states are now clearly on notice that independence not practiced well within the framework of the two major parties carries with it severe penalties."

It had not, to be sure, been Morse's objective to serve as a political-science guinea pig. Out of his lopsided defeats he sought to establish a moral victory. "I am proud of the political bed I have made for myself. But I wish to say to senators," he said in March, 1953, "that they are going to hear from me in 1954, across the country, on this matter of principle versus political expediency. They will find out in their own bailiwicks what the attitude of their constituents may be on the question of principle versus political expediency."

Despite his ineffective maneuvering on the committee issue, Morse gained more national attention than he had ever had before as the Senate's most outspoken maverick, most rambunctious independent, and the least beholden to any party ties. Demands for Wayne Morse as an after-dinner speaker mounted rapidly. In this period Morse did much speaking from the Senate as well, usually reserving every Friday afternoon for what he called the committee work of the Independent party—a series of commentaries on every conceivable subject, foreign and domestic, as well as lengthy speeches against "giveaways" of public resources, such as tidelands oil, and western dam sites. "Because the Senate has a rule of unlimited debate and Senator Morse will talk until the heavens fall—and everyone else is champing to go home for dinner—it occurs to few that his powers have been seriously abridged," observed columnist Fleeson.

Wayne Morse had lost none of his rights to be the Senate's Number-one gadfly. But in losing his committee fight, he had lost positions of added power. He was reduced to the humbling circumstances of the newest freshman in the place. His reduced circumstances were not unlike those of the elder La Follette who, as a new senator, asked to be assigned to the powerful Interstate Commerce Committee because of his interest in curbing the power of the railroads. Instead, he was given the chairmanship of the Committee to Investigate the Condition of the Potomac River Front. "I had immediate visions of cleaning up the whole Potomac River front until I found that in all its history the committee had never had a bill referred to it for consideration, and had never held a meeting," wryly observed La Follette in his autobiography.

Moreover, Wayne Morse lost his temper. His assaults upon senators on all sides cost him dearly in the moral credit an effective public man needs in the bank of his human relations. It was a costly time of trouble, a period of blaming others, especially the press, for the debacle he had brought upon himself.

Smoking Mad at the Press

On the afternoon that the Senate finally fastened upon him the ignominy of his assignment to the District of Columbia Committee, Morse strode briskly from the chamber. In a Capitol corridor he was intercepted by an Associated Press reporter, G. Milton Kelly, who asked the senator's reaction to his setback. Morse used bitterly disparaging terms to describe the other senators and what they had that day done to him, says Kelly. So in writing about the episode, the veteran AP reporter chose the colorful expression "smoking mad" to describe Morse's reaction.

When Morse saw Kelly's story, he took the Senate floor to brand it a "lie." He had not been smoking mad, he protested. He had been "amused." This is one of the most useful words in the English language for Wayne Morse. He uses it to characterize his reaction to political events which, in lesser men, would evoke anger, fear, bitterness, dismay, or disappointment.

"Of course I did not agree with the result. I said 'the fight has just started.' I said it good-naturedly, as far as the principle that I defended on the floor of the Senate was concerned. There was no anger about it. I fight hard, but I fight professionally," boomed out Morse. Growing more amused as he warmed to his topic, he described the Associated Press as a "slanted-news reporting service" with a "bunch of clever writers skilled in the use of snide, reputation-assassinating adjectives."

When the Senate that afternoon adjourned for the day, Kelly entered the chamber and approached Morse before the senator had departed. "I understand I have had the honor of being called a liar by you," remarked the veteran newsman. Morse, he related later, refused to discuss it and ordered him to leave "or I'll have you removed." When the Senate convened next day, Morse was on his feet demanding an apology from the Associated Press for the "insulting and brazen manner" of its reporter. Finally Morse made clear what was gnawing at him. Kelly's dispatch, he felt, had "smeared" him because the expression "smoking mad" created the impression "that I was a poor sport." Morse told the Senate that if Kelly "had any brains at all, he would have known he would have left that impression when he wrote that I left the floor 'fighting mad' [sic] . . ." In a word, Kelly should have protected him. He should not have informed Oregon voters that their senator was in a state of unamused fury. What would they think of his sportsmanship?

"I happen to be one member of the Senate," he thundered bravely, "who is not afraid of the press. If there is anyone in the press who thinks he is some little third-degree artist, let him get it through his skull now that I do not propose to be insulted on the floor of the Senate by any man in the press gallery. . . . I wish to say to the

AP that until I receive an apology for the conduct of their correspondent on the floor of the Senate yesterday afternoon, I never want a member of the AP ever to darken the door of my office, because as of now they are *persona non grata*, as far as the junior Senator from Oregon is concerned; and I would not give them a conference on any subject, because I do not trust their intellectual honesty, I do not trust their journalistic ethics. I think the Associated Press will understand that language."

What one must understand about this language is that Wayne Morse, perhaps more than the average thin-skinned politician, scans the press with a very subjective eye. Newspapers and their editorial writers and columnists rise and fall in his esteem in direct ratio with how they treat his latest exploits. During his first days in Washington on the War Labor Board, Morse received magnificent publicity as a colorful new figure in the often dull area of labor relations. He won editorial tributes for his tough-mindedness in standing up to John L. Lewis. How it affected Wayne Morse may be seen in a letter he wrote on one such occasion in June 1943 to Professor Andrew Weaver at Wisconsin:

> I am enclosing a copy of my decision in the coal case. I consider my special concurring opinion the most significant decision I have ever written. It apparently was good enough for Eugene Meyer, publisher of the Washington *Post* to invite me over to his office yesterday afternoon for lunch which was attended not only by his managing editor but also by his head editorial writer. I won't tell you much about what he said because even I have a streak of modesty in me. Suffice to say that he said he considered my special concurring opinion one of the most outstanding acts on the basis of principle which has come out of Washington in many a day. . . .

When Morse found a particularly glowing article about himself, he passed it along to a friend at the University of Oregon, such as he did in 1943 with a St. Louis *Post-Dispatch* article which he suggested might be circulated by the university publicity office. "Let the suggestion come from you and not from me, if you get the point," Morse wrote his friend. "It is just one of those little things which might help keep the 'personal fences' in repair back there." When he noted an uncomplimentary press reference, in these early days of his career he held his tongue, publicly.

Not until 1951, when the Chicago *Tribune* read Morse out of the G.O.P. after he defended Truman's dismissal of General MacArthur, did the senator openly scold a newspaper. Colonel McCormick then owned the Washington *Times-Herald* as well as the *Tribune*, and through these mighty organs he advised the G.O.P.: "The time has come for the Republican caucus to assemble and formally vote to bestow Morse to the Administration party, where he belongs. He is not a Republican. He retains the fiction of Republican allegiance only because he can do the Republicans more damage posing as one of them than by openly avowing that he has been an Administration supporter right along." Characteristically Morse was the one to call the Senate's attention to the colonel's advice. He called this criticism "a great personal compliment" because these newspapers are "the mouthpieces of reaction, the instruments for a type of American fascism [and] are good examples of what would happen to the Republican party if the editor of these papers ever became the true spokesman of the Republican party."

The *Tribune* responded by dispatching a reporter to Oregon to look into Morse's background. From a few anti-Morse Republicans, the newspaper developed a story which portrayed Morse as a pinko ex-professor who was a member of the Institute of Pacific Relations (then under investigation by the McCarran Committee) and a pal of Harry Bridges. From its Washington-bureau chief, Walter Trohan, the Chicago *Tribune* then published a story revealing that Dean Morse's election to the I.P.R. had been "announced by Joseph Barnes, editor of the New York *Star* and former foreign editor of the New York *Herald Tribune*." The story observed that Barnes had four times been identified "as a former Red" by witnesses before the McCarran Committee but that Barnes had denied Communist connections. Observing that Morse had been demanding an investigation of the China Lobby is the No. 1 item on the Communist party program for action on China policy, according to photostats of American party documents made available to the Chicago *Tribune*." The article sought also to link Morse through the I.P.R. to other targets of the day, including Professor Owen Lattimore, Ambassador Philip C. Jessup, Alger Hiss, Earl Browder, and Harry Dexter White.

While this assault from the far-right wing of the press was happily received by those who had grown to despise Morse in Oregon, it was another newspaper that came to Morse's defense. Editor Tugman in the Eugene *Register-Guard* dismissed the *Tribune*'s innuendo about the suspect I.P.R. as follows:

Arnold Bennett Hall, the president of the University of Oregon, was promoting the Institute of Pacific Relations and, indeed, had a dream of getting the darn thing to headquarters in Eugene. It was the fashionable thing to be Pacific-minded. Professors made summer tours to the Orient. A team of Oregon debaters traveled up and down the Pacific basin arguing with Australians, Filipinos, Chinese and Japanese. Mrs. Murray Warner was providing the treasures for the Museum of Oriental Art on the University campus. Merchants of Eugene were providing the cash for the building. Chambers of Commerce were whooping about the Pacific trade. Everybody was Pacific-minded.

Tugman allowed that Morse had done "many injudicious things in the course of his career," but joining the I.P.R. was not one of them. "This paper has supported Wayne Morse, and probably will continue to do so, for the simple reason that we believe his virtues outweigh all his faults."

The following spring, however, Tugman took Morse sternly to task for supporting President Truman's seizure of the nation's steel mills. The issue became an inflammatory one in the Senate, complete with cries for Truman's impeachment. As the only Republican senator who supported Truman, Morse felt the heat more than most. He lashed out at the press for "ignoring the seriousness of the situation" and not playing up the danger of allowing the great steel furnaces to grow cold while the boys in Korea remained in action. Specifically Morse was incensed because the papers all but ignored testimony of Defense Secretary Robert Lovett in a hearing at which Lovett answered a Morse question by saying the Pentagon was "very gravely concerned about any stoppage" in steel production. This wasn't *news*, however, for Lovett had earlier made a speech on the subject to the American Society of Newspaper Editors which was fully reported in the press. Yet Morse criticized the New York *Times*, New York *Herald Tribune*, New York *World-Telegram*, Washington *Post* and Washington *Star* for devoting only five column inches of news space to Lovett's testimony, but later devoting 979 column inches to the court decision ruling the seizure unconstitutional.

Editor Tugman wrote that Morse's "effort to blame his troubles on the press is the silliest thing he has ever done, and that's a large statement. In kindness, we diagnose this outburst as 'a tantrum' such as we've seen him throw before. Morse has great abilities, but he would be a more valuable Senator if he would think more and talk less." Morse fired back a long letter accusing Tugman of imbibing in an "emotional drunk." The newspaper published it on the front page.

When Morse bolted the party that fall, he incurred the wrath of additional newspaper editors who had earlier supported him in his Republican heyday. Shortly before the election he told a Chicago *Sun-Times* reporter that the two greatest dangers to America are "Red Communism and yellow journalism." He cited the New York *Times* and the St. Louis *Post-Dispatch* for fair journalism and the Chicago *Tribune* as "a good example of yellow journalism." Replied Colonel McCormick, "Senator Morse is a well-known liar."

From that time on, complaints about the press became a curious obsession. After the election, when Morse made his first trip into Oregon since bolting the party, crowds turned out in large numbers to hear him explain his party turnabout. When he arrived at the University of Oregon, 1000 persons were there to hear him. In this homecoming setting, where Morse and Tugman had been allied in many past causes, the senator now sought to discredit the editor before his fellow townsmen. Morse was bleeding from an editorial in which Tugman had questioned his sincerity. He could not let this pass unchallenged.

Tugman's editorial noted a dispatch I had sent to the *Register-Guard* relating that preconvention conversation in which Morse had told Alice Johnson of the Seattle *Times* and me of his thoughts about issuing a call for a new party if Taft were nominated. I had reported this remark as a kind of footnote to history, after Morse bolted the party, to show that his departure was not an impulsive act. Tugman also noted a story in the *Oregon Journal* from Roulhac Hamilton which quoted Morse right after the convention as saying that Eisenhower isn't "big enough" or "hasn't the mind" for the presidency. Tugman's point was that Morse could hardly have been sincere in later ecstatically writing from London to General Eisenhower and promising to stump the country for him.

Before challenging the editorial, Morse called in Hamilton and told him that I had denied the portion of the editorial which referred to my dispatch. Hamilton says he realized Morse was up to his old schoolboy snow-job tricks, for a secretary in the senator's outer office was trying without luck to find me. Hamilton advised Morse that the editorial looked accurate to him, as far as his contribution was concerned. When I was subsequently invited in, the senator heard the same answer. We had indeed written the stories from which Tugman quoted. Morse told me he had no recollection of telling us what we reported. I told Morse my only doubt about my story was caused by some uncertainty as to whether he regarded those remarks, made in a quiet chat just outside the Senate chamber, to be off-the-record. But the senator took the position that he had never made such remarks, on or off the record. He said this was what he intended to tell anyone in Oregon if the issue came up. I said I understood his position, and we parted amicably.

When the senator gamecock got warmed up before the huge university crowd, which included Tugman, he didn't wait for someone to raise the issue. In his effort to discredit the editor's opinion, Morse claimed that Hamilton and I had "authorized" him to say, "It's not true." Morse sought to convey that we had repudiated our stories and Tugman's editorial references to us. In fact, we had not authorized Morse to say anything, nor had we repudiated our stories. Tugman published Morse's speech on page one, flanked by contrary statements from us newsmen. We were then barred from Morse's office. Editorially Tugman observed that it appeared that Morse had "adopted the precedent of the great Theodore Roosevelt of repudiating newspaper quotes whenever they turn out embarrassing."

This was not Morse's first adoption of the Teddy Roosevelt precedent. In 1950, still a Republican, he composed a statement taking other liberal Republicans to task. He gave a copy to Charles (Doc) Watkins, an Associated Press reporter, and later telephoned Watkins twice to make changes before the story was written. The statement was newsworthy; Watkins' story hit the front page of the Washington *Star* that afternoon.

Another AP reporter, Ernie Warren, learned that Morse subsequently had written letters to several offended senators blaming the reporter for the story. Watkins covered the offices of all Pacific Northwest members of Congress for the AP, but after this incident this pleasant, thoroughly non-combative reporter stayed clear of Morse. Subsequently they met by chance in a Capitol Hill corridor.

Morse stopped and candidly apologized to Watkins. The reporter recalls the senator explained, "I had to have a fall guy, and you were it."

On his 1952 tour of Oregon after bolting the party, an *Oregon Journal* reporter, Don Sterling, Jr., sought to pin Morse down about his mounting complaints about the press. The senator said:

> Don't misunderstand me. I'm not a paranoiac—I don't have a persecution complex. But I predict in the next few years you will see the greatest campaign of lies and smears in history to get rid of the liberals in the Senate.

His bill of particulars against the press was brief. In 1947 he recalled the AP had quoted him as telling the Senate he would oppose the Taft-Hartley bill even though he thought most of his constituents favored it. He blamed the AP for not carrying his subseqent remarks explaining that he meant he was better informed on the subject than many constituents who unwisely favored that labor act. He reiterated his complaint about press coverage of the steel-seizure issue. And he cited the recent rhubarb with Tugman, Hamilton, and me.

Years later, the city editor of the *Oregonian*, J. Richard Nokes, tried to elicit from Morse a bill of particulars for his massive indictment of the press. The senator brushed the whole matter aside.

A constructive case could be made respecting the shortcomings of the American press at large, starting with its devotion to blood, sex, and society shenanigans, all of which are abysmally popular with readers. But Morse's criticism has been fiercely subjective and unspecific. In the spring of 1953 he declared, "I doubt whether in the last four months 10 per cent of the stories that have appeared in the press about the junior Senator from Oregon have had a 20 per cent relationship to the facts." He was "sad" to have to criticize the press, but "someone in public life . . . ought to stand up against a misinformed press."

His tiff with AP reporter Kelly blossomed into a full-scale attack by the senator upon the Associated Press, the world's largest news-gathering agency and a non-profit co-operative owned by the member newspapers which it serves. "I know how vicious and dangerous is the AP as a propaganda organization for poisoning the minds of the American people against any official whom they are out to smear," he said in the Senate. He suggested that a motto for the AP, using its initials, would be "Always Polluted."

There is no doubt that a wide majority of newspapers editorially prefer Republican-party candidates and policies—a fact of great usefulness to Wayne Morse in his early election campaigns. But the success of the Democratic party since the New Deal, broken only by the G.O.P.'s recruitment of a popular war hero as President in the fifties, indicates at least that the popular will is not readily determined by editorial writers. Complaints about press coverage of political campaigns, whether from Adlai Stevenson or Richard Nixon, come inevitably from the loser.

One point raised by Morse deserves attention, however, for it concerns whether or not the press affords him fair treatment in the news columns. To fortify his assault on the AP newspapers, Morse read the Senate an editorial from the York *Gazette and Daily*, a liberal tabloid published in the Pennsylvania-Dutch country. Editor C. M. Gitt, a Henry Wallace supporter in 1948, was sympathetic to Morse's complaint that the "reactionary" publishers were giving him little attention. The AP is dominated by the larger publishers, wrote Gitt, and "those persons whom the big boys in the association are interested in get the publicity and the coverage and those persons, such as Senator Morse, whom only a few of the members of the Associated Press are interested in, get practically none or very slim coverage."

There is some justification for saying that an individual newspaper may give the silent treatment to a politician who incurs its disfavor. Such a newspaper is Hearst's Seattle *Post-Intelligencer*, which periodically has acted as though Washington State Senators Warren G. Magnuson and Henry M. Jackson, both Democrats, had vanished into outer space. No matter what the senators did during their periods of banishment from the news columns, the readers of the *P-I* would find no mention of their senators in that newspaper. It is said that once when the sports editor cautiously injected Senator Magnuson's name into his column, it was dutifully deleted by higher authority. The reason for such discrimination apparently was not ideological, however. Both senators had sinned against this morning newspaper by making important announcements about new defense contracts for the Seattle area at a time during the day when this big news could be published *first* in the afternoon *Times*. Had the *P-I* been given the break, Magnuson and Jackson would doubt-less have been noble names in the *P-I* editorial offices thereafter. Even a former *P-I* reporter, Russ Holt, who was Jackson's press secretary, could not get his leader's name back in the paper for six months.

No one who has plowed through Morse's vast accumulation of press clippings, pasted neatly into a monumental stack of scrap-books, would believe for an instant that he has been banished from any news columns. In 1953, at the peak of his campaign against the press, Morse received front-page attention everywhere he went on a tour of his home state. The *Register-Guard* faithfully reported "his crowd was sympathetic to Morse's blistering attack on the Eisenhower Administration." The *Oregon Statesman,* along with a front-page picture of the senator and Mrs. Morse, carried several stories on his local visit to Salem, one of them reporting he had "a friendly audience" which "punctuated Morse's speech with several rounds of applause and kept the Senator answering questions for 45 minutes afterward." A reader complained to the *Register-Guard* about a picture of the senator on the front page of the Sunday edition which showed him with some youngsters at a tree-planting ceremony. "How can you call that stuff news, especially when you know that he'll turn right around and accuse the press of mis-representing him whenever it suits his fancy?" the irate reader asked. Editor Tugman replied:

> In covering Senator Morse, or any other public character, the news department never has any instructions except to be there and to report as accurately and completely as possible whatever is done or said. If Senator Morse, or any other public character, chooses to cry "unfair" (as he often does) that is merely one of our occupational hazards. Morse is a controversial figure (like McCarthy) and he has many of the same talents for making headlines. He has made many false and insupportable accusations against the Oregon press but that has not affected their reporting of his visit.
>
> In any showdown, the press can stand on its record, perhaps even better than the Senator. We have great faith in the ability of the people to appraise their public men in the long run. At the moment we are not quarreling editorially with anything the junior Senator says or does. This is his time to "howl"; it is our job to tell about it. It's the American way and we know no better way in public matters.

Morse's complaint has not been that the press has ignored him. "I say to the people of my state that they have not read an accurate story in the Oregon newspapers, outside of the Medford *Mail Tribune* for some five months on any controversy in which the junior Senator from Oregon has participated," he said in mid-1953. The liberal *Mail Tribune* was unique in perhaps only one respect at that time: its editor, Robert W. Ruhl, had editorially sided with Morse, even in his assault upon the AP. Ruhl's newspaper was served by the rival news agency, United Press, which faithfully reported Morse's purple adjectives about the AP.

Another Oregon newspaper, the Pendleton *East Oregonian*, equally as liberal as the *Mail Tribune*, commented that Morse "has a stuck needle. Everyone who disagrees with Morse, according to the Senator, is a liar." Noting Morse's blanket charge of unfair treatment, the *East Oregonian's* editor, J. W. Forrester, Jr., wrote, "Such a statement seems too ridiculous to warrant more than scant attention. But we can't forget that Senator Joe McCarthy has made it pay off politically and Morse is a far more able orator." The *East Oregonian*, which has always supported liberal candidates for office, notably the Neubergers, has been on Morse's black list of "reactionary newspapers" ever since—a complaint he voices with regularity upon visits to Pendleton. Morse, in a word, applies but one litmus test in determining whether a newspaper is reactionary or liberal: has it been true-blue to Wayne Morse, or has some acid editorializing made the senator see red?

To apply his test, Morse is an avid reader of what Oregon newspapers publish about him. The senator does not read all the newspapers in his state. Indeed, in late years he has canceled his subscriptions to all the Oregon papers he once received at his office. He subscribes, instead, to a news-clipping service, as do many politicians. A private enterprise based in Portland gets Morse's business. It staff of readers comb the daily prints for any mention of the name of Wayne Morse, take scissors in hand, and soon send off a bundle of fresh clips to the senator. After he has passed judgment on what sort of press he is getting, the clippings are pasted into scrapbooks.

When Morse banned a number of reporters from his office, he did not cut himself out of the news. His speeches in the Senate were faithfully covered by newsmen sitting above in the press gallery. And his office kept the press releases flowing—even to the banned newsmen. Once Roulhac Hamilton, one of the banned correspondents, found himself stuck at the last moment without a dignitary to interview on his radio program to Oregon. Although it seemed pointless, he asked Morse's office whether the senator might like to go on. A model of accommodation, Morse hiked all the way to the far end of the Capitol to the House Radio Gallery for the recording session. "He did a beautiful job," recalls Hamilton.

When the program was finished, Hamilton sought amplification of a point he thought would make a good newspaper story. Drawing back, Morse asked, "Are you asking me as a radio broadcaster or as a correspondent for the *Journal?*" Hamilton had in mind writing a newspaper story on the point at issue. He says Morse replied, "I'm sorry, but I don't give interviews to the correspondent for the *Journal!*" Off he went through the studio door.

If this seems like a weird distinction, it reflects Morse's subjective approach to the news media. Radio is very kind to him. Every week he makes a tape recording and sends copies of it to a string of radio stations in Oregon. He picks his own topic and has fifteen minutes in which to have his say, every word to be sent out on the air waves to his faithful listeners. No editorial observations by the station are injected. No one's counter views are sought. The newspapers, for all the space and headlines they give him, are ever ready to give Morse his comeuppance editorially.

The most prominent exception to criticism in the newspaper world, as far as Morse is concerned, is Drew Pearson. Speaking of the columnist, Morse told the Senate in January 1961, "I think he is the most able and the most effective journalistic muckraker we have had in the United States in our time, if not in our whole history." He said he meant the term in a highly complimentary sense as one who seeks to expose corruption by public men and corporations. Pearson's bouquets to Morse have been equally sweet over the years.

The Morse-Pearson relationship is well served by their unique usefulness to one another. Morse is adept at supplying Pearson with inside scoop material. Pearson reciprocates by portraying the senator in heroic terms.

Morse learned this trick of the trade in his first years in Washington on the War Labor Board. An item from a Pearson column in 1943 records this purported exchange from a White House conference on the coal strike of that spring:

> *Ickes:* You can't mine coal with bayonets. The fundamental issue is to settle the strike. I would have settled it if the War Labor Board had let me alone.
>
> *Morse:* Mr. President, either your Secretary of the Interior is ignorant or he is maliciously misrepresenting the facts. The fundamental issue is whether one man, John L. Lewis, shall be allowed to defy the sovereignty of the U. S. Government.

An amusing illustration of the Morse-to-Pearson pipeline is seen in a column about that auto trip Morse took with President Truman to Ball's Bluff. A Massachusetts citizen clipped the Pearson column and sent it to the President along with a photograph he had taken of Colonel Baker's grave at San Francisco. Truman examined the photograph with interest, but when he read Pearson's column he bristled. Reporting that at one point Truman nearly swerved off the road, the columnist gave this account of Morse's adventure with the President:

> Their first conversation was about the fact that the President was driving himself, the Senator discreetly inquiring when the President had last driven. Mr. Truman admitted he hadn't driven for a couple of years, but said he still remembered how. As the trip continued, it was evident that whatever the President lacked in skill as a chauffeur, he made up in zestful driving. With the Secret Service men sitting nervously in the rear, the President enjoyed every minute of it.

In his reply to Captain John J. Sheehan, Truman thanked him for the photograph but added, "The clipping you enclosed by Pearson was wrong in every particular—he never tells the truth about anything intentionally. If he does, it is by accident, and he usually lies later to offset it. There was no conversation on the subject on the way down and I am still able to drive a car as well as ever. I don't think you will find that Wayne was in any way uneasy on the trip. We had a fine visit with General Marshall and discussed the idea of the state of Oregon erecting a memorial to Baker. That was the whole program and there was nothing else to it."

Once Morse took up the cry of "yellow journalism" against the "reactionary press," he found it impossible wholly to desist. A candidate for a master's degree at the University of Oregon, Robert B. Whipple, even wrote a thesis on the subject: "The Change and Development of Editorial Attitudes of Selected Oregon Daily

Newspapers toward Senator Wayne Morse." Like Morse, Whipple stressed the shift of editorial opinion from pro-Morse to anti-Morse when he bolted the Republican party. The reverse of the coin is also true: Morse was never troubled by the press while it supported him, but once the criticism began, he quickly discerned "the great fallibility of the newspaper editors," as he put it in a letter to Whipple.

In 1955 Morse quietly dropped his indictment of the wicked Associated Press, without receiving the apology he had so loudly demanded in 1953. What he received was much more valuable and gratifying—a long, friendly article about his favorite subject, Wayne Morse, written by the AP's Pulitzer prize-winning reporter Don Whitehead. The story, complete with photo of the Morse family at tea, was given prominence in the Sunday *Oregonian*, filling four full columns opposite the editorial page. The newspaper headlined the article: "Morse Gains New D. C. Stature; Vote to Decide Senate Lineup."

The AP was not out to butter up Morse by concocting a favorable story. The story related that Morse was suddenly the key man in the Senate after the 1954 election, when the Independent senator's vote could have given either party control of the Senate. The AP was doing its customary impartial, creditable job by offering its member newspapers a lengthy profile of the senator who was suddenly big news—even though he was the same senator who had slandered the AP in bygone days of desperation. Whitehead reported that "the politicians have been forced to give a new and higher prestige rating to the rebel Senator from Oregon." No more did Wayne Morse describe the AP as vicious and dangerous, poisoning the minds of the American people.

Later correspondent Hamilton and I, after three years of banishment, were also restored to good favor. Editor Sprague of the *Oregon Statesman* in January 1955 suggested to Morse in a letter that he resume normal press relations with me on a strictly professional basis. The senator replied that this was a fine sentiment, but "I do not believe that I should be asked to hold personal interviews with a correspondent who I honestly believe is so unreliable that in order to protect myself I should have present at a conference a stenotypist to take down verbatim every word spoken between us." Subsequently Hamilton and I jointly wrote Morse to propose periodic press conferences with a stenographer present for the mutual protection of all participants. We were instantly summoned to his office, and there greeted like prodigal sons.

After a spate of jolly banter about our children and his grandchildren, the senator grew serious: "Now, as to this proposal. I see no reason in the world why grown men can't sit down in the same room together without having some stenographer present to take it all down." Without any spoken reservations, the senator ended his cold war against the working press, that day in the autumn of 1955. "But there is just one thing about this," added Morse, his brow deeply furrowed with the gravity of his next point. "There will be some who will say, 'Ah, there's Morse, making his peace with the press because he is coming up for re-election next year.'" Pondering the thought that anyone could be so cynical, we waited expectantly for the senator to conclude. Leaning across his desk and virtually embracing us with a look of humble sincerity, Wayne Morse averred, "But as long as you men don't think that is the case, then it doesn't matter to me what they say."

Mr. Hamilton, with consummate skill acquired in long years of journalistic jousting with con men in and out of public life, replied with the barest trace of mischief in his eyes, "Why, no, Senator, we wouldn't think anything like that." On this merciful note, peace was restored.

Wayne Morse's war on the press coincided with his gravest time of trouble, during his frustrating period as an independent, as a senator without a party, without visible means of political support, possibly a senator without a future. Everything had gone wrong, in one sense, as Morse viewed his troubled position as the most junior member of the Senate Committee on the District of Columbia.

Fictional though the Independent party was, it served the momentary political needs of this man without a party. Having deserted or been kicked out by the Republicans, he could not rush headlong into that party he had so frequently condemned for its alleged devotion to government by men and not by law.

Adlai Stevenson said in the 1952 campaign that the Democrats had a light in the window for Morse; and Hubert Humphrey said he would swap three Southern Democrats for Morse any day. But for Senator Morse, whose early success at the polls had been dependent upon strong utterances of contempt for the Democratic party and some of its liberal proposals, a complete transition would take at least a little time and a plausible explanation.

10. POLITICAL WEDDING BELLS

*Liberal Roots . . . Enticement . . . Oregon's Other Senator
. . . For Better or for Worse*

ONE NIGHT during the war in the Pacific against Japan, an American plane en route from Eniwetok touched down at Kwajalein, one of the myriad atolls which had emerged from geographic obscurity. A Red Cross official, Monroe Sweetland, left the plane during its three-hour stopover to seek out a young naval officer, Howard Morgan. Finding Morgan asleep in his barracks at 2 A.M., Sweetland awakened him, and the two men conferred until the visitor's plane was ready to take off for Honolulu. The discussion was about a battle front that awaited them back home in Oregon. They talked Oregon politics, little dreaming that in a decade they would mount a successful political assault in the name of Democratic liberalism that would put entrenched Oregon Republicans to rout. Nor could Morgan and Sweetland know that the man who would one day lead their charges would be an ex-college professor whose earliest political declarations denounced both the New Deal and the Democratic party to which they were so dedicated.

Sweetland, the principal figure in the precinct-by-precinct rehabilitation of the Democratic party in Oregon that was to come, was a capable organizer and a doctrinaire liberal. Born in Oregon but reared in Michigan, young Sweetland admired the La Follette Progressive movement in nearby Wisconsin, except for its isolationism. His father was a teacher and football coach at Willamette University at Salem, Oregon. Educated at Wittenberg College in Ohio and at Cornell, young Sweetland quickly plunged into politics on the far left wing. He became national chairman of the League for Industrial Democracy, which organized 120 collegiate chapters. Norman Thomas was the league's spiritual mentor. Competing with the LID for the passions of young radicals in those Depression days was the National Student Union, whose ranks were heavily infiltrated by Communists.

As a consequence of this collegiate political experience, Sweetland became a Socialist supporter of Norman Thomas for President in 1932 and 1936. He also became an ardent liberal anti-Communist. In the late thirties he was active in intra-union fighting which helped some CIO unions, such as Al Hartung's woodworkers, to put the Communists to flight while other unions were being taken over. In 1941 Sweetland was appointed an adviser to Sidney Hillman in the labor division of the Office of Production Management over the protests of some unions, notably the teamsters and Harry Bridges' longshoremen.

Howard Morgan, today a member of the Federal Power Commission in Washington, was president of the student body at Portland's Reed College in 1940 when he first met Sweetland. Sweetland came out to the campus one day as a speaker "to warn against what the Commies were up to," recalls Morgan. The Communists were then preaching the virtues of isolationism, he explained, before Germany attacked Russia. Sweetland advocated American intervention against the Axis powers. Morgan got his first taste of politics at Reed, registered as a Republican because of the predominantly one-party character of Oregon at the time, but regarded himself as a New Deal Democrat.

Morgan grew up on the wrong side of the tracks in Portland's tough Albina district. He had both brains and determination, but he lost four years getting his college degree in economics because he had to work on construction gangs (he helped build Bonneville Dam) whenever he ran out of money. Six months after he finished at Reed, Morgan married a classmate, Rosina Corbett, whose father was one of the most powerful Republicans in the state—and also one of the richest. The Corbetts had come to the Oregon territory as hardware merchants from Boston, went into stagecoach lines, telegraph service, railroading, and banking, and into the new party of President Lincoln. Morgan's father-in-law, Henry L. Corbett, owned a number of downtown Portland's largest office buildings. He had twice been president of the State Senate and once the G.O.P. candidate for governor. He personified the strength of the party which had long managed public affairs in Oregon. But his daughter was a Democrat.

Returning from wartime navy duty in the Atlantic and Pacific,

Morgan got into the American Veterans' Committee and the Young Democrats, in each case challenging and routing the young Communist element which sought to control these groups. But the prospect of routing the Republicans was more formidable. In postwar Oregon, the Republican party controlled all the state's six seats in Congress, all the high state offices, and all but a handful of the seats in the legislature. The Democrats were so poorly organized they offered candidates for little more than half the seats in the legislature. The chief figures in the Democratic party were neither sympathetic to the Truman Fair Deal nor actively concerned about much more than securing their own positions and fending off the advances of young progressives like Sweetland and Morgan. Hard work at the grass roots lay ahead.

Liberal Roots

To assume that Oregon was always the flinty one-party Republican state which it then appeared to be would be to misapprehend this Pacific coast state's political nature and to compound the difficulty of understanding why it should have given itself to so unorthodox a figure as Wayne Morse. True, the state legislature had not been controlled by the Democrats since 1878, but legislatures are notoriously undependable as barometers of public sentiment. From its admission to the Union in 1859 through World II, Oregon had taken as its governor fifteen Republicans, nine Democrats, and one Independent. It had elected roughly twice as may Republicans to the United States Senate as Democrats.

More significant, Oregon was fertile ground for reformers— the Patrons of Husbandry, who organized their Granges early in Oregon; the Farmers' Alliance, which flexed its muscles at the same time shortly before the turn of the twentieth century; the Populists, who nearly carried Oregon for their presidential ticket in 1892; the Bull Moosers and the Progressives, who found strong sentiment for Teddy Roosevelt and Fighting Bob La Follette. But for all their appeal, these third-party movements never overcame the strength of the Republicans or the Democrats in Oregon, chiefly because the older parties adopted the most popular of the reformist planks. "Scratch a Western Democrat and you find a Populist" became a common saying after the Democrats embraced the Populist objectives of free silver, the income tax, banking reform, and direct government.

America's most virile political reform movement, which sprang from agrarian discontent in the Middle West in the 1890s, also took firm root in the Pacific Northwest. There the railroads not only enflamed the wheat growers with exorbitant freight charges, but were the cause and beneficiaries of much political corruption connected with western timberlands. "The power of the trusts and corporations has become an intolerable tyranny, the encroachments of the landgrubbers have almost exhausted the public domain, and the corruption of the ballot has rendered our elections little less than a disgraceful farce," the Oregon agrarian reformers contended. While the Democrats were gaining strength in rural areas by adopting the objectives of the reformers, Professors Johannsen and Gates observed that:

> . . . the Republicans owed much to their effective control of the populous centers. In Portland it was machine control exercised crudely enough at election time by ruffians and rascals brought in for the purpose from San Francisco. For a price, these men voted as they were told, perhaps not once but several times at different polling places. Jonathan Bourne protested that Bryan actually carried Oregon only to have the victory snatched from him by Republican repeaters. The traffic in ballots helped McKinley at the moment, but it produced a popular resentment which hastened remedial legislation afterward.

This sordid episode gave new incentive to reformers who offered redemption through adoption by the legislature of "the Oregon system"—the initiative and the referendum. These became the tools of more direct government, the means by which voters could "legislate" for or against specific proposals listed on the ballot. South Dakota in 1898 had been the first state to adopt these twin weapons against corrupt legislatures, but Oregon became their best proving grounds. In eight years Oregonians had to vote up or down thirty-two proposals, including a direct-primary law, which was adopted, and woman suffrage, which was not.

The direct primary and the spirit of reform which gave it birth were transplants from Wisconsin, where Governor La Follette was conducting a one-man political revolution that would forever influence the course of free government in America. Indeed, the ties that bind men's spirits were being strongly knit between La Follette's state, where Wayne Morse was then a farm boy, and Oregon, where he would one day chance to settle and in time rise to prominence as a Republican with a reformist's zeal.

Oregon Democrats had a brief period of strength during the Wilson era, holding the governorship and both Senate seats, only to be eclipsed completely during the twenties, when the pendulum swung to the right. This was a period of reaction and violence for Oregon. It was most harshly symbolized by the flaming cross and hooded bigots of the Klan.

When Franklin D. Roosevelt swept the country before him in the thirties, Oregon Democrats lost their greatest opportunity to capitalize on his popularity and take prolonged control of the state. The cause of this impotence was the same split that was to confront Sweetland and Morgan after World War II. The conservative party leaders were hostile to FDR's social revolution. Once more the spirit of reform rose from agrarian protest, through a farmer-labor alliance, Commonwealth Federation, formed in Oregon in 1937 with Sweetland as executive secretary. Roosevelt and Ickes encouraged the Commonwealth by clearing their patronage in Oregon through Sweetland.

Commonwealth nominated a gubernatorial candidate, Henry Hess, in 1938 against the more conservative Democratic incumbent, General Charles H. (Iron Pants) Martin. But the Republicans recaptured the governorship with progressive Charles A. Sprague and both houses of the legislature and all seats in Congress. Oregon Republicans had survived the political impact of the New Deal largely because Oregon Democrats divided over their popular four-term President instead of embracing him as the agent of harmony and new strength. The dilemma of Oregon Democrats was only compounded in the mid-forties, with Truman even less a symbol of unity than FDR. Thus the Democrats were virtually eclipsed when Sweetland and Morgan returned to mastermind a recovery.

The first breakthrough came in 1948 when Sweetland ran for Democratic National Committeeman and defeated Mike DeCicco, one of the old-guard Democrats, by a narrow margin. This was a beginning, a small ledge from which to mount the jagged precipice. Even while putting across Sweetland's candidacy, the growing group of Democratic liberals was split, as liberals perennially divide and square off at one another. In that presidential-election year, a strong movement for Henry Wallace, the Progressive candidate, siphoned off much of the left-wing support Sweetland attempted to muster for

Truman. And Howard Morgan, now a rancher, was elected to the state legislature, defeating Progressive and Republican opponents.

As National Committeeman, Sweetland made periodic trips to Washington to muster all the help the Truman administration could give to a struggling local party—patronage, funds for organization work and public works for which local Democrats could claim credit. Back home, he had to contend with the dominant conservative disposition of old-guard Democrats still holding local positions of authority in the counties and in the precincts. To Sweetland and his fellow liberals, Wayne Morse was an attractive figure before he ever entered partisan politics. While Morse was still serving on the National War Labor Board in 1943, Sweetland urged him to run for the Senate against Holman. "We really wanted him to change his registration and become a Democratic candidate, but this seemed both impractical and unlikely of success," recalls Sweetland. It was still too early. When Morse became a Republican senator, he had much covert support from these same Democratic liberals. Finally events permitted them to support him openly and force a showdown that changed the entire face of Oregon's politics and, ultimately, its representation in Congress.

It was 1950. Morse was bedeviled by attacks from the conservatives of both parties during his first re-election fight. Having won renomination over Deadwood Dave Hoover in a bitter fight within the Republican party, Morse was coming up against a conservative Democrat, Howard Latourette. Sweetland dutifully went to Washington seeking party funds to help Latourette, although his heart wasn't in it. Sympathetic to Morse's liberalism, Sweetland was torn by duty to aid his party's nominee. He secured $2000 for Latourette's campaign. But Latourette rejected the financial support of what he loudly regarded as the socialistic Democratic National Committee. This act gave Sweetland and the liberals just cause to embrace Morse's candidacy openly. One of Latourette's pre-election stunts was to drop thousands of tiny air-borne leaflets over the Portland business district. On the front of the leaflet was a grim-faced Latourette, self-described as one who "has never played with Pinks or Communists." On the other side were pictures of three men described as "strange fellow travelers." They were Harry Bridges, Wayne Morse, and Monroe Sweetland. Although this was the beginning of the weird McCarthy era, Oregonians gave Latourette's Red scare little heed. With the united support of progressive-minded Democrats and Republicans, Morse got more than three out of every four votes to flatten Latourette by 260,000 votes.

The Democrats won no high offices. But Sweetland, encouraging the rank and file of his party through a monthly magazine, the *Oregon Democrat*, noted that "there were many Democratic victories throughout Oregon for courthouse jobs long monopolized by Republicans." The heavy spadework in the grass roots was beginning to pay off. To Sweetland and Morgan, Wayne Morse's triumph was a moral victory for the liberalism with which they were trying to infuse their own party. Having backed Morse, they could vicariously share in the sweetness of this victory. But agree as he might with their views on current affairs, Morse was still a Republican, whose successes were bound to hamper the growth of the new democracy they were trying to spread. Unless . . . unless Wayne Morse could be persuaded to leave the Grand Old Party.

Enticement

"After 1950," Sweetland explains, "it seemed apparent that sooner or later, Senator Morse would have to come over formally to the Democratic party, and I believe that he saw the handwriting on the wall as well." Sweetland saw the handwriting in the Republican primary when 40 per cent of the G.O.P. vote went to Deadwood Dave Hoover and John McBride in their anti-Morse campaign. "It was quite clear that they would never again let him win a nomination, and that all that was lacking as early as 1950 was the failure of the conservative Republicans to mount a substantial candidate against him. Nevertheless, Senator Morse was most reluctant to break his ties with the G.O.P."

In 1952 he finally did. This was the year Howard Morgan, thirty-eight, was elected Democratic state chairman by one vote. He and Sweetland now held the twin posts of organizational power. A tough guy in a Brooks Brothers suit, Morgan was equal to the task of knocking heads together within the organization while giving the party the image of youthful, intelligent vigor it so sorely needed. That year an old-guard Democratic state senator, Thomas R. Mahoney of Portland, was defeated for re-election and roared sourly, "Morgan and Sweetland have wrecked the Democratic party—and they can have it."

Clearly the times were now passing by these old-guard Democrats who had helped make many Oregon Republicans appear attractively modern by contrast, these unreconstructed Democrats who spent more energy flailing the liberals who threatened their party security than trying to unseat the G.O.P. Although the old-guard Democrats won few seats in the legislature, those who were successful gained a certain notoriety. The Pendleton *East Oregonian* polled newspapermen who had covered the 1951 session on their choices for best and worst legislators. "Democrats dominated the lists of worst senators and representatives," the liberal newspaper observed. "The reporters know. And, unfortunately for the Democratic party, so do the majority of voters."[1]

The proof of whether the party was being wrecked by internal factionalism or being rebuilt upon contemporary liberal policies could be secured only by victory at the ballot box, and Morgan and Sweetland knew this accomplishment depended upon finding and advancing good candidates. The quest was twofold: to encourage promising young men to enter the lists; and to entice that proven war horse who now called himself an Independent into the Democratic party. In the spring of 1953 Morgan invited Morse to be the party's annual Jefferson-Jackson Day dinner speaker, the role normally reserved for the most authentic and highest-caliber party figures. Old-guardist Lew Wallace exploded: "It is the Christmas of the Democratic party. It should have a speaker who is a registered Democrat." Morse was still registered as a Republican at the Lane County Courthouse, although by now he could outdo any Democrat anywhere, any time in heaping mementos of disrespect high upon the party of his past. Quite aside from the strategy of enticement Morgan was pursuing, the choice of Morse was designed to rally the forces of Oregon liberalism and damn the conservatives. Their speaker was given a rousing welcome. No longer did he need wear a protective cloak of conservativism in Oregon.

Sweetland, meanwhile, had gone to Washington, where he buttonholed liberal Democratic senators to ask them to back up Morse's efforts to regain his old committee posts; accompanied Morse to a committee hearing at which they jointly thumped the table against the private power companies of the Pacific Northwest for having slapped a surcharge on their customers during a temporary regional power shortage; and arranged for Americans for Democratic Action

[1] One of those rated the best was Richard L. Neuberger.

to elect Morse to its board of directors. The working alliance was being strengthened.

Morse, however, wanted *only* an alliance. He wanted to continue to call himself an Independent with assurances that the Democratic party leaders in his state would endorse his candidacy at election time. Morgan advised him that this was impossible, both for the Democratic party and for Morse. In a meeting at the home of Ken Rinke, then the party chairman of Multnomah County (Portland), the morning after Morse made that J-J dinner address, Morgan laid before Morse election statistics which showed pretty conclusively that he could not be re-elected if he ran as an Independent. He was warned that only the Republicans would win out in a three-cornered race. Morse at length acknowledged that he had drawn the same conclusion from his own analysis of election figures, but he persisted in the desire to maintain his independence, with liberal Democratic endorsement.

Oregon's Other Senator

Simultaneously in 1953, Oregon's other senator, as many referred to Republican Senator Guy Cordon, was reaching that time of decision from which most politicians shrink. At sixty-four, after a decade as the effectively conservative successor to Charles L. Mc-Nary, Cordon had to decide whether to seek another six-year term. A self-made lawyer of the old school who shrank from the public demands imposed upon a modern politician, Morse's taciturn colleague abhorred the engines of publicity which he saw men about him cranking up with daily resolve. "Newspapers," he once grumbled, "are the cause of 90 per cent of the world's troubles. They just get people stirred up over nothing."

The Senate has seldom housed a man so determined to hide his light under a bushel. Whether or not Morse's colorful performances made him all the more determined to be the silent workman, the fact was that Cordon was virtually unknown to the public at large, even in his home state of Oregon. Yet by all the normal standards of legislative workmanship, Cordon deserved a wide reputation, if only for having masterminded a long legal effort which resulted in seventeen western Oregon counties' receiving the most beneficial arrangement ever made for sharing in federal timber receipts from sustained-yield management of the old Oregon & California Railroad timberlands. It was for his legal prowess and success in this cause that Cordon was appointed to the Senate upon the death of McNary, with whom he had closely worked to pass the O&C Act of 1937. Cordon was a bedrock conservative, essentially an isolationist, a Taft man within the Senate who gave his loyalty to the modern Republicanism of President Eisenhower after Bob Taft had reshaped it to match his own philosophic aspirations. Cordon was one of the last of the old-guard Republicans who made no visible concessions to groups such as labor, who were growing in strength and demanding a larger, not a lesser, role for the federal government in modern America.

When Guy Cordon had made his decision, he called in Oregon Congressman Walter Norblad, a ten-year veteran of the House with obvious ambitions to advance to the Senate, and said, "I've decided not to run. You can run for my Senate seat." After Congress adjourned, Cordon drove to the airport to return to Oregon and announce publicly his decision to quit. But before he could board his plane, Cordon received a telephone call from the White House. The senator heard his chief, President Eisenhower, implore him not to announce his decision until he had returned to Washington and they could talk it over. Cordon agreed and kept silent. When he returned to face the obvious party appeal that he run once more, Cordon could not turn down the President, so new in office, so dependent upon experienced Republicans on Capitol Hill to implement a program the G.O.P. had waited out the long years of New Deal-Fair Deal government to put into being. Cordon had taken on the painstaking, and politically vulnerable, task earlier that year of drafting and defending in the Senate the tidelands oil bill. Could he now retire those talents when the battle was still to be decided at Hells Canyon, at John Day, or wherever the electric utility industry now opposed federal-government construction of hydroelectric dams? Cordon would do his duty and run, taking perhaps for granted that to run with party blessing was to win in safe-and-sound Republican Oregon.

Although Senator Cordon was possibly the last Republican to realize it, the time had passed when Republicans could take victory for granted in Oregon. From the precinct up, the Democrats had been rebuilding. Sweetland had discovered that Oregon ranked high among the northern and western states in percentage of unregistered but eligible voters. He reasoned that one-party domination of state politics had discouraged Democrats from registering. Many of these

Democrats were newcomers who had come to Oregon during the war to work in shipyards and aluminum plants. By stimulating the Junior Chamber of Commerce, the League of Women Voters, and even the Republicans to engage in voter-registration campaigns, Democratic leaders reasoned their party would make net gains.

While Senator Cordon was wrestling with his decision, Richard Lewis Neuberger of Portland was anxiously taking the pulse of Oregon Democracy. As one of the young avant-garde liberals who had gone to the state legislature, Neuberger was both entitled and encouraged to run for governor or U. S. Senator. But did the party with the new liberal face have the muscle to carry a major state-wide campaign? Neuberger had drawn back from a gubernatorial campaign in 1950. But in 1954 Guy Cordon appeared to the Democrats to be a ready-made target for the ambitious young man with the angry typewriter.

As a free-lance writer, Neuberger had earned considerable personal fame in twenty years of highly productive writing about his native habitat. Everything scenic or political was grist for his mill, as he turned out six books and a prolific file of articles to virtually every magazine that printed non-fiction. Much of his work consisted of serious political commentary, which appeared in the liberal journals of opinion, notably the *New Republic* and *The Nation.* The byline Richard L. Neuberger became the hallmark of the Pacific Northwest's number-one political critic.

But literary renown was not enough. During high school days in Portland, where he was a cub reporter at the *Oregonian*, another newcomer on Portland's morning paper recalls that Neuberger needed little help. "He had it from the start. And it was evident almost from the start that we had different goals. I wanted to be a good newspaperman. Dick knew from the beginning that he didn't want to stop there. Dick and I had the best of relations over many years, but there are some old-timers at the *Oregonian* who will tell you that he was a brash kid who was determined to get there at any expense." An editor recalls that he "made a lot of enemies. He always appeared to be after the next man's job." Ambition, not yet focused on political attainment, was revealed in such small things. There was the time when the *Oregonian* received a news release, written by Neuberger from the coastal town of Gearhart, reporting in dead seriousness that Richard Neuberger had been runner-up in a ping-pong tournament.

Neuberger's rise to political fame was not a one-man affair. When

he ran for the State Senate after a stint in the House, he induced his
wife, Maurine, to run for the House. Running in Democratic Multnomah County presented no major obstacles at election time. Together they became the Neuberger legislative team, outspokenly
liberal in a legislature utterly dominated by conservatives. They
were not without their victories, but much of the time this part-time
political career served as the base of operations and the fountainhead
of material that went into Neuberger's reformist articles and books.
"Evidently martyrdom suits our personalities," he once wrote of
their lonely position.

By 1954, when the time had come for a fling at the big time,
Neuberger was the best-known Democratic name in the state. This
is not to say he was uniformly well regarded. Neuberger later recalled that many people turned out at meetings during his Senate
campaign just to see what the Neubergers looked like. They were a
political curiosity that took some getting used to. Besides, it was
still not altogether respectable in many middle-class Oregon circles
to be admittedly a Democrat. Uncompromisingly liberal, Neuberger
was an apostle of the new Democracy which Sweetland and Morgan
had been promoting. Now it had come to maturity in the form of
a vigorous campaigner who challenged conservative Republicanism
on the issues. It remade the whole political complex of the state before it was over.

But Neuberger's entry into the Senate race provoked a minor crisis
within the party. Sweetland had decided to run for Congress that
year from the heavily Democratic district which embraces Portland.
The incumbent was an aged Republican, Homer D. Angell. Neuberger shortly before the filing deadline presented Morgan, the
party chairman, with an ultimatum: that unless he stopped Sweetland from running for Congress, Neuberger would either withdraw
and write a complete story of backstage maneuvers, or he would
enter his own candidate against Sweetland and campaign for that
rival. Morgan didn't need a blueprint to know that Neuberger meant
business, and that his secret candidate would be his wife, Maurine.

Returning to headquarters, Morgan encountered Sweetland and
was promptly told that the national committeeman intended to
announce his candidacy within twenty-four hours, no matter what
Neuberger or Morgan said. Morgan contrived a neat device for
heading off Sweetland. He called the Portland newspapers and gave
them a statement renouncing any intentions of his own for running

for the State Senate. At the close of his statement Morgan said, "There is no more comic and disruptive figure in politics than the party official whose unbiased search for the ideal candidate comes to a joyful end one morning in front of his own shaving mirror." Sweetland got the message and drew back.

Neither Morgan nor Neuberger wanted Sweetland to run that year. They feared his Socialist background would endanger the whole ticket because McCarthy was then riding high. Democratic National Chairman Stephen Mitchell followed Morgan's gambit by telling Sweetland that he was not alone in being sidetracked as a 1954 candidate. Robert Maynard Hutchins, liberal president of the University of Chicago, was another, Mitchell said.

The consequence of this maneuvering was that Edith Green, a former schoolteacher and public-relations director for the Oregon Education Association, became the Democratic nominee for the Portland congressional seat; Neuberger kept his secret candidate under wraps; and the Morgan-Sweetland team separated.

Immediately after the primary election of that year, Morse asked Morgan, "If I should become a Democrat, when should I change my registration, before or after the 1954 election?" Morgan asked for time to evaluate the political effects and sound out rank-and-file Democrats; but from that time on Morgan knew that Morse was ready to take the final step of his party transition. The timing remained to be determined. There was no question but what Morse was prepared to campaign for Neuberger in opposition to Cordon, his Republican colleague for eight years. Privately Cordon told friends he hoped Morse would campaign for Neuberger, so confident was he that Oregon would never stand for Wayne Morse on these terms.

Morse wanted to avoid registering as a Democrat before or during the Neuberger-Cordon campaign, so as not to be accused of trying to stampede the election of a Democrat. By the same token, he wanted to avoid registering after the election, for if Neuberger won he might be accused of simply climbing on the Democratic bandwagon. So Morgan and Morse arranged for him to obtain a registration form during the campaign, fly to Washington just before election day, fill out the form and send it by registered mail to the Lane County Courthouse, where it would arrive after the election. The stage was thus set for Oregon to get two liberal Democratic senators.

The first phase of the Neuberger campaign was to acquaint the voters with "Oregon's other senator." The man they only dimly knew as Morse's quiet colleague was portrayed as the principal villain who worked hand in glove with the special interests at the expense of the public. With vivid colors, Neuberger painted Cordon as a sinister reactionary who had piloted the tidelands oil giveaway through Congress at the expense of school children who otherwise would have been the beneficiaries of the "oil for education" plan of the liberals. He was the culprit in the Senate who was trying to put through Interior Secretary McKay's nefarious scheme to wreck full development of the Columbia Basin by cutting the private utilities in on valuable dam sites such as Hells Canyon. This incumbent senator, Oregonians were told and retold, had opposed with isolationist conviction the North Atlantic Treaty Organization to which General Eisenhower was so dedicated. He was even against free school lunches. How could they, in the middle of the twentieth century, keep a man like that in Washington?

By the time Cordon had returned from Washington in September, he was hopelessly on the defensive. While Neuberger was nightly tapping out press releases on an old Royal portable for the next day's newspapers, Cordon was floundering about, wondering how to take hold of this tough-punching challenger. His natural abhorrence of publicity and speechmaking only aggravated his problem. Most of the state's daily newspapers were coming to his rescue on the editorial pages, but how many more voters were reading Neuberger's charges on the front pages? Editor Charles A. Sprague, whom Neuberger had rightly called the "conscience of Oregon" two years before in an article in *The Nation*, brought the hurly-burly Neuberger attacks into sober perspective in his column in the *Oregon Statesman*: "Like Amos and Andy, 'we's regusted' with this type of campaigning. Cordon and McKay are not pirates and not dumb tools of special interests. They are trying to serve the public interest in all honesty and prudence. As the *Oregonian* said the other day in pointing out the fraud of the 'Stop, Thief' attacks: 'These attempts to make blackguards and looters of the public domain out of respected officials insults the intelligence and competence of the people who voted them in before.' Differences in judgment on how resources should be managed should not be exaggerated into imputing evil design in the making of decisions." Sprague abhorred such extreme charges as Neuberger's claim that Cordon evidently "plans to turn over the national forests and national parks to big timber monopolies." Sprague disagreed with Cordon and McKay on disposition of the tidelands, and he was critical of Cordon's semi-isolationist views, but his conscience rebelled at the character of the Democrats' campaign.

From the outset Morse moved into the campaign, calling Cordon "Mr. Giveaway" and adding, "I do not mean to slight Secretary McKay's claim to that honor. It's really a true case of Tweedledee and Tweedledum." Contributing five hundred dollars and sixty-one ripsnorting speeches, Morse took over the burden of blasting Cordon, with whom he had previously campaigned arm in arm, while Neuberger shifted to offering his program. It was a program of bread-and-butter liberalism for the Northwest—more federal dams, irrigation works, and conservation of timberlands, wildlife, grazing lands, from those who would exploit for private gain.

Election night, Dick Neuberger went to bed shortly after midnight thinking he had lost his give-no-quarter effort to land himself and the Democrats in gloryland, for Cordon had taken an early lead as the long process of counting ballots began. Neuberger and Morse had waged a hard-hitting campaign, but it had been forty years since Oregon had elected a Democrat to the Senate. Could they really expect to win? Next morning the outcome was less certain. As Neuberger clung to the telephone in the kitchen, receiving reports from Sweetland, Morgan, Jebby Davidson, and others who were analyzing the trends, the headlines in successive editions of the *Oregonian* told the story:

First State Returns Put Cordon in Front

Cordon Win Indicated: Control of Congress Still in Doubt

Cordon Holds Slight Senate Lead
Senate Control in Doubt

NEUBERGER GRABS LEAD
Democrats Win Control of House

Control of Senate Hinges on Oregon
Cordon Falls Behind in Photo-Finish With Neuberger

NEUBERGER IN——ALMOST
Oregon Upsets GOP Control of U. S. Senate

Neuberger Takes, Holds Senate Lead

When all the far precincts had reported, Neuberger was victorious by 2462 votes. What had tipped the balance? Surely the grass-roots work of the liberal Democrats was the bedrock foundation of Neuberger's victory, even though voter registration still favored the G.O.P. by 2411 voters. Surely Cordon was right when he later shouldered much of the blame for this loss by saying, "I have never been in any sense a politician." Surely Morse, with his personal following, had transplanted votes from the Republican to the Democratic candidate. Whatever the reasons, Neuberger's victory along with Congresswoman Green's triumph, plus Morse's plan to become a Democrat catapulted Oregon's liberal Democrats into positions of power for the first time.

On election eve, however, Morse scrapped his prearranged plan for mailing a registration form to Oregon. National Chairman Mitchell advised against it. He pointed out that Morse, still serving on minor committees, might have some bargaining power after the elections if control of the Senate were close. Mitchell also pointed out that the Senate was going into a post-election special session to deal with the censure of McCarthy, and he thought Morse would be more effective as an Independent.

The election returns made a sound prophet of Mitchell. Morse held the deciding vote. On the opening day of the new Senate session, he could make Lyndon B. Johnson either the majority leader or the minority leader, depending on whether he cast his vote with the Democrats or the Republicans to organize the Senate. Morse had announced before the election his intent to vote with the Democrats this time, but so long as he remained outside the party he might keep Johnson uneasy. Johnson immediately promised that the Oregon maverick "can have anything I have to give."

For Better or for Worse

But then, two weeks after the election, U. S. News and World Report published an interview with Morse which included this exchange:

Q—You're going to be a member of the Democratic party, aren't you?
A—No, I'm an Independent. Where did you get the idea I was going to be a member of the Democratic party?
Q—Some of the papers have reported you were going to join the Democratic party.

A—Well, if you read what's in the papers about me you'll read 90 per cent misinformation most of the time . . . It's my intention to run as an Independent (in 1956). I will say this, that it isn't Wayne Morse that counts, it's a sound, liberal cause that counts. There is a group of Democrats in our state quite different from some Democrats in some other places. They are making a great fight against the reactionary Republican machine in Oregon, and if I could be convinced that the best hope of a sound, liberal cause would be to join forces with them, I would not hesitate to do it. However, that is not my present intention, but I shall always keep myself free to change my opinion.

Sweetland responded to Morse's magazine remark with a public ultimatum that Morse would receive no party support if he insisted on running as an Independent. Morgan, fearful such an ultimatum would impel Oregon's proud senator to go it alone, retorted that he was confident Morse would become a Democrat if no one was "thoughtless enough" to confront him with an ultimatum. Next day Morse said he might become an independent Democrat. "But if I do, the word independent will be more important than the word Democrat," he explained.

When the Senate convened in January, Morse voted to make Johnson the majority leader; and shortly thereafter Johnson announced that the Democrats had awarded one of the coveted vacancies on the blue-ribbon Foreign Relations Committee to Wayne Morse. Also, Morse regained his seat on the Labor Committee.

A few weeks later, February 17, 1955, Morse flew into Portland and drove to the Lane County Courthouse at Eugene and filled out a new registration form as a member of the Democratic party. Howard Morgan watched with a smile as Wayne Morse signed his name. They went back to Portland to join in a rousing party celebration over his decision. "I will give you a fight in 1956, if you want to join under the Democratic banner for a clean, hard-hitting fight that will protect the best interests of the people against the monopolistic combine that has taken over the Republican part in the state of Oregon," said Oregon's newest Democrat, tossing bouquets to Neuberger, Congresswoman Green, Morgan, and Sweetland.

As Wayne Morse that night aroused the 600 celebrants at Pythian Hall, he left to the misty past his denunciations of the New Deal and the Fair Deal. On this night of cheering and new camaraderie it would have been unsporting to recall his words to the Young Republican convention at Salem scarcely six years before:

One of the troubles with the Democratic party is that it has made so many inconsistent and conflicting promises to so many economic pressure groups in America that I am sure it will find it necessary to revive as its theme song during the next administration the old ditty, Yes We Have No Bananas. However, the Democratic party is bound to slip on the peelings of its own promises.

Nor did anyone spoil that night's fun by recalling that only five years ago he had roughed up the eighteen-year Roosevelt-Truman era as one of "indecision, confusion and incompetency," or that only three years ago he said there was "no place for me in the Democratic party" because it has demonstrated over and over again that it stands for "government by men rather than government by Constitutional checks."

No, this was not the night to look back in anger. This was the night to start joyously into the future together. Morse's toughest re-election test was just around the corner. One for all and all for one.

After more than two years of wandering in the wilderness between the two major parties, stumbling into holes he hadn't seen, he had followed the light in the window which Adlai Stevenson had said would be there. Wayne Morse had at last found a more congenial political home, where he could freely speak of liberalism without fear of being hauled off to the woodshed. Now liberalism was in the saddle in Oregon. The Pacific coast's most conservative state suddenly had two exceedingly liberal and articulate Democratic senators, as well as a liberal congresswoman from its most populous district, with other new liberals getting set to chase other Republicans into retirement. More than the light in the window, Wayne Morse had recognized what Morgan and Sweetland rightly termed "the logic of the situation" if he was to advance his political career further and perpetuate the cherished legend of unorthodoxy. If he could become a nationally lauded senator bearing the conservative handicaps of the past, was there any limit upon his future as a brilliant, persuasive all-out liberal in the resurging Democratic party?

His marriage of convenience with the Republicans now over, his frantic and futile quest for blissful independence now spent, Wayne Morse went to the political altar once more to exchange vows with the Democrats, for better or for worse.

11. THE CONSTITUTIONAL LIBERAL

Old Soldiers Never Die . . . Steel Seizure . . . Textbook Lawyer

UNTIL Wayne Morse became a Democrat, the flexibility of his partisan attachments only confused those citizens who find the great game of politics harder to follow than a football game played on a very muddy field. Not only is it a bit dirty, which one has finally come to accept, but even a score card doesn't help to distinguish the liberal white shirts from the conservative blues. Like conservative Democrat Harry Byrd, liberal Republican Wayne Morse was often thought to be running toward the other team's goal.

For purposes of identification, Wayne Morse early in the game set himself apart as a constitutional liberal. There were many liberals, conservatives, radicals, reactionaries, right-wingers, left-wingers, and middle of the roaders. But there was only one constitutional liberal. It was an identity that he maintained throughout his transition from one party to the other. The origin of this identity appears to be Morse's early fear of appearing to be New Dealish. He was a liberal, yes, but one who respected the Constitution with fierce resistance to autocratic bureaucracy. The term seems to have conveyed that Morse was liberal on issues but conservative on methods.

Are there basic differences between a conservative and a liberal? A dictionary puts it this way: Conservative—opposed to hasty changes in political, religious or civil institutions; Liberal—free from narrowness in ideas and disposed to a democratic rather than aristocratic form of government. The liberal would never admit to advancing *hasty* changes, nor would the conservative ever confess to clinging to *narrow* ideas. These, nevertheless, are observable traits among those who adhere to these conflicting political ways; but each serves as a useful check upon the other, which is the strength of the American two-party system.

If the Republican party wasn't liberal enough for Wayne Morse, today it is too liberal to be pleasing to Senator Barry Goldwater. In his book, *Conscience of a Conservative*, Goldwater expressed irritation with conservatives who apologize for or qualify their commitment to conservativism. He cited Eisenhower's first-term remark, "I am a conservative when it comes to economic problems but liberal when it comes to human problems." This remark caused liberals to wisecrack that what Eisenhower meant was that he favored federal aid to education and other social-welfare programs, so long as they didn't cost any money. But to Goldwater, Eisenhower's statement was "tantamount to an admission that conservatism is a narrow, mechanistic *economic* theory that may work very well as a bookkeeper's guide, but cannot be relied upon as a comprehensive political philosophy."

This conservative apostle was equally indignant at Richard Nixon's admonition to Republican candidates to be "economic conservatives, but conservatives with a heart," for this played into the hands of the liberals whom Goldwater despises for claiming to be concerned "with human beings while you conservatives are preoccupied with the preservation of economic privilege and status." To Goldwater there is no place for a concession that some conservatives may be heartless; for as he views the American political dichotomy, "the root difference between the conservatives and the liberals of today is that conservatives take account of the *whole* man, while the liberals tend to look only at the material side of man's nature. . . . Conservatism therefore looks upon the enhancement of man's spiritual nature as the primary concern of political philosophy. Liberals, on the other hand—in the name of concern for 'human beings'— regard the satisfaction of economic wants as the dominant mission of society. They are moreover *in a hurry* . . ." (Italics mine)

One of Goldwater's fundamental conflicts with the Republican party during the Eisenhower administration was that it no longer resisted the *principle* of liberal federal programs to benefit this group or that, that it tried only to *reduce the cost*. He said the Grand Old Party, therefore, was fostering a "dime-store New Deal."

The point is that if Wayne Morse has used a flexible ideology to advantage, so has the Republican party; for most of its surviving politicians have been as pragmatic as Wayne Morse—if not so noticeable about it—in sensing the national mood since World War II.

To Goldwater's chagrin, the G.O.P. has quietly accepted the basic tenet of New Deal liberalism—the principle that it is necessary for the federal government to undertake certain social welfare programs financed by the graduated income tax. The difference between Morse and the party of his past, in this respect, is simply that the G.O.P. comes into the green pastures of contemporary liberalism reluctantly, hesitantly, and often only just before elections. Wayne Morse preferred these pastures all along, but found it expedient to graze among the conservatives and bray disdainfully at the grass of liberalism— perhaps reluctantly, never hesitantly, and usually just before election time.

But what of the philosophy of the constitutional liberal? First, where has he stood on the great constitutional tests of recent years?

Old Soldiers Never Die

The most dramatic constitutional crisis of recent years reached its constitutional climax on April 11, 1951, when President Truman relieved General Douglas MacArthur from the Korean command. This episode reached its emotional climax eight days later when MacArthur made his brilliant farewell address before a joint session of Congress. The deluge of telegrams that struck Washington from outraged citizens (the White House recorded 27,363 communications received in the first twelve days) exceeded anything in the experience of Western Union. The ugly mood of those protesting MacArthur's dismissal showed in many telegrams which congressmen inserted in the *Congressional Record.* "When an ex-national guard captain fires a five-star general, impeachment of the national guard captain is in order," one outraged citizen wired his congressman.

Truman went to the nation immediately to explain his bold act. "A number of events have made it evident that General MacArthur did not agree with that policy (of the government for trying to limit the war to Korea and prevent it from spreading to all Asia). I have therefore considered it essential to relieve General MacArthur so that there would be no doubt or confusion as to the real purpose and aim of our policy."

The next day in the Senate, amid heavy denunciation of the President from the right, Wayne Morse stood up and roared, "God help the American people if the day ever comes when we fail to retain civilian control over the military establishment." He belittled those who called for impeachment, saying, "as to his constitutional power to do it there can be no doubt."

Morse did not instantly support the *wisdom* of the MacArthur firing, because he had "serious and long-standing criticisms of President Truman and the State Department and the Defense Department for their policies in Asia." It had been "a mistake not to permit the Chiang government to proceed with guerrilla warfare in China" and "a mistake to bottle up his forces on Formosa," said Wayne Morse that day, but "I must raise my voice this afternoon in support of the President's constitutional power."

Morse explained his unwillingness to pass on the wisdom of the dismissal at that moment because he was a member of the Armed Services Committee, which was then about to undertake, in co-operation with the Foreign Relations Committee, a full inquiry of the MacArthur affair. As the inquiry progressed behind closed and guarded doors, the transcript of testimony, handed page by page to a military censor and then on to a horde of waiting newsmen, showed that Morse was questioning witnesses with the aggressive style of a district attorney in a hot murder trial. It was Morse who injected the sensational idea that a clandestine China lobby was spending vast sums to high-pressure Congress into its financial and military commitments to the Chiang regime. McMahon of Connecticut took up this allegation and joined Morse in urging an investigation to determine "if there is any improper use of funds to influence the foreign policy." From this point in mid-1951 Morse ranged himself with increasing vigor against the "Asian cult" in the Senate. The President's power to exercise his constitutional authority was only as lasting as his public support—his strength to resist impeachment. Morse worked to strengthen Truman's position.

In the weeks that ensued, thousands of constituents bombarded Morse with their reaction. The senator replied with a form letter which was more candid and forthright than most senators dared to be. Noting that he had been urged to support impeachment proceedings against the President, Morse said his support of Truman's constitutional authority had apparently led many of these citizens to the "general agreement" that he was correct on the constitutional issue. But many said, nevertheless, they thought MacArthur's divergent policies were right and those of the Administration wrong. What did Morse have to say about that?

First, let me say that I think a much different procedure should have been followed in removing General MacArthur from his command. It would have been much better if General MacArthur had been called back to Washington for a conference with the President, the Secretary of Defense, the Joint Chiefs of Staff, and the Secretary of State, before he was removed from command. While the record of the hearings shows that these officials were unanimous in the decision to remove him, it is possible that such a conference would have resulted in an understanding which would have either made it possible for General MacArthur to retain his command or at least accomplished his removal in a less summary fashion. In the absence of any such understanding, I think a decision to remove him would have been unavoidable. I say that because the record of the hearings to date supports the following conclusions:

1. General MacArthur was not in sympathy with the foreign policy of our government in Asia, as he has testified. We would not have two voices announcing to the world conflicting views as to American foreign policy in Asia.

2. General MacArthur has proposed bombing Chinese bases in Manchuria, including the Manchurian railroad, which is jointly administered by China and Russia, and blockading ports along the Chinese coast, including Port Arthur, which is a principal Russian port. Such action would increase the danger of Russia's immediate entrance into the war, thus bringing on a world-wide conflict.

3. The record of the hearings shows that our allies in the United Nations would not support General MacArthur's proposals for carrying the war to the mainland of China at this time. To do so involves the danger of creating such a serious split between the United States and her allies that we might find ourselves facing Russia alone in an all-out war. According to General Marshall's testimony, the Joint Chiefs of Staff unanimously opposed enlarging the war at this time as recommended by General MacArthur.

4. It has been my understanding for many months that our Department of Defense, as well as the State Department, and the President have been opposed to General MacArthur's proposals, because our defenses are still too weak and our major targets are too vulnerable to justify running any unnecessary risks of an all-out war with Russia at this time. The representations which have been made to us as members of the Armed Services Committee have been to the effect that if we became involved in such a conflict before our defenses are much stronger than they presently are, we would suffer tremendous casualties among our troops in Korea, Japan and on other Pacific outposts and also run serious danger of successful air raids against West Coast cities in the early weeks of such a war.

. . . .

I think we should fall back to a line of defense in Korea that we can hold without suffering heavy casualties and then with a unity of purpose unmatched in our history, we should devote our national energies to building up our defenses. Once we remove our present vulnerability by way of strong defenses, we then should make it clear to Russia and our allies that we have had enough of Russian aggression and will not tolerate any more. Then will be the time to issue ultimatums in regard to terms for an honorable peace.

Two months after the immediate national spasm was largely over, Wayne Morse made a swing around the country for a series of speeches in which he said the Senate inquiry disclosed clearly that MacArthur "was not in sympathy with the military or foreign policies" of the government. At no time, he told his listeners, did the chiefs of the military services in Washington agree to any policy of extending the war to China, and MacArthur's statement that he understood the Pentagon agreed with his war plans "just isn't so." Morse advocated, however, the resignation of Secretary of State Dean Acheson because "he has exercised some bad judgment and lost a working relationship with Congress." Returning from this tour, Morse said that he was convinced the people weren't with Taft and the Republicans on the MacArthur incident.

When the Senate inquiry was done, the committee members voted 20 to 3 against issuing the customary report of conclusions. Eight of the dozen Republican members, however, did sign a statement, prepared by Harry Cain of Washington, which included such statements as: "The testimony revealed only one positive plan for victory in the Korean war, the plan advocated by General MacArthur"; "There was no serious disagreement between General MacArthur and the Joint Chiefs of Staff as to military strategy in Korea"; and "We have not been convinced that Chiang lost China for any other reason than that he did not receive sufficient support, both moral and material, from the United States." Besides Cain, those who signed their names to these conclusions were Bridges of New Hampshire, Wiley of Wisconsin, Smith of New Jersey, Hickenlooper of Iowa, Knowland of California, Brewster of Maine, and Flanders of Vermont. Cain, wildly preoccupied with the whole Asiatic situation, for months had been calling for either a declaration of war against China and attack on the mainland, or complete withdrawal from Korea.

Two other Republicans issued their own statements. Saltonstall of Massachusetts said, "Our present task and duty are to deal with the present . . . and to look ahead . . . rather than look backward in anger and with recrimination." And Wayne Morse issued a statement which struck back hard at the Cain group's conclusions and reiterated the conclusions he had earlier reached and expressed in his letter to constituents.

The Democratic members of this inquiry panel adhered to the agreement not to issue any formal statements of conclusions. Wayne Morse thus became the sole member of the twenty-six-member panel to render a formal and firm judgment that President Truman was both constitutionally proper and strategically wise in taking the bold political step of recalling modern America's most legendary military figure.

"As the MacArthur case passes into history," said Wayne Morse philosophically, "it will have left another indelible lesson for future generations of Americans to profit by, namely, the preservation of a system of government by law requires that officials of government, both those in military and civilian posts, must not attempt to exceed their line of command or authority."

The Steel Seizure

The second great constitutional crisis of the time, Truman's seizure of the nation's steel mills in 1952, brought with it a personal crisis of new dimensions for Wayne Morse.

The Korean conflict, as it was euphemistically called, inasmuch as Congress had never issued a declaration of war nor ever been asked for one by Truman, was nearly two years old in the spring of 1952 when a wage dispute between the Steelworkers Union and the companies caused the government's Wage Stabilization Board to recommend a wage increase and a modified union shop as terms of settlement. The steel manufacturers protested these terms, the union called a strike, and Truman stepped in on April 8 with an order to Secretary of Commerce Charles Sawyer to take possession of the mills in the name of the United States, keep the furnaces hot, and maintain the production of steel. In a message to Congress, Truman said his act was "my duty and within my powers as President." He suggested that Congress might wish to pass legislation "establishing specific terms and conditions with reference to the operation of the steel mills by the government."

Taft laid down the blunt line of Republican attack, saying Truman had "usurped authority which he does not have." Democrats were divided on the issue, but many remained silently uncommitted. Morse went instantly to Truman's defense on the constitutional issue with words which even then—and much more so now—suggested intellectual arrogance:

> I should like to suggest to those whom I have heard today express themselves on constitutional law, whose views in my opinion would be laughed out of any freshman course in constitutional law in any of our law schools, they will never live so long as to read a decision of the United States Supreme Court holding that in this land in time of great national peril the President of the United States does not have the inherent power under the Constitution to protect the safety and security of the Nation until Congress gets off its haunches and proceeds to meet its constitutional obligations and perform its duty.

> I am becoming a little weary of hearing politicians, in an election year, proceed to attack the constitutional powers of the President of the United States because they dislike his partisanship, when they themselves have yet to take action under the Constitution, as it is their clear duty to take if they do not like the kind of action the President of the United States is taking in the exercise of his inherent power.

> . . . .

> This afternoon some snide remarks were made about constitutional liberals. Those remarks were amusing, of course; but I wish those who made them would take an elementary course in constitutional law. If they did, they would not make some of the interpretations of the Constitution which they have made.

Even had Morse's view of the Constitution been upheld by the Supreme Court, his sarcastic disdain for the views of other senators would have won him no support for a bill he that day introduced setting forth procedures and specific powers for the President to seize industrial property; or for another bill he shortly thereafter introduced to settle the steel dispute by granting a wage increase to the workers and a price boost to industry. The Labor Committee approved the first of these, but the Senate acted on neither.

The Supreme Court, however, did act. On June 2, 1952, it struck down the seizure as unconstitutional. The concluding words of the court's opinion, written by Justice Hugo Black were:

The founders of this Nation entrusted the lawmaking power to the Congress alone in both good and bad times. It would do no good to recall the historical events, the fears of power and the hopes for freedom that lay behind their choice. Such a review would but confirm our holding that this seizure order cannot stand.

In a word, Congress had never empowered the President with a law under which he could act as he had in the steel crisis.

The court's decision, read to a standing crowd of newsmen, attorneys, and interested citizens who jammed into the marble chamber, provoked a reaction in many quarters which was typified in the Senate by Senator Tobey of New Hampshire exclaiming simply, "Hooray!" But for the Truman administration and for Morse there was little to cheer about. They could take some small solace in the dissent written by Chief Justice Vinson which Morse said showed "much keener appreciation of the realities and dynamics of a system of government by law than does the majority."

Had the court split along what might be called ideological lines, as did the Senate on this great issue, liberals backing Truman and conservatives opposing the seizure, a way out for the Senate's constitutional liberal would have been straight and quick. But not so. The most liberal members of the court wrote powerful opinions against the steel-seizure act. The majority consisted of Hugo Black, Felix Frankfurter, William O. Douglas, Robert H. Jackson, Tom C. Clark, and Harold Burton. The minority members supporting the seizure were Carl Vinson, Stanley Reed, and Sherman Minton.

Morse, in his first years in Washington on the War Labor Board, had counseled President Roosevelt that he had virtually unlimited powers as a war leader to meet the necessities which military security pressed upon the nation and its people. Now he was confident that Truman possessed similar powers to resist any breakdown in steel production that might hurt the war effort in Korea. Morse's philosophy on this was ably conveyed in a speech to the Federal Bar Association during his War Labor Board days. In his case for an all-powerful executive during war emergencies, Morse made fair note of those who believe, as President William Howard Taft had put it, "that the President can exercise no power which cannot be fairly and reasonably traced to some specific grant of power justly implied and included within such expressed grant as proper and necessary to its exercising." But this was not Morse's view of presidential authority. His, he explained, coincided with that of Lincoln, who had seized railroads, telegraph lines, suspended the writ of habeas corpus, and taken other drastic actions during the Civil War. The heart of the matter, said Morse, was expressed by Lincoln when he defended these acts by saying:

> Was it possible to lose the Nation and yet preserve the Constitution . . . ? I felt that measures otherwise unconstitutional might become lawful by becoming indispensable to the preservation of the Constitution through the preservation of the Nation.

One of Morse's bright law students, Jim Landye, scolded his former dean on this occasion for defending Lincoln's order to his military commanders to suspend the writ of habeas corpus. "I am wondering if you ever read *Ex Parte Milligan*," Landye audaciously wrote Morse. "I suggest that you read it, to find out what happened to the suspension of habeas corpus when the courts got their hands on it."

Nonplussed, Morse replied that this famous court decision was not "at all in conflict with my thesis. *Remember that Lincoln nevertheless exercised the power and nothing that the court did or could do changed that accomplished fact.*"

But now the Supreme Court had ruled, six to three, against the inherent-power doctrine. Why? Not because the justices failed to reckon with the emergency under which Morse and the government attorneys said the President was duty-bound to act to avert a steel shutdown. Justice Douglas wrote:

> If we sanctioned the present exercise of power by the President, we would be expanding Article II of the Constitution and rewriting it to suit the political conveniences of the present emergency.
>
> . . . .
>
> We could not sanction the seizures and condemnations of the steel plants in this case without reading Article II as giving the President not only the power to execute the laws but to make some. Such a step would most assuredly alter the pattern of the Constitution.
>
> We pay a price for our system of checks and balances, for the distribution of power among the three branches of government. It is a price that today may seem exorbitant to many. Today a kindly President uses the seizure power to effect a wage increase and to keep the

steel furnaces in production. Yet tomorrow another President might use the same power to prevent a wage increase, to curb trade unionists, to regiment labor as oppressively as industry thinks it has been regimented by this seizure.

Justice Frankfurter observed:

The accretion of dangerous power does not come in a day. It does come, however slowly, from the generative force of unchecked disregard of the restrictions that fence in even the most disinterested assertion of authority.

Within this broad condemnation of the seizure order, Morse was overruled on a collateral contention as well. The argument had been advanced in the Senate that when Congress, during consideration of the Taft-Hartley Act in 1947, had rejected an amendment to give the President seizure powers during emergencies, it had, in effect, told the President he was not to exercise such powers. "What are we going to do," cried Morse, "when such sophomorism creeps into Senate debate?" Justice Frankfurter found this anything but sophomoric. Recounting in detail the defeat of seizure legislation by a three to one vote in the House and its rejection by the Senate Labor Committee, on which Morse served, Frankfurter said Congress had made it perfectly clear to the White House that the President in any future emergency should request special seizure powers through *ad hoc* legislation. The justice added:

. . . Congress said to the President, "You may not seize. Please report to us and ask for seizure power if you think it is needed in a specific situation."

Frankfurter noted that the only other instances of seizures of private property by order of the President had come during the first and second world wars.

Wayne Morse, as a constitutional authority, had come out on the very short end of this great national issue. This raised, quite naturally, a question of how soundly based is Morse's reputation as a constitutional expert and a legal scholar.

Textbook Lawyer

It is no intended slight to report that Wayne Morse is chiefly a textbook barrister. Except for the highly specialized field of labor law, in which he excels, Morse has never tried a case of any kind in a courtroom. He has made crime surveys, he has compiled data on prison-release procedures, he has been a labor arbitrator. But otherwise his has been the law of the academic world, as student and teacher.

As a law student at Wisconsin and Minnesota, Morse was above average but not a scholar. At both universities he is remembered more for his oratorical skill than his legal scholarship. At Wisconsin his undergraduate major was philosophy and he took a master's degree in speech; and for the twenty-seven credits he earned in law, his scholastic average was 84.4. At Minnesota, while teaching argumentation and coaching the debate team, he earned his law degree with a B average. Morse did not make Phi Beta Kappa or the Order of the Coif, the honor society for law students which is limited to the top 10 per cent of the class. When prospective employers asked about his scholastic record, Morse's law dean at Minnesota customarily added to these facts: "I believe that he is a better man than his law record indicates. He was handicapped by his full-time job." As a matter of fact, Morse held two jobs while studying at Minnesota. He taught full time at the university, and he taught a course at a Catholic seminary in nearby St. Paul. At Columbia Morse reported he was pulling As in his quick, successful quest of the relatively rare degree of doctor of jurisprudence. His thesis was on the grand-jury system.

As dean of the Oregon law school, Morse set out to fortify its reputation. When the problem of strengthening the law school was thrashed out in law-faculty meetings, two theories were advanced as to the most appropriate role the dean should play. One theory held that more scholarly teaching, from the dean down to the most junior instructor, was all that was needed. Dean Morse, however, held to the theory that the dean should be the promotor of his school, building its reputation through personal appearances. This not uncommon theory was one he zestfully undertook to implement. When he became involved in Pacific coast arbitration work, Dean Morse had ample opportunity to promote the law school in this semipublic assignment. "The students began to gripe, however, because he would tell them to read the next 100 pages until he returned," said one of Morse's faculty colleagues of the period.

During this period a law-faculty committee, after examining the curriculum in depth, reported disapprovingly of the practice of each law professor's being required to teach over a half-dozen separate courses instead of being permitted to specialize in but a few. The off-campus activities of any faculty member imposed a burden on others, the committee reported, and this proved detrimental to raising the quality of instruction. "Morse got so mad his chin quivered," recalled a participant in that faculty meeting. "He denied it hotly and replied that his activity was good for the university by giving it a name."

Oregon students, nevertheless, did well in their bar exams during Morse's reign. He was a popular professor, demanding but dynamic, offering personal attention to students when their work showed they required it. For all his stern, intense demeanor, the young professor was not above provoking classroom hilarity. In one class composed of men students there was one none-too-bright co-ed whom the boys had pegged as a husband hunter. "Would it be a crime," Professor Morse one day asked this fair member of the class, "if a man forcibly had sexual relations with his wife against her wishes?" The young lady looked pensively at the very serious professor, then shrugged in despair and replied, "Well, it might be a breach of the peace." The room was consumed in a howl of collegiate glee.

Morse didn't trouble himself to seek admission to the Oregon Bar until 1935. That year, under a new state Bar act, the admission of attorneys after July 1 would be governed by new, and presumably stricter, procedures established by the Oregon Bar itself. Morse hustled up to the state capitol at Salem and, four days before the new act took effect, was certified by the clerk of the Oregon Supreme Court, Arthur S. Benson, following completion of what Oregon Bar records simply record as "a special examination." Among those Oregon Republican lawyers who now despise Morse, this small incident is a hook upon which they hang professional disrespect for Morse's touted legal ability.

During his fifteen years at the University of Oregon, Morse was a regular contributor to the *Oregon Law Review* and one or two other legal periodicals. He wrote twenty articles, a number of them extracted from his doctor's thesis. He also contributed twenty-four reviews of such legal books as Felix Frankfurter's *The Labor Injunction*, Roscoe Pound's *Criminal Justice in America*, and Raymond Moley's *Politics and Criminal Prosecution*.

Nevertheless his methods and his manner did not fit the norm of legal scholasticism, in the view of his faculty colleagues. "He was not the plow horse, but the race horse who liked to feel the wind in his face," observed one of them. Not content to confine his energy and attention to becoming a savant of the law, Morse was irresistibly drawn into the vortex of events outside the cloistered school of law. "He had," as another colleague put it, "too many irons in the fire."

When he decided to run for the Senate, Morse traded on his professional credentials to tell Oregonians that he was opening a law office in Eugene. He approached a former student, Stan Darling, and a former law-faculty member, Kenneth O'Connell, who were considering establishing a law partnership. It was agreed that Morse should become affiliated with the firm of Darling and O'Connell, not as a partner but in the advisory capacity known in the profession as "of counsel." It seemed then to hold mutually beneficial prospects—for Morse, the solid professional tie in his home town that was likely to command wider respect than his status as an ex-professor and ex-bureaucrat; and for the two partners, the possible prestige of having a United States Senator's name on the letterhead, if Morse won the election.

The election over, Morse used this law office only as a Eugene base of operations during his periodic visits from Washington. He never handled any law cases nor threw any law business to Darling and O'Connell out of his important contacts as a senator. He never received any remuneration from the firm.

When Morse in 1946 was admitted to practice before the United States Supreme Court, he was sponsored by his Oregon colleague, Senator Cordon, and Clyde B. Aitchison, then a commissioner on the Interstate Commerce Commission, who affirmed "that his personal and professional character and standing are good." On his application for admission, Morse answered affirmatively the question, "Are you now or have you ever engaged in actual practice of law?" To the question about "the nature thereof," he replied, "Since February, 1944, I have been of counsel in the firm of O'Connell, Darling & Morse, Eugene, Oregon. While dean and professor of law, my work in the practice was confined to labor law, in which field

I served as labor arbitrator in more than 100 labor disputes and served as of counsel to industries on labor-law issues."

The firm did well until 1952, when a noticeable hostility developed among local businessmen because of Morse's mounting criticism of, and ultimate break with, the Republican party. Hearing indirect reports of this, Morse immediately asked that his name be stricken from the letterhead, and the association terminated so as not to handicap the firm any longer. Thus ended Morse's private law connections, never to be resumed elsewhere in the lucrative manner practiced by some less moralistic senators.

The law which Wayne Morse has practiced in the Senate is the public lawmaking in which every senator, lawyer and layman alike, fancies himself more or less qualified. In labor law, Morse has no peer in the Senate. As to constitutional law, Morse once told me that the late Senator Thomas Hennings of Missouri was probably the most expert in the Senate—a tribute to the senator who virtually singlehandedly defeated the Bricker amendment with the force and persuasion of his arguments against this attempt to limit the President's treaty-making authority.

On other occasions, as in the steel debate, Morse has been less than backward in professing his own constitutional expertise. Periodically he refers to his days as a constitutional-law professor—a reference which causes some wry smiles on the University of Oregon campus, where it is recalled that the constitutional-law course was taught by the head of the political-science department, Dr. James D. Barnett, not by Dean Morse. Morse's teaching specialty was criminal law; but he also taught the course in legislation which covered the broad spectrum of public law, from the initiative and referendum to legislative acts, reform measures, and constitutional devices. This, at the very least, prepared Morse well beyond the average member of Congress for the detailed toil of public lawmaking. Whether it or his other legal experience qualifies him as a constitutional expert is for the barristers to judge. It is enough to observe that even experts on the law frequently disagree, and the acclaimed expert is often the one with whom we find ourselves in maximum agreement.

No one engaged in partisan politics can avoid the temptation to mix partisan comments with constitutional judgments. Morse is no exception. As a Republican, he made a habit of scolding the Democrats for not meeting the high standards of constitutional liberalism, for practicing government by men and not by law. But when he became a Democrat, the party of Jefferson seemed instantly cleansed. "The Democratic party is the party predominant with Constitutional liberalism in our country today," he declared in a ringing oration to the Democratic National Convention in 1956. "True, we have a small minority of Democrats whose records are not liberal, but across the aisle of the Senate on the Republican side only a small minority of Republicans at best ever join forces with the majority of Democratic liberals in fighting for general welfare legislation."

As a Democratic constitutional liberal, Morse still mentions the need to preserve checks and balances, but he now insists that "the primary obligation" is to "use the executive and legislative processes of our government for the purpose of promoting the *general welfare* of all people without injuring the legitimate rights of the few." The "best test" of an administration is whether it implements "the great moral values of the Constitution . . . to meet the problems of ever-changing economic, political and social conditions from decade to decade by applying to those problems through appropriate legislation the basic human rights and economic rights guarantees of the Constitution."

Moving beyond the civil-rights guarantees of the Constitution, Morse invokes the "general welfare" clause of the Constitution to sanctify "bread-and-butter liberalism," to use the phrase of author James MacGregor Burns. Federal aid for school construction, public housing, teachers' salaries, student scholarships, school lunches, unemployment compensation, setting minimum wage levels, farmers' crop loans, increasing old-age retirement benefits, medical care for the aged, soil conservation, government-guaranteed mortgage loans, construction of dams generating cheap electricity and water for irrigation, as well as free navigation and flood-control benefits— all of these and more, in Morse's view, foster the general welfare. If other Democratic liberals smile at the Oregon senator's belated and unapologetic championship of modern advanced liberalism, they also agree that he has become one of its most forceful advocates.

Part Three

A MAVERICK'S UPS AND DOWNS

12. THE MORSE CODE

*No Half a Loaf . . . Morse Formula . . . Deficit Trouble
. . . Moonlighting*

"YOU always have to have a gadfly in an organization," says Harry
S. Truman, "and this is what these men were." The former President
was referring to the noted mavericks of recent Senate times, La
Follette and Norris and, inferentially, to Wayne Morse. Coming from
one who had been an exceedingly regular party senator, this estimate
of the value of the mavericks who bolted their party and scolded it
more often than they supported it, the gadflies who nipped at the
flanks of the regulars and irritated or stung them into actions they
otherwise would have avoided, was a tribute of generous dimension.

Senatorial greatness and maverick behavior are not, however, inter-
changeable. The Senate attracts extraordinary men, few of whom are
rated so super-extraordinary as to be called great. Among the mavericks, the proportion of greats is no higher than among the regulars.
There have been good and useful mavericks, and those of the other
stripe. That is to say, a senator is not necessarily a credit to the Senate
or a highly useful emissary of the nation simply because he has
broken ranks to defy the regulars, brave as standing alone might
appear. To be a maverick for the sake of preserving an image or a
legend of unyielding gadflymanship is to be an exhibitionist, not a
good Senator of the United States. However history may treat
Wayne Morse, it will have to grant that through his many ups
and downs he has been a maverick all the way.

Morse's maverickism is rooted philosophically in the famous words
of Edmund Burke, a conservative in the British Parliament who
scorned the practice by which other MPs took voting instructions
from their electors. Burke admonished them with these words in
1774:

Certainly, gentlemen, it ought to be the happiness and glory of a representative to live in the strictest union, the closest correspondence, and the most unreserved communication with his constituents. Their wishes ought to have great weight with him; their opinions high respect; their business unremitted attention. It is his duty to sacrifice his repose, his pleasure, his satisfactions, to theirs—and above all, ever, and in all cases, to prefer their interest to his own.

But his unbiased opinion, his mature judgment, his enlightened conscience, he ought not to sacrifice to you, to any man, or to any set of men living. These he does not derive from your pleasure—no, not from the law and the constitution. They are a trust from Providence, for the abuse of which he is deeply answerable. Your representative owes you, not his industry only, but his judgment; and he betrays, instead of serving you, if he sacrifices it to your opinion.

Possibly no senator is ever altogether free to vote his own unpressured judgment, never sacrificing it to the opinion of countless pressure groups. But seldom can anyone but the senator himself know whether he voted out of independent conviction or out of fear of disturbing an important economic interest. Given the American system by which politicians must go hat in hand to these interests for money to finance their re-election campaigns, there is hardly any way for a public man to be altogether free, if he cherishes his political future. As much as any senator, and more than many, Wayne Morse follows Burke's doctrine.

No Half a Loaf

During the 1960 civil-rights debate, a liberal senator remarked, "I think we ought to assign one of our men to vote with Wayne on every roll call, just so he won't have a chance to get out there all by himself." His dry humor was a subtle commentary on the attention Morse appeared to seek for standing alone against the "forces of compromise."

The heart of the Morse code is his attitude toward compromise. When he refers disdainfully to a liberal colleague as a "half-a-loaf liberal," Morse is holding to the La Follette creed which declared, "Half a loaf as a rule dulls the appetite, and destroys the keenness of interest in attaining the full loaf. A halfway measure . . . is certain to weaken, disappoint and dissipate public interest."

Like his rebel hero, Wayne Morse shuns halfway measures. He

often demands full measure or nothing. Following the La Follette style of arousing the public in behalf of a cause, he believes half measures tend to quiet public clamor for full-measure action by Congress, thereby postponing for a longer time the realization of full measures. As he put it,

> It is a great lesson of history that no progress is ever made by the masses of human beings without a long period of persuasion and education by the few. The elder La Follette did not obtain passage of any notable reform legislation during his years from 1885 to 1891 in the House, and his service from 1906 to 1925 in the Senate. He *did* leave the record of dissent from fatuousness and recommendation for programs which, together with the reforms he put through in one state as Governor of Wisconsin, were the basis for the New Deal.
>
> That greatest American legislator of our history, George Norris, performed his real service during those years from 1921 to 1933 when he kept alive the prospect of TVA, Bonneville, and Grand Coulee against the crushing political power of the private utilities and repeated offers to "compromise." In the case of his Lame Duck amendment to the Constitution, it took Norris ten years of failure and education before it could be passed in 1933.
>
> . . . .
>
> This educational function is one of the most important functions of the politician. It is the least popular and the least understood. Certainly it is the least appreciated by the press, where it is regarded as silly and irritating. But we must have more of it, not less.

Adherence to this code forces Morse into constant conflict with other liberals who believe, just as sincerely, that a step or two along the path toward their ultimate objective merits support. It may be a compromise, but they believe it is a worthy one. During his 1960 presidential campaigning against two fellow-liberal Democrats, John Kennedy and Hubert Humphrey, Morse summed up his differences with them on a Mutual broadcast as follows:

> They're great talking liberals, but time and time again when the chips are down they don't stand firm on liberal causes. They compromise liberal causes. And a true liberal never compromises a liberal cause; he takes his defeat today and waits for the dawn of a better day—recognizing that ultimate liberal victory is built on defeats, never on compromises. You compromise a liberal cause and you've destroyed it.

If this code makes it difficult for Morse to effect any great reform, it reveals why he so often stands alone, apparently unintimidated by the frequency of his defeats. It partly explains, also, why Morse's legislative reputation rests more on his success in stopping "bad" bills than passing "good" bills.

Morse, however, has had some success in pressing for full measures against half measures. Home rule for the District of Columbia is a case in point. In 1960 Eisenhower recommended that Congress give the District a territorial form of government—a governor appointed by the President, plus an elected legislative assembly. Morse regarded this as half a loaf and pressed for his full-measure home-rule bill—a mayor, school board, and city council, all locally elected. When the Senate District Committee accepted the Eisenhower proposal, the Oregon maverick took his fight to the Senate floor.

For some senators and a not inconsiderable number of local residents, the consequential difference here was the racial consideration: the President, they were confident, could always be counted upon to select a proper leader, meaning an upstanding citizen of *their* race; but the people could not be counted upon to be so reliable. If Wayne Morse were the most ineffective of blabbermouths that his sharpest detractors deem him to be, it is inconceivable that in this circumstance he could have persuaded the Senate to reject the bill favored by a majority of its District Committee and by the White House and to pass in its place his own more controversial measure. And yet he did.

In so doing, the Senate was probably paying tribute to Morse for devoting himself admirably to this, the civic responsibility of the Congress. Long after he had been elevated once more to posts on the powerful Legislative Committee, Morse by choice retained his place on the District Committee and pursued with continued vigor Washington's municipal problems.

The other side of this coin is that the Senate is not disposed to let Morse gain the power that accrues to the District Committee chairman, if that can conveniently be managed. A veteran Democratic senator who is a member of the inner council which manages such affairs with quiet firmness once explained to me that it was one of Nevada Senator Alan Bible's duties to remain on the District Committee as its chairman, because if he left that post, "you know what that would mean." What that would mean is that the senator next in seniority, Wayne Morse, would automatically become the

chairman. Irrelevant to the great national issues as is the work
of the District of Columbia Committee, the leaders still favor the
power of its chairman being held by regular Bible rather than
maverick Morse.

This has not disheartened nor really handicapped Morse, as
his home-rule victory indicates. The obstacle to home-rule enactment
has been the chairman of the House District Committee, Representative John L. McMillan of South Carolina, who is unsympathetic to giving the vote to District residents, over half of
whom are of another race than he. McMillan never reports the bill
out of his committee. However undemocratic this may seem, Morse,
too, has blocked what he thought was "bad" legislation, such as
an increase in the District sales tax, by threatening to talk it to
death near the adjournment hour.

Morse's usefulness to the capital city has been further demonstrated
in his insistence on creation of a school-lunch program in the
elementary schools to provide at least one daily square meal to
those 7000 youngsters which the Board of Education believes to be
in such need. Here it was a matter of prying loose necessary funds
and being willing, as Morse is usually not willing, to take less than
full measure. Failing to get funds for the 7000 initially, he settled
for 2000 and lectured the local officials that this was to be increased
the following year. In 1960 the program was doubled.

Morse Formula

As an opponent of dubious bills, Morse is more effective than in
pressing for full measures. At the close of World War II he noted
that the work of his military subcommittee had suddenly expanded,
due to many bills introduced to give away surplus military property.
From Sherman tanks rusting in the Philippines to abandoned training camps in the States, this property had some value, possibly
small but possibly great. "There were too many members of the
Congress who were making a political grab bag out of the reservoirs
of surplus property belonging to the United States," Morse advised the Senate in a 1950 speech. "It was shameful that an attempt
would be made to get for nothing for a city or county or a state
very valuable pieces of surplus property by means of the introduction
of bills and subsequent log-rolling or steam-rolling of those grab-bag
bills through the Congress of the United States." To check this

drift, the Armed Services Subcommittee devised a simple rule which the full committee agreed should be applied to all such bills passing through that committee to stop giveaways of military property. The rule was that if the property were to go for a private purpose, the recipient would pay 100 per cent of the current fair market value; and if for a public purpose, the price would be cut to 50 per cent. In fairness to all the taxpayers, no local recipient of federal property was to receive it scot-free.

What was a just rule for military transactions, Wayne Morse thought should apply equally to non-military transactions, say a veterans' hospital or an ancient postal facility which the government was willing to relinquish. Bills affecting transfers of non-military property were cleared through other committees on which Morse did not serve. Consequently Morse began to examine all property-transfer bills, insisting that they include the "Morse formula." Minor bills of this character, after clearing a committee, normally are placed on the so-called consent calendar, a docket of bills not considered of sufficient importance to require scheduling for formal debate. On a designated afternoon the clerk will call off these bills one by one by their titles; a designated group of senators from either party having cleared them in advance, they will thereupon be swiftly passed—unless one or more senators object. A single objection causes a bill to be dropped to the foot of the calendar, where it may be reached the next time the consent calendar is called. Morse or any senator can prevent any of these bills from passing indefinitely, unless its sponsors arrange to have it called up for formal debate. In that event, it becomes subject to unlimited debate and can be passed by a majority vote like all major legislation.

Since the Senate is reluctant to occupy itself long over any such minor bills, the Oregon maverick was quick to discover that his power to block these bills on the consent calendar was in itself the leverage needed to insist on the Morse formula. Thus for years bill after bill has come under his scrutiny, either to be rejected for lack of compliance or made to comply with an amendment carrying the formula. No one has challenged Morse's assertion that this formula has saved the federal government hundreds of millions of dollars.

The cost to Wayne Morse in terms of good will within the Senate, it appears, may be equally high, not because an incorruptible police-man is always despised by the racketeers, but more because Wayne

Morse has sometimes appeared the martinet rather than the wise judge. There have been cases in which the Senate has thought it unreasonable of Morse to insist on his formula, as in the 1956 case when it passed, over his protest, a bill granting .8085 of an acre of land for a Boy Scout recreational ground at no cost. To Wayne Morse it is unthinkable not to impose the same terms on the Boy Scouts of America as on the United States Steel Corporation for a patch of federal land.

A veteran Democratic senator who thinks well of Morse after long experience with him explains it this way: "He has this Morse formula. Nobody understands it, and even Wayne couldn't define it to cover all situations. But he's proud of it, and he insists on applying it to every transfer of property—whether it's a couple of acres for a ball park or what. This irritates senators. They may have helped him on some proposal, and when they want to get something approved, Morse insists on applying his formula. They can't go to him on a personal basis. He has reduced his influence by insisting on it." Why, then, does he do it? "Well, all these fellows around here are egotists. Morse is more of one than many others. He feels his people back home can understand this, when they can't understand the fine points of many other things he does."

There appears to be a good bit to this explanation. In his weekly Oregon radio talk, he periodically speaks of his latest triumph in applying the Morse formula in his fight for "economy in government." The names of other members of Congress are usually not mentioned, but they are nonetheless cast as villains against whom one bold knight fearlessly rides to the taxpayers' rescue. In one such broadcast in 1960 Morse reported to his constituents: "Politicians were dipping their political hands into surplus federal property, in no small sense I may say, for their own personal, political benefit."

How do these "politicians" react when he spoils their plans? Morse told his listeners that Senator Vandenberg once came to him, after failing to pass a bill to give federal property to the city of Detroit, and said, "Wayne, I hope you never give up your fight for the Morse formula. Although I tried to get this bill through because the city of Detroit wanted it, I want you to know I'm glad you made the fight and won." Morse then concluded his broadcast by saying, "And that happens many times on the part of other senators, although they will oppose me at the time. Once I win on the Morse formula they come to me in the cloakroom and they say, 'We're glad you made the fight.'" On what other broadcast are the vanquished villains so large-minded?

It is a cardinal principle of the Morse code to deal impersonally with big and little affairs of state. It is abhorrent to him that other senators seek to gain their objectives or to enhance their own standing in the Senate through cultivation of personal friendships, the friendly arm around the shoulder, the after-hours drink in some Capitol hideaway. "Politics is full of this kind of man, whose motivation is in his personal prestige, his entree into a kind of ruling class, the general approbation of the press and public, rather than in any progress he hopes to put into operation through political practice," says Morse. "There is many a man in politics for whom the fear of being frozen out of this inner circle is enough to produce whatever acquiescence the group is asking of him."

Morse's assertion of disdain for those whose success is secured with shrewdly dispensed personal favors is supported by his behavior. In his fierce insistence on adherence to the Morse formula, for instance, he has employed his most searing rebukes against senators with whom he has had the closest personal and ideological affinity, Aiken of Vermont and Douglas of Illinois, to name two. It is as though he has to prove quite loudly that no friend of his can soften him up or expect favorable concessions.

Just plain camaraderie comes hard to Morse, odd as this strikes those who have met him for the first time and found him friendly, gracious, even charming, brimming with amusing anecdotes from his many past adventures. He avoids forgathering with senators in their private dining room, preferring to lunch across the hall with visitors who are his guests in the regular Senate dining room. During the all-night sessions of the Senate during the 1960 debate on civil rights, the old Supreme Court chamber in the Capitol was converted into a dormitory of cots where the troops who braved the Dixie filibuster might share their ordeal together, gaining strength and *esprit de corps* for the cause. As a practical matter, their makeshift sleeping quarters were but a few steps from the Senate chamber, where quorum calls through the night brought them from their beds. Upon this senatorial togetherness Wayne Morse cast a heavy frown. The aloneness of a hard leather couch in his private office, ten times more distant from the Senate chamber, was more his style.

Senator Charles McNary of Oregon, the long-time Republican

Senate leader during the New Deal era, created the "Oregon Club," which met as a rule at the close of a day's Senate business. To these gatherings McNary invited any solid male citizen of his state who happened to be in town. There they met and became acquainted with other leading senators who enjoyed this pause for refreshment and conviviality. A regular member of this club, Guy Cordon, upon succeeding McNary in the Senate, carried on the custom. Wayne Morse, who shuns the strong beverages commonly dispensed at the Oregon Club, avoided its meetings upon his arrival in Washington. A mutual friend of both Morse and Cordon once dragged Morse to a club gathering in Cordon's office. "The mood of the group changed completely after Morse arrived," a participant reports. The easy informality, the candid give-and-take was mystically converted into the uncomfortable chitchat of polite strangers. Wayne Morse was and remains a stranger to this social custom by which others relax and let off steam.

A teetotaler, Morse is not, however, a temperance crusader. A colleague reports Morse succumbed to a single glass of wine when they once visited Paris together. During the war, Morse and William H. Lawrence, a New York *Times* correspondent, lost a bet about the fall of Singapore. They paid off in bottles of scotch.

When his office staff secretly ordered champagne for the wedding reception of one of his daughters, he grinned and paid the bill, but didn't join in the fermented toasts. Morse says this part of his personal code came from his father's admonitions against Demon Rum.

Periodically he condemns Washington's giddy cocktail-party circuit, which to him is the arena of the social climbers, political back-slappers, flattering influence peddlers, and evil influence buyers. "Too many liberals let this town get the better of them," he says. "They become black-tie drugged, duped, and doped. La Follette used to call them 'tired liberals.' No one has improved on that."

As a Pi Kappa Alpha fraternity man in college, "Wayne was a hail fellow well met," recalls a fraternity brother. The crucial difference perhaps between the college boy and the senator in this respect is that his Pi Kappa Alpha cohorts regarded Morse as a leader, even sent him once to a national convention at New York. The Senate, taking him for the loner that he is, has regarded his quest for leadership with vast suspicion, choosing to contain him behind its will to entrust leadership only to the party regulars.

But no senator, least of all an intellectually vigorous dissenter like Morse, can be safely contained by the regulars when they are embarked upon a delicate enterprise whose success demands quiet assent. In the spring of 1960 certain wives of members of Congress prevailed upon their husbands to introduce legislation to permit four acres of pleasantly wooded park land in Washington to be developed as a headquarters of the Congressional Club. This innocent organization, comprising only wives, mothers, and daughters of senators and representatives, sent to each member of Congress a letter explaining everything the ladies considered relevant to their request: their old headquarters was "inadequate for many of our functions, the location [on New Hampshire Avenue] has deteriorated and the parking facilities are woefully meager"; "the club has been seeking a site which would lend itself to the prestige and needs of the organization"; "There is no involvement of Federal funds." Upon this cheerful and prestigious site along Massachusetts Avenue's "embassy row," the ladies had determined to erect a $350,000 structure, assuming the Congress would co-operate by gracefully granting their wish for a ninety-nine-year lease to the park land, rent free.

Mrs. Joseph L. Miller, not a club member but the recreation chairman of a local citizens' group, protested that the proposal smacked of nepotism. Congressman Joe L. Evins of Tennessee gallantly defended the club ladies against this "pretty farfetched objection" to their splendid plan for utilizing "surplus lands." At which point the tiger roared, "This is a clear violation of the Morse formula. It is also a shakedown of the taxpayers." Possibly this influenced the ladies in later abandoning their rosy plan.

The Morse code extends to matters of personal finance. As Gunther observed, Morse did not place his wife's name upon the Senate payroll by designating her as an office employee, a device not infrequently used in the past by members of Congress to shore up the family exchequer. When he travels on Senate business and takes Mrs. Morse with him, he insists on paying her expenses and making public note of this, to the discomfort of some others who have been criticized for taking their wives on official junkets all about the world. A State Department official recalls that once after the Morses returned from a Latin American trip to which he had been assigned, the senator asked for a statement of the cost of their return flight on a government aircraft. He had earlier insisted on paying the added cost of hotel accommodations caused by his wife's presence. But the State Department replied that it cost the government no more to fly the plane to Washington because of Mrs. Morse's presence on it, so the senator should forget it. Soon thereafter a check from Morse arrived at the State Department, in the amount of the cost of commercial air rates for the same flight. "We had a devil of a time figuring out what to do with that check," reports the official.

It is a Morse ritual to introduce in each new Congress his pet bill which would require members of Congress and those government officials earning $10,000 or more to make annual public statements as to the sources and amounts of their private income. This, as the Senate knows, is a gadfly bill. Drew Pearson says he first suggested it to Morse in 1946 following the columnist's disclosure of stock-market manipulations by Senator Elmer Thomas of Oklahoma. Its purpose for Wayne Morse is to question the propriety of public men accepting private income in any way connected with their public duties—say, a lawyer-senator whose firm enjoys a substantial industrial clientele whose interests in Congress the senator may also serve. In this foggy area, each man must now be his own arbiter of propriety. The theory of the Morse bill is that public disclosure might nudge a man to draw the line closer to the side of unquestioned innocence of conflicting interests. As a serious legislative proposal, the bill has received no congressional attention, not even from Morse beyond the speechmaking stage. The committee in which it is always pigeonholed can recall no request from Morse for hearings on its merits. Nothing short of heavy public indignation, provoked by some disclosure of scandalous graft, is likely to stir the Senate to submit to Morse's idea. For years the Senate's payroll was a closely held secret, long after the House had opened its books to public scrutiny. Morse frequently was critical of this secrecy, but it was not until a Scripps-Howard newspaper series on congressional nepotism suddenly placed Capitol Hill on the defensive in 1959 that the Senate at last relented and ordered a statement to be published quarterly of the names and salaries of all its staff employees.

During the mink-coat and deep-freeze tempest, Morse received a sterling-silver tray and goblet from an Oregon businessman whose firm had benefited by some of the senator's activities. "I am sure this was sent in good faith," Morse told a reporter, "but this is the kind of thing that we must put a stop to" because a senator should not take gifts for "doing the kind of work he is supposed to do in his job as senator." He sent back the gift. A year later, after his bolt from the Republican party had inflamed many a G.O.P. stalwart, he received a pair of silver cuff links and a tie clasp which he did not send back. Businessmen from his home town had had them made specially for Morse by a jeweler who fashioned the image of the south end of a northbound horse to convey their sentiments about the senator. Morse offered the jewelry to the first worthy charity that asked for them, and promptly accepted the bid of Arthur E. Lorenzen, an Oregon rancher, who gave $250 to a community hospital at Hermiston. Morse publicly reported the whole episode, turning it to his political benefit.

Deficit Trouble

No one, as far as I know, has ever questioned Wayne Morse's financial honesty. His intellectual honesty, however, was challenged on a financial matter not long after he bolted the G.O.P. It arose in the midst of the Republican theme of "cleaning up the mess in Washington" in the 1952 presidential campaign. On September 18 General Eisenhower was in Iowa, promising to drive the "crooks and cronies" from Washington. Senator Nixon was whistle-stopping up the Pacific coast toward Portland as the news hit the front pages about an $18,000 fund from contributions of California business-men to defray earlier political expenses of the young Senator from California. By the time Nixon's train reached Morse's home town, Eugene, the New York *Herald Tribune* had editorially called for Nixon to withdraw from the ticket and the Democrats were in full-throated outcry. At Eugene, Charles O. Porter, later elected to Congress for two terms, had rounded up a posse of young Demo-crats from the University of Oregon, armed them with double-bar-reled signs, and galloped down to the depot to meet the varmint. "No Mink Coats for Nixon, Just Cold Cash," said one of the signs. In this political Western, curses cut the air, fists flew, Porter made a citizen's arrest on a belligerent local Republican, but Nixon escaped to the north without a scratch.

Meanwhile, back in Washington, Wayne Morse made the charita-ble observation that "It is too early to jump to a conclusion until we have all the facts in the case." He told an interviewer, "I don't think there's been any proof that Nixon's been corrupt." He noted that senators without personal means are handicapped in what is "rapidly becoming a rich man's club." He said he had to make speeches for a fee to earn $600 to $700 a month to defray expenses his salary doesn't cover.

But several weeks after Nixon's famous Checkers speech, when it had been proposed that the presidential and vice-presidential candidates make public statements about their income, Morse accused Eisenhower and Nixon of "stalling" and said it was a "simple matter to turn over to the press their office copy of their tax returns." The Portland *Journal*, which was backing the Democratic ticket, gave Morse's statement prominence on its front page October 11, a week before Morse announced he would vote for Stevenson. A few days later the *Oregonian* reported that two prominent Portland bankers had raised a fund of about $13,500 to meet Morse's political debts in 1945 after his election to the Senate. Wayne Morse, it suddenly appeared, was the beneficiary of privately donated funds just as Dick Nixon had been.

The bankers' fund for Morse was different from Nixon's fund in this respect: the bankers raised the money to pay off a campaign deficit which hung over Morse after his successful 1944 campaign, whereas the Nixon fund was designated to meet current political expenses of Nixon during his service in the Senate. Morse's campaign deficit, about $15,500, had been paid by a personal friend, E. D. Conklin, a San Francisco businessman. Morse was endeavoring to repay Conklin from speaking fees. He had whittled it down by about $1500 when his Eugene editor friend, William M. Tugman, heard about it and advised that his campaign backers ought to raise some more money to take the load off their newly elected senator. E. B. McNaughton, then president of the First National Bank of Portland, agreed and soon raised about $6000. McNaughton mentioned the matter to E. C. Sammons, president of the United States National Bank, one day at the Arlington Club.

Sammons had become acquainted with Morse in his university days when the banker had served as chairman of the finance committee of the State Board of Higher Education. In those days when Sammons went before a state legislative committee in support of funds for an educational program, he frequently took Dean Morse with him as an advocate. "He was a crackerjack, none better," recalls Sammons, long a respected civic leader in Oregon. When he pitched in to help wipe out Morse's debt, Sammons sent letters to leading businessmen suggesting they each chip in $250. Many followed that suggestion. Sammons put in $500 himself, and Aaron Frank of Meier and Frank's department store put in $1000. A few small checks for $10 and $25 also came in, but $250 was the average donation. Sammons told his business friends that Morse wanted to be like a judge when he got to the Senate, that lifting this burden would make it possible for him to be a better senator for Oregon than if he were out making speeches for pay. In about a month Morse's financial slate was clean.

Before the reporter wrote his story, he telephoned Morse in Washington for comment. Said Morse, "I've never handled my campaign money. I don't know how much it was. That's what bothers some of those fellows out there. *They can't give me money and so they can't tie me up. The reason these guys haven't been able to handle me is that they haven't been able to get me under obligation to them.*"

Was Morse ignorant of the identity of his benefactors? Sammons showed me carbon copies of personal letters Morse had written to each of them thanking them for their contribution. And what of Morse's remark imputing evil designs to these benefactors? "I told Wayne Morse," says Sammons, " 'I'll never ask you for a thing. If you'll do as you say you will, be like a judge on the bench, listen to the evidence and act accordingly, that's all I want.' And he said that he would."

Sammons later served as the finance chairman of Morse's 1950 re-election campaign. The banker says he respected Morse's financial integrity, which he felt was demonstrated when Morse, in 1945, declined a $3500 contribution to his deficit fund offered by a Washington lobbyist and another for $5000 from the CIO. The senator in those days had a rule against accepting financial help from unions, an idealistic one that he later abandoned when pressed by the grim realities of underwriting a hard election contest. But as a freshman, his code was ideally high.

What, then, was all the shouting about? For one thing, there was nothing wrong with the McNaughton-Sammons kitty which erased Morse's campaign deficit. It was handled in the best of possible fashions, and the contributions to it were no different from the many made before the election by the same persons among many others. Raising money from private donors to conduct election campaigns is one of the cruelest burdens placed upon public men in this country. The wonder is that there is not more crookedness than there is. And yet who is to know how many ostensibly objective acts of government—a rider on a bill here, a change in specifications for a government contract there—are designed to please, if not to favor, the most generous underwriters of election campaigns? But so long as this is the system, it was far better for Morse's deficit contributions to be solicited by two respected leaders of the business community than for the senator himself to be soliciting financial aid in Washington, where money passes hands most easily with a wink or a nod in the name of friendship but in the interest of very special consideration.

In the second place, Morse's benefactors were Republicans, as was the senator, when they helped him. It was one thing for them to help lift his burden when he first sallied forth to be a good Republican senator; but it was impossible for them to feel glad about it when Morse a few years later turned scornfully upon the Republican presidential and vice-presidential ticket. Sammons said that "since Wayne has jumped off the reservation and refused to support Ike and Nixon, they [the contributors] have lambasted me. They've been sick about it and so have I."

When the Morse fund story came out, at a time of general sensitivity about ethics in government, the senator obviously felt placed on the defensive. When in such a position, the Morse code calls for him to slash out at the motives of his adversary and take a holier-than-thou attitude which is designed to protect his Legend from all tarnish. When he struck back at "these guys" by suggesting they had tried to obligate him with their financial contributions, but that he had eluded their wicked designs, he disheartened some of his earliest and strongest supporters. The *Oregonian* said editorially the next day, "One trouble with Oregon's junior Senator seems to be that he will not credit others with honesty he claims for himself." Bill Tugman, recalling this episode, said, "A truly big man might have had a word of gratitude for them, even while regretting political breaks. In slurring his loyal friends, Morse slurred himself."

About this same time another $1200 contribution came to light. A wealthy Eugene lumberman, George E. Owen, explained to reporter James G. Welch:

He didn't ask me for money, but he let me know of the need. He emphasized the great expense of his office and that he was financially embarrassed. He said there was an unpaid balance of $3600 that he owed on a printing fund. But I gave him the money without specifying what it should be used for.

In August 1951, Owen sent the senator a check for $1000, which Morse endorsed for deposit in his personal account in the Riggs National Bank of Washington, D.C., and Owen also sent Morse $200 in currency.

When he made this matter public on October 22, Owen was "disillusioned" with Morse because of the senator's defection four days before from the G.O.P. Owen thought of himself as a liberal Republican who had approved of Morse's course in the Senate. But when Morse backed Stevenson, Owen added, "I'm no New Deal Democrat." Owen said he could see no difference between Morse's taking this contribution and Nixon's having a fund based on similar sources for similar political expenses.

When reporter Welch called Morse for comment, the senator said there was "no comparison" between this and the Nixon fund. "Mine is a question of open books. The fund was not concealed. It's been pretty well known," said Morse. He explained that it was used to cover the expenses of reprinting copies of his speeches, which are mailed to thousands of Oregon voters. But since Owen was now displeased with him, Morse returned the $1200, and Owen passed it on to the Republican campaign fund.

Six weeks later Morse made a lengthy radio speech over a Eugene station to explain his "reprint fund." Material published in the daily *Congressional Record*, Morse explained, is available from the Government Printing Office in the form of reprints marked "Not printed at government expense." The member of Congress who orders the reprints is charged for them. Using the type already set up for printing the material in the *Record*, the cost of reprinting is low. (This helps explain, incidentally, why the *Record* is so full of irrelevant material, for if a person wants several thousand copies of a speech he has made, the most influential-appearing way is to have his senator or congressman insert it in the appendix of the *Record*, after which the reprints can be readily ordered and purchased through the congressional office.) Morse told of inserting a number of speeches in the *Record* which were delivered by George

Stringfellow, vice-president of the Thomas A. Edison Company, West Orange, New Jersey, after which reprints were paid for and sent to Mr. Stringfellow.

For the most part, Morse's reprint expenses are for his own lengthy addresses. To underwrite these reprints, he can dig into his own account, or he can make an arrangement with some private organization to supply copies they would like to have if they will pick up the tab. "As a matter of courtesy, the usual practice is for such groups to have printed enough copies to cover their needs and to cover my relatively small mailing list," explained Morse. "Once the order is placed for the first 1000 reprints, additional copies cost comparatively little."

Offering a year-by-year accounting of the number and cost of speeches or other insertions which he had reprinted, Morse said his printing bill for his first eight years in office came to about $17,000 for 227 publication orders. Most of these were the senator's own speeches, in and out of the Senate. There were a few oddities such as clutter each day's edition of the *Record*, among them one entitled, "Historic Shrines in New Jersey," which Morse ordered reprinted for his friend, Stringfellow, who paid $129.70.

Morse reported that he had paid about half of his $17,000 printing bill with his own funds. The balance had been met by various organizations which requested reprints of certain material. These groups ranged from the Potato Growers' Commission of Oregon ($21.49) to the labor unions, who wanted copies of Morse's speeches during the Taft-Hartley struggle of 1947 and paid $1350 for them. The CIO paid another $1049.95 in 1952 for reprints of Morse's speeches supporting Truman's seizure of the steel mills, and the AFL paid $1441.19 for other labor speeches in 1949. The G.O.P. Senatorial Campaign Committee invested $1279.72 in reprints for distribution during Morse's 1950 re-election campaign.

Morse's radio talk afforded insight into the talkative nature of Congress. To the dismay of visitors in the galleries above, a senator may break into what is charitably called debate on the pending bill and deliver a wholly irrelevant talk on some obscure topic; or, if he is more sensitive to the impatience of others, he may simply receive permission from the presiding officer to have it "inserted" in the *Record*, which means to have it published in the next day's edition without his having to read it aloud in the Senate. By the reprint route, an arrangement with some organization will soon place copies of that talk in the mailboxes of hundreds or thousands of voters, at no cost to the senator. The topic may be utterly non-controversial—say, New Jersey's historic shrines; but more often it is a burning issue to some group. In 1949, for example, when Morse came out against the Columbia Valley Authority bill, the Idaho Reclamation Association paid $350 for reprints of this speech, which coincided with that group's viewpoint. Three years later, when Morse came out in favor of the federal Hells Canyon dam, this same Idaho reclamation group opposed the dam and showed no interest in acquiring copies of that speech. The Idaho Hells Canyon Association, a group formed to promote the dam, paid $201.70 for copies. Other groups which paid for Morse speeches in this period included the American Legion, Oregon Medical Society, National Milk Producers' Association, National Nut Growers' Association, League for Free Palestine, and the Non-scheduled Airlines.

Moonlighting

By this accounting, it cost Morse over $1000 a year of his own money to pay for reprints. Where does this money come from and why should he incur that heavy expense? The money comes from what an Oregon Republican official, Peter Gunnar, once called the senator's "moonlighting." Morse has for years carried a heavy schedule of lectures, which take him to all parts of the country and earn him a substantial supplemental income beyond his government salary. "These speeches do not interfere with my work in the Senate," says Morse, "because I never accept a lecture engagement without the express stipulation that it will be canceled even at the last minute if my work in the Senate calls for my remaining in Washington on the day or evening of the lecture."

Obviously there is an ethical question that goes quite beyond relatively harmless absences from his office while on the lecture circuit. There is the propriety of accepting thousands of dollars each year from private organizations. Many public men accept speaking fees, so in one sense this practice is honored by its wide usage. Alben Barkley did much lecturing, especially when his wife's illness confronted him with huge medical bills. When I once asked Morse whether he had to sell any of his prize bulls to put his three daughters through college, he grinned and replied, "No, I'd just make a few speeches. You might say it was the same thing as selling my bull."

Senator Morse says his standard speaking fee is $500, plus travel expenses. But the fee sometimes is higher. One senator tells of a labor official in his state who asked for Morse as a speaker but became highly indignant when the Oregon orator advised that his fee would be $1500. *Newsweek* reported in 1959 that Morse went to Wisconsin for a speech to a labor group for a $1500 fee. Marquis Childs reported a decade ago that Morse then made $15,000 a year from speaking fees, in addition to his senatorial salary of $22,500.

Morse's speeches and the groups he addresses are, at least, a public matter for all to see and evaluate. Some other senators who enjoy private income on the side keep it most private, although it may come from economic interests which gain or lose on the turn of critical decisions in Washington. Some own oil companies, broadcasting stations, plantations and farms, law firms, or investments in airlines, railroads, utilities, or corporations bidding for large defense contracts. This is not to suggest automatic dishonor for all senators in this position. Each senator is the keeper of his own conscience. But these same senators demand strict accounting from all appointed cabinet officers and their chief subordinates to be certain they have divested themselves of all conflicting financial interest. Senators excuse their own conflicts by explaining blandly that the people can always replace them with better men at election time if their conduct is questionable.

However one may judge it in relation to what other senators do, Wayne Morse's moonlighting income raises unavoidable questions: Is his outspoken behavior partly professional mavericksim which pays off in many speaking invitations? Is it proper for a senator on the Labor Committee to take fees from labor organizations whose interests ride on virtually every vote he casts in his committee work?

Wayne Morse dismisses such questions with an assertion of his honesty and independence. He justifies taking fees on the basis of need, for he exceeds the standard allowances for office expenses and must cover the difference from his own funds. Speaking fees have also helped fulfill Wayne Morse's need to become a cattleman.

Morse makes many speeches, he maintains, for educational purposes (a value which could be sustained by accepting only travel expenses). Speechmaking is a major weapon in the liberal's assault on the status quo. As Morse puts it:

The reactionary forces in and out of the Senate would welcome the silencing of the liberals in the Senate, because as the watchdogs of the people's interest it has been the liberals who have time and time again forewarned the people of the many injustices and selfish schemes cleverly covered up in the language of much of the legislation proposed by selfish economic interests whose spokesmen speak for them in the Senate. The liberals can point with pride to the fact that on innumerable occasions, it has been the tenacious debating of the liberals battling away with speech after speech that has forced many changes in legislation pending before the Senate, which changes resulted in a better protection of the public interest.

Morse notes that liberals are often ahead of their times, and sometimes they are defeated at the polls for proposals which years later are adopted. Liberal reformers are always the target of reactionary defenders of the status quo, and to reach the public with his views is the liberal's aim in making speeches and sending out reprints, says Morse.

Another factor which plays a large part in Morse's behavior is his pride of authorship. Time after time he has said to me after finishing a vigorous Senate exposition, "Best speech I ever gave. You've got to get that. It's very important." Having delivered it, Morse wants others to read it. News accounts are always abbreviated. Reprints of the full text offer the only true measure of satisfaction. A college student wrote to Morse in 1947 to compliment him for standing up to Senator Kenneth Wherry, a pugnacious Republican from Nebraska. By return mail the student received this reply:

> Your letter of April 9 was most kind. Among so many brickbats coming into my office it certainly is a relief to receive such a nice bouquet once in awhile for what I am trying to accomplish here in the Senate.
>
> In response to your expressed interest in my work, I am sending you copies of some of my recent speeches on various topics currently being discussed in the Senate which I thought you might like to have.

The student was not even a prospective Morse voter. He lived in Pennsylvania. When Morse was on the War Labor Board, he did the same thing. He inundated friends and former faculty colleagues with copies of his written decisions. No one who shows the slightest interest goes away empty-handed. In 1960, when he was an announced presidential contender, the senator received this communiqué:

Wayne, baby
    Like I feel you might be the *leader*. So send me some jazz, you know man, like the Morse code.

Later,
Daniel Thompson

Out of the conviction that even beatniks will profit from his educational endeavors, Wayne Morse sent citizen Thompson reprints of his speeches. Such non-discrimination is prescribed by the Morse code.

13. THUNDER FROM THE RIGHT

*Resisting McCarthyism . . . Duke . . . Censure Heroes . . .
Wire Tapping*

DURING the five-year reign of terror of Senator Joseph R. Mc-
Carthy of Wisconsin, senators of reputed courage and widely acclaimed liberal persuasion quaked and fell silent. Before the suddenly
attained power of this national demagogue, two branches of the
federal government were effectively besieged for many months.
Not only were liberal thinkers threatened, but here was a challenge
to the very constitutional presumption that one branch is always
checked and balanced by another to guard against tyranny. At the
crest of his tumultuous reign in the early fifties, there were no checks
or balances pressed against McCarthy and his peculiar seditionist
actions. Encouraged by Taft, appeased by Eisenhower, unchallenged
by most of the Senate liberals, McCarthy quickly gained his mysterious political power.

There was, to be sure, more to the success of McCarthyism than
the failure of defenders of the Constitution to move against him
with dispatch. No politician ever walked the American stage, as
Richard Rovere described it, with "a surer, swifter access to the
dark places of the American mind." McCarthy was the fearless hero
to the jingoists, the isolationists who hated Eisenhower as much as
Roosevelt and Truman, and other right-wing elements whose despair
with the times found a cathartic outlet in McCarthyism. As certainly as McCarthy exploited and enlarged the fear of communistic
forces among the American people at large, he held at bay for
several years those forces of rational righteousness which at last
crashed down upon him in 1954 to end, with blessed swiftness,
McCarthy's personal reign, if not all of the fears provoked by this
thunder from the right.

Wayne Morse, more than most other senators, sniped away at

McCarthy during his ascent to power. Also Morse played a key role in McCarthy's ultimate collapse. Yet between the rise and fall, when McCarthy stood at the peak of his potency in 1953 and early 1954, Wayne Morse strangely shifted his position. In so doing, Morse joined the many senators and civil libertarians who had retreated to whatever safe ground they could find. Unlike many liberals, Morse had no history of left-wing affiliations for the Red hunters to exploit. He had been against communism before it was fashionable or politically needful to damn the Reds. Wayne Morse, as the expression of the times went, was a clean liberal.

Morse's strange shift of position may be explained by the theory of several senators that Morse can be handled only by tough-guy methods. Perhaps because they themselves tried friendly persuasion and calm reasoning without success, they were impressed with the results achieved by a no-nonsense labor leader. The incident occurred in a meeting in 1953 when Morse, during his wild fight for his committee seats, boldly told a group of labor officials he thought he would go into New York and campaign against Senator Lehman, whom on other occasions Morse had called the "father of liberalism." Instead of registering shocked awe, Joe Beirne of the Communications Workers is said to have grabbed Morse by the lapels and retorted, "You do that, you S.O.B., and I'll punch you right in the nose." The next day, the story concludes, Morse's office issued a statement in support of Lehman.

Joe McCarthy is not known to have grabbed Morse by the lapels, but he slyly converted Morse, at least temporarily, from an annoying critic into a safe champion of the congressional responsibility to investigate. Perhaps only another tiger can terrorize the tiger in the Senate.

Resisting McCarthyism

In the period of McCarthy's rise, Morse was one of the first to align himself against the Wisconsin Senator's disregard for elemental fairness. When McCarthy launched his 1950 barrage against alleged subversives in the State Department, Morse asserted his willingness to have any allegations of subversive activities or persons adequately investigated. Indeed, when the Tydings inquiry into McCarthy's first charges brought a conflict of procedure between the Truman administration and the Senate on the issue of opening government loyalty and FBI files to the Senate investigators, Morse proposed that Truman open these files to the Tydings Committee members, a step the Administration was unwilling to take.

But in May of that year, 1950, when Senator Margaret Chase Smith drafted her widely acclaimed "Declaration of Conscience" and invited Morse to sign it, he unhesitatingly joined her and five other Republicans in warning against "techniques that if continued here unchecked will surely end what we have come to cherish as the American way of life." In selecting signatories, Mrs. Smith explained to me that she asked those senators who she was confident shared her conviction about the danger of McCarthy's guilt-by-accusation technique and whose home states gave the declaration wide geographical sponsorship. Besides herself, from New England she chose Aiken of Vermont and Tobey of New Hampshire. From the middle Atlantic coast came Ives of New York and Hendrickson of New Jersey, from the Midwest Thye of Minnesota and from the West Morse of Oregon. If the declaration bravely gave heart to respectable elements who wanted some sign that courage and rationality had not altogether evaporated from the Senate, it caused McCarthy to pause no longer than was needed to belittle these fellow Republicans as Snow White and the six dwarfs.

Later, Morse helped the late Senator McMahon of Connecticut foil McCarthy when the Wisconsin Senator said his whole campaign against the State Department would "stand or fall" on the case of a mysterious Mr. X, described as "a Moscow-born Communist high in the State Department." McMahon challenged McCarthy by introducing twenty-one affidavits supporting the loyalty of Mr. X, and Morse revealed the name of McCarthy's victim, which peeled back some of the fiction. Mr. X was not high in the department, only a lower-rank economist; and he had come from Russia because he was driven out with his family by the communists. McCarthy bounced back with a document he claimed was a secret FBI report proving the man to be a Red agent. The FBI reported the document was a forgery. McCarthy raced quickly on to his next allegation.

At one point Morse declared, "I'm still waiting for the first case when Senator McCarthy can establish his burden of proof. I want proof—not accusation; I want proof—not smear; I want proof—not character assassination." When he received letters chastising him for not supporting McCarthy, Morse in these early years of the Red hunt dispatched a standard reply in which he said:

I think you are overlooking the fact that guilt by association is a very dangerous policy to be following in the United States Senate. You and I and everyone else in the country can be made the victims of such a policy. Therefore, I think I am fighting for a basic American principle of justice when I take the position that Senator McCarthy should either have had the proof in his possession before he made his accusations or he should not have made the accusations.

I am very much disturbed about the fear psychology which is sweeping America and which is taking the form of false accusations and smear charges against fellow Americans. It is the type of campaign of arousing suspicions against one's neighbors which characterized Hitler Germany and which characterizes Communist Russia today.

McCarthy never won wide acclaim in Oregon, although there, as everywhere, he had his intense admirers. From members of this segment of the G.O.P., McCarthy in August, 1951, accepted an invitation to speak at a Republican party picnic at Portland. In trying to drum up interest in McCarthy's coming, Mrs. Louise Gronnert said in a letter to Republicans, "The time has come for us to end this role of 'His Majesty's loyal opposition' and start an old-fashioned slugging match for survival . . . to give more than lip-service to the courageous leaders who are making what may be our last free fight for American traditions, if we lose this opportunity."

Reaction to this from editor Charles A. Sprague typified the sentiments of liberal Republicans when he wrote in the Salem *Statesman*: "We believe in free speech in Oregon, so let this adept at the technique of the Big Lie have his say, and let who will attend. But if the Republican Party is to endorse McCarthyism it deserves to be laid in a grave both wide and deep. And to win the presidency by condoning McCarthy's tactics would be to obtain office under false pretenses." Wayne Morse shunned the McCarthy picnic. Generally, Morse's criticism of McCarthy was backed by the leading newspapers of the state who, more often than he, gave McCarthy unshirted hell from the start to the finish of his reign.

While McCarthy was gaining most of the headlines in 1950 and 1951, another Senate sleuth with only lesser instincts for publicity, Senator Pat McCarran of Nevada, had utilized his chairmanship of the Judiciary Committee to probe the Institute of Pacific Relations, of which Professor Morse had once been a casual member, in quest of insidious influences on American policy in Asia. Morse was never implicated in any of the committee's findings. To his home-town editor friend, William M. Tugman, Morse wrote in August, 1951:

The McCarran investigating committee needs to be watched very carefully by the press of the country. It is almost getting to the point that if one insists that guilt should be established by judicial procedures in this country rather than by accusations of politicians taking the form of character assassins, he becomes suspect as a subversive. I recognize that pounding away as I do upon the basic principles of constitutionalism is rather abstract argument for many people, but nevertheless I am convinced that it can be discussed in terms of examples which will make most people come to realize that their individual rights are always endangered when any clique in either political party resorts to the Big Lie technique."

In this letter Morse added that the "obvious partnership between Taft and McCarthy is frightening. There is no doubt about the fact that a dangerous form of American fascism is working through the reactionary wing of the Republican party."

Morse's proposed remedy for the excesses of Senate investigators was a new set of rules of procedure governing their hearings to mitigate the tendency of zealous committee members to abuse hapless witnesses. Chiefly Morse recommended that all witnesses have the right to be accompanied by an attorney who could advise the witness and interpose objections, as in a courtroom, to questions from senatorial prosecutors. The height of McCarthy's abuse of customary procedures brought Senate hearings on this whole procedural problem, but no action on any of many proposed reforms.

In addition to the procedures of investigating committees, Morse objected vigorously to the use of lie detectors at the Pentagon in screening job applicants for sensitive security positions, a practice which was secret until Morse exposed it in a Senate speech in January 1952. The New York *Times* reported that the Atomic Energy Commission also had experimented with the polygraph before hiring persons for "highly sensitive jobs and also on several thousand other employes on a periodic basis after they had been hired." Calling the practice "repugnant, foreign and outrageous," Morse threatened to press for a legislative ban if the government agencies didn't abandon it. He said his protest caused Defense Secretary Lovett to ban the practice in his department; but Drew Pearson later reported that Lovett's order, limited to his immediate staff, was only a gesture.

The 1952 elections carried McCarthy to the peak of his supremacy. Besides winning re-election himself in Wisconsin, McCarthy was thought personally to have influenced the outcome of eight other Senate contests in which Republicans were elected. If the elections

turned more on the strength of the Eisenhower sweep that fall, a
driving part of that year's Republican momentum in the land was the
force McCarthy exerted against what he called "twenty years of
treason." In any event, the Republicans took command of the
Senate by the margin of 48 votes to 47 for the Democrats. Wayne
Morse, then a declared Independent, voted with the Republicans on
the issue of controlling the Senate; but even had he voted with the
Democrats to equalize the votes of the two parties, this tie could
have been broken in the favor of the Republicans by Vice-president
Nixon.

Duke

With Republican-party control, McCarthy gained the Senate's
greatest weapon of personal power, the chairmanship of its chief
investigating committee. By virtue of these events there passed to
McCarthy the authority to hire a staff (such as Roy Cohn and G.
David Schine, who gallivanted through Europe fingering controversial
books to be burned in American overseas libraries, and whose later
behavior provoked the Army-McCarthy hearings); to subpoena witnesses and documents; to establish the agenda of the committee's
work; and to set the tone of its entire operations.

As Rovere observes in his definitive book on this period, *Senator
Joe McCarthy*, on the opening day of Congress in 1953, as this advent
of new power lay before the Wisconsin wild man, it was thought by
some that "there might be one man in the Senate willing to come
forward with the suggestion that McCarthy just had no right to be
there. The decisive moment came. . . . No voice was raised. He was
sworn." There was a solid base upon which to mount a challenge,
for all through 1952 McCarthy had ducked and weaseled away from
a probe of his financial affairs conducted by the Senate Subcommittee
on Privileges and Elections. However strong the case against seating
McCarthy in January, 1953, to have raised a voice in challenge would,
in all likelihood in those days of fear, have been a prescription for
political martyrdom. Wayne Morse has often *talked* like an eager
candidate for martyrdom, the man of principle who would willingly
become a martyr to the causes he advances. Many times he has said,
as though to defy the counsels of caution, "Here is one senator who
is not afraid to be defeated," or "If I go down, I'll go down fighting."
But here in January, 1953, a veteran of combat against Taft, an

audacious challenger of the popular general in the White House, Wayne Morse did not volunteer for liberal martyrdom against this worst scourge of liberalism in his time.

Whether or not there were any who might have suggested to Morse that he take on McCarthy, there were those who counseled him to try to hamstring the operations of the investigating committees by cutting off their operating funds. For all his authority, a committee chairman can conduct far-ranging investigations only so long as he has funds with which to pay investigators and the massive expenses which accrue as witnesses are subpoenaed and brought to Washington for questioning. But before the question of funds came up, McCarthy announced that he had subpoenaed a west coast promoter, Russell W. Duke. McCarthy slyly observed that Duke had received assistance from time to time from Wayne Morse. All Duke's records had been seized in a garage in San Francisco, added McCarthy, and in due time his committee intended to embark upon an investigation of influence peddling by Duke. Morse instantly declared his innocence of any improper activities respecting Duke. "My files will show that I extended to Mr. Duke the same courtesy extended to every other constituent who came to my office for assistance in connection with any legitimate problem they might have with the government."

Duke was not just another Oregon constituent. From an obscure figure in a fight for control of a Portland local of the Boilermakers Union, Duke began to dabble in politics, attaching himself to Morse's entourage in the manner of political hangers-on who habitually infest campaigns for high public office. A con man of some ability, Duke took to representing various Portland and San Francisco interests in tax dealings with the federal government. He frequented Morse's office when in Washington, and the senator, who never turns away a flattering admirer, refused to take stern measures to dislodge this talkative interloper. Later Morse said he warned Duke "to stop representing himself as having some connection with my office." The most important observable favor Morse did for Duke was to push through Congress a bill that would have financially benefited a group of Duke's contractor clients who had built the Appraisers' Building in San Francisco, and who felt aggrieved because government wartime controls had cut their profits below expectations. President Truman vetoed the bill.

Two weeks after Duke was hauled into a secret examination by McCarthy's committee, the Senator from Oregon suddenly stood up in the Senate as a champion of congressional investigations and an outspoken opponent of those who would hamstring the investigations of McCarthy and Senator Jenner of Indiana, McCarran's successor as head of the Internal Security Subcommittee. Out of the context of these prior events, Morse's remarks that day might puzzle anyone who regarded him as a champion of liberty, as a watchdog of individual rights, as the conscience of the Senate. When Jenner offered his committee's resolution requesting $150,000 to continue investigating alleged subversion, Morse was on his feet in an instant. It should be observed here that Morse held no fondness for Jenner. When Morse lay in a hospital with a fractured jaw from being kicked in that famous horse episode, it was Jenner who gleefully went about the Senate soliciting contributions to buy the horse a bale of good hay. Nevertheless these factors were now subdued in what was one of the strangest colloquies of Morse's career. Indeed, it serves as a small classic example of how the tensions of the McCarthy era often transformed black into gleaming white. What follows is the complete text of this exchange from the *Congressional Record*, January 30, 1953:

Jenner. I am glad to yield to the Senator from Oregon.

Morse. If the Senator will permit, I should like to propound a series of questions dealing with the resolution. I may say at the outset, the questions are aimed to bring out the position of the junior Senator from Oregon, that the appropriation requested by the committee should be granted.

My first question is this: Does the Senator from Indiana agree with me that there is in the body politic of our country among our people, a great deal of concern over the question as to whether there exist in our country subversive elements which, in case of an all-out war with Russia, would work to the detriment of our security?

Jenner. I do not think there is any question about that.

Morse. Does the Senator agree with me that if, as a result of the work of the committee, one such element should be detected and his or its activities prevented, the relatively small amount we are asking to have appropriated for the committee would be repaid to our people many times over in the benefits derived?

Jenner. I certainly do.

Morse. Let us be frank, as I know the Senator from Indiana always is. I am referring to no Member of the Senate, but does the Senator agree with me that there are those in this country who seem to be in opposition to the granting of any increase in funds for the investigation of subversive activities to which the Senator has referred, because for their own reasons, none of which is good, they do not want the Congress to put itself in a position where it will have the funds to detect subversive activities in this country.

Jenner. How is Congress going to be able to discharge its duty to the people unless it has the funds necessary properly and intelligently to represent the people of the country?

Morse. That goes to my next question. Does the Senator agree with me that in spite of the fact that there is much criticism today about the investigatory activities of the Congress, it nevertheless happens to be one of the great functions of the Congress in protecting the country from fraud, corruption, subversive activities and wrongdoing against the public interest?

Jenner. That is correct.

Morse. There is no question about the investigative power of the Congress of the United States being one of the great bulwarks of a free people against oppression and wrongdoing. Is not that correct?

Jenner. That is correct.

Morse. Does the Senator from Indiana agree with me that there are those who are apparently in opposition to the granting of the funds which the committee is asking for because they claim they do not like the methods or the techniques of the investigations of this and some other committees of the Congress?

Jenner. I presume that is correct.

Morse. But is not the answer to that not only a refusal to deny the funds necessary for conducting fair investigations, but also an effort on the part of the Members of the Congress, in keeping faith with their duties, to see to it that congressional investigations are fair, if it is alleged and proved and shown that they are not fair?

Jenner. That is correct.

Morse. If the Senator will yield further for a brief comment, I think the last question I have put goes to the kernel of the problem before us today. As my colleagues know, I put my cards on top of the table, and in recent days, since the Senator from Indiana and the Senator from Wisconsin have been quoted in the newspapers to the effect that more funds were needed for their committee work representations have been made to me that I ought to do what I can to try to block the granting of those funds.

My response has been that I not only will not be a party to an attempt to block them, but that I even have doubts as to whether the committees are asking for sufficient funds properly to conduct the investigations. I intend to accept the figure for which they have asked. I serve notice on the floor of the Senate today that I am going to be no party to any organized drive in this country. I care not how sincere the intentions of those conducting it may be, to prevent the Senate from doing the investigative job which needs to be done. The members of the committee sit here under a great public trust, and I am not going to assume or presume that they will not live up to that trust merely because some persons do not like some of the committee members personally.

So far as I am concerned, Mr. President, I am not going to indulge in a presumption of guilt against anyone, including any colleague in the Senate of the United States. I am going to hold fast and true to a great principle of American justice, namely the presumption of innocence, and the assumption that trials, investigations and hearings are going to be fair and in keeping with American principles of justice, until someone shows me that such an assumption is not justified. If that is demonstrated, then I will deal with the issue when it arises. But I here and now disassociate myself from any movement which seeks to prevent the granting of funds necessary to enable the Senate to conduct an efficient and thorough investigation of subversive activities.

To the Senator from Indiana, I say I wish him well in the investigation. I think the attitude of the Members of the Senate should be to judge the Senator on the basis of the procedures which he follows. I have no reason to believe that those procedures and the conduct of the committee will not be in keeping with the high standards of American justice and fair play.

Jenner. I thank the Senator from Oregon.

After questioning Duke behind closed doors, McCarthy's committee dismissed him, but with the admonition that he could be recalled at any time because he was being kept under a "continuing subpoena." Duke skipped off to Canada beyond the reach of McCarthy. Four months later McCarthy asked the Senate to cite Duke for contempt. In so doing, McCarthy made a convincing case for investigating Duke and his connections. It was a tale of a man who mysteriously obtained inside information on who was in tax trouble, who for a fee promised to secure favorable settlement with the Internal Revenue Service.

McCarthy said he wished to emphasize, however, that his staff "made a complete investigation and they reported that there was no evidence whatever to indicate any wrongdoing of any kind on the part of the Senator from Oregon." Morse expressed his appreciation for McCarthy's clearance and added that his office gives equal service to any Oregon constituent who comes in seeking assistance in arranging appointments with government officials. "I have never asked a government official to consider a complaint or a problem raised by any constituent of mine except on the basis of the merits of the matter," explained Morse. "No compensation, financial or otherwise, was ever paid to me for any service I ever rendered a constituent in connection with carrying out any of my work or duties as a Senator." As though anticipating the question of why he had aided Duke, Morse said, "I do not keep an FBI agent in my office to check into the background and business dealings of constituents who may visit my office. They are entitled to the kind of courteous service which I have rendered to all my constituents, including this particular one."

The Senate cited Duke for contempt for his failure to return from Canada upon McCarthy's command. When apprehended in Cleveland in November, 1953, Duke was returned to stand trial for contempt. The District Court for the District of Columbia declined to convict him. The McCarthy concept of a "continuing subpoena" without any fixed date was a phony, the court ruled. McCarthy promptly announced he would renew the Duke investigation.

The surmise in Washington at the time was that McCarthy was chiefly interested in discrediting a Washington attorney, Edward P. Morgan, who had had a few business contacts with Duke. Morgan, although an ex-FBI agent, had incurred McCarthy's displeasure as counsel for the Tydings subcommittee during its 1950 probe of McCarthy's original charges. Morgan and Morse shared a speaking platform at Peoria, Illinois, in behalf of Adlai Stevenson in the last days of the 1952 presidential campaign. Morgan on that occasion called McCarthy a "political faker and a phony United States Senator" and Morse told the assembled Democrats that "McCarthyism is a dangerous threat to the freedom and liberty of every American . . . because it substitutes trial by accusation for trial by proof." It was only a few weeks later that McCarthy pulled Duke into his web.

Although no evidence of impropriety was ever offered against Morse in his dealings with Duke, the Oregon Senator had reason to be uneasy as long as Duke was being held in tow for a possible sensational public hearing. For Morse knew what many in Washington by then knew, that McCarthy was a quick and brutal manufacturer of phony charges which suited his momentary purpose. The impact of McCarthyism had already been amply demonstrated when the Wisconsin Senator went after senators who had defied him, notably in the defeat of Tydings in the Maryland campaign of 1950. If one so conservative as Tydings was vulnerable in that era of hysteria, was not a more liberal senator the more vulnerable?

Senator William Benton of Connecticut bravely called for McCarthy's expulsion from the Senate and triggered off the Senate inquiry into McCarthy's finances—an episode which ultimately contributed to McCarthy's downfall. But Benton, defeated for his bravery, went down before McCarthy's mysterious momentary political power, as did perhaps a half dozen others in the 1952 election.

Censure Heroes

McCarthy's grip of mortal political fear upon the Senate was not broken until two gentle-spoken New Englanders challenged him in 1954. One of these was Boston attorney Joseph N. Welch, whose great national contribution was simply being *what* he was—a reserved and kindly gentleman with an unyielding reverence for justice secured through obedience to the law—throughout the televised army-McCarthy hearings in which McCarthy for the first time was seen by millions as precisely what he was. The other was a quiet, religious Vermont Republican Senator, Ralph Flanders, who in March, 1954, began to criticize McCarthy for "doing his best to shatter that party whose label he wears." Flanders also belittled McCarthy's anti-communist efforts by recalling that when McCarthy ran for election in 1946, he welcomed the support of "the CIO at a time and a place where the CIO was dominated by the Communists." Senators Cooper of Kentucky and Lehman of New York praised Flanders for his bravery.

In June Flanders stood up once again—a smallish, round man looking very much like an old gentleman being awakened in an easy chair of his private club. McCarthy, he said, was a senatorial Dennis the Menace, but he likened his anti-communist activities to the methods of Hitler—"to strike fear into the heart of any defenseless minority." He followed with a resolution calling for McCarthy's removal as chairman of the Investigating Committee. Noting that McCarthy had refused to answer the charges inherent in the 1952 probe of his financial affairs, Flanders suggested that a "Fifth Amendment Communist" now had a parallel in a "Fifth Amendment Senator." At this point Morse suggested perhaps the investigative jurisdiction of McCarthy's committee might be transferred to another committee "for the good of the objectives of fair investigations." Lehman, the first liberal Democrat to speak up, followed Flanders' lead with his own resolution to strip McCarthy of his powerful position. If courage is contagious, it was now beginning to spread about in the Senate.

On July 30, 1954, Flanders introduced his censure resolution, and Wayne Morse at last said something of what he thought, that McCarthy had indulged in "political thuggery." But, he urged, the censure resolution should be referred to a committee, there to be weighed with calm deliberation against a bill of particulars against McCarthy. Morse was then among several to file such a bill.

Meanwhile, Humphrey of Minnesota had introduced a resolution to outlaw the Communist party, a device designed more to protect its liberal advocates from right-wing hysteria than to protect the country from the furtive adherents of the Communist party. As Humphrey told his biographer, Michael Amrine, the first colleague he consulted was Morse. "Senator Morse not only enthusiastically approved of the bill but asked for the privilege of co-sponsoring it," Amrine quoted a Humphrey memo. "He was joined with eighteen members of the Senate who asked for the opportunity to co-sponsor it." When Amrine later asked Humphrey whether he thought the bill had done any good, Humphrey said it had saved several liberal senators from defeat in the 1954 elections.

By the time the Humphrey bill came up for a vote, the Flanders censure resolution had been referred to a special committee headed by Watkins of Utah. The Humphrey bill then passed the Senate with the votes of eighty-five senators. As Morse was making an argument for the bill, McCarthy turned upon him with bristling sarcasm: "I find that at the same time those who are the most active in sponsoring general laws against Communism are the loudest in their screaming against those who pick up the individual Communists by the scruff of the neck and expose them to public view. . . . The nice little boys would pass a resolution against the skunks, but the nice little boys did not help us dig them out. I find that the nice little boys in the Senate object to our methods, but they do not have a single skunk pelt to show. They do not like to see the job done. They do not like the odor that goes with skunk hunting."

Morse retorted that McCarthy reminded him of the days when

suspected cattle thieves were strung up by the necks in order to stop rustling. "But it soon became apparent out on the great frontier that what was happening with false accusations was that innocent people were being strung up by the neck time and time again and that lynch law was a form of blackmailing innocent people." Morse said McCarthy's procedures "closely resembled lynch law," and that personal liberties required protection from "trial by accusation" and "guilt by association."

For forty-five minutes Morse and McCarthy snarled at one another, fists clenched, arms waving, barely parted by two of those quaint little Senate desks. Twenty other senators watched with solemn glee. Clattering his fist down on his desk with the reflexes of one accustomed to banging a gavel, McCarthy called on Morse to name one out of 536 witnesses whose rights had been abused before his committee. Morse said McCarthy's procedures "resulted in unfairness to every witness." It continued like this:

McCarthy: I think the junior Senator from Oregon is guilty of the most fantastic, dishonest name calling, even though I like the Senator personally, when he accuses . . ."

Morse: I love these kisses of death.

McCarthy: When he accuses me before all the newspapermen and before 160 million people of being guilty of using the lynch law, and then will not tell me whom I have lynched.

Morse countered that McCarthy's "one-man committee" methods should be supplanted by a rule that a committee cannot function unless a majority of its members are on hand, so that fair-minded senators can check abuses by unfair senators. That, replied McCarthy, would be a great gift to the communists. Allowing that their rhubarb had reached the absurd stage, Morse ended it by renewing his plea for adoption of improved committee procedural rules: "The responsibility for [McCarthy's] action rested more on the Senate as a whole than on the junior Senator from Wisconsin, because he is the agent of the Senate. He is chairman of a committee which is responsible to the Senate. So long as those are the rules of procedure which apply, I do not think he deserves nearly as much criticism for those procedures as does the Senate as a whole for not having changed them."

Few senators, it must be added, were willing to be so bold with McCarthy, even so late as this. There were no perfect acts of courage in the Senate during those dark days of the early fifties as the sun-shine liberals waited for the storm to abate. When called to muster for a march against a tidelands oil bill or any other safe economic issue that readily aroused their supporters, the liberals eagerly responded. But the call for a raid upon the lair of the horny ogre of Wisconsin brought only echoes bounced from the shiny, empty desks. Such were the years characterized by Herblock's memorable cartoon, "Pussyfootprints in the sands of time."

If the Senate's censure vote knocked him from grace, the 1954 elections toppled McCarthy from power. By the barest possible margin of one vote, control of the Senate passed to the Democrats, and McCarthy was reduced to a relatively powerless minority senator. McCarthy himself blamed Eisenhower for this cruel loss, contending that the White House had not given sufficient support to his friend Senator Welker of Idaho, who was that November defeated by young Frank Church. The truth was that Welker's erratic behavior had so displeased Idahoans that even a "Dear Herman" letter from Eisenhower couldn't save him from defeat. McCarthy would have had much stronger basis for blaming Wayne Morse for his fall from power—for it was at this juncture that Morse switched his vote of allegiance to the Democrats and brought into the Senate by the narrowest of election margins a Democratic colleague from Oregon, Richard Neuberger. Had Morse retained his earlier allegiance to the G.O.P., all other things being equal, the Republicans—and Joe McCarthy—would have remained in power in 1955, despite the censure vote by which this respectable institution rapped McCarthy's knuckles, *but only for offenses against the Senate.*

Morse merits credit for this consequence, whatever other reasons impelled his political transition in its final phase. That it brought McCarthy's final collapse is but an accident of history, yet no less meaningful in national effect.

Wire Tapping

Dealing with McCarthy was only part of the problem of unrest and anxiety which subversive activities—those of the communists and those of the senator—had caused. The McCarthy era brought a deluge of bills assertedly designed to tighten security, make it tough on spies, give law-enforcement agencies new weapons. The Smith Act, as amended in 1948, had made it a crime to teach or advocate the overthrow of the United States by force or violence. Morse had voted for this act, under which about 100 Communist officials were rounded up in five years. Although an ex-professor, Morse had expressed no sympathy for the argument that academic freedom was here placed in jeopardy. Speaking to the graduating class of the FBI Academy in 1949, he said it was evident that Communists were trying to infiltrate colleges. While witch hunts by those who opposed academic freedom itself were to be guarded against, Morse rejected "the logic of some of our educators who are arguing these days that the preservation of academic freedom in the colleges of America requires the recognition of a right of teachers to become Communists and retain their teaching positions." Such teachers, said Morse, are not seeking to lead students through objective analysis of governmental philosophies but are so devoted to their indoctrination objectives that they slant their teachings away from facts."

After the congressional investigations of subversive activities had gained wide attention, the parade of witnesses "taking the Fifth" caused numerous lawmakers and Eisenhower's Attorney General, Herbert Brownell, Jr., to call for a method of mitigating this hardship which the Constitution imposed upon the investigators. Brownell wanted a bill to grant immunity from prosecution to a witness for any disclosures he might make once he shed the protection of the Fifth Amendment against self-incrimination. Senator Kefauver, after his crime investigation of 1950, had recommended an immunity bill. In either case, the congressional motive was the same: to elicit more information from witnesses.

When the bill came before the Senate in 1953, Taft was dubious for fear it might lead to "immunity baths" for talkative witnesses. Other leading private attorneys or legal authorities expressed doubts or opposition, but the American Bar Association endorsed it. Several liberals opposed it, notably Lehman of New York and Cooper of Kentucky, on grounds that it would negate a basic constitutional right. No roll-call vote was taken when the bill was passed by a standing vote in the Senate, but ten senators—Lehman, Cooper, Magnuson, Kerr, McClellan, Jackson, Stennis, Hennings, Murray, and Hayden—announced their opposition. To this one fundamental statutory change which was an outgrowth of the McCarthy era, Wayne Morse raised no objection.

Against the second thrust, a bill to legalize use of wiretap evidence in federal court, Wayne Morse moved with scholarly vigor. Brownell had urged this measure upon Congress in the spring of 1953, explaining that it was to be limited to cases involving national security. The House Judiciary Committee, before approving such a measure early in 1954, considered extending its application to kidnaping cases. On the House floor one safeguard, along lines recommended by Washington attorney Joseph L. Rauh, Jr., of Americans for Democratic Action, was inserted to require that the Attorney General secure a federal court order. Only ten congressmen stood up against this wiretap bill that April day in 1954 when 377 of their colleagues voted for it.

Months before the bill reached this plateau, Morse had threatened to filibuster if necessary to stop it from becoming law. In January he and Senator Homer Ferguson, Michigan Republican, were highlighted as chief spokesmen on either side in a debate published by *Newsweek* magazine. To Ferguson, "wire tapping for investigation of crimes involving national security and defense, and crimes like kidnaping, is a sensible adjustment between the liberties of the individual and the need for protecting the nation from its internal enemies." The senator cited the Judith Coplon espionage trial in which the government's case had collapsed because its incriminating evidence, gained through wiretaps, was inadmissable in court. Quoting J. Edgar Hoover's arguments for adopting "modern techniques" to fight treason, Ferguson warned that "the people of our country should not have to wait until our country is destroyed in order to learn who the plotters against us are."

To Morse, wire tapping "is a cover-up for lazy, inefficient, unimaginative, ruthless law-enforcement administration." Noting that the Constitution forbids unauthorized search and seizure, Morse said, "We cannot legalize safely a wiretap apparatus for police surveillance of the privacy of the homes of America and not run the risk of sacrificing, in the name of law-enforcement expediency, our hard-won protections against secret police tactics. . . . What is a nation profited if it gains security and loses its liberty? . . . There is no room in America for a substitution of police espionage for vigilant and unfailing adherence to democratic principles and fair methods of law enforcement."

The wiretap bill, it was obvious from the overwhelming House vote, would be hard to defeat. With the ranking Democrat on the Judiciary Committee, Pat McCarran, allied with the Administration in support of this measure, hearings focused more attention on *how* it could most safely and effectively be done—not *whether* it was sound policy. Even the American Civil Liberties Union, which noted that it had always opposed wire tapping as destructive of personal liberties, asked that if Congress insisted on adopting this bill, the practice should not be sanctioned without a court order and should be limited to security and kidnaping cases. John J. Gunther of A.D.A., however, opposed the whole idea and urged, instead, that Congress outlaw all wire tapping "as an intolerable violation of civil liberties."

In this uncertain atmosphere Morse made a series of Senate speeches condemning wire tapping as a police-state method. With detailed references to the first constitutional debates on the issue of personal privacy, as sanctified by the Fourth Amendment, Morse declared, "Wire tapping—secret listening to words spoken in the home, or surreptitious interception of a person's confidential communications to his family, friends, associates, lawyer, doctor, or priest —is an insidious kind of intrusion upon personal privacy. It would be impossible, in my judgment, to authorize its use and at the same time provide safeguards consistent with the spirit and purpose of the Fourth Amendment," which provides in part:

> The right of the people to be secure in their persons, houses, papers and effects against unreasonable searches and seizures shall not be violated and no warrants shall issue but upon probable causes, supported by oath or affirmation, and particularly describing the place to be searched and the persons or things to be seized.

A wiretap, argued Morse, is comparable to a general warrant because it can never be selective or specific. Rather, it intercepts and eaves-drops on all, the innocent with the suspect.

In the strict sense, Morse's persuasive case against *all* wire tapping was irrelevant to the bill advanced by Brownell. Wire tapping as such was already legal, and it had for years been employed by federal and local law officers among others. It is illegal only to *divulge information* gained by wire tapping. It was only this portion of the law which would have been altered, to permit wiretap information to be legally divulged in court against a defendant.

Yet there is no gainsaying the probable effectiveness of Morse's attacks on the bill in the highly emotional atmosphere of the time. The bill cleared its subcommittee by a 3 to 2 vote, but in the full Judiciary Committee it faltered on a tie vote. Chairman Langer refused to vote on the bill and break the tie. He explained that he could not possibly be objective about the merits of this bill. Wild Bill Langer recalled that twenty years before, his telephone in the governor's office at Pierre, North Dakota, had been tapped when he was having a feud with the Interior Department. He had despised the practice ever since. Thus did the wiretap bill fail.

Was Wayne Morse's oratory instrumental in causing its defeat? When only one vote proved the margin of defeat, who is to say with certainty what combination of forces among the many then in play brought the seven individual senators to their decision to oppose the bill? It is perhaps enough to say, as a triumphant Kennedy aide said after the eyelash 1960 election outcome, "When you win, never try to figure out why you didn't lose." In those days of hysteria, Wayne Morse spoke out against a bill that appeared certain to pass. Undoubtedly, this gave strength and courage to those who deeply wished to brave this thunder from the right.

14.   THE NOBLE FILIBUSTER

Confederate Retreat . . . Necessity and Survival . . . Atomic
Power . . . Meeting Mr. K

THE SENATE of the United States is the highest place in American public life where a maverick can find long and useful fulfillment. Unlike the House of Representatives or the agencies of the other branches of the government, the Senate is the dissenter's rightful place. For it is a solemn constitutional purpose of the Senate to be the highest realm for effective dissent. Here little Rhode Island is as powerful as mighty New York. Here every minority—be it sectional, racial, economic, religious, or simply political—can and must be heard if but a single senator rises and claims his right to speak in its behalf. The power, the guarantee, of effective dissent lies in the rule of the Senate which permits a senator to talk as long as his strength or his sense of fitness permits.

Fighting Bob La Follette's general order number one to his senatorial rebels was, "Never vote for cloture." Never vote to halt an ongoing debate by invoking a gag on those senators who wish to speak. A squad of dissenters, each taking his turn talking and then yielding only to a compatriot, can conduct a successful filibuster for weeks on end, if the dissenters make no slip. Only cloture, the vote of a two-thirds majority to close debate on the pending business, can stop a filibuster.

A cruel slip quashed La Follette's most vigorous filibuster effort against a currency bill in 1908. Speaking for over eighteen hours, he set a new long-distance speaking record before yielding the floor to Gore of Oklahoma. By prearrangement, Gore was to speak two hours and then pass the baton on to Stone of Missouri, the next man in the rhetorical relay. Gore, who was blind, yielded the floor to Stone on schedule and sat down, not realizing that Stone had stepped into the cloakroom momentarily and was not in the chamber at the critical moment. Advocates of the currency measure instantly seized control, demanded a vote, and passed the bill.

Wayne Morse has outdone La Follette in marathon oratory. But, violating the La Follette order, Morse has voted for cloture and perennially advocated a change in the rules to make cloture easier to achieve. Morse has thus been the most frequent user of the filibuster method while advocating a rules change that would curb it. "There is an inconsistency on the face of it," he once conceded when Senator Brewster of Maine confronted him with this fact. "But filibusters can be motivated by different reasons."

This sounded as if it were simply a question of whose ox was being gored. Not so, said Morse. He explained that a badly motivated filibuster was one designed to prevent any vote at all and thereby to kill a controversial bill; but a noble filibuster was one designed only to delay a vote to permit public reaction to be felt by senators, in hopes of changing the outcome. Columnist Arthur Krock called this an "ingenius" distinction, adding, "It does not change the basic purpose of a filibuster, which is to prevent a majority from doing what it wants to do."

As Walter Lippmann has observed, "the crux of the question is not whether the majority should rule but what kind of majority." The Constitution calls for several kinds of majorities. On the most solemn issues—overriding a presidential veto or amending the Constitution, to cite two—a two-thirds majority of all senators is required. While many liberals have opposed the idea of a two-thirds vote to halt a filibuster, Lippmann says that it is "vital to our liberties to preserve the principle that for great issues . . . there should be required more than a simple majority. For we must never forget that majorities are not always liberal and that they may be quite tyrannical."

Morse's position is a pragmatic fusion of the value of extended debate and the necessity to bring an issue to a vote. He proposes changing Rule XXII so that only a majority of those senators voting on the motion would be needed to impose cloture. Once cloture has been imposed, each senator would be entitled to speak for one additional hour on the pending bill, or he could yield his time to a colleague. The practical effect of Morse's plan would be to permit a maximum of 100 hours' debate (which would take twenty days at the usual Senate pace of afternoon sessions, or four to five days if the Senate went into round-the-clock sessions) before the final vote on the controversial issue.

Wayne Morse is the victim of counterpressures. When he is making an address to a crowd of students or writing an article of liberal doctrine, the political theorist comes to the fore and he damns the filibuster as an evil device of a willful, reactionary minority. But when he steps into the feverish pressure chamber of Senate politics, he justifies using this "evil device" as a noble weapon in the service of a higher good.

Unlike La Follette, Morse must in theory scorn the filibuster because of the times in which he lives. When La Follette proudly used the filibuster against the economic and international proposals he opposed, he was a hero to his Wisconsin followers, for the filibuster was the natural weapon of a great orator in a legislative chamber which permitted unlimited debate. La Follette made no effort to disguise his intent to filibuster to death what he deemed to be unsound legislation.

Today, however, filibuster is a nasty word in the Northern provinces of contemporary liberalism because it has come to symbolize Southern resistance to civil-rights legislation. In his freshman term, Morse first witnessed the power of the filibuster as the Southern Democrats talked to death Truman's Fair Employment Practices Commission bill. He wrote an indignant article for *Colliers* deriding such patriarchs as Tydings of Maryland for saying, "Majority to Hades . . . let us not fool ourselves with the silly thought that majorities are always right," and Russell of Georgia for lauding the filibuster as a "bulwark against oppression by a mere popular majority." Morse chastised the Senate leaders for not holding the Senate in continuous night-and-day sessions to exhaust the filibusterers and "abolish once and for all the filibuster travesty."

Confederate Retreat

In the civil rights struggle in Congress, the modern equivalent of the slavery question of the 1850s in its devisive implications, the chief weapon of either side is power, not persuasion. To the shrinking Southern minority, the filibuster—or the threat of its use—is the visible weapon of their power. Everyone has seen its past effectiveness to snarl Senate business and prevent legislative action.

In recent years, however, two civil-rights bills have been enacted, the first since the Reconstruction era when the Radical Republicans were punishing the South. The Southern senators sternly resisted with powerful filibuster tactics, but at last acceded to the overwhelming majority, which favored some kind of bill. This did not mark the end of the filibuster as the ultimate weapon. Rather, it illustrated the use of the invisible weapon in the strategy of Russell's dwindling confederates.

Ever since civil rights became a major political issue in the mid-forties, the invisible weapon of Russell's forces has been their ideological coalition with the conservatives of the Republican party. While the Southerners were openly cannonading with the filibuster, the Republican heirs of the Great Emancipator were openly condemning such resistance to civil rights; but both were finding that common objectives were better served by easy-does-it measures than by the overnight reforms of the liberals. The 1957 civil-rights bill was finally enacted because it contained scarcely any of the liberals' proposed reforms. By the amendment procedure, it had become a bill which the Southern politicians felt they could "live with," and one the Northerners could point to as a political achievement. Russell ceased firing with the filibuster when it seemed wiser to retreat a few yards than to risk possible annihilation of the fundamental position of the Old South, which the bill did not threaten. Wayne Morse called the bill a "sham" and voted against it.

The 1957 act created a Civil Rights Commission to investigate discrimination against minorites; a Civil Rights division in the Justice Department; and new authority for the United States Attorney General to seek court injunctions against local and state officials who obstruct voting rights. If this was the sham Morse termed it, it was a first step in the right direction. The Justice Department initiated several suits, one of which restored 1377 previously registered Negroes to the voting lists in Lousiana, and another which abolished "white primaries" in Fayette County, Tennessee. The Civil Rights Commission, to which President Eisenhower appointed a distinguished group of leaders from both South and North, observed that racial discrimination in housing was nationwide (a point most Northern liberals have conveniently ignored) and that laws were inadequate to guarantee voting rights in the South.

The consequence was the 1960 drive for voting-rights legislation. The 1960 act called for elaborate legal procedures by which courts could declare Negroes qualified voters if need be. Roy Wilkins of the

NAACP said these procedures compelled the Negro to pass more check points en route to the ballot box than if he were trying to reach the gold reserves in Fort Knox. The bill also contained penalties against officials who destroy voting records, and it gave the Justice Department access to these records. It also made it a federal crime to cross state lines to escape punishment for bombing and arson or to threaten citizens by telephone or other interstate facilities. This time Wayne Morse said he believed some achievement was evident. He voted for the bill.

In this struggle the Southerners conducted one of the longest filibusters of modern times. The debate ran from February 15 to April 8, with grueling round-the-clock sessions that lasted for nine consecutive days of this period. As one Southerner talked, others bargained and gradually succeeded in gathering enough support for eliminating the provisions of the original bill most distasteful to them. This invisible weapon, the cloakroom bargaining in which the gentlemen of the Old South are superb, once more resulted in a compromise—a small advance along the road to equal rights, and a small retreat by the men from Dixie. Again it was the filibuster by which the South held the North at bay while the bargain could be struck.

An amusing illustration of the strategic use and misuse of the filibuster occurred in 1957. After succeeding in stripping the bill of so-called Title III, which would have empowered the United States Attorney General to initiate court action to protect those deprived of civil rights, the Southerners met in Russell's office and agreed to cease firing and let the bill pass before the liberals made it tougher. But Senator Strom Thurmond of South Carolina broke ranks and filibustered for twenty-four hours and eighteen minutes, eclipsing Morse's tidelands oration by nearly two hours as the longest in history. (Thurmond, however, was aided by several restful quorum calls which allowed him to take his seat, whereas Morse spoke without interruption.)

Russell was furious with Thurmond. He and other Southerners received many angry letters asking why they had not fought as hard as Strom.

In the next civil rights fight, Senator Olin D. Johnston of South Carolina, the last of the quivering-jowl Southern politicians, blustered to reporters that he had a 400-page speech in preparation that would outdistance Wayne and Strom combined. When his opportunity for

historic notice arrived, Johnston lasted only ninety minutes. After
all that build-up, a reporter told him it appeared he had been
bought off. "Ah have not been bought off," retorted Olin the Solon
with a show of magnificent indignation. "Mah feet got tired and so
ah quit."

Necessity and Survival

During World War II, when the government evacuated Japanese-
Americans from their homes in Pacific coast states to inland relocation
camps, the American Civil Liberties Union in 1942 was considering
making a fight against the treatment of these citizens. Dr. Frank
Graham, president of the University of North Carolina, and a
colleague of Morse's on the War Labor Board at the time, asked
Dean Morse what he thought of the ACLU proposal. Morse took
a completely pragmatic position. He defended the evacuation practice
and opposed making a fight. In a communiqué to Dr. Graham,
Morse said:

> As a liberal and a staunch defender of civil liberties, I am enough of
> a realist to recognize that these are times when we have to ex-
> pect liberties to be abridged in order that we may have the opportunity
> to restore them after the war. It is my opinion that neither one of the
> resolutions of the American Civil Liberties Union would constitute a
> contribution to liberalism in America. A pressing of them will simply
> antagonize a large section of our populace against the cause of civil
> liberties. We all have to make our sacrifices, and I think that citizens of
> Japanese, German and Italian nationalities are going to have to expect
> to make theirs in the form of being moved out of military zones if, in
> the judgment of those entrusted with the prosecution of the war, they
> should be moved out . . .
> It is an unfortunate policy in many respects, but realism convinces me
> that it is the only safe course we can follow. . . . One such citizen, be
> he a Fifth Columnist, could destroy the Bonneville Dam or the Boeing
> Aircraft plant or anyone of the other strategic military objectives on
> the West Coast. My answer to the ACLU is simply "Why take a
> chance?" . . .

Morse subsequently learned that a former law student of his of
Japanese ancestry had decided to test the constitutionality of the
evacuation law. The National Student Relocation Council's Portland

branch asked Morse whether he could recommend the young man, "who wishes to continue studying in an eastern or midwestern college or university." Morse wrote back that he was "well acquainted" with this former student, but he understood the boy was in difficulty for defiance of the evacuation law. "I should like to withhold my judgment in the matter until I know the full details of the situation and can judge it on the merits," replied Morse. "I am sure you will understand my position in this matter."

From the Multnomah County Jail in Portland nine months later, the student wrote to his old dean to seek a recommendation, apparently unaware that Morse had declined to give him one the previous year. Once more the busy Washington official replied: "I wish to say that I am not sufficiently familiar with the facts and circumstances surrounding your case to pass any judgment on it at this time. I have been so busy with my work . . ." This time the boy had applied for induction into a Nisei combat unit. Morse said he would give military authorities his opinion of the boy as a student, "which was a favorable one." But he did not let the boy off without a lecture on the theme that "when nations are at war, the laws of necessity and survival must supersede any application of peacetime doctrines if the application of such doctrines appear to threaten the safety and security of the nation."

When he became a senator, Morse strongly supported Truman's civil-rights proposals; and when they were killed off, Morse must have observed that the Southerners won the political war because they followed his doctrine of "necessity and survival" and used the filibuster to defeat the liberals. It was only a year after the Fair Employment Practices Commission bill had been filibustered to death that Morse himself in 1947 launched his first filibuster.

This, to be sure, was a noble filibuster. It was a ten-hour oration against the Taft-Hartley bill. It was the longest Senate speech in more than a decade, since Huey Long's famous fifteen-hour rendition of bayou recipes for pot likker, turnip greens, and corn bread as a protest against a New Deal bill. Morse, on the occasion of his debut as a filibusterer, had a flamboyant accomplice, Senator Glen Taylor, the Idaho minstrel. At issue was whether the Senate would override Truman's veto of the Taft-Hartley bill. Confident of the necessary two-thirds majority vote he needed to beat Truman, Taft was pressing for an immediate vote. Everyone knew what the issues were, in any event, so a discussion for the purpose of illuminating other senators was unnecessary. But Wayne Morse would have none of this fast shuffle.

Under Senate rules, no vote can be taken until the last senator has spoken the last thought that throbs within his brain. Morse and Taylor decided that the only chance of upholding Truman's veto was to create a considerable disturbance about Taft's quick-vote plan, arouse the public with oratorical splendor, and hold off the vote for several days until public reaction could be felt on Capitol Hill. Between them they held the Senate in session over eighteen hours for its longest session in two decades. Taft finally decided that it was wiser to defer a vote over the weekend, as the filibusterers demanded, than to martyr them by holding the Senate in continuous session until they dropped of exhaustion.

Morse's debut was a notable success by the common political criteria. He had made his point, and he had become a national weekend conversation piece, with his heroic features on most newspapers' front pages.

But in substance, in the avowed purpose of a noble filibuster to educate the public and allow time for public sentiment to congeal and to influence a vital Senate vote, what was the result? Taft's private forecast was that he would override the veto by the same 68 to 24 vote by which the Senate earlier had passed the bill. Morse, in this one last charge against Taft's forces, hoped to break the lines. A switch of only five votes would kill the bill.

Instead of extending the rose of persuasion in the cloakrooms, Morse characteristically slashed with the steel of oratory from the Senate floor. Not a vote was changed. When the roll was called, Taft held every one of his original sixty-eight votes. The noble filibusterer had won his first battle for delay, but had lost his first war.

In 1953, when the Eisenhower administration urged passage of the tidelands oil bill, the liberal Democrats on April 1 opened their attack. Taft once again was the leader of the Senate majority. No hurry this time. Let the Democrats talk.

But by mid-April, as Senator Lister Hill of Alabama was in the midst of a 45,000-word speech against the bill, Taft finally used that nasty word filibuster to describe the goings-on. Why, scoffed the gentleman from Alabama, how could Mr. Taft say such a thing?

On April 24 Wayne Morse started a speech with the concession that the three-week debate had "many characteristics of a filibuster" but it was not "an *extreme* type of filibuster." But after he had spoken his scheduled eight hours, the Oregon orator felt sufficiently warmed up to talk at some length. Into the night session he talked; into the wee hours, eclipsing the record of the Louisiana King fish; into the dawn, catching up with the all-time eighteen-hour and thirty-five minute record of old Bob La Follette. On he went, greeting senators as they arrived at their desks for another day's work, but always relating everything to the tidelands question and its broadest possible implications. No turnip-green recipes for Morse. When he finally sat down, after speaking for twenty-two hours and twenty-six minutes, Wayne Morse was the new champion of marathon talking.

The tidelands debate, he later explained, had not been receiving adequate attention in the press to arouse people sufficiently to bombard senators with letters of protest. The oil companies, the White House, and conservative interests at large were making their weight felt, and the only hope of stopping this "giveaway" was to reach the people. Morse said he tried to "break the newspaper blockade" by dramatizing the issue. But what happened? Well, Wayne Morse's picture was in virtually every newspaper in the country that weekend, and countless citizens wondered how anyone could possibly perform this great feat of physical endurance. "The news stories," grumbled Morse, perhaps with justification, "were devoted mostly to what I ate during the marathon."

On May 5, after five weeks of debate, the Senate passed the tidelands bill, 56 to 35, without any significant modifications. Once again, a noble filibuster had effectively won the battle for delay, but failed to prevent any alteration in the bill at issue.

Atomic Power

The following year came the most successful noble filibuster of modern times. The Eisenhower administration proposed to let private industry into the atomic-energy field, until then a government monopoly. Under the generalship of Senator Lister Hill, twenty-five senators were mustered for duty. "Put me down for six hours a day from now until Christmas," bravely volunteered young Senator Gore of Tennessee. By careful preparation, this band of liberals sustained a marathon debate which went round the clock day after day for nearly two weeks—the longest continuous session in Senate history. The dramatic elements of the affair attracted wide attention. Even the staid New York *Times* devoted three columns on its front page one morning to a photograph of the champ, Wayne Morse, cat-napping in his shirt sleeves on an army cot. The New York *Daily News* converted this picture into an editorial-page cartoon in which the sleeping figure was identified as "Wayne Morse, the Mouth," and the caption was "Sleep that knits up the raveled sleeve of GAB." Morse confined himself to what he called relatively brief speeches this time, running six, eight, and twelve hours each. "Batting practice," he called it.

The filibuster was inspired by the discoveries of Herbert Roback, an aide to Congressman Chet Holifield of California, and other technicians who had carefully dug into the maze of technical language in the complex atomic matter and passed on their findings to senators for ammunition as the battle mounted. Morse was one of the most effective users of this intelligence. The chief objections to the Administration's proposal were that it would authorize private development of atomic power plants without any preference to non-profit public agencies; failed to authorize the federal government to build atomic electric plants; authorized compulsory licensing of atomic patents to private firms for five years, after which government control of these valuable patents would lapse. Morse and company charged that it would enable a handful of private corporations, which had acquired atomic experience while fulfilling defense contracts, to gain a stranglehold on atomic power development and a monopoly through patent control.

Whether the public educational intent of this noble filibuster was achieved is impossible to determine. Richard L. Strout of the *Christian Science Monitor* was dubious. "The issues involved were reported only briefly in the press as secondary to the spectacular delaying tactics," wrote Strout. "These issues were tremendous, but complicated and confused." But there is little doubt that the Senate was educated. The bill was modified in significant respects as a result of the extended debate. By a 45 to 41 vote, an amendment was added to authorize the federal government to build atomic power plants and to give preference in sale of power to public power agencies. The five-year patent clause was extended to ten years, although the House later insisted on reducing it to five years; and all patents would revert to the government if the owner violated the anti-trust laws. (The major failure of the liberals was in trying to eliminate authorization for what later became the celebrated Dixon-

Yates power contract, which had nothing to do with atomic energy as such.)

One reason for the greater success of the Southern conservatives in forcing changes in bills which they filibuster is that many of them are committee chairmen, powerful men, bargaining from strength; while most Northern liberals have little or none of this bargaining power—a source of continuing frustration to them.

In some of his delaying efforts, Morse has had talkative allies. On other occasions he has made a one-man effort. Often only the threat of a lengthy oration has been sufficient to discourage intended action which he opposed. Although Morse customarily says he never tries to prevent a vote on an issue, this is the heart of his strategy in implementing the Morse formula. In the atomic energy debate, which did come to many votes, he candidly handed his critics a remark which they have never forgotten: "This is a filibuster. I never sail under false colors."

If one takes Arthur Krock's definition of a filibuster as any effort to prevent a majority from doing what it wants to do, Morse has used the device year after year. The most common occasion for it usually arises near the end of the session, when impatience to adjourn is driving Congress to make hasty, often ill-considered, decisions. The Oregon Senator is usually good for a few long lectures on the evils of running out on the American people.

Meeting Mr. K

The most interesting preadjournment filibuster by Morse came in 1959, a hectic Labor Day weekend. The leaders were pressing a swift legislative cleanup schedule. Goading them was a worrisome premonition. It was that Soviet Nikita Khrushchev, soon to arrive in Washington for his first visit, could not agreeably be denied the high privilege accorded countless other visiting heads of foreign states— the opportunity of addressing a joint session of the House and Senate. This specter of the dictator of the communist world mounting *their* podium to receive all the blessings of dignity and respect which it affords was an apparition quite unacceptable to many members of Congress. How could they ever, to put first things first, explain it to the grass-roots patriots before election time?

Happily, there was one act of congressional magic which could dispel this premonition. So it was that the leaders, with rare bipartisan harmony, quietly planned for Congress to adjourn by September 12, three days before Khrushchev's arrival. To meet this deadline, the Senate would work through the holiday weekend, said Majority Leader Lyndon B. Johnson of Texas, obeying the canvassed wish of some eighty senators who were "anxious" to make haste.

Unhappily, Johnson failed to consult the one senator most apt to set these plans awry. Wayne Morse's reaction came as a written declaration to Johnson: "I do not intend to yield to your dictatorship." Morse had other plans for that weekend—a speech to a labor group and a visit to the Oregon State Fair, where he was exhibiting his cattle. If the majority leader insisted on holding the Senate in session through the holiday weekend, Morse threatened to stop all business by reading a three-volume history of the labor movement in highly audible tones from the center of the Senate chamber. Johnson's refusal to back down brought Morse's declaration of parliamentary war. Against the vaunted superior skill of Johnson, his own party leader, only a foolish exhibitionist or a skillful, battle-scarred warrior would willingly draw his sword.

Johnson opened by seeking unanimous consent that the Banking and Currency Committee be permitted to meet during the session of the Senate to expedite work on a housing bill.

"I object," announced the Senator from Oregon.

The parliamentary duel was on. Wayne Morse, with the thrust of sharp objections, reduced Johnson, for all his fancy maneuvers, to momentary helplessness in leading the Senate toward swift adjournment. Johnson was compelled to recess the Senate for two hours to permit the committees to function, for under the Senate rules the objection of but one senator can prevent committees from meeting simultaneously with the Senate session. After the Senate reconvened, and Johnson sought to dispense with the reading of the *Journal*, the minutes of the daily sessions, Morse again objected. Johnson, powerless to do more than grumble sarcastically about the waste of public funds inherent in Morse's dilatory tactics, waited impatiently while the reading clerk droned on through page after page. Even the clerk's manner did not escape attention. Morse caught him flipping pages too rapidly, halted the reading to inquire whether he was skipping anything, was advised by the presiding officer that he was reading *about* the labor reform bill just passed. Morse insisted that every word of that bill's 14,000-word text be read aloud. The Senate was immobilized for two more hours as the clerk droned on.

Why was he doing it? Basically, Wayne Morse was being his rebellious self. He was here rebelling against a condition of the congressional mind. Like a hibernating bear, the Congress drowses through the late winter, slowly comes to consciousness in the spring, develops a ravenous appetite for a hopper full of new and sometimes indigestible bills, and by Labor Day is surly and easily provoked to anger if further restrained from its natural urge to lumber off to the woods and caves far from Washington. Only the tiger braves this bearish mood.

Morse's beastly behavior, initially provoked by irritation with the holiday work schedule, soon gained a nobler cause. In that Saturday morning's Washington *Post*, columnist Roscoe Drummond tried to relieve congressional anxiety over the coming of Khrushchev by advising "that neither protocol nor precedent nor courtesy requires Congress to invite Mr. Khrushchev to speak." But, concluded Drummond, "Congress certainly ought not to run for cover during Mr. Khrushchev's presence in Washington by rushing to adjourn before it finishes its business." Arriving that morning with Drummond's piece in hand, Wayne Morse made it the central theme of an hour and a half lecture to the Senate in justification of his dilatory tactics. "As a member of the Senate Foreign Relations Committee, I believe that any planned walkout on Khrushchev will be interpreted in many parts of the world where we are trying to win men's minds to the cause of freedom as an affront not only against Russia, but against our own professed ideals of peace," Morse declared.

Alexander Wiley, senior Republican on the Foreign Relations Committee, worried about what would happen if Khrushchev should invite himself up to the Senate, and under Rule XXXIII [allowing "members of national legislatures or foreign countries" to visit the Senate floor during sessions"] the Communist dictator should amble into the chamber. "And if by a quirk of fate he were recognized while on the floor of the Senate [could he possibly be ignored?] . . . we might then experience a real filibuster," exclaimed Wiley. "Once recognized, the likelihood would be that he would not yield to anyone." It was a nightmarish thought the portly Wisconsin Senator could not dismiss. Morse could. The rules implied that outsiders were granted access to the chamber only upon invitation, said Morse, not merely on their own volition. Unconvinced, Wiley asked for a ruling from the chair. Vice-president Nixon ruled that Morse was right. Khrushchev could not take the Senate chamber singlehandedly, at least not without a by-your-leave.

The Senate Foreign Relation Committee had met with Mikoyan and Kozlov, two of Khrushchev's top deputies, during earlier Washington visits. Morse said it would be well if senators could similarly question the Soviet Premier to assist them in appraising the future course of action to follow in relations with Russia. Seeing no sign of a concurrence with this view from the Senate leaders, Morse relentlessly continued his one-man campaign to keep Congress in town until Khrushchev arrived ten days hence. Just as doggedly, the Senate inched its way into the night, successfully passing one bill before quitting after midnight.

When Labor Day arrived, Morse was at his post, interrupting with parliamentary inquiries so thick and fast that Johnson pleaded with Vice-president Nixon "for protection of my rights." In the polite jargon of the place, Nixon told Morse to keep still. Morse had a rosebud in his lapel, his signal to the Senate that he was planning a lengthy speech, one so long that the rosebud would be wilted long before the senator was. A Labor Day lecture on the history of the workingman's rise to organized strength seemed both appropriate and useful in engaging the Senate for much of its day. After enjoying the threat, however, he gallantly switched tactics and presented his rose to Senator Margaret Chase Smith. By this time newspaper editorials were pouring in, scorching and praising Morse, but all of them recognizing him as the hair shirt of the Senate.

On the fourth day of the siege Johnson conceded failure in the drive to get through by the end of the week. "We have more than 100 bills for the Senate to consider," he lamented. But then without explanation, Morse quietly lifted his blockade. The Senate that day whipped through eighty-three bills, sixty-two more on Thursday, and twenty-one on Friday. Lyndon Johnson, the leader who brought legislative automation to the Senate, had regained control of the machinery.

The end of the parliamentary war had come quietly in Johnson's office with only Senator J. William Fulbright of Arkansas co-operating in the truce talks. Morse later told of this meeting in a newsletter mailed to thousands of Oregon voters:

> After I made my point that the Congress should stay in session until Khrushchev arrived in Washington and the Senate Foreign Relations Committee could meet with him, Senator Johnson called Senator Fulbright, and me to his office and we discussed the matter. Senator

Fulbright, chairman of the committee, told Senator Johnson that he agreed with me that the Foreign Relations Committee should treat Mr. Krushchev the same as other foreign high government officials. It was agreed that the Russian ambassador in Washington be advised that the Foreign Relations Committee of the Senate, plus any other Senators who might wish to come to the meeting, would be glad to meet with Mr. Krushchev at a coffee hour in the Foreign Relations Committee room in the Capitol at 5 P.M. on September 16th if such a meeting could be fitted into his schedule. Senator Fulbright and I each called the Russian ambassador, with the result that arrangements were made.

When the Senate finished its work at 6:22 A.M., some six hours before Mr. Khrushchev's big jet landed in Washington, the Congress of the United States, with no further objection from Wayne Morse, adjourned for the year, happy to refer to the Foreign Relations Committee the role of host to the Soviet dictator. Morse, gratified with this result, wrote his constituents:

The meeting with Mr. Khrushchev lasted for an hour and 35 minutes. Many Senators expressed to me, after the meeting, their appreciation for the position that I had taken in regard to the matter. . . . Certainly we were sobered by our meeting with him. He is a tough and intelligent adversary who knows the objectives which the leaders want for Russia. He proved to us that our struggle against communism over the next century will be no easy task, and that Americans had better wake up to these facts of life before it is too late. . . . I am proud of the part I played in bringing it about.

The story is incomplete without its ironic postscript. In the meeting in Johnson's office, one fact apparently was withheld from Morse— that the plan to have Khruschev up before the Committee had been initiated by Fulbright *before* Morse had expressed this idea on the Senate floor. But, the crafty Johnson must have thought, why spoil the possibilities of this coincidence by revealing it? Fulbright willingly sacrificed pride of authorship in order that Johnson might pacify Morse, a small price to pay for the resumption of expeditious action on the Senate floor.

Convinced that he had inspired the meeting with Khrushchev, Morse could consider his truce with Johnson honorably efficacious. Better still, to take credit for the outcome was a neat answer to criticism, such as the Portland *Oregonian* editorial which described him as "the albatross Oregon has hung around the neck of the United States Congress."

Lyndon Johnson, whose skill as majority leader derived partly from knowing the idiosyncracies of his colleagues, knew how to tame the tiger for the moment. But Wayne Morse could start roaring again any time he wished to embark on another noble filibuster.

15. MARCHING INTO HELLS CANYON

Historic Giveaways . . . Ideological Giveaways . . .
Defeated on Two Fronts . . . Arm-twisting at the White
House

LESS than a month after the new Eisenhower administration laid hold upon the government in 1953, Wayne Morse began a series of speeches dedicated to Senator George Norris, the insurgent conservationist Republican from Nebraska who sponsored the New Deal TVA legislation. Said Morse in this warning and prophecy:

> I hope that by the time I conclude the series of speeches which I intend to make in the next few months, I shall at least have broadened the understanding of the American people so that they will indubitably realize that they, and they alone, own the streams and the other great natural resources of the United States. These resources do not belong to the private utilities of our country. The forests do not belong to the lumber companies of our country, to be used for exploitation purposes. The public domain does not belong to those who would seek to so use it that they would change the western plains of America into an eroded China. The public domain belongs to the people of our generation in trust for future generations of Americans, and in the great natural resources fight which will be waged in this Congress against an administration which, in my judgment, unless it is checked, will exploit our natural resources for selfish interests. I see an arousing of the American people to a clearer understanding of their vested interest in their own natural resources. . . . If we are not constantly on guard, the movement which is under way to exploit our natural resources will take the form of law.

What seemed to others, even liberals, like an exceedingly premature cry of "wolf" soon had others joining in to castigate the new administration. The new President, quick to implement his campaign promises to Texans, recommended that Congress pass a tidelands oil bill. Although the liberals resisted this bill, there was little doubt of the outcome, for Congress had previously passed tidelands legislation but Truman had vetoed it. The major unanswered question now was what other resource proposals would the new G.O.P. regime make?

Concern on this score reached the bipartisan stage when Senator Aiken, the Vermont Republican, expressed his worries about "the determination on the part of certain groups to acquire unto themselves the natural resources of the United States which have always belonged to the people." Aiken deplored schemes of private interests to "seize Niagara Falls" or "grab the power from the Saint Lawrence [seaway] development" and said he was convinced "this great raid which has been building up will reach its climax very soon. I believe that President Eisenhower will soon be under greater pressure to permit the raiding of natural resources than any other President has been put under for a generation."

The day the Senate passed the tidelands bill, May 5, 1953, the governors of the western states were invited to lunch with the new Secretary of the Interior, Douglas McKay, who himself had been Governor of Oregon until Eisenhower picked him for the cabinet. At this meeting McKay revealed that the new administration was going to junk plans for building a federal dam in Hells Canyon in the Snake River on the Idaho-Oregon border. This decision, ratified by the cabinet two weeks before, was then announced publicly at a news conference in which McKay was flanked by these smiling western governors, Republicans all. Only Governor Earl Warren of California made it a point to advise a reporter that his presence did not necessarily constitute an endorsement of the Hells Canyon decision.

Bringing in the executives of the sovereign states symbolized plainly the policy switch from the federal government to private enterprise. The new businessmen's administration was determined to stop Uncle Sam from doing business which could be handled by "local interests," in this case Idaho Power Company. This power company qualified magnificently because it was local in so many places: in Idaho, where it reaps the fruits of a virtual monopoly in the electric business with the highest consumer rates of any utility in the Northwest; in Maine, the state in which it is incorporated and where its stockholders hold their annual meetings; and in the great financial centers of the East, where its most substantial owners take comfort in Idaho Power's steady earnings.

A Washington public-relations counselor who knew McKay personally tells a story, never confirmed by Eisenhower administration officials, that he was visiting with McKay in his office at the Interior Department some weeks before the Hells Canyon decision was announced. McKay handed him a report to read while he answered the white telephone on his desk, his direct line with the White House. When the call was completed, McKay turned to the man and, so the story goes, said, "You can tear up that report. The White House has just changed my mind."

The report in the visitor's hands supported the high Hells Canyon federal dam.

As a governor who had previously favored federally built dams in Oregon's Willamette Valley and had never opposed the large Columbia River dams which the New Deal had brought to the Northwest, McKay sympathized with the full and comprehensive river development epitomized by Hells Canyon dam. McKay, however, was neither a strong nor a brilliant advocate. He was, in Washington parlance, "a nice guy." McKay utterly revered Eisenhower; and Sherman Adams, on the other end of the white-telephone line, was Eisenhower's brisk, demanding chief of staff. As an old army man, Douglas McKay cheerfully took his orders and tried to make the best of things. Unhappily for him and for his President, his best was not good enough. The new Republican administration was soon faced with an onslaught of criticism which began with Wayne Morse's Norris memorial speech. It gathered bipartisan strength, gained momentum from the organized conservation groups, and added a new political epithet, *giveaway*, to the voters' vocabulary as tidelands and Hells Canyon were followed by Al Sarena, Dixon-Yates, the partnership power policy, the grazing bill, atomic patents, and oil leases on wildlife refuges. But were these genuinely insidious giveaways?

Historic Giveaways

The names of the conflicts were new, but the problem here was as old as America's westward expansion, settlement, and economic development. At its roots it is this: How does a capitalistic, democratic society apportion, with fairness to all, the vast riches of its natural resources so as to enhance the public welfare?

The conflict of ideas today among opposing forces is not greatly different than it was in the time of Washington, Adams, and Jefferson, when basic resource policy was first debated. As Secretary of the Treasury, Hamilton espoused the view of many Eastern interests that the vast public lands of the Western territories should be sold in large tracts to speculators who would convert them into small tracts for sale to settlers. Many influential Easterners owned western land which they wanted to sell before the West was thrown open to settlement. Madison favored dumping all land on the market at once to pay off the national debt. Washington also owned western land but took a western-minded stand against speculators and in behalf of selling the land at prices that would accommodate small, stable settlers. When Congress passed the land act of 1796, offering settlers 640-acre tracts at $2 per acre, it "set the rhythm of American soil development for a century to come."[1] Here was the basic policy governing the great land resource: that in this land of self-government there would be wide and equal opportunity for individual development, free of exploiters, unlike the policy adopted in Canada of fostering loyalty to the crown by making enormous free land grants to loyalists and government officials.

In succeeding years Congress made land-purchase terms more attractive, adopting a pay-as-you-go policy which stimulated migration to the West. It was not until the advent of the railroad in the West that the greatest giveaway to a few corporate interests was carried forward under the congressional policy of subsidizing the transcontinental lines through vast land grants. Under the policy of giving the railroad company twenty square miles of land in alternating blocks on either side of the completed rail line plus generous government loans, great engineering hardships were surmounted in the companies' zeal to press ahead and to span the continent. The great scandal of the period, investigated by Congress, showed that Union Pacific's backers had created a separate construction company, the Credit Mobilier of America, through which they drained off huge profits by charging the railroad unreasonably high costs for building the transcontinental line. The stockholders of Central Pacific Railroad employed similar enriching devices. Through this giveaway program, the nation gained its first great East-West transportation system; and some of the most substantial private fortunes of the West were amassed by Mark Hopkins, Collis P. Huntington,

[1] *The Growth of the American Republic*, Morison and Commager, 1937.

Leland Stanford, and Charles Crocker, who each left no less than forty million dollars at his death.

By the turn of the twentieth century, however, fortunes were being made at every hand by the exploitation of what seemed to many like unlimited resources with which to satisfy the raging appetite of the maturing industrial giant. In 1892 the New York *Tribune* compiled a list of the nation's new millionaires and found 178 in lumber, 113 in coal and lead mining, 73 in gold and silver, and 72 in oil. When Theodore Roosevelt became President, he was astonished to discover that of the original 800 million acres of virgin timber, less than 200 million acres remained standing—and four fifths of that had passed into private hands beyond the reach of government-imposed conservation regulations. Water-power sites on the nation's rivers had been acquired by private owners who had no thought for such unprofitable considerations as flood and erosion control or watershed protection.

Taking prompt and broad advantage of the Forest Reserve Act passed by Congress in 1891 but used only sparingly by Harrison, Cleveland, and McKinley, the first great conservationist in the White House set aside 150 million acres of timberland for a national forest system; and, at Senator La Follette's suggestion, Roosevelt withdrew from public entry some 85 million acres in Alaska and the Northwest, pending a study of their mineral and hydroelectric potential. In his energetic fashion, TR also aroused public opinion in favor of conservation, against careless exploitation. He cracked down on land frauds, made western cattlemen pay for grazing their vast herds on the public domain, and created the Bureau of Reclamation under the 1902 Reclamation Act, the opening wedge for the magnificent irrigation works of the West from Grand Coulee Dam on the Columbia River to Hoover Dam on the Colorado River.

After Roosevelt promoted the conservation movement, there followed, ironically, the classic giveaway scandal, Teapot Dome, during the Harding administration. At La Follette's urging, the Senate investigated this episode and found that Interior Secretary Albert Fall had arranged to have transferred to his department's jurisdiction naval oil reserves in the western states which he then quietly leased non-competitively to friends in the oil industry, Doheny and Sinclair, who rewarded Fall with the tidy consideration of $400,000 for his co-operation. These disclosures brought court action canceling the fraudulent leases and imprisoning the principals. The Teapot

Dome, named for the Wyoming oil reserve, was the classic scandal because it brought together a high public official and a powerful private economic interest for the purpose of exploiting public resources for mutual financial gain.

Ideological Giveaways

With the possible exception of the Dixon-Yates episode, in which a non-paid consultant to the government was implicated in a conflict of interest involving the banking firm with which he was permanently associated, the giveaways attacked by Morse and the conservationists during the Eisenhower administration do not fit the mold of Teapot Dome and other lesser acts of fraud which troubled Harding, Grant, and other Presidents. Rather, they fit into Hamilton's more sophisticated mold. They were perfectly legal, based upon new interpretations of old laws or newly enacted or proposed laws urged upon Congress by the Eisenhower administration; and they did not, nor were they meant to, privately enrich public officials. Just as Hamilton's proposal for disposition of western lands was for what he deemed to be the high national purpose of strengthening the economic interests of the East, the controversial proposals of the Eisenhower era were advanced with the same determined passion that Taft gave to his labor fight, and for essentially the same reasoning: to strengthen the private economic sector against what the victorious Republicans regarded as the threat fostered by twenty years of New and Fair Deal administrations. Just as the Taft-Hartley Act was the Republicans' answer to the threat of growing labor power, the decision to abandon the federal Hells Canyon dam, to execute the Dixon-Yates contract, and to advance the partnership power policy constituted the Republicans' answer to the grievance of the private electric utility industry against the rapid growth of public power from TVA to the Columbia Basin after the great electric utility trusts were demolished in the New Deal thirties.

The national consequence of ideological giveaways can best be judged by historians with the 20-20 vision which hindsight affords them. The exploitation and profiteering in the railroad land grants are easily deplored, but the national consequence of the completion of the transcontinental railroads was quite breath-taking.

There is a yet finer distinction to be drawn respecting ideological giveaways. It is that too often the high national purpose, which Hamilton and the railroad land sponsors hoped to serve, has not been truly present. Too often the impelling force has been the dogmatic use of "free enterprise" as a magic shibboleth to justify any form of exploitation of the public domain. Teddy Roosevelt articulated this distinction by a reference to the countless ideological giveaways which had legally been executed before he took office. He said:

A narrowly legalistic point of view toward the natural resources obtained in the Departments and controlled the Governmental administrative machinery. Through the General Land Office and other government bureaus the public resources were being handled and disposed of in accordance with the small considerations of petty legal formalities instead of for the large purposes of constructive development, and the habit of deciding, whenever possible, in favor of private interests against the public welfare was firmly fixed.

A number of the officials of the Eisenhower administration quickly reverted to the old "habit of deciding, whenever possible, in favor of private interests." To General Eisenhower, the new leader who was vastly unschooled in such fine points of public administration, this approach was not "against the public welfare," as TR had maintained. Quite the contrary. Columnist Arthur Krock in April 1953 encapsulated the move as follows:

Methodically, and at a more rapid pace than he is proceeding to carry out some other campaign pledges, the President is taking the government out of competition with private business to the utmost practical degree. . . . Arrangements are in train for the disposal to private industry of synthetic rubber factories built and owned by the government. The Attorney General wants to drop the criminal antitrust proceedings that were started by the Truman Administration against the big oil companies. This is on the President's direct order. . . . Mr. Hoover's recommendations, to reverse "twenty years of creeping socialism in the field of federal electric power," will be seriously studied. . . . The Secretary of Commerce, Sinclair Weeks, wants to sell to private operators the government's inland waterway barge line. A determined move is in the making to return a considerable measure of the control of farm credit to the financial community. . . . It was to assure this approach that the President-elect formed his cabinet of "eight millionaires and one plumber". . . .

This is quickly materializing some old and more recent issues between the Republicans and Democratic parties—on conservation, public power, big business, monopoly, credit control and interest rates on government paper foremost among them. . . .

Defeated on Two Fronts

In Congress the year before, Wayne Morse had introduced legislation urged by the Truman administration to authorize the Bureau of Reclamation to construct the Hells Canyon dam. As the chief advocate of this federal project, Morse led the outcry against McKay's announcement as "a shocking betrayal of the public interest" and further proof "that the Eisenhower Administration would be a tool of American monopolies."

McKay's decision had the effect of ending the government's earlier opposition to the plan of Idaho Power for building its own hydroelectric facilities in this reach of the turbulent Snake River where the Bureau of Reclamation had hoped to build one huge federal dam. The utility company had then to apply for a fifty-year license from another agency of the government, the Federal Power Commission, whose final authority was vested in five commissioners appointed by the President. The Eisenhower administration, like its predecessors, maintained that the Power Commission was an independent body; but just as surely as the new power policy of encouraging local utilities was announced, this Republican philosophy was soon reflected in the decisions rendered by the new power commissioners appointed by Eisenhower.

Idaho Power met a forceful challenger, however, when a National Hells Canyon Association was quickly formed at the grass roots of the Pacific Northwest by representatives of fifty-six organizations in five western states, chiefly the Grange, Farmers' Union, AFL-CIO, and local public-power groups. Led by two former Interior Department officials from the Truman administration, C. Girard Davidson and Mrs. Evelyn N. Cooper, the association intervened in the FPC proceedings and battled against the utility's lawyers through 20,000 pages of testimony, the longest record in the history of the FPC. The presiding examiner, William J. Costello, a career civil servant who was not insensitive to the subtle but nonetheless powerful influence of the new administration's power policy, reached twin conclusions: First, that the high federal dam would be "the better investment and the more nearly ideal development of the middle Snake," and secondly, that due to the unfavorable "political climate," exemplified by the Administration's insistence on the Dixon-Yates contract for the TVA area, it was obvious that the federal dam could not be built in the foreseeable future. Therefore the Idaho Power Company should be issued a license. In August, 1955, the FPC ratified Costello's conclusion, but dropped any mention of the engineering superiority of the high dam over the more modest facilities the company proposed.

Morse, meanwhile, was trying to head off the hombres at the pass. If he could get his Hells Canyon bill enacted into law, it would estop the utility for all time from going ahead. This was a futile hope during the Republican-controlled Congress of 1953–54. In 1955, with Morse now a registered Democrat, his new party companions pitched in to help the Hells Canyon cause and to bolster Morse's re-election prospects for 1956. Hearings were held by the House and the Senate Interior Committee, but a coalition of Republicans and a few Southern Democrats who opposed the bill kept it bottled up until 1956, when suddenly two new circumstances broke in Morse's favor. In the House committee a Colorado Republican, J. Edgar Chenoweth, broke the solid Republican ranks against the bill after he was quietly advised by the Democrats that a pet reclamation project for his state was doomed if he remained adamantly opposed to Hells Canyon. Chenoweth's switch gave the bill clearance by a 15 to 13 vote. In the Senate committee, it was a significant change in membership which broke the barricade. Long of Louisiana, who is said to have pledged to a Northwestern Republican that he would never vote for Hells Canyon out of gratitude for the other's support for the tidelands oil bill, was transferred to a new vacancy on the Foreign Relations Committee upon Senator Alben Barkley's death. In his place on the Interior Committee went a Hells Canyon bill supporter, W. Kerr Scott of North Carolina, whose vote cleared the Morse bill for floor debate.

As the showdown neared in the Senate in 1956, the White House exerted such pressure on Republican senators that several of them told Allen Drury, then a New York *Times* correspondent, that it was "as great as that applied on any issue" since Eisenhower took office. Lobbyists for the natural-gas and oil industries teamed to help electric utility officials buttonhole their friends to oppose Morse's bill, causing one legislator to report he was kept up all one night by these intense devotees of private enterprise who sought to dissuade him from backing Hells Canyon. The organized conservationists, public-power groups, and the labor unions were active in behalf of the bill. Into this whirlpool of pressure one other element was introduced. Senator Eastland of Mississippi is said to have advised the Democratic leaders that he would be delighted to support Hells Canyon, if only it were not the cause of such grief to Welker of Idaho, a good friend of the utility. Welker, after all, had brought comfort to Eastland as a member of his Judiciary Committee by voting to pigeonhole civil-rights bills. It wouldn't be sporting, or politically wise, to arouse Welker by voting for Hells Canyon, now would it?

Representatives of the rural electric co-operatives, a public-power group strongly supporting Hells Canyon, approached Senator Russell. They later reported that this field general of the Southerners said he surely would be pleased to be more co-operative, if only Morse and the other Western public-power diehards would share some of *his* region's concern on the racial front. Oregon's Democratic National Committeeman, Jebby Davidson, made these same rounds, sweet-talking the Southerners in the unmistakable drawl of his native state of Louisiana. "I'd like to help Wayne on this one," replied one man of Dixie, "but down in my state there is only one issue—civil rights. If Wayne would be willing to recognize that, maybe we could reach an understanding." Morse at the time told me that upon hearing this indirectly, he sent back word for the Southerners to "go to hell."

When the roll was called, Morse was ten votes shy. The Hells Canyon bill was defeated, 51 to 41. Eight Southern Democrats voted with forty-three Republicans to overcome the Democrats' natural majority. Only two Republicans bolted to vote for the bill. Coming on the eve of his campaign for re-election, his first attempt at election as a Democrat, this was a bitter climax for Wayne Morse's most hard-fought legislative cause.

The Hells Canyon bill was doomed in any event, for the President's veto power could not have been circumvented even had all the Democrats been aligned with Morse. But in the misty world of politics where clear pictures such as this are avoided, the Hells Canyon bill's demise in 1956 represented a *personal* defeat for Morse simply because it occurred in *his* realm. If it had faltered in the

House or on the President's desk, the Hells Canyon cause would have been just as dead, but the politics of it would have been much more comforting for Wayne Morse, who could then have blamed the defeat wholly upon the failings of others. The defeat in the Senate, to be sure, was not wholly Morse's failing. It is questionable whether any senator on that occasion could have passed that bill. But his obstinate adherence to the Morse code—not only declining to bargain with the Southerners, but declining with a curse—assured defeat by a decisive margin.

The Eisenhower administration was delighted with this outcome. It saved the President from the necessity of vetoing a hot item, and it appeared then to enhance Republican prospects in Oregon against Morse's re-election. It seemed to fortify the G.O.P. charge that Morse talks big but accomplishes little. But Morse, too, found these events useful. They contributed to the idea that Wayne Morse was the number one target of the G.O.P. that election year. Though the Republicans never put it so bluntly, their actions gave credence to this image of liberal martyrdom which Morse sought.

Arm-Twisting at the White House

A year and a half earlier the White House had been the scene of a meeting in which Sherman Adams and Attorney General Herbert Brownell had placed a firm armlock upon the governors of Oregon and Washington to encourage them to run against the two most troublesome Democratic senators from those states, Morse and Magnuson. Although denying at the time an exclusive Seattle *Times* story to this effect, Governors Patterson of Oregon and Langlie of Washington nevertheless later announced their candidacies.

Paul Patterson had attained the governorship upon succession when McKay resigned to enter the Eisenhower cabinet in 1953. When Patterson ran for the office in the 1954 election, he won by a handsome margin, unhurt by the Democratic gains which brought Neuberger's Senate victory that same election. An able lawyer with a quiet manner which fostered confidence, Patterson was politically unblemished by past controversies. In all respects, he appeared to Republicans to be the man to beat Wayne Morse, the one to whom they could confidently hand the long black whip for the massive public flogging to which they had sentenced that betrayer of the party which never forgets. Here in 1956, as he prepared for the uncertain role of a Democratic senatorial candidate in Oregon, Wayne Morse was confronted with the most able and attractive challenger of his career.

After announcing his candidacy on January 28, the governor three nights later went to the Arlington Club, Portland's most exclusive businessmen's haven, there to take counsel from his advisers for the campaign ahead. As John Higgins, William Ireland, and Ted Gamble sat in an upstairs lounge with their fifty-five-year-old candidate, Patterson silently slumped back on the davenport, unconscious. Before a hastily summoned physician could administer effective aid, Patterson died, within ten minutes of his coronary attack.

The leadership vacuum thus created was not readily filled. To those Oregon Republicans who turned to Interior Secretary McKay in hopes he would take on Morse, McKay said he liked the cabinet just fine. "A job for a younger man," is the way the sixty-two-year-old party warhorse sized up the grim task of tackling Morse when I asked him about it in an interview March 5. Two other highly respected Republicans stepped forward. They were Lamarr Tooze, Portland attorney, and Philip S. Hitchcock, ex-state senator with the reputation of a persuasive moderate liberal. But at 2 A.M. on March 9, the deadline for candidates to file at Salem, Tooze and Hitchcock were each awakened by a telephone call inviting them to breakfast at Portland's Multnomah Hotel. Their caller was Douglas McKay, who had slipped undetected into town by using a pseudonym on the hotel register and on the passenger list of the aircraft which had brought him flying home from Washington.

Over breakfast, McKay advised his two friends that he was that day going to Salem to file against Wayne Morse. Tooze, ever deferential to McKay's pleasure in the matter, was so pleased that he volunteered to drive McKay to Salem. Hitchcock, however, balked. His refusal to withdraw brought immediate consternation and dismay to McKay, who had been led to suppose that the skids had been greased for the eleventh-hour surprise launching of his unopposed candidacy. Who had masterminded this maneuver? And what had converted McKay from an unwilling contender into one who now asked more willing contenders to step aside?

Behind this move were essentially the same men who had four years before rebuffed Morse at the Salem meeting of the Republican convention delegation. "We paid for one or two very sketchy polls," John Higgins later told me. "McKay stood up pretty well. I supported McKay, and I got him to come out here and run." One of the party's most wealthy backstage participants in Oregon, Higgins was a former senior partner of the prominent New York law firm, Sullivan and Cromwell. As head of the firm's litigation department, Higgins had been impressed with the potential of a young district attorney, Thomas E. Dewey, and tried to hire him in 1932 at triple his public salary. Dewey at first accepted, but then had to decline after New York Republican leaders told him his prospects for the governorship were excellent. Higgins years later ran Dewey's 1948 presidential campaign in Oregon, and retained over the years his influential connections with the leaders of the party nationally and with the Eisenhower administration.

The poll arranged by Dewey and Higgins became the lever for prying McKay loose from his cabinet seat. One official says it showed that McKay's support among Oregon voters was in the mid-forties, Morse's in the high thirties. Sherman Adams says in *Firsthand Report* that the poll "showed conclusively" that McKay could lick Morse "by a comfortable margin." So, two days before the Oregon filing deadline, Adams and Republican National Chairman Hall, Attorney General Brownell and Postmaster General Summerfield showed McKay the poll at a breakfast meeting and put the heat on him to run. Whether McKay thought he had any clear alternative when so confronted by the president's top political advisors, is not clear. Adams reports that McKay set two conditions: that Adams convince Mrs. McKay, which Adams says he did; and that he have no opponents in the primary, which Adams promised but couldn't deliver because Phil Hitchcock refused to bow out. McKay later explained that he decided to run sometime between that breakfast meeting Wednesday and an 11 A.M. appointment with Eisenhower Thursday. Finding the Chief Executive "pleased" with his decision, McKay climbed aboard an airliner that afternoon for Portland. The hasty nature of his decision was indicated by McKay's failure to notify even his closest political adviser in Oregon, William L. Phillips of Salem. Also, elected party officials were advised after the fact of McKay's sudden move.

Amid the confusion created in McKay's Multnomah Hotel suite when Hitchcock balked, party officials entered upon the scene to debate the proper course. State Chairman Wendell Wyatt and Phillips tried to dissuade McKay from running. National Committeeman Jess Gard was equally certain McKay should run. Newspapermen, upon discovering this little drama, were told by McKay he was uncertain of his course. Press wires immediately flashed this first intimation of McKay's candidacy to Oregon's afternoon newspapers, but what came in on the White House news printer was the element of uncertainty. A press release had already been mimeographed and awaited distribution to reporters at 3 P.M. eastern time, noon at Portland. A series of transcontinental telephone calls involving McKay, Hall, and Adams, in which McKay at one point plaintively exclaimed to Adams that Hitchcock "refuses to withdraw," soon concluded the confusion. McKay set out for Salem to become a candidate for the Senate; and the White House, only an hour behind schedule, issued a mimeographed copy of a letter signed by Eisenhower which read: "Dear Doug: Your decision . . . is worthy of the highest commendation."

In suite 417 in the Senate Office Building the next morning, Wayne Morse was almost beside himself with joy. For months he had been daring the Republicans to run McKay against him for a test of voter sentiment on his allegations about giveaways of natural resources. In a contest between Morse and McKay, who was the more likely fellow to be placed on the defensive before the average voter: the one charged with betraying a political party by deserting it, or the one charged with betraying the public's inheritance in forests, rivers, and other resources? Adding to Morse's delight were the needling observations of his Democratic allies. "No one in history has ever taken on this much hard work in order to get fired gracefully," observed Democratic State Chairman Howard Morgan. The McKay episode reminded Monroe Sweetland of the Biblical story of Uriah, and it evoked from Senator Douglas the recollection that "if a figure around the court of Kaiser Wilhelm became unpopular, he was sent to the most dangerous portion of the western front."

Unquestionably McKay had become one of the more controversial cabinet officers, standing firmly behind those Administration decisions which had so aroused the organized conservationists and partisan critics. It was a big leap, however, from this fact to the conclusion that McKay had been dismissed when he was thrust into the Oregon Senate race. A dispatch of mine at the time brought a call from Brownell to deny a report that he had assured some of McKay's critics that the Secretary of the Interior would soon be separated from the Administration. Confirming that he and Adams and Hall had discussed in advance the strategy by which McKay might be induced to run, Brownell said, "I don't think that [meaning giveaway criticism of McKay] entered into it at all." The plausible logic of Brownell was that it made no political sense to drop McKay from the cabinet because of his supposed vulnerability to criticism and simultaneously urge him into a Senate contest which the Republicans badly wished to win.

There was, nevertheless, no sign of hesitancy at the White House in relinquishing McKay's cabinet services. The poll which Hall pressed into McKay's palm during their breakfast meeting was a straw grasped by those who were anxious to give McKay this new assignment. That poll was characterized by an Oregon Republican official as "totally meaningless in light of the fact that there was such a huge proportion of undecided (voters) and it was so early, before any issues were framed." McKay was not fired; nor would he ever have been let out, any more than Agriculture Secretary Benson, because he was under fire. To General Eisenhower, Captain McKay was simply reassigned, as recommended by Chief of Staff Adams, from headquarters command to put down that most distasteful rebellion on the western front. Undoubtedly to the general, it was an unconscious soldierly expectation that his captain would return victorious from the field to receive the honors owing to the triumphant.

The rebellion of Wayne Morse was not that readily put down.

16. THE OREGON UPRISING

Morse vs. McKay . . . Emancipating the Indians . . . Al Sarena and Big Meadows . . . Time for a Change

IT IS doubtful that the White House had any realistic intelligence in advance of the Oregon uprising of 1956. Or perhaps it was simply a case of blind confidence that Wayne Morse's cry of "Giveaway" represented a mere one-man rebellion. In any event, dispatching a cabinet officer to the front instantly transformed Oregon into a battleground of national significance.

For Wayne Morse, the more immediate problem was his first venture into a Democratic primary. His opponent for the Democratic nomination was a filling-station operator from Hood River known to his neighbors as Woody Smith. Upon branding Morse a phony Democrat, the challenger unfurled his full name, Woodrow Wilson Smith, and his slogan: "Democrats are born—not made." Smith even filed suit against Morse on grounds the senator was not an eligible contender for the Democratic nomination, a lame but attention-getting action which the courts readily dismissed. (Actually there had been a slip-up in the completion of Morse's registration as a Democrat that winter's day when he suddenly appeared at the Lane County Courthouse to switch parties; but neither Smith nor the Republicans were thorough enough to catch it.)

Ignoring his unknown challenger, Morse remained in Washington throughout the May primary campaign and easily won the Democratic nomination. Smith, however, received 38,959 votes, which showed a hard core of resistance to Morse from the conservative element in the Democratic party. These were voters unlikely to be won over to Morse, so long as his opponent was suitably conservative. Could Morse hope to pick up enough moderate or liberal Republicans to offset this loss?

In these circumstances, it is not difficult to perceive the *theory* upon which conservative Republicans advanced in pitting McKay against Morse. Theoretically all good Republicans would vote against their betrayer; and joined by conservative Democrats, they could defeat Morse with a solid, conservative Republican candidate with a state-wide reputation and an attractive vote-getting record. This theory soon fell victim to the dynamics of the campaign.

The initial dynamic was the indignant reaction to the way in which McKay was pushed into the race. Salem editor Charles A. Sprague, a former Republican governor himself, wrote editorially: "The *Statesman* objects to the commissioning of a candidate by the Republican national chairman or by the White House as was done with McKay. . . . We think Hitchcock should stay in the race both because of his splendid qualifications, and to repudiate the notion that Oregon is a province of the G.O.P. GHQ." Hitchcock persuasively argued that he was the more likely Republican to defeat Morse. "I'm strong in the areas where Morse is strong," he said, referring to labor and minority groups. "I'm not on the defensive, as McKay necessarily would have to be. Nor am I an unwilling candidate as McKay, by his own admission, is." Paul Harvey, the AP bureau chief at Salem, said Hitchcock was the only state senator he ever saw who could cause votes to change in the legislature by making a speech. McKay, the ex-governor, won the nomination—but by fewer than a majority of the Republican votes cast! McKay received 123,281 votes to 99,296 for Hitchcock, while two minor contenders, Elmer Deetz and George Altvater, gained 26,695 votes between them.

If Morse was in trouble with the conservative Democrats, obviously McKay faced difficulties he had never before confronted in his undefeated political career, which started in the mayor's chair at Salem. Each side sought comfort in statistics: Morse in the 72,000 ballots by which his vote exceeded McKay's; and McKay in the 14,529 ballots by which the total vote of all the Republican candidates exceeded that of the two Democrats in the primary. What everyone knew with certainty was that Wayne Morse vs. Douglas McKay was to be a horse race down to the wire.

To Douglas McKay, this campaign was far more than an attempt to punish a turncoat. He wished to defeat Morse, he explained, to "check the leftward drift in Oregon which he represents. Maybe socialism is too strong a word, but he and a lot of other left-wingers have been trying to lead this state away from the sound, sensible principles that have prevailed here for almost a century."

Born of pioneer Oregon stock (McKay's grandfather had worked for Dr. John McLaughlin at Fort Vancouver when the Oregon territory was being opened to settlement and fur commerce) and in poor rural circumstances, McKay studied agriculture at Oregon State College, but became an auto salesman during the Roaring Twenties. Eventually he built his own successful Chevrolet-Cadillac agency at Salem. He brought to political life an unshakable faith in the free enterprise system. Although a wealthy man, McKay salted his campaigning with references to his humble beginnings—selling newspapers, driving a meat cart, or discovering at age sixteen that underwear was not always made from flour sacks. A wisecracking, affable man who parted his hair down the middle, McKay was always at pains to show that his high station had not changed just plain Doug. A pet joke which delighted Oregonians was: "When we were in Rome, Grandma [his pet name for his wife, Mabel] asked me, didn't I think Saint Peter's was beautiful? 'Sure,' I said, 'but have you seen the '55 Chevies?' "

McKay's indictment against Morse began with one of the senator's more outrageous remarks that President Eisenhower was "completely lacking in all political morality." Said McKay, "He must either prove his charge or himself be convicted of lacking political decency and being a disgrace to the Senate." The indictment continued with the observation that Morse had been completely irresponsible in shifting parties and was basically unresponsive to the desires of Oregon voters; that he had become so ineffective in the Senate that in nine years he had been able to pass only 24 of 488 bills he had introduced; that Morse stood squarely against the leadership of Eisenhower, whose program McKay would foster—namely, further reduce big government and big taxes; further increase security against hazards of unemployment, sickness, and age without added cost of bureaucracy and without surrendering control to the politicians; expand federal-local partnership for electric power, highways, schools, and housing, while keeping control of these efforts close to the people; leadership toward peace. Oregonians seemed certain to support Eisenhower's re-election that November, so how could they fail to eliminate his most persistent critic, McKay was saying, and give the President a man who would be for him, not against him?

To strengthen his appeal, President Eisenhower came winging into Oregon to envelop Doug McKay with the warmth of his smile and an endorsement that was authentic Eisenhowerese: "Put someone in public office upon whose word you can depend. I bring this name to you in that connection: Douglas McKay. Of course, I have not known him nearly as long as many of you in this audience, but I saw him under those special conditions where on a meeting of the minds on a difficult subject, each one bringing in his opinion, his convictions, on what should be done—I shall always testify to this, to Douglas McKay—he never pulled his punches on what he believed to be right. That was what was done as far as his *recommendations* were concerned." However McKay must have felt at being implicitly credited with *recommending* the controversial policies which others had drafted, loyal Doug McKay never intimated that he had been a better conservationist than the White House had permitted him to be in the early high-pressure days of the new administration.

To Wayne Morse, the difference between the two senatorial contenders represented national issues which he reduced to the simplest household terms. The tidelands oil bill was a giveaway of the best hope of better education for children and relief from heavy school taxes because it killed the "oil for education" plan of the liberals. The Administration's 1954 tax-reduction bill had given seventy-three cents of every tax-relief dollar to corporations, only nine cents to families earning $5000 or less. The Administration's anti-inflation tight-money policy was the cause of the home-building decline and the consequent slump in Oregon's chief industry, lumber, and the decline in Oregon workers' paychecks. Administration opposition to a domestic parity wheat bill was preventing Oregon wheatgrowers from securing higher prices. The Administration also opposed increases in social security benefits, as well as in the minimum wage to protect Oregon labor from cheap labor in the Southern states. The Taft-Hartley Act should be revised to avoid legalistic warfare weighted against the unions. McKay's Hells Canyon decision, among other giveaways, would mean high profits for the utilities and higher electric bills for Northwest consumers and industry. The choice for the Senate, as Wayne Morse sized it up, was, "Public interest vs. private interest."

In this, his first Democratic campaign, Morse showed quick mastery of the approach to the voters which his new party circumstances demanded. His technique was the same, of holding out a promise of better things to come to every recognizable segment of society—from the farmer to the veteran, the pensioner to the small businessman, the teacher to the unemployed mill hand. But where the promise of earlier campaigns had been to rescue these folks from the wicked bureaucrats, now the promise was to utilize the services of a benevolent federal government to rescue them from exploitation by the wicked, powerful private interests.

Unlike McKay's easygoing, folksy manner, Morse's campaign manner was stern, humorless, evangelistic. Apparent to all was the zealot in his nature, as he lectured the voters with a relentless gleam in eyes deeply set beneath bristling, dark brows. No one was ever heard to call him "Good Ol' Wayne." He was temperamentally incapable of sauntering down a city sidewalk, shaking hands at random and introducing himself, making small talk. In a meeting hall, a labor temple, he could mount his soapbox and take the hide off the opposition, then hustle through the room shaking every outstretched hand. The difference was that they had come to him, to hear his speech; but voters sought at random in the streets, in the mills, held an unknown and possibly hostile attitude that Wayne Morse preferred to avoid.

After observing his technique, Cabell Phillips wrote in the New York *Times* that Morse is a superb politician because against his glacial manner he balances two political attributes: he has an inexhaustible store of indignation, and he is brilliant, articulate, and persuasive. Also he noted that Morse could usually "sell" an audience and move them to spontaneous outbursts of applause and cheering, although the unsold "often find him pedantic and not a little sanctimonious—a view, incidentally, which is shared by some of his Senate colleagues. His favorite and most evocative posture is that of a free agent unfettered by any obligations save that to his own conscience. It is in this vein that he explains, at nearly every meeting, his switch of party affiliation, and apostasy for which his opposition constantly excoriates him."

Beyond excoriating his shift of parties, the G.O.P. pulled together a 350-page *Documented Record of Senator Wayne Morse*, a compendium of anti-Morse statistics and comment calculated to place him on the defensive. Republican State Chairman Wyatt observed that Morse in years past had silenced many critics by telling them to look at his record. "It was relatively safe to make such an offer, for few persons have the time or the background to examine Senator Morse's voluminous and contradictory record," said Wyatt. While the Republicans' version of Morse's record showed the usual slant of partisan literature, it magnified the senator's ideological flexibility by simply reprinting his own varied remarks over the years. Also, a researcher had calculated that Morse oratory in the Senate from 1945 to 1956 covered 4192.3 pages of the *Congressional Record* at a cost of $320,410.76 to the taxpayers. There was no countering calculation of the dollars Morse had saved the taxpayers with his Morse formula. It asserted that Morse in eleven years had missed over 100 roll-call votes, due to absenteeism which increased as his outside speaking schedule became more intensive and more lucrative. It didn't say that Morse's attendance record has been about average for the Senate.

Oddly, the *Documented Record*, was larded with quotes from Morse's criticisms of the Eisenhower administration, apparently on the theory that Morse was shamed by these remarks. But Morse boasted of this part of his record as proudly as if it were a combat medal of honor. This, after all, was the story he was repeating at every hamlet and crossroad in the state, of his tireless battle in Washington against the marauding interests.

More embarrassing to Morse was a newspaper ad which displayed a large meat grinder under these words:

> How Neuberger made Hamburger of Morse. What is Wayne Morse's real character: Don't take our word for it—take the words of a man who knew Wayne when, Democratic Senator Richard Neuberger. They were written in the days when Mr. Neuberger was a free-lance writer—using his lance to make mincemeat of his future colleague.

Here the Republicans opened a wound for which there was no salve. They quoted from the earlier, obscure writings of Neuberger before he was a senator campaigning all over Oregon in Morse's behalf. The most widely quoted Neuberger description of Morse was from a 1950 article in *Frontier* magazine:

> This lean man with the swarthy black mustache and lantern jaw has reduced to an exact science the technique of leading a political double life. No Parisian roué ever dashed more expertly between boudoir and counting house than does Morse between the dinners of the A.D.A. and the annual banquets of the West Coast Lumbermen's Association. The advantage of having the breadth of a vast continent separating his spheres makes it possible for a man as nimble-witted as Morse to carry off the Jekyll and Hyde performance.

Another Neuberger commentary on Morse, 1947 vintage, gained new currency in Oregon editorial columns in 1956:

> As the attacker, the denouncer of others, the militant critic, Morse has few peers in the Senate. But he himself mixes little mortar to close the breach which he thus exposes.

In the liberal journals, such as the *New Republic*, Neuberger had nicked Morse repeatedly during his earliest Senate days for cosying up to the substantial Republican financiers and giving strength to the whole Republican ticket with his massive indictments of the Democrats and their more liberal program.

Neither Morse nor Neuberger paused to try to defend this page from the past. Now they were allies. Morse's 1954 campaigning, which had helped pull Neuberger through to victory, was now fervently reciprocated. Neuberger and his popular wife, Maurine, stumped the state for Wayne Morse as though their own political future were at stake, as indeed it appeared to be. A Morse victory would enlarge and consolidate the Democrats' gains of the year before, and a McKay victory would jeopardize Neuberger's chances of re-election when he faced the voters once more. No one could envision the strange tragedy that lay ahead.

The failure of the Republicans' campaign against Morse was fundamentally their failure to arouse the electorate at large by some basic charge of wrongdoing against him. Only the most diehard partisans objected to his bolting the G.O.P. Thus they failed to place Morse on the defensive, failed to divert him from pressing his offensive against McKay and the Administration. A large part of their difficulty lay in the personal difference between the two candidates. McKay too often showed symptoms of foot-in-mouth disease, notably when he quipped, "The issues don't amount to anything. It's the votes that count." If Morse ever planted his foot in his mouth he would plausibly argue that that was exactly where the public interest compelled him to place it.

The success of the Morse campaign was fundamentally the success which the Democrats realized in arousing Oregonians about issues which many voters keenly felt. If the issues had been more remote, Morse might have failed to convince Oregonians that the G.O.P. candidate was not just Good Ol' Doug. But McKay's Interior Department had become implicated in a succession of local controversies which had emotional reverberations.

Emancipating the Indians

The case of the "emancipated" Klamath Indians was probably the most telling. The Eisenhower administration early urged upon Congress a new Indian policy which sought the end of federal guardianship over those tribes whose members were declared to be capable of sustaining themselves in the competitive world. In its first year the McKay administration sent Congress ten bills to terminate federal trusteeship over 66,000 Indians living in ten western states, roughly a seventh of the total remaining Indian population. It is not the purpose here to challenge these bills in toto, some of which were overdue, nor to challenge the heart of this Indian policy. It is enough to observe, on the matter of policy, that the Interior Department has historically vacillated between overprotection of the Indians as living archaeological museum pieces rather than American citizens and, at other times, underprotection to the advantage of non-Indian livestock, lumber, and mining interests who coveted Indian resources. The case of Oregon's Klamath Indians suggests the latter.

On the Klamath's million-acre reservation near the California border of southwest Oregon grew a vast forest of Ponderosa pine valued at about 100 million dollars. So long as the government supervised the tribe's interests, this timber was managed on a sustained-yield plan. That is, trees were cut for saw logs and marketed to nearby lumber companies at the highest bid; but the amount of timber cut each year was sufficiently low so as to guarantee a permanent yield of lumber at that rate.

From these planned timber sales, the 2000 members of the Klamath tribe gained a steady cash income which averaged about $3000 per family annually. Other income from farming and working for wages off the reservation raised the average Indian family income to $4000, comparable to non-Indians' living standards in the area. The Klamath termination bill, sponsored by Utah's Republican Senator, Arthur V. Watkins, and Oregon's Republican Congressman Sam Coon, offered the tribe three alternatives: 1. They could organize a private corporation to assume control and management of the tribal property; 2. They could designate a new trustee in the government's place to manage or liquidate the property; 3. If they failed to take any action, the Interior Department would direct a trustee to "liquidate the assets so transferred and distribute the proceeds to members of the tribe."

A small faction of tribal members worked in behalf of the last alternative, which proved popular because it offered each tribal member the pleasant prospect of receiving over $40,000 in cash. This would be possible because "liquidate the assets" meant put the great pine forest on the auction block. The bill sailed through the Republican-controlled Eighty-third Congress with no opposition, its effect widely unrecognized until the Portland *Oregonian* editorially sounded the alarm months later. The newspaper predicted that the reservation would be spoiled for those Indians who wished to stay on, while those who left with their new fortunes "would wake up with deep-throbbing headaches in a few weeks, their money gone and no reservation to go back to live on. Congress should give the tribe some control over liquidation of its assets beyond those flimsy controls in the termination bill."

If the Administration had been naïvely unaware of the devastating implications of liquidating the tribe's assets in its zeal to reduce bureaucratic controls, a more charitable judgment would be in order. But McKay's assistant secretary in charge of Indian affairs, Orme Lewis, a Phoenix lawyer, pointed out to Congress that termination "may result in abandonment of sustained-yield management practices presently enforced by the federal government. Accelerated cutting would result eventually in serious injury to the economy of the entire Klamath Basin." Here was the crux of the matter. Did the government have a public responsibility to prevent this injury to conservation values? The McKay administration thought not. "This asset is private property belonging to the Klamath Indians, even though held in trust by the United States for the tribe, and the provisions of the proposed bill governing termination of special federal relations affecting forest management have been designed to conform to the concept of tribal and individual Indian holdings, as private property," Assistant Secretary Lewis explained. In short, the old habit of deciding in favor of private interests at the expense of the public interest in conservation had taken hold at the Interior Department.

The Oregon Council of Churches, newspapers, and state educators aroused concern for the fate of the Klamaths. Morse was in no position to do any finger-pointing at McKay, for he had not raised any objection when the bill passed the Senate on the consent calendar in July 1954. But by election time it was McKay and not Morse who was on the defensive. Morse and Neuberger had put through a bill to defer termination for two years, pending changes in the act. This was a telling case because McKay, in promising to support protective changes, had to admit by implication that the Interior Department had not acted wisely in its haste to liberate the Indians. With the Democrats and the organized conservationists that year crying "giveaway" for many other reasons, the Klamath case lent an element of credence to that massive arraignment.

Al Sarena and Big Meadows

If Morse's escape from any blame in the Klamath debacle is a cause of wonder, his skill in eluding embarrassing circumstances (first demonstrated in the Montgomery Ward seizure during his first campaign) was better exhibited later in the campaign when the *Oregonian* pinned a giveaway proposal on him. For two years the Democrats had been berating McKay and his Interior subordinates for granting title to 475 acres in the heart of Oregon's Rogue River National Forest to an Alabama firm, Al Serena Mines, Incorporated. Neuberger had run against Cordon using this giveaway as an issue. Morse had called for a congressional investigation. In unprofessional, partisan fashion, a joint House-Senate probe was conducted, but Morse was not a participant.

The bad odor caused by the character of the investigation did not, however, obscure the fact that the Al Sarena decision was a legal and ideological giveaway. It was legal because the company had applied for the land under the 1872 mining act which permits public land to pass into private ownership if the applicant has made modest efforts at extracting ore and can show that the land has enough mineralization to "justify a prudent man" to continue investing time and effort. It was a controversial case because the Forest Service tried to protect its valuable timber from passing into the hands of the Al Sarena firm by challenging the validity of fifteen of the twenty-three mining claims. In the normal course of administrative proceedings conducted by the Interior Department's Bureau of Land Management, the Al Sarena company had lost its case when assays of the fifteen disputed claims twice revealed only negligible mineral content.

When the Eisenhower administration took over, the company

appealed over the heads of the civil service employees who had
denied its wishes. McKay's new solicitor, Clarence A. Davis, was
readily persuaded that the lesser bureaucrats had been hamstringing
free enterprise. He dispatched an order to the Bureau of Mines for
another set of samples to be tested for mineralization. Davis left no
doubt what outcome he desired when he wrote to his subordinates:
"I am aware of the peculiar nature of the area that they say is
mineralized and want to approve patent for them if the assays afford
us the well-established legal basis therefore. All people concerned
should therefore co-operate in obtaining samples and assays upon
which no doubts will be harbored by anybody."

What then occurred cast doubt into many neutral minds. The rock
samples, previously taken to experienced mineral-testing laboratories
on the Pacific coast, this time were shipped all the way to Mobile,
Alabama, the home town of the Al Sarena firm, to an assayer whose
chief experience was in testing building materials. The results were
favorable.

The great fiction perpetrated by the company, and by the Interior
officials when they were called to account, was that the Al Sarena
firm wanted title to the land to develop further its mining potential.
In years past, without title but with its legal mining claims, Al Sarena
and its predecessors had mined over $16,000 worth of gold, silver, and
lead from the property. What it could not legally do—and what it
now plainly wished to do—was to cut and sell the valuable government timber on the land, valued at over $100,000. A memo in the
bulky Interior file on the case shows that Al Sarena officials pleaded
for a favorable decision on grounds that they faced financial ruin if
turned down. Selling the timber would bail them out. A few years
after the Davis decision, Al Sarena sold the property to a logging
operator. No attempt was made to extract, as Neuberger delighted
in phrasing it, "one thimbleful of ore."

Wayne Morse's indignation over this giveaway was abruptly interrupted in mid-campaign when the *Oregonian* discovered that he
had quietly introduced a bill just before Congress adjourned that
year to give 550 acres of Siskiyou National Forest to an Oregon
lumber company in order to settle an ancient dispute of ownership.
The property had been made a part of the national forest system
by one of Teddy Roosevelt's proclamations, but the state of Oregon
had overlooked this and sold the land in 1912 for $4200. Not until
1949, after title had changed hands several times, did the con-

flict of title become known. The state, which presumably was orig-
inally at fault, said it could do nothing more than refund the $4200
it first received from the sale, although the timberland was valued
at $300,000 by this time. The federal government was unwilling to
give up its legitimate claim of ownership. So Wayne Morse agreed
to introduce a bill to convey title "to the state of Oregon or its
successors in interest," which meant to the lumber company which
had "bought" the property but now couldn't cut the trees. The
Oregonian chided Morse for sponsoring a special-interest bill instead of urging that the case be settled in the courts.

Like Houdini performing on the vaudeville circuit, Wayne Morse
went into a brilliant escape act before a Willamette Valley gathering the next night. The purpose of the bill, he explained

> was to enable a Senate Committee to determine whether the federal
> government should convey to the state of Oregon or those who later
> purchased it, a tract of land to which they thought they had full
> ownership. I introduced the bill on request of constituents who believe
> they have been wronged by the federal government. It was my clear
> duty to attempt to get them a hearing. If the hearing were to show
> that the constituents are wrong and the government is right, I would
> vote against the bill.

What could be more fair than that? Or a more ingenius theory of
the proper duties of a member of Congress, to introduce *any* bill
that *any* private interest wishes enacted and then to let the chips
fall where they may. But there was more:

> My bill would require consideration by a Senate committee. If passed
> there, it would require a Senate vote. The complete sequence of House
> action and presidential signature would also be necessary before the bill
> could become law. The safeguards of the public interest inherent in
> my bill were a far cry from those followed in the Al Sarena case. My
> bill was open to the clear white light of full public disclosure of all
> the facts. Al Sarena, on the other hand, was handled in the dim
> shadow of administrative action behind closed doors without public
> notice or cross-examination of witnesses.

Not willing just to escape blame, Morse seized upon this case
to cast further aspersions on Al Sarena and McKay. Then came the
daring climax:

What the *Oregonian* has called the Big Meadows case involves another smear. I shall reintroduce this bill in the next session of Congress, and will work to assure that the issues in the case are resolved fairly and in the public interest.

Never one to concede a point to a critic, Wayne Morse characteristically converted this dubious proposal into a noble quest for truth.[1]

A host of other factors influenced the election outcome. Labor put all its organizational and financial strength behind Morse. Businessmen did well financially by McKay, but had nothing comparable to labor's Committee on Political Education (COPE) for getting out the vote. It was the most expensive election in Oregon history. Morse reported spending $266,431 and McKay reported $229,680, but knowledgeable participants say the total came near to making this a million-dollar battle. G.O.P. Chairman Wyatt alleged that over $500,000 had been spent on Morse's campaign.[2]

[1] But after the campaign, the bill never reappeared. Portland Attorney Robert F. Maguire, a Republican who strongly supported McKay but also represented the lumber company, publicly defended Morse's action in behalf of his client. He said it would have been difficult to get the case into the courts because the government must give its consent to be sued; and if they had started cutting timber to provoke legal proceedings, they would have faced criminal prosecution. Maguire worked out a settlement later by which the state selected another tract of federal timberland in lieu of the disputed tract, and turned it over to the lumber company.

[2] Two years after this bitter campaign, the White House considered appointing Wyatt to the U. S. Tax Court, a lifetime judgeship which requires Senate confirmation. An able attorney, Wyatt had supported Morse's Republican campaigns (even as a Marine in the South Pacific in 1944 he sent a $25 contribution to Morse's first campaign); and Morse had twice been an overnight guest in Wyatt's Astoria home. When Wyatt telephoned from Oregon to see if the senator would object to the appointment, Morse invited him to Washington to discuss it. Upon his arrival, Morse advised Wyatt that he had decided against clearing the appointment, and he foreclosed all further discussion of the matter. Morse refused to explain his action to the press, but other Democrats say he exercised political vengeance chiefly because of Wyatt's charge about high spending. (One Democrat says Wyatt made a pretty accurate estimate.) Also Morse apparently held Wyatt responsible for the Republicans' use of a "cropped photograph" from *Life* magazine which showed Morse standing alone in the Senate chamber. One other senator who showed in the picture was trimmed out, apparently to fortify the point that nobody listens when Morse orates. The whole affair was patently absurd. The photo had been taken surreptitiously (no photographs are ever allowed of the Senate in session) during the atomic power debate of 1954 when the liberals talked in relays without any expectations of holding a crowd of attentive colleagues in the chamber. If anything, the cropped-picture incident was probably an asset to Morse.

Morse believes the climax of the campaign came in mid-October, when he and McKay appeared on the same program at a luncheon in Portland's Benson Hotel. McKay spoke first, scoring Morse severely for lack of integrity and untrustworthiness in betraying the loyalty of countless Oregon citizens who had sent him to the Senate as a Republican. As Morse rose to answer, amidst boos and catcalls, he reached into his coat pocket and withdrew a telegram which even his campaign aides didn't know he had cached for just such an occasion. It was one he had received four years before from the then Governor McKay during the tidelands oil bill debate of 1952. Morse put on his spectacles with a dramatic flourish and proceeded to read the wire aloud:

"Advised that President will veto Holland submerged land bill. Hope that you can conscientiously and wholeheartedly vote to override veto. We felt the bill is of utmost importance to Oregon and strongly urge passage. But if you cannot support it may we ask you to please refrain from voting? Congratulations on fine vote in recent primary. Regards. Douglas McKay."

Pausing while he took off his glasses, Wayne Morse surveyed his hushed audience, turned and pointed a long finger at McKay and roared, "When my opponent sent me that wire he disqualified himself for all time from holding political office. It means he advised me to walk out on my convictions, to walk out on my intellectual honesty. That I have never done and never will do!"

The effect was electrifying on the audience. Moreover, by happenstance the program had been recorded by a Portland radio station for broadcast that night. This happened to be the day President Eisenhower came to Portland to boost McKay. The station broadcast the President's talk and followed it immediately with the recording of the dramatic luncheon encounter between Morse and McKay, obviously with a huge, state-wide audience. By sheer good luck, Wayne Morse gained maximum impact with his haymaker punch. "If there was any one thing that turned the campaign, that was it," Morse said one night years later as he carefully returned that old yellow telegram to his "asbestos file" in his office safe.

The Republicans, too, attempted a startling surprise. They ran a large newspaper ad which asked the senator:

DON'T YOUR PERSONAL ACCOUNTS SHOW THAT YOU
MAKE MORE MONEY FROM OUTSIDE SPEECHES THAN
YOU DO AS A PART-TIME SENATOR? YOUR SALARY IS
$22,500 A YEAR. ISN'T THAT ENOUGH?

The Republicans apparently knew exactly how much he had made
in outside speaking fees, for I understand they somehow secured
information based on Wayne Morse's personal income tax returns.
Morse ignored the question, and the G.O.P. failed to press for an
answer. So a potentially explosive issue never materialized.

Independent polls showed Morse ahead throughout the campaign
and easily the favorite of the younger voters. Women voters showed
a slight preference for McKay. When voter registration was completed, the Democrats had a decisive edge, their first major breakthrough as a majority party in Oregon. They had 451,179 registered
Democratic voters to 413,659 Republicans. Many Republicans
switched parties to stick by Wayne Morse. Morse once again had the
advantage of running under the banner of the majority party. However, his victory margin over McKay was twice as great as the Democratic registration margin over the Republicans.

McKay, nevertheless, ran a strong race. He gained more votes in
his defeat than any candidate who ever ran for governor or senator
in Oregon, except for the man who defeated him. Morse had set
the record for the heaviest vote in his 1950 campaign as a Republican
when he was re-elected with 376,510 votes. In 1956, as a Democrat,
he won with 396,849 votes, to secure his reputation as the biggest
vote getter in Oregon history—an honor which subsequently passed
to Senator Maurine Neuberger in 1960.

Despite Oregon's preference for Eisenhower over Stevenson, Morse
helped put Oregon Democrats to their most successful election. A
new Democratic governor, Robert D. Holmes, was elected; Democrat Al Ullman, a leader in the grass-roots Hells Canyon crusade,
defeated Congressman Sam Coon, who had opposed the Hells Canyon dam and sponsored the Klamath termination bill; and Charles
O. Porter replaced G.O.P. Congressman Harris Ellsworth, who had
defended the Al Sarena decision and sponsored power bills criticized
by the Democrats. The only surviving Republican, Congressman
Walter Norblad, had kept his distance from all the giveaways, as he
does from all controversies which might conceivably backfire against
him politically. The rebellion which Doug McKay had been assigned

to put down had developed into a sectional revolt. It spread to neighboring Idaho, where Democrat Frank Church defeated Idaho Power's ardent defender, Senator Welker. It helped Senator Magnuson easily defeat Governor Langlie in Washington State.

Time for a Change

Morse's stunning victory jarred the Eisenhower administration; its most enlightened politicians knew that it was time for a change. There was to be no appearance of the elephant wheeling about and fleeing toward the scorned New Deal. No; easy does it. McKay's successor, Fred A. Seaton, even talked publicly as though everything would go on pretty much the same at the Interior Department. The late Tom Stokes noted this in a biting postelection column which concluded: "Douglas McKay was beat—but Fred Seaton is here to carry on for him, just as if the voters of the Pacific Northwest had never said a word." When Seaton saw the column, he called in the skeptical columnist for an exclusive preview of changes to come.

Spreading maps over his big desk, the new Interior boss traced the course of the Snake River after it plunges through Hells Canyon and reaches a place whose name alone augured more tranquil things. There, at Pleasant Valley, Seaton told Stokes, he planned to build a big government dam that would demolish the charge that the Administration was giving away all the good dam sites to the private power companies. Seaton's plan would wreck the hopes of a new combine, Pacific Northwest Power Co., for taking advantage of the Administration's power policy by building its own dams in the Pleasant Valley area. Stokes began his exclusive column: "Cabinet officers as well as the Supreme Court often follow what Mr. Dooley called 'the eliction returns.'"

Fred Seaton knew that decisions had to be made that would still the cry of giveaway, even though the Administration's critics overlooked its imaginative resource conservation achievement in starting the long-planned $1 billion Upper Colorado River Basin development. This is a vast network of federal dams, irrigation pumping stations and transmission lines which will eventually bring greater agricultural and industrial wealth to arid areas of Wyoming, Utah, Colorado, New Mexico and Arizona. The chief project is the 700 foot Glen Canyon dam, which compares reasonably well with the scrapped Hells Canyon dam in the Snake River. The difference is that the utility companies favored government construction of Glen

Canyon but opposed the federal Hells Canyon project because it interferred with Idaho Power Co.'s plans.

Experienced as a White House troubleshooter, Seaton had what the sensitive Interior post demanded. He meticulously examined the implications of each decision before he approved it. More important, he sought advice from the conservation organizations—National Wildlife Federation, Wildlife Management Institute, Izaak Walton League, American Nature Associate, National Audubon Society, National Parks Association, Wilderness Society and others—which had swooped down upon the giveaways in full-throated cry.

Seaton pleased them in his first move. He got the White House to scrap a reorganization plan for the Fish and Wildlife Service, developed in McKay's regime. In its place went one sanctioned by the conservationists. Eased out in the maneuver was John L. Farley, whose appointment as head of that agency illustrated the early ways of the Administration. Ralph A. Tudor, McKay's undersecretary, later told the yarn in the *Saturday Evening Post*:

> Even before I left for the capital to take on the new job, my friends in the banking business were telling me that I must 'do something about the Fish and Wildlife Service.' Complaints about Fish and Wildlife continued to reach me at my desk in Washington, 90 per cent of them were from bankers. This puzzled me at first, for it would seem more logical for unhappy bankers to be writing the Secretary of Treasury. It turned out, however, that apparently every banker on the West Coast is a duck hunter. Fish and Wildlife has a rough job, for among its many duties it must tell people when and how long they can hunt and how many ducks they can take—and evidently it is impossible to satisfy a duck hunter.
>
> I turned the tables on the complainants in this instance by making them talent scouts. My reply to them was that the best way to start improving the Fish and Wildlife Service was to get the best man available to head it—and had they any suggestions? The upshot was that they had, and that is how John L. Farley, ardent fisherman, former schoolteacher, businessman and onetime executive officer of the California Fish and Game Department, came to head the Fish and Wildlife Service.

Farley may have pleased the duckhunting bankers, but his administration of Fish and Wildlife Service was rebuked by a unanimous report of a House committee for granting more oil leases on wildlife refuges than all previous administrations combined.

As Seaton tried to follow the Oregon "eliction returns" with new policies, he ran afoul of Sherman Adams, just as McKay had, especially in his idea for a government-built dam at Pleasant Valley. The Hells Canyon diehards also frustrated this plan in Congress. Columnist Stokes explained why Adams was a doctrinaire private-utility adherent:

> His attitude reflects a widespread antagonism in New England among businessmen against federal power development. They have resisted development of their rivers for production of cheap electric power by comprehensive federal development. This failure is a factor in migration of so many mills to the South. Because of that migration, much of it to the TVA cheap power territory in the Southeast, you find deep-seated hostility toward TVA among New England's members of Congress. That is shared by Sherman Adams. . . . It is he who is the real driving force in the Administration's war on public power development. Credit should go where credit is due.

It is a strange irony that while Adams was doubtless the unseen power who was never called to account or publicly rebuked for the giveaways, as was McKay, he ultimately left Washington under a cloud—after Wayne Morse played the small but key role in the congressional investigation of the Goldfine case.

Besides quashing the giveaway cry, Seaton's great positive achievement, which coincided with Morse's attitude, was in getting President Eisenhower to reverse his official attitude toward the admission of Alaska as a state. McKay had personally favored statehood, but passively accepted the word from the White House that Eisenhower opposed it.

Here again, the heart of the matter was whether the Administration was going to side blindly with those business interests who pleaded for a policy they deemed privately beneficial. The large salmon packers based at Seattle led the opposition to Alaska's admission. They feared Alaska taxes would be raised and that fish traps, long outlawed in the states, would be abolished. For years the power of these colonial-minded absentee interests frustrated the statehood crusade led by Ernest Gruening and E. L. (Bob) Bartlett, now Alaska's two Democratic Senators, and two Republican publishers, Robert B. Atwood of the Anchorage *Times*, and C. W. (Bill) Snedden of the Fairbanks *News-Miner*. But for Seaton's skill in securing Eisenhower's passive co-operation and in rallying Republican support to go with northern Democratic support, the Union would not have been extended to the Artic—thus clearing the way for Hawaii's subsequent admission—during the Eisenhower era.

Had Wayne Morse lost to McKay, what solace and strength would this outcome have given those who resisted Seaton's changes? Morse's victory had wide ramifications. It even brought McKay, before his death, his greatest achievement in the role of United States representative on the International Joint Commission. Through this agency an agreement was reached with Canada by which both nations are to build a series of related dams on the upper Columbia River, sharing hydroelectric and flood-control benefits far beyond what either government could accomplish alone or by turning the job over to local utilities.

More directly, Morse's attacks against the giveaways forced a moderation of those Administration policies that would have made Teddy Roosevelt writhe in anguish. The Republicans, in Professor Morse's school of hard knocks, had learned their lesson the hard way. The good fight had been won, and the people had been educated. Fighting Bob La Follette would surely have telegraphed: "Congratulations, you did both."

17. NEUBERGER

The Cribbing Case . . . Mr. Conservationist . . . Seeds of Disunion . . . End of the Honeymoon . . . Self-reform

RICHARD Lewis Neuberger, of all the many political figures whose careers meshed with that of Wayne Morse, was the least probable man for the crucial—quite possibly decisive—role that fell to him at the peak of his promising senatorial term. As a University of Oregon student, he gave eloquent testimonials to his admiration for Dean Morse. He was rescued from a deep campus crisis by the intervention of the Dean. He was the beneficiary of Morse's vigorous campaigning when he gained election to the Senate by a whisker. His breakthrough as the first Democrat elected to an Oregon Senate seat in forty years in turn assisted Morse's re-election as a Democrat in 1956. Between them these two intelligent, aggressive comrades in arms, Wayne Morse and Dick Neuberger, turned Oregon's politics upside down before most Republicans realized that their safely conservative state suddenly in the mid-fifties had acquired the most ardently liberal senators west of the Appalachians.

The stranger-than-fiction climax of this tale is that Neuberger and Morse at length embarked upon the Senate's most bitter personal feud. And, in the end, Neuberger came closer than any prior adversary to piercing the Achilles' heel of this seemingly invincible warrior. How and why did it happen?

Professor Morse, at thirty-one, became dean of the law school the year that Dick Neuberger, a curly-headed nineteen-year-old freshman, entered the university. The year was 1931, and both men were visibly untouched personally by the economic distress of the Great Depression. Neuberger came from a moderately well-to-do Portland family which had a successful restaurant business. He grew up in a big house on the edge of a fashionable residential area of Portland, attending the public schools with children of the more comfortably fixed families. As a classmate of Neuberger's recalls, using a status symbol of the Depression, the Neuberger family "drank copious quantities of fresh orange juice at a time when oranges were a luxury."

From Lincoln High School, Neuberger went to the *Oregonian* for a year to learn the rudiments of reporting. His zeal for journalism was focused upon the athletic world. When he arrived on the university campus the next fall, he immediately captured the sports editorship of the student newspaper, the *Daily Emerald*, and became most influential with the athletic crowd. He idolized the football coach, Doc Spears, defending him editorially even in the gloomy aftermath of a 51–0 drubbing perpetrated by the merciless lads from Southern California. With the backing of the graduate manager of athletics, Hugh Rosson, Neuberger became editor-in-chief of the *Emerald* his sophomore year, an unprecedented advancement. This higher and broader editorial responsibility marked the beginning of Neuberger's political awareness. Upon assuming the editor's chair, he announced: "The *Emerald* will be conservative in whatever it does. Radical opinions and bolshevik tendencies will have places in neither its news or editorial columns. It is the opinion of the writer that a paper can oppose an existing order without turning radical in doing so." If this suggested that young Neuberger had little sympathy for liberal thought, a front-page column by the editor later that fall of 1932 left no doubt. It was headlined: "Why I will vote for Hoover." (It may gratify his liberal admirers to know that Neuberger was taking editorial license. He did not, in fact, vote for Hoover, for it was not until the following year that he attained voting age.)

The account of young Neuberger's conversion to liberalism is best told by his college roommate, Stephen B. Kahn. In an essay written upon Neuberger's election to the Senate, Kahn wrote:

> Over our typewriters in the journalism building he would mock my admiration for Walter Lippmann. I, in turn, would rib him unmercifully for being oblivious to the economic depression, which was forcing half the students to drop out of school because they could not pay the $30 tuition fee.
>
> . . . .
>
> By 1933 the Depression had cut the University's enrollment in half. I repeatedly called Dick's attention to the world's woes, and pushed copies of *The Nation* and the *New Republic* under his nose. . . .

I lured him down to the local Salvation Army yard to watch men splitting wood for a meal. Again, we visited a nearby cooperative farm where awkward city folk were trying to wring enough to eat from their over-mortgaged acres. Dick sat down and ate the meager stew from a rough plank table, and tasted his first margarine. . . . It made Dick realize there were hungry women and children a couple of miles from his comfortable dormitory. . . .

Between us we concocted "the Oregon *Daily Emerald* Low Cost Living Plan for Hard Pressed Students" and filled the pages with starchy menus which would sustain life for $1.62 a week. This gained Dick the enmity of the fraternities, nearly all of which were struggling to keep afloat. When the Oregon legislature threatened to cut teachers' salaries drastically, Dick rounded up Butch Morse, Oregon's star end, and me and led a protest demonstration to the Senate chamber at Salem. . . . His editorials began to recognize the nation's problems, and the efforts Franklin D. Roosevelt and a Democratic Congress were making to meet them.

Here were the roots of the emergent political crusader and reformer. Editor Neuberger suggested that the annual Homecoming game between Oregon and Oregon State be held at Portland, and a third of the ticket receipts be allocated to feed the hungry that winter. Later he rapped his sophomore class for holding an extravagant dance when a Portland newspaper was reporting "1300 families huddle over fuelless stoves, pleading help to get wood."

The summer before his junior year, in 1933, Dick's Uncle Julius Neuberger, a navy physician, took him to Europe where he visited Germany at a time when developments under the Nazi party were not yet widely known. Returning to New York, he spoke to the editor of *The Nation*, Ernest Gruening, now a senator from Alaska. The result was his first article in a reputable national magazine.

Upon returning to campus that fall, he entered Dean Morse's law school. During Neuberger's editorship the previous year it had become apparent that he admired the vigorous law dean. He had referred to Morse as "a Roscoe Pound of the future." He had acclaimed the dean for "bringing to the law school a liberal atmosphere and a militant fearlessness that will send forth men who will make new traditions before they will be held back by old ones." By the end of that year the editor wrote: "from the same legal stamp that produced men like Louis D. Brandeis, Benjamin N. Cardozo, Harlan

Fiske Stone and Oliver Wendell Holmes comes Wayne L. Morse."
The news pages, too, were sprinkled with favorable stories about
Dean Morse that year, suggesting that increasingly high standards
were being established in the Oregon law school. Dean Morse, in a
word, got an exceedingly good press when Dick Neuberger was
running the press.

The Cribbing Case

With Neuberger's new obsession with political affairs and social
conditions there came a corresponding decline in his popularity with
his old athletic buddies and with the fraternities—the leaders who
traditionally controlled campus politics. It was in this context that
Neuberger became ensnared in a personal crisis. His interest in
politics led to much off-campus campaigning in 1934. He campaigned against the Zorn-McPherson bill, the proposal on the ballot
to merge the university with the state college; and he beat the drums
for the liberal independent gubernatorial candidate, State Senator
Peter Zimmerman. Neuberger cut so many law classes that Dean
Morse at length warned him that attendance was not optional. One
of these classes, Legal Bibliography, a relatively simple course in how
to conduct legal research, got short shrift from Neuberger. The weekly
assignment, as Kahn recalls it, consisted of looking up certain legal
problems. "Almost invariably the men checked their answers among
themselves before turning them in," says Kahn. "But Dick was too
busy campaigning to bother looking up indices. He just borrowed
his neighbor's solutions and turned in the same answers."

For years the law school had operated under an honor system
against cribbing in exams. "A five-year student board, composed
entirely of fraternity men, supervised the honor system," recalls Kahn,
"and they learned from the 'grader' that Neuberger's answers in
'Legal Bib' were always identical with another student's. Here was a
chance to 'get' Neuberger! Promptly they hauled him up before
them for violation of the honor system. They contended his action
was tantamount to copying during an examination. Dick's prominence made it a *cause célèbre*."

The student board convicted Neuberger of cheating and recommended his dismissal from school. At this point Roscoe Nelson, the
prominent Portland attorney who headed the State Board of Higher
Education until he resigned after being blasted by Dean Morse in the

PLATE 9   Morse never shied from happily meeting with newsmen, especially when the mikes and cameras were turned on, as in this 1953 scene outside the White House where he had just lunched with President Eisenhower. He subsequently waged war with the press, including the author (center with striped tie). Editorial cartoonists loved his controversial nature, and sometimes portrayed him heroically, as did Walt Partymiller in the York (Pa.) *Gazette and Daily* in 1953 after Morse criticized Ike's cabinet appointments.

THE CRUSADER FOR THE PEOPLE

SENATOR MORSE

SENATE OK

ROAD BLOCK TO CABINET APPROVAL

OBJECTIONS BASED ON PRINCIPLE

PLATE 10 Dramatic events erupted between these two poses for press photographers. At top, Morse displays arm-around-the-shoulder solidarity with Republican Douglas McKay at the 1952 GOP convention shortly before he bolted the party. Below, eleven months later, he breaks bread with liberal Democrat Monroe Sweetland before addressing Democratic fund-raising dinner and informally consummating new political alliance.

Edmund Y. Lee

PLATE 11   The Senator's most loyal admirers are his younger sister, Mrs. Caryl Kline, wife of a college professor, and his wife, Mildred. Mrs. Kline once ran for Congress from Syracuse, and in 1961 President Kennedy sent her to represent him at ceremonies marking the birth of a new African nation, Sierra Leone. Below, Mrs. Eleanor Roosevelt joins Morse and Robert D. Holmes in a box supper during 1956 campaign when Morse won his first election as a Democrat and Holmes became Oregon's governor. In a subsequent article, Mrs. Roosevelt suggested Morse as presidential material, a conviction shared by the Senator's sister and wife.

Photo by Allen deLay, for the The Oregonian

PLATE 12 After Senator Morse abandoned his independent status and registered at the Lane County Courthouse as a Democrat under the pleased watchfulness of Democratic State Chairman Howard Morgan (*above*), he and Senator Richard L. Neuberger led the party to a new peak of power with conquest of five of Oregon's six congressional seats. In addition to Neuberger on Morse's right is (*below*) Representative Al Ullman and on his left Representatives Edith Green and Charles O. Porter.

© 1954 *Buffalo Courier Express*

© 1953 *Denver Post*

PLATE 13   Lee Joseph Roche caught the Luce affair in his cartoon of the tiger in the Buffalo *Courier Express*, and Paul Conrad sized up the official Democratic party reaction to Morse's presidential aspirations in his cartoon in the Denver *Post*.

General Eisenhower

Maurine and
Richard L. Neuberger

John F. Kennedy

Clare Boothe Lu

Robert A. Taft

© 1957, *The Oregonian*

Joseph R. McCar

Mark Hatfield

PLATE 14 Among his many adversaries Wayne Morse has numbered many former friends or political allies, notably the late Senator Richard L. Neuberger as depicted by the *Oregonian's* cartoonist, Art Bimrose. Here are Morse's chief adversaries.

William Jasper K

William M. Tugman

Lyndon B. Johnson

Harold L. Ickes

Douglas McK

PLATE 15 This dramatic Medford *Mail Tribune* photo captured Wayne Morse as he assaulted Mark Hatfield's integrity during the gubernatorial campaign of 1958. Tucked beneath one arm is a volume of Oregon Supreme Court reports from which Morse quoted court testimony in a teen-age auto accident case involving Hatfield. The charge backfired and Hatfield won decisively over Democrat Robert D. Holmes.

Photo by Leo Rose

PLATE 16 Morse was rescued from the agony of the collapse of his presidential quest when President Eisenhower appointed him a delegate to the United Nations in 1960. Above he chats with India's Krishna Menon. In 1961 he returned to his Senate office *(below)*, gained new positions of power in the Senate, but faced an uncertain future alternating between new bursts of anger and an optimistic smile.

famous 1934 Homecoming speech, asked editor Tugman to determine the reasons for Neuberger's prosecution, stating that "if Richard is guilty of anything dishonorable I won't lift a finger for him, but if he is being persecuted because he is Jewish . . ."

Tugman, upon investigating, reported back to Nelson that "Dick is not being persecuted because he is Jewish, and he is not in my opinion guilty of anything dishonorable because students say that copying in Legal Bib is an ancient custom; the trouble grows out of old campus feuds, and if the boy ever wants to be a lawyer he'd better go someplace else." Tugman says he took the matter up with Dean Morse, who had initially "washed his hands like Pontius Pilate, claiming that it was not for the dean to interfere with duly constituted student government." Tugman replied that "you can't surrender faculty authority to a bunch of adolescents in a situation like this."

Neuberger, with roommate Kahn as his defense counsel, appealed the conviction of the student board to the law faculty. All the formalities of due process were invoked. Recalls Kahn:

As defense counsel, I pointed out that the honor system had never been codified. And in Oregon every crime was required to be set down in the statutes. Wayne Morse had taught me that. Moreover, I argued, there was no intent on Neuberger's part to commit an act which could be termed dishonest. I put student after student on the stand, and invariably each admitted he "checked" the correctness of his answers with other students before turning in assignments. It was no less honest to copy the entire solution, I maintained, than to check one's answers with another student. Undoubtedly it was lazier. But certainly it could not violate any precept of honor if "checking" were countenanced. With tears starting in his eyes, Neuberger faced his judges and said: "Gentlemen, I have never done a dishonest act in my life."

Four of the five law professors who sat as judges voted to convict. The majority opinion was rendered by Orlando John Hollis, now dean of law. The lone vote of acquittal was cast by Dean Morse. He did not defend the act but he did exonerate Neuberger of any dishonorable intent. As Kahn recalls the outcome, "the administrative officer of the University, in whom all disciplinary power was vested, upheld Morse's decision, and all charges against Neuberger were dismissed."

If Dean Morse saved Neuberger from disgrace, he also diverted him from going further into the law. At the close of the dean's course in criminal law, he gave Neuberger a lower mark than the bright student thought he deserved. When he appealed to his professor to re-evaluate his final exam, Morse invited Neuberger to go over it with him. When they had finished, the dean leaned back and said this second reading had convinced him that he had been hasty in marking the exam. Transfixing his ambitious pupil, Morse said he had been much too generous in marking that exam. He then and there lowered Neuberger's grade ten points, flunking him.

The dean advised his student that day to give up his quest of a law degree and concentrate on writing. Telephoning the boy's parents in Portland to drive home the point, the dean is reported to have said, "This boy is a fine journalist. But he's no lawyer, and I doubt whether he ever can be. At any rate, I haven't got the time to try to make him one."

Neuberger did not then and there accept this advice, and he later continued law studies at a Portland night school before determining to pour all his creative effort into magazine writing. Nor did Neuberger take kindly to being scholastically booted out of criminal law. Kahn says Neuberger never forgave Morse for this, and it is his belief that Neuberger's personal feelings toward Morse emerged in the many articles he later wrote that were not nearly so glowing with encomiums as his student editorial tributes to the dean had been.

Neuberger left the university without taking a degree. He did so in order to wage a state-wide campaign against certain compulsory student fees charged by the university of all students. Poor students who couldn't afford textbooks shouldn't be taxed to support dances and football games, argued Neuberger. The attorney general of the state upheld the student's challenge to the legality of the fees. But a bill introduced and passed by the legislature made them legal again, until Neuberger sponsored a referendum on the issue and organized a Student Relief Committee to carry the issue to the voters. It was in this cause that Neuberger left school to beat the bushes from Astoria to Klamath Falls for votes. Kahn said he warned Neuberger not to drop his studies at this point. "If you ever run for public office, they'll say you were kicked out of school for cheating," Kahn recalls telling his roommate. "But in his usual headstrong manner, Neuberger pooh-poohed the warning."

His referendum campaign was a thumping success. In a special election January 31, 1936, compulsory fees were abolished by a vote of more than three to one against the bill. Thus Dick Neuberger launched his successful political career. He also advanced upon his successful writing career at this point when he and Kahn collaborated on a biography of Senator George W. Norris, *Integrity*, which earned critical praise.

Fifteen years later, when Neuberger was thinking of running for governor, Senator Morse circulated a letter which warned against the use of the old cribbing incident against Neuberger. For a Republican senator to do this for an aspiring Democratic politician demonstrated a generous spirit. Neuberger backed away from the gubernatorial race, biding his time until 1954, when he ran for the Senate. Early in this campaign the cribbing charge was raised for the first time since campus days. State Circuit Judge Carl E. Wimberly, a long-time friend of incumbent Senator Guy Cordon, without Cordon's advance knowledge or consent charged that Neuberger had been expelled for cheating. Neuberger pulled out the letter Morse had written in his behalf four years earlier and brandished it in self-defense. "I have always been of the opinion that the decision [not to expel Neuberger from the university] was correct in light of all the facts and circumstances of the case," Morse had written. "Therefore any rumors or accusations against Mr. Neuberger in regard to this matter I think are most unfair and I am pleased to deny them."

As political smears often do, Judge Wimberly's assault backfired. Some of Oregon's most ardent Republican newspapers deplored the attack on young Neuberger, whom they had not the slightest intention of supporting for the Senate. Neuberger's victory margin was so slender that one might find it hard to dispute the remark of the exasperated Republican State Chairman, Ed Boehnke: "That fool judge has just cost Guy this election."

Mr. Conservationist

As Neuberger's book, *Adventures in Politics*, showed, he came to the Senate no babe to the wily way of politics. He came with the same eager zeal for stirring things up that he showed on the campus and in his stormy career as a state legislator. He came, also, without much sense of restraint as a freshman, and with a flair for publicity that matched that of Wayne Morse in some ways. His first escapade to gain national attention was his charge that President Eisenhower had violated a law of the District of Columbia by having squirrels trapped by White House grounds keepers and exiled to the wilds of West Virginia because of their propensity for digging up the President's practice putting green. The White House was embarrassed by the sympathy engendered for the squirrels at the expense of Ike's beloved form of recreation but Press Secretary Jim Hagerty denied that any traps had been set. While editorial cartoonists had a field day and the country chuckled, Neuberger engaged upon this first national crusade without the slightest trace of lightheartedness. "I think we've got him now," he told me earnestly the day his legal aide discovered the anti-trapping ordinance. But what District Attorney, an appointee of the President, would be so bold as to investigate the gardens of the national estate on Pennsylvania Avenue for evidence that the rights of these bushy-tailed rodents had been transgressed?

Although many thought that the senator and not the President looked the more ridiculous in this incident, Neuberger knew exactly what he was doing in one important political respect. He was saying, in effect, to all of the organized and unorganized conservation-minded citizens, the countless thousands who yearn to protect all the feathered and furry friends of woods and hills and parks, "I will be your champion. No matter whom I have to battle, I will defend conservation principles." Wayne Morse later, in another episode, called Neuberger the Senate's "Mr. Conservationist," a title his junior colleague was proud to hold.

Together, Morse and Neuberger formed the least inhibited senatorial team, slashing out at one policy after another of the new Eisenhower administration, but with special zeal against the giveaways. It was Neuberger, probably more than Morse, who discredited the partnership power policy by which the Republicans hoped to permit the utility companies to become partners with the government in building and financing new dams. The utilities were eager to install generators for the huge amount of electricity that comes from a major Columbia River dam, if the government would pay for the profitless features—navigation locks, fish protection, and flood-control facilities. In a series of debates with Sam Coon, the Republican Congressman who was later defeated, Neuberger disparaged the partnership policy with this simile: this partnership will be about as fair as one in which two fellows go into the department-store business, one partner operating the elevators and the other the cash registers.

Until the Eisenhower power policy was formulated, all dam building on the Columbia had been a federal undertaking. The grass-
roots defenders of this program rose up against the partnership idea.
These were the same public power, farm, and labor organizations
which supported the Hells Canyon effort. When Morse and Neuberger challenged the utilities, they received powerful support from
these groups.

In Congress, Morse and Neuberger blocked all bills to authorize
partnership agreements between Oregon utilities and the government; and, allied with other influential Northwest Democrats such
as Senators Magnuson and Jackson of Washington, they secured federal appropriations to build as federal projects those dams the utilities
proposed as partnership ventures. Largest of these was the million-
kilowatt John Day dam on the lower Columbia.

In short, the Northwest liberals successfully defended and advanced the Columbia River development program which began during the New Deal when Roosevelt launched the federal dam-
building era with the Grand Coulee Dam in central Washington and
by "giving Charlie McNary his dam" at Bonneville on the Oregon-
Washington border. Since then the powerful Columbia, second only
to the Mississippi in size, has been harnessed by a succession of great
dams built by the Army's Corps of Engineers and the Interior
Department's Bureau of Reclamation. Another federal agency, the
Bonneville Power Administration, has built the transmission lines
which link the powerhouses with the market areas—but local utilities,
the private power companies and the rural electric co-operatives and
public utility districts, buy power wholesale from the Bonneville
Administration and market it to householders and industry throughout the Pacific Northwest.

Seeds of Disunion

Despite the early political success of their alliance, Wayne Morse
and Dick Neuberger at length were at one another's throats. Perhaps this was inevitable. Both men were ardent self-expressionists,
unaccustomed to following anyone else's lead, intense by nature,
and equally capable of rubbing others the wrong way.

To counter Republican taunts that Oregon Democrats would rue
the day they enticed Wayne Morse into their party, the two senators
and the state's three Democrats in the House—Edith Green, Al Ull-

man, and Charles O. Porter—held weekly breakfast conferences for the announced purpose of planning joint legislative efforts for Oregon. From their offices tumbled a cascade of press releases stamped with the names of one and all. So obvious was this act of one for all and all for Oregon that they resembled the Rockettes, kicking and wheeling in precise unison, oblivious to the danger that someone would sooner or later get out of step and kill the act. This purposeful oneness survived its initial misstep, but not its second.

Both senators provoked a certain wariness within the delegation. Neuberger had an odd habit of publicly defending his colleagues from some allegation which, if they had had their druthers, they would have wished Neuberger to ignore instead of repeating. Morse made his colleagues edgy for the first time when he violated a minor understanding concerning a new power proposal advanced by Portland General Electric Company. Thomas Delzell, the utility's board chairman, and Robert H. Short, his executive assistant, had advised the Oregon delegation they wished to discuss the matter. The delegation members agreed that they should form a common position in a letter to the utility signed by one and all. Before the joint letter could be perfected and dispatched, Morse impatiently fired off his own reply, speaking as head of the delegation, without notifying Neuberger. The Neuberger office didn't like this violation of teamwork, but no hostilities developed.

The first difficulty to plague Oregon's Rockettes developed as Congresswoman Green and the Neubergers, who had never been close, each fell victim of unsubstantiated suspicions about one another. The Republicans had been craftily predicting that Neuberger's intent, after his own election to the Senate, was to get his wife elected to the House so that the Neubergers could become a husband-and-wife team in Congress, as they had been in the state legislature. As a writer on state politics, Neuberger had penned many a piece on their joint exploits in the Oregon legislature.

Mrs. Green, perhaps more than anyone else, found it impossible to dismiss this idea, for it was her Portland congressional seat that Maurine Neuberger would seek if this was, indeed, their objective. When Neuberger wrote an article for *Harper's* entitled "My Wife Put Me in the Senate," when he placed his wife's portrait next to his own at the top of his monthly newsletters, which were mailed to thousands of Oregon voters, when he constantly employed the marital "we" in describing his legislative actions in Washington, Edith

Green became more certain than anyone that the build-up was advancing toward this fancied Neuberger objective.

On the other hand, Neuberger grew equally suspicious that Congresswoman Green somehow represented a threat to him when he faced re-election in 1960. His projection of Maurine to the fore was probably not only his way of paying the respect he genuinely felt for his wife, but a methodical appeal to women voters that might serve him well in any future election campaign, especially if he were challenged by Mrs. Green. The result, to be sure, was that suspicions mounted, and any slight became a major grievance. When the then Democratic Governor, Robert D. Holmes, came to Washington, to cite but one petty episode, Mrs. Green held a modest reception for him in her office after working hours and invited all other members of the Oregon delegation, their wives and employees and the press. But once the punch bowl had been drained, the governor was taken to dinner by Mrs. Green. The Morses were also invited. The Neubergers were not, a slight not lightly taken by Maurine Neuberger. When Wayne Morse was called upon to settle the ensuing dispute of right and wrong in a private meeting, this skilled veteran of keeping peace on the Pacific water front failed utterly to achieve more than a surface show of conciliation. The breakfasts went on, but the snap, crackle, and pop thereafter came not from the cereal bowls.

There was yet no sign of hostility between Morse and Neuberger, however. Whatever he might have thought of Morse's earlier "political double life," Neuberger in early 1957 wrote an article for *Progressive* recommending Morse as the Democratic candidate for President in 1960. But soon the seeds of disunion began to germinate. The catalytic agents were civil rights and Hells Canyon.

Morse's Hells Canyon bill, defeated in the Senate in 1956, was reintroduced in 1957. The National Hells Canyon Association, after losing out to Idaho Power Company at the Federal Power Commission, had gone into federal court in an effort to overturn the FPC decision, or at least to delay the utility from using the license granted by the FPC. On April 1, 1957, the Supreme Court declined to review lower-court decisions upholding the utility's license. The end of the long fight appeared at hand. The power company, already at work in the great canyon, and the Eisenhower administration had won. Morse, Neuberger, and the public-power forces had lost.

Suddenly one unexpected act turned this picture awry. The Office of Defense Mobilization advised Sherman Adams that it was planning to award Idaho Power a fast tax write-off for sixty-five million dollars of its investment in these new power facilities. Before this decision was publicly announced some two weeks later, Idaho Power stock on the New York exchange surged to a new high for the year. The public announcement of the tax break for the utility company provoked a full-lunged protest. Senator Kefauver turned loose the Senate's Anti-trust and Monopoly Subcommittee staff to investigate. Kefauver's hearings turned up no evidence of collusion between beneficiaries of the rise in Idaho Power stock and those government officials who made the grant. But they did focus attention anew on a set of sharply contrasting circumstances which breathed new life into the Hells Canyon crusade.

The Administration, in defending its preference for the utility's lesser plan for harnessing the middle Snake River, had emphasized that the money would come from private capital resources rather than from the taxpayers. The theme of the Federal Power Commission decision and of the Justice Department's argument against a Supreme Court review was that this private project would be achieved "at no cost to the government." No sooner had the courts dismissed the last appeal than the company was handed a tax deduction which, government officials told the Kefauver subcommittee, would cost the government some eighty-three million dollars. Only one high Administration official, Interior Secretary Seaton, had warned that it was "most inequitable for the federal government now to assume any portion of the cost." Seaton's warning was ignored by Adams and ODM Director Gordon Gray.

Watching the build-up of public and senatorial indignation over the tax write-off which the Kefauver hearings helped generate, Lyndon Johnson waited until the peak moment, then called up the Hells Canyon bill once more. As the utility's defenders felt the ground shaking, Idaho Power magnanimously returned the hot tax write-off certificates and announced that it would take no tax advantages. Morse called it a "deathbed repentance." It came too late. The Senate, after three days' debate, passed the Hells Canyon bill by a 45 to 38 vote. Five Republicans (Mrs. Smith of Maine, Aiken of Vermont, Cooper of Kentucky, Langer of North Dakota, and Wiley of Wisconsin) crossed over to join forty Democrats in what amounted to a spanking for the Eisenhower administration.

Six years after first introducing the Hells Canyon bill, Wayne

Morse had at last been successful. Here was sweet vindication, for he had won *his* battle in *his* realm. There was less doubt than ever that Eisenhower would veto the bill if it reached his desk. but then it would be all the easier for the Democrats to charge the Administration with responsibility for giving away Hells Canyon. (Once more, however, this vexing situation was averted by the Administration. The bill was bottled up successfully in the House Interior Committee. A solid Republican line-up against the bill was strengthened by two Southern Democrats and the curious defection of Adam Clayton Powell of New York, who was reported to have been safely sitting in Sherman Adams' office when the committee vote came against the Hells Canyon bill.)

The Hells Canyon bill came up in the midst of the most titanic struggle the Senate had witnessed in years on civil rights. Senate liberals had devised a strategy for avoiding the traditional demise of all civil-rights legislation. At the instant that a new civil-rights bill reached the Senate from the House they would move it be taken up immediately as the Senate's pending business, thus preventing its customary referral to the Judiciary Committee, headed by Eastland of Mississippi. Morse and Neuberger both attended this conference and concurred in this strategy. But shortly thereafter Morse did the unexpected. He publicly denounced this strategy as "parliamentary expediency."

Douglas of Illinois hastily called another liberal caucus, there accusing Morse to his face of betraying their cause. Morse replied that upon reflection, he realized that he could not agree to this move to bypass a standing committee because it violated the accepted procedures by which the Senate does its legislative business. Then he stalked out of the caucus, took the floor once more to blister the liberals for expediency. Highly aroused, Douglas fired back, "I think what the Senator from Oregon is trying to do tonight is kill civil rights."

It was on the next afternoon that the Senate passed Morse's Hells Canyon bill. Douglas and the Republicans noticed that this time a number of Southern Democrats, led by Russell of Georgia, voted for Morse's bill, changing their votes of the year before.

The question which only the inner Wayne Morse can possibly answer is whether he had hoped his ringing denunciation of the liberals' strategy would soften up some Dixie dissidents to support his bill.

Neuberger, torn by personal fondness for Douglas and a strong

conviction that the liberals were doing what was right and necessary, nevertheless defended Morse's honor. Both publicly and privately
he dismissed the suspicion that his colleague had made a deal.

But while defending Morse's honor, Neuberger grew uneasy in
his alliance. For three years he had been as aggressively partisan
as Morse in advocating liberal causes or blistering the policies of the
Eisenhower administration. Yet now he silently winced when Morse
branded Eisenhower and Dave Beck as the same sort of immoralists.
When Republicans upbraided Morse in the Senate for that assault
on Eisenhower, Neuberger tried to rescue Morse—not by defending
Morse's attack, but by noting that many of these Republicans had
not been so eager to defend Eisenhower's policies as his person. But
Morse's attack on Eisenhower's integrity troubled Neuberger.

The practical problem Neuberger faced was that he and Morse
might have overworked their "one for all and all for one" act to the
point where he would be blamed for Morse's unpopular acts. Wayne
Morse had not consulted him before comparing Eisenhower to Beck,
but Neuberger wondered how many citizens in Oregon would stop
to consider that. A letter which one of Neuberger's staff assistants
received during this period crystallized this fear in his mind. As
Neuberger told me about it, this constituent expressed strong dis-
taste for Morse and raised the question whether Neuberger was any
different. Guilt by association has many facets, not the least of which
is the old saw that a man is known by the company he keeps, or a
politician is known by his alliances. In his first years in the Senate
Neuberger had coveted this alliance as much as Morse for personal
political security. But now the alliance was causing Neuberger a
new sense of insecurity. If Wayne Morse only wouldn't go so
far!

End of the Honeymoon

With strategic deliberateness, Neuberger sought opportunities to
draw slightly, but noticeably, apart from Morse. Morse's charge of
"parliamentary expediency" against the other liberals in the civil-
rights fight was the first crack in the alliance. Neuberger didn't challenge Morse's remark in the Senate, but when Morse sent reprints
of his speech containing this charge to many Oregon voters, Neuberger seized upon it as criticism aimed specifically at him. Paul
Douglas, who took a fatherly interest in Neuberger and who was

deeply aroused against Morse's tactics, offered to write a letter of commendation about Neuberger's civil-rights record. In an eloquent testimonial, mailed to a list of Oregon voters supplied by Neuberger, Douglas said:

> I want to tell you what a tower of strength Senator Neuberger has been throughout this whole battle. He has been one of the men we could depend upon in every emergency. He has been resolute in his courage, and diplomatic in his language, and highly honorable in every relationship on and off the floor.

Morse's name wasn't mentioned in the Douglas letter, but the implication was strong that Douglas was drawing a vivid contrast between the two Oregon senators which highly favored Neuberger.

Morse was incensed. He dashed off a letter to Neuberger and another to Phil Reynolds, head of the Portland branch of the National Association for the Advancement of Colored People, in which he said he was "saddened by Paul Douglas' conduct in respect to mailing a letter to many people in Oregon which was interpreted by many of my civil rights friends as a snide attack on me, which it was."

On the civil-rights bill, Neuberger voted for it, "however limited and modest" it had been rendered by amendments and deletions. "Where would this nation be today if all senators during our past history had allowed themselves the luxury of opposing each piece of legislation which failed to dot every 'i' or cross every 't' to suit their own particular taste?" Morse replied that the bill had been so weakened as to be meaningless, adding, "I will never knowingly vote for what I consider to be a sham." Neuberger then reminded Morse, in this exchange in the Senate chamber, that they had both supported the Klamath forest bill even though not altogether pleased with its final terms, which were less than Morse thought the Indians deserved. Morse said Neuberger was guilty of the fallacy of false analogy, for the Indian bill was not completely unacceptable to him, as was the civil-rights bill. Morse then voted with the Southern opponents of the 1957 civil-rights bill, the first passed by Congress since the Reconstruction era.

These expressed differences on a public issue caused no more than a ripple of comment by the public, for the letters which figured in this episode were then very private matters. Soon Neuberger saw a fresh opportunity to disassociate himself from Morse's attacks on the

popular President. Not long after the civil-rights episode, Morse accused Eisenhower of being "politically immoral" for accepting a king's
ransom in gifts for his Gettysburg farm, from trees and shrubs to
cattle and farm machinery. (Morse, curiously, finds nothing "politically immoral" in accepting money for speechmaking—the better
to equip his own farm.) Rising several days later with a mild essay
in rebuttal, Neuberger said the President was simply the victim of a
dubious practice which past Presidents had made traditional. "I do
not criticize Mr. Eisenhower. He is not to blame for this situation,"
Neuberger declared. In case anyone in Oregon missed the point, he
extended a public invitation to the Eisenhowers to spend their
vacation on the scenic Oregon coast. He knew the President had
other preferences, but that was hardly the point. It was a gimmick to
nourish the carefully planted idea that Dick Neuberger was not
Wayne Morse's boy.

If this was too subtle for many citizens, Wayne Morse got the
point. In his office on the fourth floor of the Senate Office Building, the man of letters called in a secretary and dictated a note to
his young colleague down on the third floor. Neuberger's defense of
Eisenhower could be taken "as an indirect slap at me." This and
the Douglas' letter would only provide fuel for Republican attacks
on both of them, warned Morse with professorial formality. Although his words were relatively light as a reprimand, they carried
an implication that was exceedingly heavy. It was that if Neuberger
disagreed with Morse he had better keep quiet, for to voice disagreement was to slap him—and Wayne Morse was not noted in any
quarters for taking a slap with a smile. From one who never displayed the slightest hesitancy to slap at others when he found their
position disagreeable, this was a peculiar demand. For Neuberger, it
was an intolerable one.

Neuberger refused to get into line. Instead, he dropped a broad
hint to me that all was not what it seemed on the surface in their
relationship. Obviously Neuberger wanted to get the whole thing
out into the open. Under questioning, neither of the combatants
could long maintain the surface fiction of unity. Morse assumed a
professorial posture, as though his letters were those of a dean to a
freshman who needed a stiff reminder about his undeferential conduct. Neuberger assumed the posture of the shaken comrade in arms
who never would have believed his fellow man could be so beastly.
"This whole episode has disillusioned me with political life," he re-

marked over and over. If he had it to do over, he said he would not write any magazine articles booming Morse for President.

In the political quarrel which ensued, a contrasting feature was that Morse tried to hush it up and Neuberger deftly nudged it into public view. Morse wanted to spank his junior colleague, but in the privacy of the U.S. mails. Neuberger knew the only gain in a quarrel with Morse was to be derived from the sympathy it would arouse for him among Oregon's many Morse haters—among them many newspaper editorial writers. When my first dispatch, describing the end of their honeymoon, was published, Morse sent a member of his staff to ask Neuberger to join him in a statement which would describe the dispatch as baloney. Neuberger refused. Morse then issued a public statement describing the story as "nonsense" because "Dick Neuberger and I are close personal and political friends and we shall remain so, much to the consternation of our mutual political enemies."

Neuberger a week later issued a skillfully phrased statement which served to confirm that he and Morse had differences in "our personal attitude toward President Eisenhower." This was the point Neuberger had set out initially to make. But then he turned to the Republicans who had gleefully greeted the news of the split. "Certain partisan politicians in Oregon [who] are shedding crocodile tears over the fact that Senator Morse and I have disagreed recently" need only review the Morse-Neuberger record in Congress to be assured that "we can disagree . . . and yet team in harness for the benefit of Oregon," said Neuberger, listing many public-works improvements which he said had stemmed from their joint efforts. "The two Oregon Senators are not carbon copies of each other. But when the welfare of Oregon is at stake, the record speaks for itself as to our teamwork and mutual effectiveness."

Passions had a chance to cool in the autumn months of 1957 between congressional sessions, so when the Oregon Democrats in January renewed their breakfast conferences, no sour notes toward one another were voiced. Morse, however, led off the discussion by lamenting that Governor Holmes had passed out too many jobs to Republicans. Several others joined in the spirit of the occasion. As usual, this gossip soon leaked into the newspapers. Morse instantly issued a statement to the press to head off the notion that he and other Oregon congressional Democrats were sore at the governor. "I am amused by Oregon newspaper rumor stories concerning that meeting," Morse said, adding a glowing testimonial in behalf of the governor. But in a letter circulated to his colleagues, Morse bristled, "It is unfortunate that someone on the delegation or someone on the staff of someone in the delegation who attended the meeting did not respect the confidential nature of our delegation meetings."

Neuberger, in a letter to all hands, replied that he felt no need to issue any statement to the press "because I was not the member of the delegation who spent approximately half an hour criticizing Governor Holmes, his personal staff, and many of his appointees." The fat was in the fire. Virtually every subsequent difference became a battleground, as these two fiercely combative senators struggled, each desperate to secure himself. The delegation breakfast meetings continued, but only as a kind of mask of harmony to hide the dark frown of factional intrigue. The Morse-Neuberger alliance at last collapsed.

The behavior of both men in this political relationship bore out their adherence to the doctrine that politics is a kind of war which unites or divides men of power, as each determines his own self-interest.

Self-reform

Neuberger, however, did more than war with Morse. He undertook a basic self-reform as a senator. He had come to the Senate from a successful career as a political essayist. As a new senator, he adopted a pattern for which his past experience ably fitted him. On a typewriter at his elbow in the Senate Office Building, Neuberger pecked out pungent reformist essays which he then delivered in a dry, flat monotone in the Senate chamber so they would be published in the *Congressional Record*. He wanted to reform virtually everything, from the ancient system for appointing committee chairmen by seniority to the practice of senators' deleting or expanding their remarks made in the Senate before the *Record* is published. Midway through his term Neuberger concluded that the needling, goading tactics by which he had advanced his causes theretofore should be superseded by a win-friends-and-influence-senators approach. Sheathing the rapier of the critic, Neuberger now came forward with the hand of friendship to senators of both parties and to the Eisenhower administration to "get things done for Oregon."

Why did he do this? One very tangible problem confronted him as chairman of the Indian Affairs subcommittee. He had drafted a bill designed to save the Klamath Indian's pine forests from swift private cutting. Pointing the finger of accusation at past Republican mistakes would not get that bill onto the statute books. But having lunch or breakfast with key officials in the Eisenhower administration, making kindly gestures toward Senate Republicans, and hard shirt-sleeve work in committee would—and did—save the timber. Mr. Conservationist earned his title not by assaults on squirrel trappers but by adopting the constructive legislative habits which characterize senators who truly serve their state and nation.

Also there was no better way to draw further contrast between himself and Morse. When asked whether he had concluded that Oregon could no longer afford to have two gadfly senators, Neuberger nodded gravely. Perhaps he would have made this shift without any of these pressures which played upon him. One of his oldest and closest friends says of his metamorphosis: "My explanation is that he one day realized that he had arrived at the top. No longer did he have to fight and bite and kick his way up the hill. He was there. Having arrived, he wanted the esteem of all of the people of Oregon. He was there and he wanted to settle down to the hard job— no more tricks—of being an able statesman, one who would have a permanent place in Oregon history. This decision was made, I am sure, before the bout with cancer." Neuberger's "get things done" program began at least six months before his doctor detected a malignancy.

Neuberger's self-reform provoked a crisis of dual dimensions for Wayne Morse. The broken alliance tended to bear out earlier Republican predictions that Morse would become the center of discord in his newly adopted party. As Neuberger got things done, he tended also to demonstrate what critics had often said of Morse: he never accomplishes anything. Editorial writers all over the state began to see Neuberger in a fresh, pleasant light; and by contrast they saw Morse in gloomier light than ever.

The second dimension of the political crisis which now plagued Morse was provoked by Neuberger's raising a fundamental challenge to Wayne Morse's bread-and-butter liberalism. Neuberger was a member of the Senate Post Office Committee when Eisenhower's Postmaster General, Arthur Summerfield, urged an increase in postal rates to reduce the postal deficit and finance postal improvements. As a liberal Democrat, Neuberger began with the standard conviction that the postal service to the people need not, as a matter of sound public policy, be maintained on a self-sustaining financial basis. But as he listened to testimony and began to analyze the alternatives and implications of his position, Neuberger changed his stand. His vote gave the Administration the slender margin it needed to get the postal-rate bill to the Senate floor.

When news of this committee vote reached the chamber, Morse immediately denounced the vote of approval as "brazen" and "unholy." Tipped off about Morse's attack just as he was sitting down to lunch, Neuberger hurried from the Senate dining room to the chamber, where he found his colleague castigating the press for making "a grab bag out of our nation's mail bags. I am one senator who does not propose to let the newspaper editors and magazine publishers get by with this avarice, when they seek to impose upon the taxpayers of this country this unconscionable burden that we are already paying by way of the post office deficit." Morse seemed to be objecting to raising first-class rates from three cents to four cents, or to five cents as the Administration wanted, when second-class rates for publications were not put on a pay-as-you-go basis. But in the next breath he said, "I do not take the position either that second and third-class mail users should pay a higher rate. I take the position that they could pay more than they do now. But I still say that second- and third-class mail is also vital to the educational processes of the nation."

Neuberger could stand the suspense of Morse's tightrope act no longer. He interrupted to point out that the postal bill provided rate increases for all classes of mail. He then observed that postal workers were eager for a pay raise—and the liberals were backing their wage demands; a post-office building program was on the drawing boards—and liberals were complaining only that it was overdue; he mentioned the constant demand by Democratic liberals for federal funds to develop Pacific Northwest resources, particularly the mighty Columbia River with its network of magnificent hydroelectric and flood-control dams; and he recalled that he and Morse were among those demanding repeal of the transportation tax, which penalized western shippers. "Legitimate as these needs are," argued Neuberger, "we cannot always advocate only the spending of public funds and the lifting of burdensome taxes. We cannot always evade the responsibility of facing up to the need to collect revenue."

Dick Neuberger, the New Deal liberal, had not merely made a case for raising postal rates. He had exposed the soft underbelly of bread-and-butter liberalism. Some way, somehow, costs must be met.

A government which spends is a government which must collect. A government which invests tax dollars in needed social programs must raise the capital or the national debt.

Wayne Morse sought to counter with logistical tricks. "I have listened to many non sequiturs in my thirteen years in the Senate, but I have never listened to one that is more absurd than the one my colleague has just made when he pointed out that Senators from the Northwest are sent to Congress from time to time for the purpose of securing large public works and that therefore a five-cent postage stamp ought to be imposed upon the people of the United States in order to do something to reduce the Post Office deficit."

Neuberger, however, wisely obtained a letter of support from the Democratic chairman of the Senate Appropriations Committee, the venerable Carl Hayden of Arizona, who said, "By voting to cut down the postal deficit, you were actively assisting me to provide more federal funds for dams, locks, transmission lines, reclamation projects, harbor dredging, and other needed public works in the state of Oregon. Federal funds, first or last, have to come from the taxpayers of this country. When we must divert such funds to cover postal deficits, it means less money for public improvements in such regions as the Pacific Northwest. I want to thank you for your courage in not flinching from the question of a five-cent postal rate."

Next, Morse countered with tear-jerking imagery. He would never vote to increase the cost of a poor widow's letter to her son serving his country in Korea. It was the liberal's duty to protect the little people, and low postal rates represented one of the first lines of defense. But, persisted Neuberger, it was not the little people who were filling the most mailbags. Testimony in committee showed that "by far the majority of the users of the mail, in terms of volume, including first-class mail, are various businesses throughout the country. But when a deficit exists, it has to be made up by the general taxpayer, out of their individual income taxes; and they are making it possible, for example, for very large department stores and utility companies, in sending out their billings, to mail them at a reduced rate, below that recommended by the experts, statisticians and accountants in the Post Office Department."

Characteristically refusing to concede a point, Morse shifted fuzzily to a defense of business use of the mails: "That is part of the service they have a right to expect of the government. It is part of the educational process about which I have been talking, and for which the Post Office was set up in the first place. The fact remains that the so-called average letter writer to whom my colleague has referred is going to be hit if a five-cent postage rate is adopted."

Next day, with a night to muse over Neuberger's telling point, Morse returned to the floor, once more the champion of the little fellow instead of the business houses. "When we refer to the fact that businesses use first-class mail to send out their bills—whether they are private utilities or department stores or what not—I wonder whether anyone really thinks that the businesses pay for that postage?" he asked. The answer was, No, of course not, for they would pass it on to their customers. "By increasing the rate on first-class mail we would be increasing the burden on the so-called little fellow, the general consumer in the United States."

By such logic, one might defend reducing corporation income taxes because taxes are passed on to the little fellow in the cost of products. Or higher interest rates on bank loans could be defended as ultimately to the advantage of the little depositor, whose interest rate on his savings would be increased as a result.

Dick Neuberger had pierced Wayne Morse's liberalism through its Achilles' heel. No matter how Morse twisted and turned, he could not escape the fallacy of something-for-nothing which Neuberger speared through the opening in Morse's armor.

Neuberger used the same lance when Morse and other liberals offered an income tax reduction bill to stimulate the economy in March 1958, when unemployment was reaching troublesome peaks. Reciting all the federally financed programs he wanted expanded, Neuberger told the Senate, "I do not wholly understand senators who say, 'I favor, on the one hand, very large tax cuts, and on the other hand a great increase in federal spending.' I do not believe that is possible. I do not believe the American people think that is possible, unless we do devaluate and cheapen the worth of the dollar that they spend at the grocery store for food far more than they ever gain in tax reductions. . . . It seems to me that the two positions are mutually inconsistent, and that I would be validly subject to the criticism of inconsistency and hypocrisy if I were to advocate them."

The college boy who Dean Morse had said would never make a lawyer had become a senator in his own right and, at last, in his own way. Although never a match for Senator Morse in sheer oratorical skill, Dick Neuberger suddenly became the most formidable opponent Wayne Morse had ever encountered.

18. LOVE THINE ENEMIES

Morse-Neuberger Feud . . . Cancer . . . The Hatfield As-
sault .   . "The Other Fellow May Be Right" . . . Maurine
. . . Everyman's Burden—Self-centeredness

IN THE summer of 1959 the office of Senator Wayne Morse issued
a statement to the press which mentioned one of the least publicized
of Senate gatherings. It stated that the Reverend H. P. Sconce of
Hermiston, Oregon, "accompanied Senator Morse to the weekly
Senate Prayer Breakfast, at which a group of Senators meet to discuss
the application of Scriptural teachings to their daily work. Morse is a
regular member of the group."

This Morse press release related that after the prayer breakfast, the
senator and his guest recorded a conversation for broadcast over a
string of Oregon radio stations, and the preacher had this to say:

> I was deeply moved at that meeting this morning when the Senator
> in charge of the meeting delivered the message on the Beatitudes, and
> on the meaning of 'blessed are the peacemakers.'
>
> When it was over, I felt the Nation was in good hands.
>
> I have lived for 25 years in Oregon; I know it from Brookings to
> Astoria, from Astoria to Milton-Freewater, and down to Lakeview,
> and I wish all the people of Oregon knew you more for what you
> actually are, and for what you really stand for.
>
> I wish they knew you for the wonderful influence you have here in
> Washington, because I heard it from so many Senators around the
> Capitol. . . .

It must, indeed, have been an inspiring experience for a man of
the cloth to break bread with powerful men of state and watch them
nod approvingly as a colleague recalled the Master's teachings. His
wish to give a testimonial in behalf of Senator Morse to the folks
back home was understandable. The senator's desire to exploit this
testimonial for favorable publicity was just as understandable, for at

this stage a growing number of Oregonians thought that Wayne Morse had horns, a tail, and the other attributes of the devil. It seemed apparent to this Oregon minister that the contrary was the case. As he put it, "I wish all the people of Oregon knew you more for what you actually are, and for what you really stand for."

We have seen, in large measure, what Wayne Morse stands for. His moralistic lectures on the need to translate human values into legislative practice, to improve the whole moral tone of government and private life, to turn from materialism toward spiritual values have inspired thousands of citizens, especially students, who yearn for mankind to rise to new heights of civilized conduct. In his periodic acts of lonely courage, he has also captured the imagination of many citizens who have viewed him as the white knight of American politics—Everyman's senator, fighting Everyman's battles without fear or favor. This is the Legend of Wayne Morse.

But the events which immediately preceded this radio broadcast tell us more about the inner man and something of the degree to which Wayne Morse practices what he preaches.

Morse-Neuberger Feud

When the Morse-Neuberger alliance crumbled, Congresswoman Edith Green and Congressman Al Ullman lined up on Morse's side and Congressman Charles Porter sided with Neuberger in a series of factional tiffs. To observe simply that the senators completely lost contact with one another on a personal basis is to miss the depths to which their mutual distrust and bad feelings fell. But the breakdown in speaking relations helps explain the final stage of their feud. The spark was a minor bill which Porter had piloted through the House and which Neuberger planned to push through the Senate. The bill's purpose was to transfer to the city of Roseburg, Oregon, a small tract on which stood an old house which some citizens thought would make an interesting local museum. The federal government had acquired the property at no cost to the taxpayers. Lillie Moore, the long-time owner of the property, had willed it to Uncle Sam instead of to the city in order to spite Roseburg's city fathers, who had long before incurred her displeasure in an altogether unrelated land deal. Mrs. Moore had hopes her house might become a museum, although this was not so specified in her will.

So a bill was introduced and enacted to give the ancient dwelling to the city, providing it was moved to city property for conversion into a museum. The government could then use or sell the valuable downtown real estate on which it had stood. After this bill was enacted, however, engineers discovered the house was too fragile to be moved from its foundations. So Porter introduced a second bill to transfer the land to the city at no cost.

As Porter recognized, there was a question whether this proposal would violate the Morse formula—that familiar rule which Morse has applied to countless property-transfer bills to force local beneficiaries to pay part or all of the fair market value. Porter wrote Morse a letter seeking to show that this case was uniquely outside the confines of the Morse formula, inasmuch as the property came into federal possession only through a personal quirk of an old lady. It would be no net loss now for the property to be deeded to the city for creation of the museum Mrs. Moore had suggested. Chances that the government would ever create such a museum were exceedingly slim. Morse replied that he would have to study the matter.

On the day that the bill was called up on the Senate consent calendar in August, 1958, Morse objected to its passage. It violated the Morse formula, he declared, and unless the city agreed to pay half the land's dollar value, he would block the transfer. He emphasized that he had always assured other senators in blocking their bills that he would never play favorites in his home state.

Neuberger was prepared for the occasion. He produced a letter from the Library of Congress Legislative Reference Service offering the opinion that this case did not require application of the Morse formula. Morse was not impressed by someone else's opinion on this, his specialty. He maintained his objection, and the bill was not passed. All this might have been avoided had the two senators been on speaking terms, but their only mode of communication now was via the mails. Returning to his office, Neuberger dictated a chiding note to Morse:

Dear Wayne:
    You may recall your letter of July 11, which stated that irrespective of any differences which might exist between us: "I shall continue to offer to work with you at all times on any matter or problem that involves the welfare of our State and our Senatorial duties in representing the people of the State and of the Nation in the Senate."
    I regret that you evidently did not feel this applied to the bill to transfer the Lillie Moore property to the city of Roseburg, before

that bill reached the floor yesterday, there to be met by your objection to its enactment. I had no prior notice that you believed H.R. 6995—Charlie Porter's bill to authorize this conveyance—to be in violation of the "Morse formula" in the form in which it came before the Senate yesterday. Charlie informed me that in his view he, too, had no such prior notice until you actually took the floor to object to its passage.

Neuberger then reviewed the legislative history of the bill, including the observation that the bill had been before a Senate committee for over five months and Morse had not asked for any changes in it until the day it came up for Senate action. Neuberger suggested that Morse had ambushed the bill instead of making known his objection in advance. Upon receiving this communiqué from his junior colleague, Morse dictated a quick reply:

Dear Neuberger:
You have a lot of guts to write me the message contained in your letter of August 5th. It is further evidence of your untrustworthy tactics. You and Porter were familiar with my long-standing opposition to this bill and your bill on the Lillie Moore property. The cowardly attempt in your letter to pass the buck to me for your failure and Porter's failure to consult with me about your two bills is but further evidence of your complete untrustworthiness as a colleague.

It is obvious in view of your oft repeated amoral conduct that you and I simply agree to disagree.

Thus the differences between the senators reached the stage of ugly words. Both men had past experience in this business of postal combat. Neuberger had had an explosive exchange of letters with Howard Morgan, the state Democratic leader who he at one stage suspected would be his opponent for re-election in 1960. Morse, of course, was a skilled man of letters.

The two senators were quite different, however, in one respect: Morse could lash out with ugly words and be buoyed up by the experience; Neuberger became nervous, anxious, fearful in such ordeals. Perhaps wisely realizing his emotions might get the better of his reasoning, Neuberger made a revealing decision as his feud with Morse mounted. He assigned his legal assistant, a capable young lawyer, Hans Linde, the task of drafting all further letters of reply to Wayne Morse. Quite the contrary, Morse took counsel from no one on how to handle Neuberger. In his early Senate days his impulsive strike-back trait had been held in check somewhat when hot-tempered replies sometimes were torn up the next day because a coolheaded personal secretary deliberately neglected to mail them the night they were dictated. But now no one checked the flow of angry words. Neuberger's reply to the Morse allegation about "amoral conduct" was as follows:

Dear Wayne:
I regret the abusive and intemperate tone of your letter to me of August 5. I do not propose to trade insults with you, but I merely want to point out that a hearing was held on the Lillie Moore bill before Senator Hubert Humphrey's Subcommittee on Government Operations on July 29. At that time I appeared before the subcommittee and testified in behalf of the legislation sponsored by Congressmen Porter and myself. The fact that neither you nor any member of your staff submitted testimony regarding the legislation at the hearing would certainly indicate to us that you had no objection to our bill.

Furthermore, Charlie Porter himself has told me that he had no reason to believe you would interpose objection on the Senate floor to passage of the measure. Lacking any evidence to the contrary, Charlie and I proceeded to seek passage of the bill.

However, I again urge you to let our bill pass because of the precedent set when the Lillie Moore house was transferred in 1956 without your objection. Should this proposal be unacceptable to you, I am willing to join with you in an amendment to the bill providing that the city of Roseburg pay 50 per cent of the fair market value—although I still regret the apparent necessity of such an inclusion.

Can we join in offering the amendment as soon as possible to avoid having the Lillie Moore property bill lost in the adjournment rush?

With good wishes, I am

Sincerely,

Wayne Morse lost no time in replying the next day. It should be noted that postal combat between senators is aided by the swift and frequent mail deliveries senators receive through a post office located in their office building. On the day Morse dictated and dispatched the following letter, August 7, Neuberger received it and sent his reply:

Dear Neuberger:

Your letter of August 6 is in keeping with your record of trickiness in your relations with me. I had no knowledge of the hearings before Senator Humphrey's subcommittee on the Lillie Moore bill just as you have no knowledge of scores and scores of hearings that are held before Senate committees. The fact is that neither you nor Porter ever conferred with me about your bill. Just common ordinary courtesy placed such an obligation on both of you. At no time did either one of you ever raise the Lillie Moore bill matter at one of our delegation breakfasts. One of the major purposes of those breakfasts is for a discussion of just such matters. Both you and Charlie Porter had every reason to believe that I would object to the bill. Apparently you thought if you could get the bill to the Senate calendar then you could get by with this violation of the Morse formula.

I shall oppose any amendment at this time in the Senate to the Lillie Moore bill. I have made clear to Charlie Porter that I will continue to object to the bill until it comes over to the Senate from the House with the Morse formula written into it. Both of you are making a tragic mistake in the way you are handling this matter.

Very truly yours,

The reply read:

Dear Wayne:

I profoundly regret the continuing abusive nature of your letters to me. Neither Charlie Porter nor I ever has resorted to trickery in sponsoring the Lillie Moore bill and you know it. We have been open and above-board about the entire matter. We do not have to consult with you about everything that we do, any more than you must consult with us. There are not enough hours in the day for that.

On August 5, you criticized and attacked my fisheries protection bill, S. 3185, and introduced amendments to weaken and change it. I introduced the bill as early as January 29, 1958. I do not recall you ever conferring or consulting with me about my bill, S. 3185, before you attacked it at great length. Yet I am not resentful or angry. That was your right. In the pressure of events here, you did not have to confer with me before you disagreed with my bill. I have never expected or asked you to do so.

I only hope that, somehow, you can subdue the terrific personal resentment you seem to have against me, so we can work together to the best interests of our state and nation.

With best wishes, I am

Sincerely,

The next day, August 8, they had another exchange.

Dear Neuberger:
I understand very well why you are upset over my letters because at long last you now realize that I have had my fill of your deceit, trickery and completely untrustworthy tactics as a colleague.

Your fisheries bill, which you mention in your letter of August 7, is but another example of your lack of teamwork with the Oregon delegation. It was a bill which you should have brought up at one of our delegation breakfasts for discussion before you ever introduced it. Each member of the delegation had a great deal at stake in respect to the implications and effects of your bill.

It is obvious that you do not know what the word teamwork means. When I made my speech the other day in the Senate on both your fisheries bill and the Lillie Moore bill, I paid you a courtesy that you never pay me. I instructed Jay McDonnell to call your office and advise you that I was about to make a speech on matters of interest to you. In doing that I extended to you much more cooperation than your record of lack of teamwork with me entitles you to. My disrespect for you has become so complete that there is no basis on which you and I can work together.

                                                    Very truly yours,

Dear Wayne:
I am completely at a loss to account for the venom contained in your letters to me.

Let us suppose that Charlie and I were derelict in not notifying you about the Lillie Moore bill. Is that any reason for you to accuse me of every abysmal quality which words can describe?

I was not notified by you that you were going to denounce on the Senate floor as "parliamentary trickery" the stand taken by 12 other Senate liberals and me in favor of placing the Civil Rights Bill on the calendar. That fact certainly did not cause me to hate you, or to direct toward you accusations of deceit and trickery.

Supposing somebody does slip up, in this hectic atmosphere, and does not give all the notice he or she should regarding a particular bill or speech. So what? Is that a cause for abuse and slander?

You are a brilliant man with wide knowledge of public affairs. I urge you not to damage yourself by harboring personal malice against me which can only damage you far more than it damages me. I bear you no ill-will. I bear you no malice. If I have done anything to offend you in this Lillie Moore legislation, I apologize and I hope you will forgive me.

I was trying to help Congressman Charlie Porter and a good many Roseburg people by promoting a piece of legislation close to their hearts. The farthest thought from my mind was to offend or annoy you.

With good wishes, I am

Sincerely,

Three days later Morse sent back a lengthy reply in which he said the Lillie Moore bill "was just the straw that broke the camel's back." What, then, had caused the venom that spewed forth from Wayne Morse? This is how he explained it in that letter August 11 addressed to "Dear Neuberger":

What has hurt me so deeply over the many months has been your many actions of inexcusable disloyalty to our friendship. No one could have tried harder than I have tried to teamwork with you. The saddest thing about this unpleasant experience is that I started my service with you in the Senate after the historic election of 1954 with a deep personal fondness for you. I defended you against your critics. I boosted you at every opportunity. By the end of your first term in the Senate, I started advocating your re-election to the Senate in 1960. In many speeches and public statements I labeled you, for example, "Mr. Conservationist in the Senate." I talked in most complimentary terms about your services on Senate committees. In fact, the record is replete with so many proofs of my loyal support of you and my manifested desire to teamwork with you in carrying out our responsibilities in the Senate that I shall always be at a complete loss to understand why you proceeded to undercut me.

No good purpose can be served at this time in any further discussion of this personal tragedy. Even as recently as Friday night a very able radio commentator came to me and gave me an account of representations that you made to him months ago about me that were so fictitious in nature and unjustified that his accounts left me feeling sorry for you. I have had so many similar reports given to me which, added to your snide undercutting of me in your writings, speeches and correspondence, have forced me to the conclusion that a re-establishment of our friendship is almost hopeless. Apparently you think that such wrongs can be committed by you and then when I finally react against them, you need only say you are sorry and all will be forgiven.

What you and I have to think about now is the procedures and policies we should try to follow in the interest of our best service to the people of Oregon as long as each one of us holds the great public trust which is ours as members of the Senate. The obligations therein entailed transcend the sadness of a broken friendship.

I hope it will be possible for us to develop a working arrangement between each other and our offices that will make it possible for us to work cooperatively together at least on an impersonal basis in respect to specific legislative problems as they arise in connection with our work in the Senate which is of importance to Oregon. The people of Oregon are entitled to that teamwork and cooperation in their interest irrespective of what you and I may think of each other personally. To that end I intend to devote myself.

It certainly would make me very pleased and happy if after the passage of a year or two such a new relationship between us might re-establish the personal regard that once existed. However, that very much to be hoped for relationship is a matter for future events to determine.

In the meantime, for whatever you may consider it to be worth, I suggest a gentleman's moratorium on personal attacks. I shall await with interest not your words but the record of action you make in respect to our Senatorial relationships. The old saying that actions speak louder than words is very much in need of application in our relationships.

This fall you and I have a very important task awaiting our attention in Oregon. We need to devote ourselves untiringly to the campaign in an endeavor to re-elect Bob Holmes, Edith Green, Charlie Porter, Al Ullman, and also to help elect to offices now held by Republicans such men as Bob Thornton and the other Democratic candidates. There is no justification, in my opinion, for that campaign being weakened by charges and countercharges relating to a broken personal and political friendship between us.

It is my suggestion that when we are confronted, as we will be, with charges that our relationships have reached a Humpty-Dumpty condition, we each say in effect that whatever differences may have developed between us have been buried and that we have pledged to each other that the Democratic party of Oregon and all the people of Oregon can count on us to cooperate on legislative matters involving the welfare of our state and our nation reserving the right to vote on each issue in accordance with our individual judgment based upon our honest convictions. It seems to me that only by such an understanding between us can we hope to carry out our responsibilities in the Senate.

I think it is also clear that, in view of the unfortunate developments in regard to our personal friendship, the only hope of re-establishing the mutual respect that I would like very much to have exist once more between us is that we follow such a course of action as I am suggesting in this letter.

Neuberger may not have altogether relished the depths to which his relationship with Morse had plunged, but the last thing he now wanted was to hide his difficulties with Morse behind some new façade of party unity. With each new expressed difference he had become a greater hero to many Oregonians. He especially cherished the backing of those editorial writers who loved to take sides against obstreperous Wayne Morse. Republicans who once openly despised Neuberger were taking on a new tone of respect for this man who battled Morse and also talked about the need for fiscal responsibility. As Neuberger viewed it, this was no time to kiss and make up with his angry colleague, not when he had become expert in pricking Morse's thin, taut skin. To Morse's invitation that they outwardly, and quite ceremoniously, bury the hachet, Neuberger sent back this reply on August 12:

Dear Wayne:

I am glad to note from your letter of August 11 that you recognize that your utterly abusive, venomous and defamatory letters of August 6, August 7 and August 8 could not stand as the final record of your views toward our mutual responsibilities in representing the people of Oregon in the Senate. As I have previously written you in reply I cannot fathom what could have led you to write me in that vein; and I doubt that those letters would find much understanding with any objective observer.

There is nothing particularly novel in the approach which you suggest for the future, as stated in the last two pages of your August 11 letter. If you will review my letters to you and other members of the delegation over the past several months, you will find that this approach is in essence similar to what I have consistently urged—particularly in consideration of the implications for the Democratic campaign to which you refer in the last two paragraphs of your second page. Accordingly, I welcome your change in tone, and particularly your evident reconsideration of your August 8th announcement of refusal to work with me any further. Such an attitude clearly could have resulted only in great damage to the interests of our state in the Senate.

While I shall thus be ready, as before, to discuss with you all matters bearing upon the proper representation and protection of those interests, I do not care to leave unanswered all the self-serving, special pleading that is also again contained in your letter of August 11. Upon review, you will find that your recent series of accusations against me have been so vague, unspecific and rhetorical that it is hard for me even to understand what, percisely, I am supposed to have done—let alone to meet your nebulous allegations with factual answers. However, certain facts do need to be kept on the record.

1. You suggest "a gentleman's moratorium on personal attacks." Such a course requires only your concurrence, not mine. I do not concede, as you do, having engaged in any personal attacks; to the contrary, I have unfailingly stressed that occasional policy differences need not involve personal antagonism. It is you, not I, who has chosen to place these differences on a personal basis.

You have accused me, without specification, of "undercutting" you. You have repeatedly accused me of "character assassination." You have referred to completely vague "overwhelming evidence" against me; but you have specified only one alleged conversation with an unidentified radio commentator concerning equally unidentified representations I am alleged to have made to him about you. I deny it; I do not know either whom, or what representations, you could mean.

It has been your letters, not mine, that have contained the terms "disloyal," "untrustworthy," "amoral," "cowardly" and "snide." It has been your letters, not mine, that have hurled accusations of "trickery" and "deceit."

I shall gladly concede, without contest, your preeminence in the use of personal invective and imprecations. If you now wish to call a halt, on your part, to this kind of thing, I shall be only too pleased.

2. If we are to have a moratorium, however, I hope that it will apply to private and public statements alike. *On the same day*, August 6, that the Congressional Record appeared with your statement, in your Lillie Moore speech (p. 14861), that "there is no personal animosity or ill feeling on my part toward either of my colleagues who are involved on the other side of this issue"—i.e. Charlie Porter and me—you wrote me a letter accusing me of "untrustworthy tactics," "cowardly attempts," and "amoral conduct." If those terms are merely a dispassionate discussion of a legislative disagreement, I would be interested to see what terms you would consider appropriate in a case of "personal animosity or ill feeling."

I do not see how a moratorium can be based on that kind of performance, particularly in view of the fact that it has evidently not been your intention to treat your abusive letters to me as a personal or confidential matter. I am informed that you have taken pride in displaying them to representatives of outside groups as well as to members of Senate staffs—I cannot imagine why. If you really believe that any goal can be served by public and press discussion or these vitriolic attacks in your letters to me, that would be a source of great wonder.

If you intend to express publicly the views you suggest toward the end of your latest letter, I hope that these will also square in the future with the terms of your private correspondence.

3. Further to keep the record straight, you have written me that you had me informed of your proposed attacks both on Charlie's Lillie Moore bill, H.R. 6995, and on my FPC bill, S. 3185.

With respect to H.R. 6995, I was informed after you had begun to speak. In that instance it was not important, as I had decided that in any case no useful purpose could be served by taking the time of the Senate to discuss, on the Senate floor, the detailed merits of the evidence pro and con of a property disposition which is wholly limited to the local interest of our state. Both Charlie and I have expressed our willingness to accede to an amendment of the bill to satisfy your objections.

With respect to S. 3815, contrary to your letter, I was not informed of your intention to speak in opposition to it. As I regard this bill as a matter of more than local importance, I intend to speak in defense of my bill at an early date, and I shall notify you in advance on that occasion.

So much for setting straight the record in response to your accusations.

In conclusion, Wayne, I think you must realize that you cannot expect others to carry the entire burden of good personal and working relationships with you, if you will not concede to others at least a reasonable proportion of the pride in personal principles, honesty and integrity which you are habitually and continually claiming for yourself.

I do not believe that I have apologies to make for my side of our recent exchanges. I am prepared at any time to submit the whole record to objective, impartial and disinterested public judgment. Nevertheless, I am also prepared to repeat once again that I seek no personal controversy with you, and that I bear you no malice or ill-will. If you are now prepared to proceed on that basis, in conduct off just as much as on the Senate floor, it will certainly make life easier for all of us, as well as avoiding the unfortunate consequences in Oregon of which I have so often expressed my apprehension.

With good wishes, I am

Sincerely,

To Wayne Morse, this was the last affront. He sent back his answer on August 13:

August 13:

Dear Neuberger:

I am amused by your letter of August 12 which reflects again your sanctimonious holier than thou attitude. I am perfectly willing to have you make public our correspondence and let the public be the judge of our differences.

Your psychological escapism of fain [sic] innocence whenever your hand is called in respect to your disloyal conduct toward your colleagues in the delegation is well known. It had been my hope that my bluntly notifying you in my correspondence that at long last I had decided to acquaint you with the fact that your well-known tendency to put Dick Neuberger's selfish personal political interest above the welfare of the delegation would cause you to pause long enough to mend your ways and to try to work out a better relationship within the delegation. Your letter of August 12 convinces me that my hope was really a hopeless one.

When you were a student of mine, I found you amoral. I had hoped over the years that you would mature and develop a character of moral responsibility. Your relations with me in the Senate have proven that I was mistaken in placing that hope in you.

In regard to the notification that I had sent to your office in respect to H.R. 6995 and S. 3185, I did not send any message to your office in respect to either bill. When I saw you were not on the floor, I asked that your office be notified that I would like to have you come to the floor because I was going to discuss some matters of interest to you. That certainly should have been enough notification for you to know that I was seeking to extend to you a floor courtesy that you have yet to extend to me.

I shall always be satisfied to stand on the record I have made since you came to the Senate in an endeavor to try to get along with you. However, I have regretfully come to share the view of some others that it is impossible to teamwork with you.

What our relationship can be while we are both in the Senate in view of our mutual obligations to the people of the State of Oregon is a great puzzlement to me. My disrespect for you is so complete that I think it is perfectly clear in light of your August 12 letter that there is no basis left for any personal relationship.

I have tried hard to cover up our personal differences in the hope that some way somehow they could be reconciled. Thus when I try to extend such a protection to both of us in a public statement, you are

vindictive enough to seize upon that as evidence that my public statements are contrary to my private views. Unfortunately, you demonstrate time and time again your inability to draw distinctions and your
tendency to argue by false analogy. Thus, my statement on the floor of
the Senate quoted by you in your letter of August 12 that "there is no
personal animosity or ill feeling on my part toward either of my colleagues who are involved on the other side of this issue" was a statement of fact.

I fully understand the reasons for the course of action you and Charlie
followed in the Lillie Moore case. It has not been my opinion that
either one or both of you at the time you introduced your legislation
were seeking to do me harm. It is my position that you both made a
bad mistake in judgment by not discussing the matter with me personally. It was exactly the kind of a problem that should have been
ironed out at one of our delegation breakfasts or in personal conference
among us.

My criticism of you for untrustworthy and cowardly attacks and amoral
conduct to which you refer was based on the totality of your record in
your relationships with me. However, it is obvious that you and I have
become so far apart in our personal relations that any further attempt
to try to repair them is a waste of time and I do not have the time to
waste.

From now on I intend to work with you on a strictly impersonal basis
on issues arising in the Senate that affect the welfare of our State and
Nation whenever we find ourselves in agreement on those issues. When
mutual friends come to me, as they have, in a good faith desire to act
as emissaries in an endeavor to end what they have referred to as the
feud between us, I shall continue to give them my reasons for my complete disrespect for you.

I fully expect that you will continue to write me letters as long as I
answer yours. Therefore, I wish to notify you that this is the last personal letter you will receive from me.

                                              Very truly yours,

Cancer

When Dick Neuberger returned to Oregon upon the adjournment
of Congress soon after being verbally banished by Morse, he dropped
in to see Dr. Mort Goodman, his friend and family physician, before
driving to the scenic Oregon coast for a brief rest with his wife.

A sore in his mouth was nothing to worry about, Dr. Goodman assured him, but as long as he was there why not have a quick physical examination. Thus it was that a malignant testicular tumor was discovered.

A confirmed hypochondriac who kept his desk drawer loaded with pills of every description, Neuberger nevertheless had not suspected the cancer within him. The operation was relatively simple, but months of daily radiation treatment lay ahead. The senator's activities were severely restricted, but one thing now came to him in unlimited supply—an outpouring of good will. His newly earned stature as a successful legislator was instantly enhanced by the general sympathy and hopes of many in both parties that he would win his battle with a dread disease.

The big election contest in Oregon that fall of 1958 involved neither senator, for only the governorship was at stake. Democratic Governor Holmes was being challenged by Secretary of State Mark Hatfield. Neuberger did what his physical limitations would permit, throwing the weight of his prestige into public statements and a large "Why I'm for Bob Holmes" newspaper ad. Morse returned to Oregon to find Holmes' effort sagging. In the style that has made Morse one of the toughest campaigners many political observers have ever seen, the senator began stumping the state.

But Morse did not limit his attacks to Republicans. Upon reaching the Pendleton area, he blasted that city's daily, the *East Oregonian*, as a "reactionary" newspaper. J. W. Forrester, Jr., its liberal editor, answered the charge in an editorial which was widely reprinted thoughout the state in other newspapers:

We think the record will refute this typically abusive charge by Oregon's senior Senator. The *East Oregonian* has been a leader for many decades in the great cause of public development of the Columbia River. It was one of the few daily newspapers in Oregon advocating the high damn at Hells Canyon. It was one of three daily newspapers favoring the victory in 1954 of Richard L. Neuberger, first Democrat to be elected to the Senate from Oregon in 40 years. This year the *East Oregonian* is urging the election of Governor Robert D. Holmes and Representative Al Ullman [both liberal Democrats]. We could cite this newspaper's support of many liberal causes, all well known to Morse. It is obvious that the principal sin committed by the *East Oregonian* is that we have not supported Wayne Morse in all his election cam-

paigns and all that he has done in public office. But how does a newspaper with consistent principles go about supporting Senator Morse,
whose principles are taken on and off like a sweater? . . .

Today, Wayne Morse is denouncing the private power companies, but
the campaign records of 1944 and 1950 reveal the substantial financial
assistance which Republican Wayne Morse received from private utility
stockholders and directors in those election campaigns.

Today, Senator Morse is making numerous speeches about ethics in
government, but newspaper clippings of 1952 disclose how he was
accepting financial donations from an Oregon lumberman to pay for
Congressional Record reprints. . . .

Today, Senator Morse cannot find words too abysmal with which to
denounce the Republican party, but when he ran for re-election in
1950 he proudly reprinted praise of himself from such Republican
stalwarts as House Leader Joe Martin and Sen. William F. Knowland.
How does a newspaper of consistency follow the record of Senator
Morse with any degree of faith or assurance?

We could refer to innumerable other examples of the strange and
shifting career of this brilliant but misguided Senator from our state—
this man who, almost by rote, questions the integrity of all who disagree with him—this man who has called some great liberals in the
United States Senate, "phony liberals." How tragic that a mind so
incisive should be devoted almost wholly to negativism and abuse.

Once more, Wayne Morse alienated a possible supporter by his
self-centered appraisal of one of the strong liberal journals of Oregon.
This attack was symbolic of one of his major political shortcomings.
Instead of skillfully mustering the forces and persons which could
lend cohesive strength to the liberal causes he espouses, he has
periodically caused divisive weakness by his intolerance of differences
from the Morse line. Consequently his capacity for effective leadership has been undermined by his inability to accept public criticism
and perhaps profit by it. As editor Charles A. Sprague once advised him, "Permit yourself the luxury of being wrong once in a
while." The Morse code makes no such standard allowance.

The Hatfield Assault

In the gubernatorial campaign the Democratic strategists probed
for a vulnerable spot in the record of Mark Hatfield, the attractive
thirty-six-year-old challenger. He had been a political science in-

structor at Willamette University at Salem, had dabbled in local
G.O.P. politics until he ran for the legislature and finally for Secretary
of State in 1956. Midway through his first term in that state office,
Hatfield angered some Republicans by crowding State Treasurer Sig-
frid B. Unander out of the race for governor—but that was at most
a showing of high ambition, a sign that Hatfield was thinking first of
Hatfield. There was not much in his public record for the Democrats
to shoot at.

Facing a poverty of solid issues, the Democrats turned to a report
that Hatfield had run over a child with an automobile. Governor
Holmes, however, made it clear to his advisers that he was opposed
to any attempt to exploit this melancholy episode. Other political
warriors were not so ready to discard it. One report had it that this
had been a hit-and-run case, another that Hatfield had driven without
an operator's permit for some years.

Wayne Morse wanted to know what the facts of the case were. A
Democratic attorney, Dan Poling, searched the files at the state
capitol. Whether or not Hatfield had ever driven without a license
could not be established. Democrats continue to believe that Hatfield, as Secretary of State, used his authority to "clean up the records"
to obscure any such past misdeeds. But the record of the auto
accident was there in black and white at the State Supreme Court,
where a suit for civil damages had been decided. A report on the
accident was given to Morse's assistant, Charles Brooks, by Holmes'
campaign manager, Harry J. Hogan, who says he advised Morse "that
we didn't want to use the case in the campaign."

To Mark Hatfield, this accident had for years been a political
time bomb. Knowing that sooner or later it might go off at the
most unexpected moment, Hatfield wrote out a brief statement the
year he entered politics, 1950, just in case anyone ever mentioned
that accident. In his files, under "A" for accident, the statement
remained through one successful campaign after another. "We heard
whispers that so-and-so had been leafing through the record either
at the Marion County Courthouse or the Supreme Court," recalls
Hatfield's political associate, Travis Cross, but no one raised the
matter publicly. What were the facts of this case which soon was to
explode in the gubernatorial campaign?

One spring evening in 1940 when Hatfield was a high school
student, he had gone with his parents to the home of friends
several miles south of Salem for a picnic supper. At about seven
o'clock, as planned, Mark started back to Salem alone in his mother's

Chrysler to attend a high school band practice. As he testified in the damage-suit trial, before he reached the scene of the accident he saw a group of children walking along the road and slowed down to thirty to forty miles per hour. After passing the children, he next saw a little girl standing on the right side of the road. He recalled he eased up on the accelerator and pulled slightly toward the center of the road to avoid passing too close to the youngster. The transcript of the trial then reads:

Q—Then as you proceeded further down the road, Mr. Hatfield, what happened?

A—I got approximately opposite the Lane mailbox, and like a streak of light or something just like a swish, a streak across my eyes, I didn't see a thing, you might say, and then——

Q—You say a flash of light?

A—I guess then I heard a noise, and even yet I could not feature what had happened, because it happened so fast. That is entirely what happened, first a swish, a flash across my eyes, that is what occurred."

The auto had struck a second little girl who was crossing the road from the left side to join the girl whom Hatfield had seen on the right. The two girls, Alice, seven, and Doris, eight, had been sent across the road to deposit milk in a box located at the base of their mailbox. Doris had gone first with a quart, placed it in the box, re-crossed the road and was waiting for her younger sister. Their father, Harold Lane, was milking his cow when he heard a terrible scream. When he reached the road, he found his wife with Alice in her arms. A few neighbors were standing around. So was Hatfield, who had parked up the road. The Lanes gathered Doris and their baby daughter, Frances, into the family car and rushed to Salem with injured Alice.

As they reached the hospital Hatfield pulled up next to them, got out of his car and said, "Oh, I don't know how it happened. I didn't see her, I didn't see her." Mrs. Lane asked him to take care of her baby while they took Alice into the hospital. He took Frances into his arms and followed the Lanes to the door of the emergency room. There the doctor found that it was too late. As the Lanes left the room, they met Hatfield carrying their baby. He said, "It wasn't my fault, she ran out from behind some bushes and ran right into my car. You don't blame me, do you?" When Mrs. Lane told him Alice was dead, Hatfield turned away in agony and declared, "Oh, my God, I didn't see her, I didn't see her in time."

The Lanes subsequently filed a suit for civil damages in Marion County Court. No criminal charges were lodged against Hatfield. When the case came up for trial in October 1941, over a year after the accident, Hatfield was nineteen years of age. It was a routine damage suit. Testimony focused on whether Hatfield could have seen the child or whether she had darted out from the weeds along the road. The only witness to the accident was Doris, then aged nine. She testified that Alice had placed a pint container of milk in the box in the weeds, had then looked both ways before recrossing the road. She offered no explanation of why the child crossed when Hatfield's car was coming down the road. Mrs. Lane testified that Alice was four feet tall and that the weeds around the milkbox were eighteen inches high, so the weeds "wouldn't be more than waist high." Photographs introduced as evidence showed some weeds as high as the wooden crossbar on which the mailbox was fastened. The milkbox at the foot of the post was not visible in the photographs, apparently obscured by weeds.

The court received testimony that if the child had bent over, as she had probably done to place the milk in the box, she would not be seen because of the weeds. Inspection of the Hatfield car showed the child almost made it across the road before being struck by the right front fender and headlight. Should Hatfield have seen the girl, or should the girl have seen the car? These questions were not clearly answered by the testimony. The County Court awarded the parents $5000 damages.

Hatfield's lawyers appealed the case to the State Supreme Court. The defense hung its plea for acquittal on this allegation: "That said mailbox was placed in, and entirely surrounded by, thick tall grasses; that on account of said thick tall grasses so growing and being at and about said mailbox and of said Alice Marie Lane being concealed therein, said defendant was unable to, and did not, observe her presence."

Justice Percy R. Kelly, in rendering the verdict of the Supreme Court, noted that Hatfield had testified that he had seen only what appeared to be a flash of light across his path just before his car struck the child, and that during cross-examination by Wallace Carson, the Lanes' attorney, there ensued this exchange between the attorney and Hatfield:

Q—You desire to be understood as saying you couldn't see the little girl that was killed because of the grass and the mailbox?

A—Yes, I didn't see her at any time.

Q—And it was because of the grass, you couldn't see through or over the grass?

A—I could not see through the grass, I could not see over the grass. I couldn't see any mailbox there at all."

The attorney then introduced photographs showing the mailbox in full view. Justice Kelly's opinion stated: "There is no testimony sustaining defendants' allegation set forth in their answer to plaintiff's amended complaint. We are convinced that this is not a case where the victim darted out from a place of concealment into the path of an oncoming automobile." The high court upheld the award of damages. These are the facts available to anyone who examines the court records.

Five days before the 1958 election, at Klamath Falls, the city where he had eighteen years before made his debut as a political speaker with a bold denunciation of the New Deal, Wayne Morse fired his blast at Hatfield. But outside the meeting hall, the explosion was like the proverbial tree that crashes to earth in an uninhabited forest— it made not a sound, for there wasn't a newspaperman present to record and transmit the news.

Finding not a line in the morning papers, Morse drove the next morning to Medford where he and Charles W. Brooks, his field representative, dropped in to tell Eric Allen, Jr., managing editor of the Medford *Mail Tribune* what Morse had said at Klamath Falls. "I think I was the first newspaperman in the state to know about the Hatfield attack," recalls Allen. "Wayne, with a sort of eager glee, told me about it and the fact that he was going to do it again. I had an immediate and almost instinctive bad reaction to it." One of Allen's reporters was assigned to cover what Morse that day told 200 listeners in a Medford theater.

"Some years ago," the senator gravely informed his audience, Secretary of State Hatfield "killed a precious seven-year-old girl by negligent driving of an automobile. Being called as a witness before a jury, Hatfield gave testimony that the jury rejected and the Oregon Supreme Court rejected as well." From the crook of his arm, Morse took Volume 173 of the State Supreme Court reports and read selected excerpts.

The point of going back eighteen years, said Morse, was that the case showed the Republican candidate "cannot be believed under oath as a witness." He likened what he termed Hatfield's "false testimony" to "evasive language" which characterized his campaign literature. Hatfield "ducks and dodges" the real issues, Morse contended. Quoting a statement by Hatfield that he would "take [electric] power out of politics," Morse said, "I thought he believed in democracy. We're not going to "take power out of politics" and put it in the control of McKee." Paul B. McKee, head of Pacific Power and Light Company, is the "power behind Hatfield" and the person "chiefly responsible for getting Mark Hatfield into running in the first place," charged Morse. "Hatfield is thoroughly, intellectually dishonest. Hatfield cannot be relied on."

When Morse then made his way down the aisle of that Medford theater, a lady approached him to ask the question that crossed the minds of thousands of Oregonians who had always associated Wayne Morse with his own vows of high principle:

"Why did you do it?"

"I don't intend to let a man run for public office who lies to a jury. I don't intend to let a man lie to a jury and get away with it," came the brusque, determined reply.

At Salem and Portland the more sensitive detection devices of politicians on both sides of the Holmes-Hatfield race had picked up the initial shock wave from Klamath Falls. Democratic National Committeeman G. Girard (Jebby) Davidson put in calls to party leaders in an effort to stop Morse from repeating the charge. It was too late. Morse the afternoon of the Klamath Falls speech had told Governor Holmes' manager, Hogan, by telephone he intended to use the Hatfield incident that night, despite Hogan's reminder that the governor was strongly opposed to such an attack. At Salem Hatfield received a telephoned report of Morse's Klamath Falls speech at 11:30 that night. Reaching into his "A" file and extracting his eight-year-old prepared statement, Hatfield deleted a few of its original words and had it reproduced for distribution to the press when the Morse attack next day made boldface headlines throughout the state. Hatfield's statement said:

> The entire case is a matter of public record and the Supreme Court reports in every law office in the state carry the final chapter of the tragedy. To have brought it up again in an effort to shatter a reputation at this particular time will bring on a recurrence of great grief to all who were involved in the regrettable accident of 18 years ago. Those who conspire to profit thereby have my compassion.

On the Democratic side there was a swift scurrying for cover. Morse's blast was disowned by virtually every prominent Democrat in the state. Governor Holmes remained mum momentarily, but when a wave of indignation began rolling across the state he, too, disavowed Morse's action. He went on television with Congresswoman Green in a program hastily planned to replace a film in which Morse was to have appeared as a Holmes supporter. The governor told his audience that if such techniques as the personal attack on Hatfield were necessary to be re-elected, "then I do not want to be governor that badly."

The *Oregonian* newsroom was deluged with irate readers' phone calls, expressing shock and anger at the Morse attack. The drab campaign had come to a roaring climax. Characteristically Morse bulled ahead, repeating and recasting his attack. "In these speeches," Morse declared at Baker three days before the election, "when the people of Oregon really analyze this matter, every mother, every father, every grandfather of every little child in Oregon will understand the soundness of my point of view."

There was no question that young Hatfield, climbing fast and now reaching for the highest rung on the state political ladder, was ducking the hot issues on which the Democrats tried to pin him down, was refusing to become identified with the policies of the Eisenhower administration which had cost McKay so heavily two years before, was not advertising even that he was a Republican— a successful tactic used the same year by Nelson Rockefeller in his campaign for Governor of New York. Hatfield conducted a personality campaign, in which he sought to convey the impression of an attractive, intelligent, reasonable, nice guy with vigor and fresh ideas for improving state government by providing better service for less taxes. It was a smartly conducted campaign, compared to Holmes' fumbling, well-meaning efforts that weren't registering. Even the simple but proud announcement in mid-campaign that Hatfield's bride of that summer was expecting a baby seemed blessed with magnificent timing.

Wayne Morse tried to pierce the challenger's attractive exterior. Recalling his experience as a teacher of young people for twenty-one years, he said, "In that time I had many a teen-age boy in class. When a boy has a pattern of low intellectual standards as a student, follow him through life and you'll find he has the same pattern. Now take a look at this student's standards, under oath."

Neuberger sought to disavow the Morse attack and simultaneously discredit the Republicans who were weeping aloud over this "vicious" act. He recalled that in his own campaign for the Senate, he had been the victim of several personal attacks from supporters of his Republican adversary—notably the college cribbing charge, and a low-key, unfavorable reference to him as a Jew. Neuberger said Morse's smear "should not divert attention from Mr. Hatfield's real disqualifications for the governorship—principally his reckless and irresponsible campaign promises of both lower taxes and higher spending."

But no one could divert attention from the Morse attack. The Chief Justice of the State Supreme Court at the time the case was reviewed, J. O. Bailey, said the Senator was in effect contending that every litigant who loses a case in court is a liar, which "is simply not true."

Night before election, Morse wound up his part in the campaign with a five-minute television report at the dinner hour. His finale was characteristically bold:

"The lightning of bitter political criticism is striking around my head these hours. It is no new experience for me. In my position as Senator, I have the duty of following where the facts lead even though the facts may not be politically popular at the moment. My abiding confidence in our political system of self-government is that once the people have the facts and reflect upon them, a majority of the people also will follow where the facts lead. I hold to the view that the life of a candidate for office should be an open book in respect to any conduct which pertains to the candidates' qualifications for office. Throughout this campaign for the governorship of Oregon I have charged and documented my charges that the Republican candidate has been evasive, equivocal and all things to all people on vital issue after vital issue. . . . Such misrepresentations based upon intellectual unreliability honeycomb Hatfield's campaign literature. In my speeches in Klamath Falls, Medford, Riddle and Baker, which have caused such an emotional uproar in the state, I only pointed out as an old teacher that it long has been my experience that when intellectual unreliability is present in the mind of a student, it usually carries forward into adult life.

"My references in those speeches, to the unrealiability of the testimony of Mark Hatfield when he was 19 years old and a second year college student and testified as a witness to an accident in which he was involved a month before he was 18 years of age, were made because his testimony links directly with his tendency to make misrepresentations in his campaign literature. I considered it my duty to forewarn the people of Oregon of this pattern of behavior possessed by the Republican candidate. The full responsibility of these disclosures is mine. . . . Bob Holmes disapproves of my discussion of his opponent's qualifications, as do some of my other Democratic colleagues. However, each one has to keep faith with the dictates of his conscience. I have done so. I have no regrets and now, irrespective of what our differences may be, I plead with each voter of Oregon to go to the polls tomorrow . . ."

No regrets, no backing down, no apologies to the sensibilities of others. Why should there be? The senator was keeping faith with his conscience!

Mark Hatfield the next day was elected governor by 60,000 votes. The best-informed post-mortems agreed that Holmes would have lost in any event; but Morse's bombshell exploded any chance of a last-minute recovery, and widened the victor's margin because of sympathy for Hatfield. In the crushing hours of defeat which fell over the Democrats, Wayne Morse picked up the telephone and called Bob Holmes. "I lost the election for you, I lost the election," he mourned. In a telegram to Hatfield, as though it were for *him* to concede defeat, Morse said crisply: "The supreme court of politics, namely the ballot box has rendered its verdict. You win. Congratulations."

Back to Washington flew Morse, to his Maryland farm where his cattle offered no rebukes to their overseer as they looked up placidly from their pastoral munching, back to his horses and dog who promised unflinching loyalty to this strangely vituperative man, no matter what he said or did. Wayne Morse went back to the place he has come to treasure most as a restful sanctuary from the slings and arrows of daily political warfare. But he did not rest.

Governor-elect Hatfield invited Morse to return to Oregon for a conference to discuss state problems. As Oregon's senior member of Congress, he was asked to bring all his colleagues along. Morse rejected it as political window dressing that would serve no constructive purpose. His office was open to Hatfield any time the governor had any problems in Washington. Neuberger stepped between Morse and Hatfield, with a swipe at both: "It will be very unfortunate if the great and urgent needs of our state are neglected while Senator Morse and Governor-elect Hatfield jockey politically for

1962." Neuberger adroitly portrayed the other two chief political figures in Oregon as men less interested in solving grave public problems than in seeking personal political advantage. Neuberger and Hatfield later had tea. "Empty gestures," hooted Morse—"political window dressing." Certainly not much more.

Two weeks later, Neuberger, in a speech at the annual Good Government luncheon of the Portland Junior Chamber of Commerce, called for an end to personal abuse and character assassination in politics. He referred specifically to Morse's attack on Hatfield and the personal attacks on himself in 1954 as "precedents in Oregon in which spokesmen of both major political parties have crossed the line to personal abuse in an attempt to win elections." Neuberger was now riding Morse's abusive behavior for all it was worth politically. It was more than Morse could stand. When an enterprising pair of newsmen stopped by his office in the Senate Office Building shortly thereafter, Morse gave them an earful of what he thought of Neuberger—indeed, what he had called Neuberger in the hot letters they had exchanged a few months before. One of these newsmen, Sam Shaffer, of *Newsweek*, pursued this good lead to Neuberger's office. Applying the lever of what he had learned from Morse, Shaffer pried loose the entire file of Morse-Neuberger letters from a Neuberger aide who made the spot decision, without calling his ailing boss in Oregon. If a story was going to be published about name-calling between the Oregon senators, the reporter had better see the whole context, Neuberger's assistant, Lloyd Tupling, decided. Shaffer's exclusive story was a mild sensation in Washington and in Oregon. When it appeared, Morse sent a press release to the Senate press gallery which said:

When the break between Senator Neuberger and me developed over a period of weeks in the last session of Congress, I tried on several occasions, including one breakfast meeting with my Democratic colleagues in the Oregon delegation, to work out a basis for reconciliation. My attempts failed. In such situations there sometimes comes a point at which it is best to simply agree to disagree and bring an end to personal relationships. Senator Neuberger and I reached that point. At that time I was not aware that my colleague, Dick Neuberger, was seriously ill. In fact not until I reached Pendleton, Oregon, on August 31, 1958, did I learn for the first time that he was suffering from a malignancy. It is my judgment that his illness explains psychologically even more than he may know his conduct toward me.

Everything, even a colleague's cancer, became grist for Wayne Morse's grinding mill of personal rationalization and self-righteousness. His words and deeds mocked the Legend of Wayne Morse as the man whose only master is high principle. He was now driven by the whip of quite another master. Why had this brilliant man, this capable political figure, this man who espouses a high code of ethics—why had he made so many grievous errors that did violence to his reputation in all these areas?

It is not that Wayne Morse doesn't know better. Indeed, at a Senate Prayer Breakfast during this period of his feud with Neuberger, Wayne Morse led the devotions. His text: Christ's great commandment, Love Thine Enemies. When Morse had completed a faithful and eloquent testimonial to the virtue of Christ's teaching, the irrepressible Senator Alexander Wiley of Wisconsin piped up, "That's swell. That means you're going to lay off Neuberger!" There is some difference among senators present as to whether Morse held his tongue or growled a rejoinder to Wiley, but it is clear he made no commitment to love his enemy, Neuberger. When one senator asked him to make such an effort, Morse is said to have replied, "I'm not going to commit political suicide."

But in these events and subsequent actions against Neuberger, many political observers wondered whether Morse weren't slashing his own wrists. In April 1959, at an Oregon Farmers' Union meeting, Morse called Neuberger a "rubber stamp" for the Eisenhower administration. Still burning over the postal-rate debate they had had, Morse said Neuberger "is discriminating against every farmer in America by his proposal to raise the rates on letters." When Neuberger took exception to this criticism, Morse took the final step. He pledged to campaign against Neuberger's re-election the following year by telling the voters about his "sorry record." Neuberger expressed "regret" that Morse thought so poorly of him and his record— but Neuberger, in fact, was delighted with the prospect of being opposed by Morse. He knew that his own political stock had taken a sharp rise after he incurred Morse's wrath. Later Neuberger told a friend he had had a nightmare one night that had awakened him in a cold sweat. In the midst of his re-election campaign, dreamed Neuberger, Morse had suddenly embraced him and told the people how much he liked Dick Neuberger. That, explained Neuberger, was the most frightful thing he could imagine happening to him in 1960.

If Morse kept firing away at him, he was confident he would win in a landslide by picking up Republican sympathy votes from Morse haters, as well as the normal Democratic vote he might expect.

"The Other Fellow May Be Right"

This showdown was never to take place. At his home in Portland, where he had gone to recuperate from a series of seemingly minor maladies, Senator Neuberger died of a cerebral hemorrhage on March 9, 1960. To those who had grown to love and admire him, who had watched him change and grow in his short Senate career, who had hoped and prayed for his complete recovery from cancer, who had believed as he had that this battle had been won, death by a sudden stroke came as a cruel climax.

It was a solemn Senate which convened at noon that day to note with eloquent words the passing of one of its young favorites. All eyes were on one senator, waiting to hear what Wayne Morse would say. Neuberger plainly had gained wide sympathy within the Senate during his simultaneous bouts with cancer and Morse. Now that the battle was done, what would the survivor say in eulogy?

Before he went to the Senate chamber, Morse telephoned Neuberger's office and asked to see the late senator's aides. He told them he planned to make the customary formal announcement to the Senate of his colleague's death and follow with a eulogy based upon Neuberger's life story. He asked for and was given background material. Flanked by these aides, Wayne Morse marched to the Senate chamber.

Sitting in the press gallery above, I wondered but one thing as the chaplain opened with a prayer of tribute and we waited for the senatorial eulogies to commence. Now that the young man who had gravely challenged his supremacy was still, now that the threat was gone, would Wayne Morse now do what he could not earlier do? Would he love his enemy? Would he this day, in this place, humble himself in sorrow?

Rising quietly at his desk, the senior Senator from Oregon was recognized by Vice-president Nixon.

Mr. President, it is with sad and heavy heart that I announce to the Senate this morning that last night my colleague, Richard L. Neuberger, passed to the Great Beyond. On the basis of such information

as we have up to this hour, the immediate cause of his death appeared
to be a massive cerebral hemorrhage.

In the words of the great poet, John Freeman, "Last night a sword-
light in the sky flashed a swift terror on the dark."

Mr. President, Dick Neuberger wrote a great chapter in Oregon's
political history. He loved young people, particularly students. His
political record will for generations to come inspire young people who
study it. Oregon and the Nation have lost a courageous leader, one
whose voice and pen will be sorely missed in this time of national and
international crisis.

The senator then extended condolences to the family and gave the
Senate a biographic sketch of Neuberger's writing and political
career. He went on:

Mr. President, among the great things for which Dick Neuberger
stood, I suppose there is none that he would more appreciate having
mentioned this morning than his great record in the field of natural
resources. Dick Neuberger was a conservationist through and through.

But Dick Neuberger was dedicated to the cause of enlightened conservation. He truly believed that our generation has a solemn responsibility to see to it that we leave to future generations of American boys
and girls a heritage of natural resources untrammeled by waste and
selfish interest in our time.

Morse then read a list of the legislative accomplishments of which
Neuberger felt proud. He paid tribute to him for writing in the
last newsletter before his death an appeal for an end to racial
discrimination. Morse then cited a recent article Neuberger had
written for the *Reader's Digest* entitled: "The Best Advice I Ever
Had." Morse read the key section of the article to the Senate which
related that a Canadian Mountie had once told Neuberger that he
retained the affection of people by following this rule: "No matter
how decisive things seemed to be on my side, I always kept in mind
one thought: the other fellow may be right." Morse continued:

Then Dick wrote: "Perhaps because of the impressive dignity of the
man, his advice has lingered in my memory and guided me. It has
given me second thoughts in situations where once I felt all too sure of
myself."

Mr. President, it is due to this fallen leader to say that he put into practice, as a mode of conduct, this bit of advice, which he attributed to this Canadian Mountie, who told him on that day: "Always keep in mind one thought; the other fellow may be right."

What did Wayne Morse think of this philosophical advice? He didn't say. He went on to tell of his colleague's courage in fighting cancer, that here was "a man who was not afraid to die," who "knew the probabilities were great that he would never return to this body" when he went home to Portland a few weeks before for a rest. He concluded by quoting Edwin Markham's verse about Lincoln, he "leaves a lonesome place against the sky," and said:

We will all be lonesome because this fallen leader is no more in mortal flesh, but his record will live on as his monument.

These generous remarks belied much of what Wayne Morse had said in angered combat through the long months of feuding with Neuberger. But in his formal eulogy there came forth no words of sorrow for past misunderstandings, no apologies for past ugliness, no concession that the other fellow might have been right. Wayne Morse let pass the first, best moment in which to repent and thereby to soften hearts which had hardened against him.

The mood of Wayne Morse on this melancholy day was perhaps best typified by his remark to me later in the day. "How did you like that for an unhypocritical speech?" he asked rhetorically, exuding the satisfaction that characteristically envelops him when he has delivered a tough speech. He was proud of his day's performance.

On the Air Force jet which flew to Portland with a delegation of dignitaries to attend Neuberger's funeral, Wayne Morse was a lonely man. As other senators fraternally forgathered for bridge and conversation, the surviving Senator from Oregon was left alone in an isolated seat. He passed the time reading *Advise and Consent*. In reflecting upon his thirty-year association with Neuberger from the campus to the Senate to the grave, this senator knew that truth is far stranger than the fiction he held in his hand. Ironically, he later ventured the critical opinion that *Advise and Consent* was not fair because senators aren't as vicious as Allen Drury's novel portrays them. (Neuberger thought Drury's Senator Van Ackerman was patterned on Morse.)

In the Jewish temple where the service was held, a succession of prominent men who had been Neuberger's friends arose to speak a last farewell. By prearrangement with the senator's widow, those who followed the rabbi were Governor Hatfield, Senator Lyndon B. Johnson, Palmer Hoyt, former Governor Holmes, Supreme Court Justice William O. Douglas, Senator Paul Douglas, Senator Ernest Gruening, and Dr. Paul Steiner, Portland Unitarian minister. The man who had had more to do with Dick Neuberger than all of these was passed over. Also the man the Neuberger's most admired in politics was unable to be there to pay tribute, but Mrs. Neuberger attached a pin to the inside of her husband's coat lapel that paid its mute tribute. Dick Neuberger went to his grave wearing an Adlai Stevenson campaign button.

Maurine

Neuberger's death, at a critical political hour in Oregon, came just two days before the deadline for candidates to file the necessary papers at the state capital. Neuberger, although weak and ailing, had wanted badly to seek re-election and to win overwhelmingly. On the Monday of his last week, he had lunch with a Portland attorney, Jack Beatty, who was to have managed his campaign. Beatty was so struck by Neuberger's appearance of poor health that he decided the senator ought not to run, although he did not voice this opinion. He subsequently began preparing a statement for Neuberger to issue, withdrawing as a candidate. Tuesday the senator was stricken before the statement could be made public. Early Wednesday morning he died without regaining consciousness. With no time for the customary amenities, all of Oregon's would-be United States Senators and their friends were thrown into a hectic thirty-six hours of orbiting before the Friday filing deadline.

National Committeeman Jebby Davidson, maneuvering adroitly, led the procession to the Neuberger home to persuade the senator's widow, Maurine, to become a candidate for that high office. Governor Hatfield indirectly got word to Mrs. Neuberger that he would be pleased to appoint her to serve out the last few months of her husband's term—but only if she did not become a candidate for a new six-year term. Congresswoman Edith Green, acting on a faulty piece of political intelligence, flew to Portland in the confident belief that Mrs. Neuberger did not wish to run but wanted the appointment. Congressman Porter also flew to Portland with a hope and a prayer, but quickly joined Davidson in persuading Mrs. Neuberger to run. Wayne Morse's political aide, Charles Brooks, indirectly advised Mrs. Green that Morse would support her if she ran. But by the time she arrived upon the scene, Mrs. Green discovered Mrs. Neuberger's candidacy was ready to be announced. She knew what every other Oregon politician knew—that no one could possibly challenge the widow Neuberger in a primary with any expectation of success.

Morse did not linger in Oregon after the Thursday funeral service, nor did he personally engage in the backstage maneuvering. Davidson approached him at the Portland airport before Morse returned to Washington and asked what he thought of the developments which resulted in Mrs. Neuberger's decision to run. The man who had not been consulted said coldly, "Jebby, I couldn't disapprove more of what has happened."

In her successful campaign over Republican Elmo Smith, Senator Maurine Neuberger received Morse's blessing in several campaign speeches which he delivered in Oregon. But it was not the usual campaign stumping tour, for Morse in the fall of 1960 was engaged at the United Nations as a member of the United States delegation to the General Assembly. Upon her election, Morse wrote Mrs. Neuberger a letter of congratulations; and upon her arrival in Washington she asked him to escort her down the center aisle for the swearing-in ceremony. In so doing, she was following custom. Had she shunned Morse and asked a senator from another state, she would have been following the independence of Ohio's freshman Senator Stephen Young, who refused to have his senior colleague from Ohio, Frank Lausche, escort him down the aisle in 1959. Mrs. Neuberger, however, had no wish to renew the hostilities with Morse which had engaged her husband before his death. As the new Senator Neuberger and the old Senator Morse came down the center aisle, the Senate rose to a man to salute her arrival. The Morse-Neuberger feud was over. A wary truce was now in force.

The prospect for lasting peace between these two Oregon senators is as uncertain as Wayne Morse's next move. On the dark side is the irrefutable fact that Morse has at one time or another been furious with each and every one of his Oregon Democratic congressional colleagues for acts he regarded as disloyal to him. Only a brave or foolhardy forecaster would confidently predict Mrs. Neuberger would escape similar difficulty. On the bright side is the fact that Maurine

Neuberger is unlike her late husband in a way that may serve her well.

In one of the last long conversations I had with Dick Neuberger a few months before his death at the close of the 1959 session of Congress, he fell to philosophizing about his wife. For years Neuberger had told the world about his legislative partner as though she were the better half—a masterful public-relations effort which had its culmination in her easy victory by the highest number of votes ever cast for an Oregon Senator. But this quiet day in his office, Dick Neuberger was not trying to promote a favorable story. "You know, I did something today I thought I'd never do," he offered. "I told Maurine to go downtown and buy herself a mink coat." He recalled an early political meeting at which he was scheduled to speak. When his wife put on her sable, Neuberger blanched at the thought of her wearing so luxurious a garment to a rural gathering. He asked her to change. She balked and said she would wear her sable or he could go alone. Neuberger relented but held his breath. Instead of icy stares that cost him votes, Neuberger concluded that his wife did him proud at that meeting.

"My wife is wonderful," he mused admiringly. "She has no fears. She has no sense of danger, either physical or political. I've got so many fears I'm neurotic, but Maurine isn't afraid of anything." In admitting a personal weakness to emphasize a strength of his partner, Neuberger was probably exaggerating, as often he did, but nevertheless offering a clue to his ambivalent conduct. Neuberger wanted to be liked by everyone—other senators, page boys, newspapermen, waiters, elevator operators. He went out of his way to seek their friendship and good will. When Oregon daffodil growers periodically sent huge batches of their flowers to Oregon's congressional delegation, Dick Neuberger climbed into his car and delivered little bunches around Washington and left them on the doorsteps of friends. Those deliberately excluded from this friendly behavior were those he thought posed a threat to him, real or fancied. Every politician has some fear of his next opponent, but Neuberger conjured up disproportionate fears and acted accordingly to neutralize or to diminish the striking power of the object of these fears.

Everyman's Burden—Self-centeredness

Morse, for his part, has a trail littered with broken friendships. Those who have differed with him and survived as friends are a rare species. One of these is Owen Scott, editor of the influential weekly magazine, *U. S. News and World Report*, a fraternity brother from Wisconsin college days. Friends of both men tell a story of the conservative Scott and the liberal Morse locking horns on a contemporary issue some years ago. In those days Morse kept his livestock on Scott's Maryland farm. But the more he thought about the argument, the less he could abide the idea of his stock remaining one day longer on Scott's farm. Into the country that night rushed Morse to rescue his menagerie. Climbing trees to fetch chickens, Wayne Morse did not let the sun rise before he had transferred his animals to the farm of a former employee, Helen Keifer. The two men were later reconciled through the good offices of their wives, who are intimate friends.

Perhaps a senator deserves an extra measure of compassion. He is subject to enormous daily pressures and frustrations. He is often caught between demanding, and usually powerful, constituents. Circumstances routinely defy the actions which are demanded. He nurses along a pet proposal and, more often than not, is helpless to avert its ambush by conflicting forces. These daily experiences, and more, he is expected to take with unruffled dignity. Small wonder that so much steam of indignation is expended in the Senate chamber for every pound of pressure that actually moves the great wheels of government.

Although Senator Morse avails himself of this safety valve, he frequently has plenty of steam left over. When the steam level is below the critical mark, Wayne Morse is good-natured. He is smiling, ribbing others, even poking a little harmless fun at himself, and always prepared to tell an adventure yarn from his stormy past. The most noticeable lines on his face are smile wrinkles, not the deep, downward furrows of a perpetual sourpuss.

But when the pressures mount, when impatience and anger push the steam level past the critical mark, when the inner tiger begins to roar, Wayne Morse snaps and snarls at those who cross his path, and at the poor working girls who scurry to answer his insistent buzzer. Then the trouble begins.

When a capable secretary announced she was quitting after a rhubarb with the Senator, he instructed another secretary to try to patch things up for him. He indicated he was ashamed of himself, according to this account, but he couldn't bring himself to apologize to his employee or admit his error. Wayne Morse apparently suffers some remorse in the disruption of personal relations, but he shows little talent for making amends. After he had once chastised another secretary in a temperamental outburst and ordered her out of his office, he is said to have blurted out to an associate, "I don't want to be hateful," and bolted into his washroom. The witness to this scene says it was a rare moment of agonizing for Wayne Morse.

This trait which faults so much strength has caused Morse no end of personal and political hardship. In 1958, shortly before Morse made his charge against Hatfield, he was driving from his Eugene home to the local fairgrounds to look at some of his horses. At the wheel was an old friend, Paul Washke, a physical-education professor at the university, and in the rear sat D. F. Pickert, who had worked for Morse since the thirties as a part-time handyman around his small estate. As they drove along, Washke turned to Pickert and remarked that Morse had just made a blistering speech at Oregon City criticizing "your old pal." Pickert asked whom he meant. Washke said, "Eisenhower." Pickert says, "I told him Ike had forgotten more about war than the ordinary man will ever know." Morse's reaction was violent. Says Pickert, "I never saw a man go so nuts in my life. Wayne got very abusive. I tried to calm him down. He said, 'You can just get the hell off my ranch.' I'd been working for him so long it hurt, it really hurt bad. I asked him, 'What's wrong with you?' 'You didn't vote for me at election time.' I says, 'No, I'm a Republican and I didn't vote for you or Doug McKay, either one. I plead neutral.' He says, 'You're either for me or against me, and you're against me.'"

Pickert says they had never before had an argument, that Morse entrusted him with blank checks for buying stock and machinery and paying bills. He had lived in the house itself for about a year before this incident. In 1956 Morse asked him if he had voted. Pickert replied that he had. Morse didn't press him to say how he had voted. As a lifelong Republican, Pickert had campaigned for Morse among the sawmill hands in Morse's two Republican campaigns. After Morse became a Democrat, Pickert continued to campaign for Republicans. When someone pasted a Morse bumper

strip on his car in 1956, he tore it off. When a photographer from
the Eugene *Register-Guard* once took pictures of Pickert and Morse
working on his estate, Pickert later asked the newspaper not to
publish his picture "with a damn Democrat."

In the year before his dismissal, Pickert had been privy to a few
political discussions in the Morse household upon the senator's
periodic visits home. "They would talk about different men, different politics, but never did I say a word about it to anyone. If
I'd wanted to spill a few things, I could really turn loose." Pickert
thinks he was fired because local Democrats urged Morse to hire a
Democrat in his place.

News of the firing leaked out several months later and provoked
a spate of head shaking and chastising editorials. Morse replied:

> My employe was not discharged because he was a Republican. Nei-
> ther was he discharged because he was a supporter of President Eisen-
> hower. He was discharged because I discovered that he was not loyal
> to the position of trust which he occupied in my employment.
>
> This part time employe lived rent free in my home and was really a
> member of the family circle. . . . In that relationship, he was present
> at many discussions within my home, both political and otherwise, that
> involved matters of confidence, and privileged information. When I
> discovered that he was not loyal to my friendship, and confidence, I
> released him. . . . I am very sad about that fact that it became neces-
> sary to terminate this employe's services, but the facts left open to me
> no other course of action.

A political firing? Morse tried to escape this conclusion by publicly
accusing his long-time employee of disloyalty.

In the Hatfield and Pickert episodes Wayne Morse demonstrated
his willingness to sacrifice the feelings and attack the reputation of
a fellow human being when it seemed to him a necessary means to
a desired political end. Those who have long known him agree on
one observation: self-centeredness, Everyman's burden, burdens
Everyman's senator to an extraordinary degree.

Wayne Morse loves humanity in the mass and at a long arm's
length. But often when humanity has taken the form of a single
person with individual aspirations and values which interfered with
the momentary interests of Wayne Morse, humanity has been in for
a very difficult time of it. Senator Douglas one day accused Morse,
apparently in jest, of being more interested in "the plight of wild

geese than the plight of humans." This may not be an altogether unjust indictment.

One Sunday in 1959 during a visit to Morse's Maryland farm, I found the senator hobbling about with a cane due to a slight accident. The senator's youngest sister, Caryl, to whom he is devoted, was there with her family from Pittsburgh for the weekend. As the hour for their planned departure neared, Morse conceived it of monumental importance that everyone pitch in to help finish a task. All members of the family dutifully went to work. Even to the outsider it was plain that only the senator failed to perceive the anxiety everyone else showed about the delayed departure of Caryl's family for the long trip home. Morse was completely absorbed in the task at hand—tacking up each and every one of the red, blue, and yellow ribbons his livestock had won at county fairs that summer.

Later, when the family had gone at last, we stood against an auto fender chatting in the twilight. A lonely chicken chanced to cross in front of us. Morse's eyes were on it like a hawk. "That chicken is sick," he observed. "I think she is looking for water." Into the house he hobbled for a pan of water; placing it on the ground, the lame but faithful protector of his flock then chased that chicken all over the yard until he had caught her. His diagnosis had been correct. The chicken was thirsty. His perception, he remarked, had probably saved the bird's life.

Wayne Morse, the farm boy, had early learned to be sensitive to the needs of his chickens and ponies. He had later learned to stick up for the humanitarian liberalism of Bob La Follette. But somehow he had neglected to learn to live at peace with other individual humans when their interests did not precisely coincide with his. More than that, Wayne Morse had climbed the hill of success by the rocky path of contention rather than the quieter road of reconciliation. In his first days in the Senate, Morse jousted with all of the esteemed leaders. When one day he was particularly rough on Alben Barkley, the Democratic leader, a Republican colleague, Senator Saltonstall, approached Morse in the cloakroom and suggested he go back and tone that down a bit. "Leverett," said Wayne Morse to the gentleman from Massachusetts, "I've got where I am in this world by being against people."

Yet Morse has performed deeds of kindness for individuals. A man who has known him for years and considers him completely self-centered says, also, that Morse will "do anything for you if you ask him." He is no modern Scrooge, denouncing all civility as so much humbug. In his University of Oregon days, he once helped rescue financially an Oregon editor who he believed had been let out by his newspaper because he was "too liberal." Rallying friends to place some funds in an account to tide the man and his family over until he could get another job, Morse was a good Samaritan when it counted for this family.

Within this man of many gifts there are, obviously, conflicting instincts. With his appealing arguments in behalf of civil rights he has mixed an unappealing assortment of uncivil wrongs. For all his admirable Biblical preachings, he has demonstrated little love for his enemies. Worse, he has struck with inhumane ferocity against individual humans.

Always there has been the tiger's instinct for survival. For to Wayne Morse, politics is a dense jungle. His adversaries, real and fancied, are numerous; and in fiercely battling them, his combat code is the survival of the fittest. He once wrote a friend about his feud with Ickes and explained, "I let the law of self-preservation control my answer to him."

In these, the worst days of Wayne Morse's political career, there was a powerful driving force which no one then clearly recognized. Soon it was to emerge and illuminate one of the final and fundamental mysteries of Wayne Morse.

19. "I HAVE NO ILLUSIONS"

"A Machiavellian Plot" . . . *"Phony Liberals"* . . . *The Children of God* . . . *The Hypothesis*

ENCOUNTERING Wayne Morse one day in a Capitol corridor, a colleague stopped to say he had heard talk about Morse as a vice-presidential possibility for the Republican party that year, 1948. To this suggestion of national advancement, the Senator from Oregon replied, "They're just trying to kid me. I know my place in politics. I am a political irritant."

In this self-appraisal, Wayne Morse that day was realistic about the role a maverick must be content to play in American politics. He can be an effective irritant who forces action which the counsels of caution and prudence would avoid. He can be the watchdog who barks at dubious legislation, arousing the public in order to send such bills to a deserved grave. These important tasks, and others, he can and must forthrightly undertake to fulfill his role. But with these accomplishments, the political irritant must be content. It is not for him to lead a nation from either its highest or next highest office. These are roles for other men, trained in other skills, accustomed to other ways.

Nevertheless, those who have regarded Wayne Morse as a brilliant, persuasive, courageous, fighting senator have periodically suggested that he would make an admirable candidate for President or Vice-president. For many years he had a stock answer to this suggestion: "I have no illusions about my role in American politics."

It would surely have been an illusion for Morse to believe that he, the bold maverick who challenged all comers with daring defiance of party regularity, might one day hope for the support of the many key politicians and sectional interests upon which the candidacy for the highest office is quite dependent. The man who can put together the right combination of delegates going into a party con-

vention is, least of all, a political irritant within his own party, as
Wayne Morse had long been. If Morse hoped to be Eisenhower's
running mate in 1952, surely it was a monumental illusion to
think that this great honor might pass to him after his many fights
with the party leaders.

Whatever his secret hopes of 1952 might have been, Wayne Morse
eight years later announced that he was a candidate for President
of the United States. He revealed, openly for the first time, that he
yearned to be more than a political irritant. Or did he? Isn't it
more likely that he jumped into the scramble for the Democratic
presidential nomination in 1960 just for the thrill of political combat? Many seasoned Washington observers believed this was the case.
Unable to take Morse's candidacy seriously, they could not believe
that Wayne Morse took his own candidacy seriously.

This may have been the most mismanaged, ill-conceived, short-
lived, and chuckled-at presidential bid of recent memory. But
those who have known Wayne Morse for many years have no doubt
about one thing: Wayne Morse wanted to be President with no
less intensity than others who have contended and fallen short of the
pinnacle.

The parallel between Dean Morse's strange campaign for the presidency of the University of Oregon and Senator Morse's quest for
the Democratic presidential nomination in 1960 is unmistakably
clear.

Wayne Morse says he became a candidate for President when, looking around at his fellow senators—Kennedy, Humphrey, Symington,
Johnson—who were contenders, he said to himself, "Why not?"
It seems apparent, however, that Morse nurtured the idea of
reaching the White House for years before he openly declared
himself. His triumph over McKay in 1956 made him a Democratic
party hero in his own right. After the 1958 elections, in which he
crisscrossed the country making campaign speeches for Democratic
senatorial candidates, he was heralded again for his mighty oratorical
endeavors which helped elect such newcomers as Young of Ohio,
McGee of Wyoming, and Engle of California. In 1959, when he
brought Clare Boothe Luce to book, the cheers for Wayne Morse
from Democratic partisans were thunderous. Only a detached realist
would keep his head and know, as Vandenberg used to say, "All this
shall pass." Wayne Morse, driven by ambition, could be neither detached nor realistic. And, once again, he could not keep his head.

"A *Machiavellian Plot*"

In the feud with Neuberger, Morse's fighting instincts drove him into combat, but what apparently caused him to lose his head and slash out wildly was the damage Neuberger inflicted on his presidential hopes. Neuberger had written an article booming Morse for President. Interestingly, it appeared in the *Progressive*, the liberal magazine published at Madison and founded in 1909 by Fighting Bob La Follette to further the reform doctrines of his Progressive movement. In view of subsequent events, this April 1957 article makes fascinating reading.

How would Neuberger make the case for a maverick as a presidential prospect? He began with the sort of imagery which typified his colorful writing:

> In America today the political anchor is up and the moorings are loose. No hawsers fasten the frigate of politics to ancient and accustomed wharves. Charted waters have been left behind. The compass no longer responds predictably to orthodox magnetisms. Even the electoral stars in their courses now defy time-honored rules of political astronomy.

This led into a rundown of curious political events, such as President Eisenhower's winning re-election without carrying either the House or Senate for his party; traditionally Democratic southern states backing the G.O.P. presidential candidate; of "traditionally Republican states like Iowa, Oregon, and Kansas" electing Democratic governors. "Amidst such deep and catacylsmic political changes," wrote Neuberger, it was time to recall Lincoln's favorite couplet from *The Present Crisis*, by Lowell:

> *New occasions teach new duties,*
> *Times make ancient good uncouth . . .*

The new duty of the Democratic party, as Richard L. Neuberger saw it, was to nominate its most famous newcomer and long-time maverick, Wayne Morse; the ancient good which was now uncouth was the old notion that a party regular must be chosen. He wrote:

In my opinion, the times and the challenge confronting the Democratic Party demand just the type of outspoken, forthright and militant program Wayne Morse would bring to the party's nomination. The Negro vote, the labor vote, and the liberal vote all have been shaken loose from their normal Democratic allegiance—particularly in the great metropolitan areas where the fate of key states is determined. Wayne Morse would return these nomads to the Democratic corral.

Neuberger reported that since making a speech at San Francisco in November 1956, advancing Morse as a contender, "the response has been enthusiastic, spontaneous and continuous." He allowed that others might contend for the prize, notably Senators Humphrey, Clark, Kefauver, and Douglas. "And Senator John F. Kennedy of Massachusetts," suggested Neuberger, "might make an appealing and attractive running mate for Wayne Morse or any of these other Democratic leaders of liberalism."

Neuberger contended that Morse's "unique advantages and qualifications . . . fall into no fewer than ten categories:

1. "Wayne Morse has been prominent in both parties." Americans are not hidebound in party affiliations, he said. Witness the popularity of Willkie, La Follette, Norris, Borah, McNary, and Earl Warren, who "have worn party robes only loosely." None, however, became President. Lincoln, who started in politics as a Whig, was his only example of presidential success.

2. "Wayne Morse has been consistently in favor of a strong civil rights program. Anybody in doubt that such a position is indispensable to Democratic success in 1960 must be incapable of understanding arithmetic. . . . In the Harlem area of New York, President Eisenhower registered gains averaging 12.5 per cent. Principally as a result of this, the Democratic margin in the nation's largest city dropped from 55 per cent to 51 per cent—far too narrow to swing strategic New York State.

3. "Wayne Morse has fought for labor benefits and against labor racketeering.

4. "Wayne Morse was one of the first members of Congress to assail the Eisenhower proposal for 'partnership' with the private utilities.

5. "Wayne Morse has political courage." He cited his bolt of the G.O.P.

6. "Wayne Morse has fought militantly for fundamental free-

doms." Neuberger cited his opposition to McCarthy and wire-tapping legislation.

7. "Morse has been more critical of President Eisenhower than has any other Senator. . . . If Eisenhower's popularity continues at the phenomenal rate of 1956, the Democrats may not be able to win anyway in 1960. . . . But if Eisenhower's inadequacies and pro-crastinations become evident to the average voter, what Democrat is in a more strategic position than Wayne Morse to say, 'I told you so?'

8. "Morse is one of the most powerful and tireless orators of all time.

9. "Wayne Morse has the requisite age and physical condition. Because he was born with the century, Morse will be exactly sixty at the time of the next Presidential election. . . . Morse possesses a cast-iron constitution. Although I am twelve years his junior, I find it exhausting to maintain his pace during a campaign. Morse does not drink or smoke (habits I share with him), and he carefully avoids rich foods in order to keep his weight at fighting trim." Neuberger was using literary or political license here. Morse avoids eating chocolate cake and brownies only when he can't get his hands on these favorite rich foods. He keeps in trim by eating steaks, straw-berries, and bologna sandwiches. Neuberger skillfully interjected the idea that he shared Morse's puritanical habits. This virtue, he was convinced, was good for votes in church groups. (Apparently this caused Neuberger to claim to be a teetotaler when, in fact, he enjoyed the fermented brew of his German forebears.) Morse's recreation, Neuberger went on, is his Maryland farm which "might be more acceptable in rural areas than golf or quail shooting."

10. "Wayne Morse has a profound religious and spiritual interest." He cited the churchgoing regularity of the Morse family, adding, "A strong sense of the power of prayer and of the influence of the Supreme Being gleams through an impressive speech which Morse delivered against capital punishment last year in the Senate at the time that the death sentence was being proposed in connection with dope-peddling crimes."

Finally, Dick Neuberger offered his personal endorsement. "People ask if he is not too harsh and strident and arrogant—an opinion perhaps inspired by his fiery, pounding political speeches. My own experience as Morse's junior Senate colleague is the best refutation of such an impression. Politics is a profession notorious for its jealousies. It rivals the theater in this respect. Yet I have never felt the slightest envy because of Senator Morse's greater fame and prestige. He has not tried to impress upon me his longer experience and service. We have worked together as harmoniously as two Senators could."

When this 1957 article came out, Morse grinned like a pussycat, but flicked his tail nervously about its effect. Neuberger hadn't consulted him in advance and he wasn't sure whether he should howl or purr. Inasmuch as the article scratched his back quite thoroughly, the tiger cat purred.

This grand stack of trumps held by Wayne Morse for President collapsed like a house of cards in Neuberger's mind once the harmony in their relationship vanished. When he admitted to me that if he had it to do over again he wouldn't have written this article, he pointed to Morse's personal shortcomings as the feet of clay he had not previously detected.

Wayne Morse was furious. "A Machiavellian plot," he snarled. Not only did Morse regard Neuberger's change of heart as the most severe act of personal disloyalty, but he concluded that the whole sequence had been craftily plotted to set him up as a presidential contender much too early so that he was certain to be toppled before convention time three years hence. The proof, for Morse, was that Neuberger was the first to repudiate his own idea that Wayne Morse should be the Democratic candidate. Neuberger aides were convinced that this was not in Neuberger's mind, that he saw it simply as a good topic for a provocative magazine article that would flatter his colleague, if nothing more.

The effect of the ensuing feud was damaging, indeed, to Wayne Morse. His abusive condemnation of his young colleague grew out of his frustrating dilemma. Without solid support from his own state, how could he possibly embark upon a presidential campaign? It was this frustration which probably drove Morse to announce in late 1959 that he would campaign against Neuberger and his "sorry record" in the spring primary of 1960. Everyone but Morse seemed to recognize by then that Dick Neuberger, thanks in part to his twin battles with Morse and cancer, was virtually unbeatable. But no one had quite lost his head as completely as Wayne Morse.

Several Oregon Democrats had proposed earlier that Morse be Oregon's favorite-son candidate—but purely as a convention-holding operation until the trend could be sensed, and perhaps a bargain struck with a promising contender who needed Oregon's votes. The

Young Democrats of Oregon, in convention at Salem in April 1959, adopted a resolution favoring Morse for favorite son. Congresswoman Edith Green endorsed that move when she appeared at the convention. Morse did nothing to spike the idea when he delivered the main address.

Indeed Morse was then making speeches outlining the precise qualities the next candidate must have—"a brilliant man, dedicated to the principles of constitutional government"; a "humanitarian who places the general-welfare clause of the Constitution above tax dodges and special-privilege legislation"; and most of all, one who is not a "pussyfooter." This description was about as subtle as his letters twenty-five years earlier describing the qualities of a university president. Who but Wayne Morse could measure up?

The favorite-son idea did not catch fire. The split with Neuberger plus Morse's attack on Hatfield in late 1958 had hurt his prestige badly. Perhaps to disassociate himself from a *feeble* favorite-son drive, in July Morse filed an affidavit with Oregon's Secretary of State declaring "without qualification that I am not now and do not intend to become a candidate for the presidential or vice-presidential nomination."

Congresswoman Green took Morse at his word and shortly thereafter flew to Oregon with Senator Kennedy for a few days of campaigning which greatly impressed her. She later accepted Kennedy's request that she head his Oregon campaign. Neuberger and Congressman Charles O. Porter endorsed Adlai Stevenson, and soon most Democratic leaders in Oregon were backing one of the recognized contenders. None of them urged Wayne Morse to rescind his "I shall not run" declaration.

But a retired Oregon logger and long-time party worker, Gary Neal, believed that Morse was the man of the hour. He observed that Morse was "tickled to death" over the Young Democrats' favorite-son proposal. Also Neal held a strange conviction that all the liberal Democratic leaders were plotting to gang up on Morse, so he took it upon himself to start a petition drive to place Morse's name on the Oregon primary ballot for President. "I thought it better to have the fight in 1960, when if he lost it wouldn't put him out of office," Neal explained. In August, the month after Morse issued his "I shall not run" declaration, Neal was approached by Morse's field man, Charles Brooks, who wanted to know whether Neal had started circulating the petitions as yet. Neal informed him that they

would soon go out. Brooks made no effort to dissuade him from this
endeavor, says Neal. With three hundred dollars of his own money
Neal ordered petitions printed and mailed to party workers in all
thirty-six counties, urging endorsements of Morse for President. He
says he was helped by Jack Churchill, a Morse loyalist.

After enough signatures had been secured, Neal says he had a
telephone call and a letter from Morse in which the senator advised
him against pursuing this petition drive. "I think he wanted to make
it appear that he was being drafted," says Neal. "I don't think he
intended for me to quit." Morse made a public display of his request
to Neal to desist from this campaign. "When he called me, I figured
it was for the record so it would appear that we was [sic] forcing him
to run," the old logger says. "I told him he was going to be on the
ballot." Neal says the petition drive "went better after he called" and
made a public request that Neal cease and desist.

From among the nearly 4000 petitions mailed out, about 1000
were returned by party workers who explained that they were all for
Morse—but as a senator, not as a presidential candidate. Only two
were returned with anti-Morse sentiments attached. Neal collected
5145 signatures, not an overly impressive number, but many more
than the 1000 required by law to place a presidential candidate's
name on the ballot. This, then, was the vehicle for Morse's entry into
the race—a move which he repeatedly said was against his wishes.

"Phony Liberals"

In Congress, that summer of 1959, Wayne Morse found an issue
on which to mount his campaign. Senator Kennedy had deftly led
Congress to enact a compromise on a controversial labor-reform
bill. This was the legislative climax of the sensational McClellan
Committee investigation of corruption in the labor-management
field. When it came time to write legislation designed to guard
against abuses in the labor field, conservative business interests aggressively lobbied for basic changes in the nation's labor laws that
would further restrict union activity and power. As between the
more moderate Senate bill which Kennedy, Morse, and others
sponsored, and the more restrictive House measure known as the
Landrum-Griffin bill, Kennedy averted a complete stalemate between the two houses by developing a compromise version which was
endorsed by AFL-CIO leaders, who reluctantly decided it was the

best they could expect. As a member of the committee which worked out the labor compromise, Morse dissented vigorously. In the Senate he and Langer cast the only "nay" votes when the bill finally passed.

A few weeks later, after we had spent an afternoon at his Maryland farm, Morse suddenly ventured the opinion that Hubert Humphrey had made a serious political error in voting for Kennedy's compromise bill. A secretive smile crossed Wayne Morse's face. "Wait until you see my next newsletter," he added. In it he cut loose at all those who had voted for what he termed the "Kennedy-Landrum-Griffin bill." No sound liberal could have squared that vote with his liberal professions, contended Morse. Here was his issue.

From that day forward for many months, Wayne Morse used this shibboleth to attack other senators who were presidential prospects. They were merely "phraseological liberals" or "phony liberals" or even "gutless wonders." If his fellow Democratic candidates didn't enjoy this tough talk, the officials of the Teamsters' Union did. Given Teamster President Jimmy Hoffa's hatred for the Kennedy brothers and the Teamsters' history of support for Morse, it was natural that they would now seek to use Morse—and he them. Morse and the Teamsters co-operated to make and distribute widely a film in which the senator rebuked his party's front-running presidential contender. Following an introduction by Hoffa, Morse let fly:

> Let us not forget that the chief architect of this bill in conference, Kennedy, apparently thinks so little of the bill that he doesn't want to have his name associated with it. But it is still true, "ye shall know them by their fruits." And make no mistake about it, this bill would not have passed the conference or the Congress if the Senator from Massachusetts had supported me in my opposition to it. Political opportunism rode rough shod over the Congress of the United States in the passage of this bill. . . . But this kind of legislation that was passed is going to rise to plague not only labor and industry, but to plague the public because it's not fair labor legislation.

Even in remote Alaska, Morse's film was shown on television. Under the auspices of the most discredited labor leadership in the country, the most unlikely presidential bid of 1960 was advanced.

Morse tossed his hat into the ring formally just before Christmas, but the AP story that went out from Washington on the occasion stated in its second paragraph that the senator was "obviously not a serious presidential candidate." He was going to enter the Oregon

presidential primary just because he "likes a political scrap." The AP
was doing what almost everyone was doing, taking for granted that
Morse was not a serious contender, as he himself had so declared six
months earlier.

Even his adopted party could not—and would not—take his bid
seriously. At the Sheraton Park Hotel in Washington, the Democratic
National Committee on January 23, 1960, held a gala "presidential
campaign kick-off dinner." All eyes were fixed on seven presidential
prospects who shared the platform: John Kennedy, Lyndon Johnson,
Stuart Symington, Hubert Humphrey, Robert Meyner, "Soapy" Williams, and Pat Brown. Everyone was there that night but Adlai
Stevenson, who declined because he said he wasn't a candidate, and
Wayne Morse, who wasn't invited.

A man of less compulsive drive would that week have bowed
silently to the inevitable. Not Wayne Morse. He asserted and reas-
serted: "I am a serious candidate." But asserting it did not make it
so in the public mind. Columnist Doris Fleeson dubbed him the
"mischief maker" in the Democratic race. "He is not embarked on a
serious effort to win the presidential nomination, and he would not
get it if he did," she wrote in February. Columnist William S. White
said Morse was simply playing a "wrecker's role."

Plagued by this image, Morse plunged into three primaries, the
District of Columbia, Maryland, and Oregon—and reluctantly stayed
out of the primary in his native state of Wisconsin for lack of funds.
There was a certain theoretical logic to this strategy. Kennedy and
Humphrey were to meet in Wisconsin. Next came the District of
Columbia primary, in which Morse and Humphrey were entered.
Morse was expected by many local observers to win that one, because
he had championed many District causes, notably home rule. Next
there would be West Virginia, where Humphrey was given a good
chance against Kennedy. So if Morse beat Humphrey and then
Humphrey beat Kennedy, theoretically this would "prove" that Morse
was the strongest of the three contenders, certainly a man the party
could not ignore. Capping it would be certain victory for Morse in
the Oregon primary over any and all outside rivals. So went the
theory.

When Kennedy mopped up Wisconsin with Humphrey, it seemed
even more certain that Morse would win in the District of Columbia
over the Minnesota Senator. Morse had the backing of labor officials
and of A. L. Wheeler, local Democratic leader. But apparently

Wheeler was simply using Morse as a vehicle in his own quest for re-election. Wheeler had sought to tie up with Humphrey and had been rejected. Humphrey allied himself with a slate of liberal rebels led by attorney Joseph L. Rauh, Jr., an A.D.A. leader, who challenged Wheeler's long supremacy.

The Children of God

If religion was a big factor in the West Viriginia and Wisconsin primaries where Kennedy was running, race became a none-too-subtle issue in the District. With a population almost equally divided between whites and Negroes, Washington, D.C., had the only presidential primary in which candidates sought to exploit racial affiliations. After Morse allied himself with a labor official, J. C. Turner, who was running for re-election as national committeeman, Humphrey forces recruited Frank S. Reeves, a Negro attorney who challenged Turner. Morse quickly charged his opposition with making "appeals to racism." He was privately fearful that Washington Negroes would go down the line for the Humphrey-Reeves slate on election day if the alternative were an all-white Morse ticket. Humphrey also induced Jackie Robinson to make public appearances for him in a Negro section of the capital.

"This is a sad development in American politics," said Morse nobly. "I am convinced that it means no good either for the voters whose votes are sought on the basis of race or religion, for the candidates who seek them."

Humphrey called the "racism" charge "nonsense." So Morse tried a countermove to match Humphrey. A sample ballot mailed from Morse headquarters declared that one reason for voting for Morse was that his slate of convention delegates was "50 per cent more fully integrated than any other slate of delegates and alternates." To make sure no one missed the point, photographs of all members of Morse's slate were included.

When Morse opened his campaign headquarters in Washington, he told an applauding crowd of local admirers of both races how he happened to become a champion of home rule. Some senators had privately warned against home rule, he said, out of fear Washington would elect a Negro mayor. When he heard this, Morse assured them, it was the signal for him to pitch in with all his vigor in behalf of an elected-mayor home-rule bill.

On the Sunday before election Morse spent the day visiting Negro churches, speaking from the pulpit. In each church Morse retained the dignity he sometimes loses in hell-fire and damnation oratory in the Senate chamber. To the parishioners, who had seldom seen a white man in their service, much less a United States Senator, this was an occasion which merited attentive curiosity. Wayne Morse gave them a skillful performance. He was the senator, he reminded them, who had called local officials before his committee to account for the lack of a school-lunch program. He didn't have to tell his listeners that it was the children of their race who most desperately needed this program. He talked of his championship of civil rights and he mentioned his integrated slate of convention delegates.

Finally in each church he offered the *pièce de résistance*. It was a discussion which he said had once taken place in the Senate when he was advocating a District social welfare program. A Southern senator arose and bluntly asked whether it wasn't true that most of the beneficiaries of the program would be Negro youngsters rather than whites.

Morse told the story with a dramatic re-enactment of the debate. In each case the congregation fell into a hush. Mothers holding babies somehow quieted them. Old men nodding in their seats awakened and waited. Young people stopped wriggling in their seats. All eyes were fixed on Senator Morse in the pulpit.

"And I said to that colleague, 'The Senator is quite correct.' Then I paused. And then I replied, 'But they, too, are the children of God.'"

As the senator's words floated down to these children of God, here and there a head nodded, a woman ventured a quiet smile, an old man muttered, "Amen." They had heard it, as they had heard many words, words, words so often before. But could they believe it? Did this white man care for them as children of God—or chiefly as prospective voters two days hence?

On election day the District's voters rendered a verdict of indifference. As between Humphrey and Morse for President, they showed little enthusiasm—but if they had to make a choice, it was not to be Wayne Morse. Only 19,436 Democrats voted, and of these 6239 could not bring themselves to select either contender. Humphrey received 7831 votes and Morse 5866. Morse's "more integrated" slate of delegates nosed out an unofficial Stevenson slate, but Humphrey's slate went to the convention.

For the first time in his long political career, Wayne Morse had lost an election. Again, instead of making a graceful concluding bow, he bulled ahead into Maryland, where he was hopelessly matched against Kennedy. A landslide loss in Maryland on top of his initial defeat set Morse up for the final debacle in his home state. Early in the year Kennedy told me he had no hope of defeating Morse in the Oregon primary. All he hoped to do was run well ahead of all other nationally recognized contenders whose names, by law, were placed on the ballot unless they individually signed affidavits of no candidacy.

Morse roared into Oregon with the charge that Kennedy was "wallpapering" the state with huge amounts of campaign expenditures. Chiefly he reverted to his "phony liberal" contention, and came near to pleading with Oregon Democrats not to discredit one of their own whose prestige would mean so much in elections to come.

It was too late for either tough talk or pleas for mercy. On the crest of a string of six straight primary victories, John Kennedy breezed through Oregon with the glamorous presence of a winner, a soft word about Morse, and a glint of confidence that took hold with the voters. Advance straw polls had indicated a horse race between Morse and Kennedy. But when the votes were in, Morse was swamped by Kennedy, 146,000 to 91,000.

The result proved conclusively what a sand-castle candidacy this had been. The first wave of voter sentiment in the District tumbled in the roof, the second wave that rolled in from the residents of the Chesapeake Bay state broke down the walls, and the final wave in Oregon obliterated the foundation with humiliating finality.

How could he seriously have believed that he had a chance? Besides members of his inner circle who encouraged him to believe it, there was a handful of labor officials who were disgruntled over the Kennedy compromise on the labor-reform issue. They were at least willing to run with Morse's hounds in hope of cornering the fox from Massachusetts. Then there were the private citizens who wrote in to encourage him.

The Gallup poll for March 27, 1960, showed just how strong Morse's following was. Six per cent of all Democrats polled and 9 per cent of all Independents indicated that their presidential preferences lay among four contenders—Bowles, Meyner, Williams, and Morse, each registering about the same strength. That would mean that Wayne Morse was the presidential choice of 1.5 per cent of the

Democrats and just over 2 per cent of the Independents, a pitiful minority. But in the mind of an ambitious man, a whisper of approval can sound like a chorus, and one flatterer can sound like a multitude. Wayne Morse did, after all, become possessed by the great illusion— until the force of events in 1960 shattered it once and for all.

The Hypothesis

Suppose, for a minute, that you followed this rocky trail. Suppose you are a United States Senator, fifty-two years of age, highly intelligent, well informed after eight years on Capitol Hill, so highly regarded by newspaper correspondents and political-science professors that they rank you as the best man your party has in the Senate. Suppose, also, that you have gained a wide national reputation, are a powerful and persuasive orator, possessed with courage and great stamina. And you have a powerful, driving ambition to go to the top, to be the leader—but this among all traits you cannot admit, perhaps not even to yourself. Lincoln had it, Teddy Roosevelt had it—but it was perfectly respectable for them to have had driving ambition, for they became great Presidents. They were entitled to it, people would readily say. People might not say that of you. They might even hoot at your dreams of reaching the top. People can be merciless in belittling a public man. Better admit to no ambitions. Thank those who suggest it, but tell them you have no illusions.

Your party is heading into a great crisis at its national convention. The isolationists are led by the senator with whom you have had more outspoken disagreements than any other. If he were nominated, you could not in all honesty support him or the party. But the internationalists in your wing of the party have persuaded a most attractive leader, a general, to do battle in the convention for the presidential nomination. Even in this, you were the wisest of them all, the first in the Senate to advocate the general's candidacy. You are making one daring attack after another against Mr. Isolationist. You are already fighting the general's cause.

Is it not permissible to cherish a secret hope that your time has come, that there are those who will recognize that you would make a splendid running mate for the general? Would not a powerful speech sweep the delegates? In any event, if the general wins at the convention, the party will go forward to victory and your future leadership in some high capacity will be assured. The general wins.

It marks a historic event, you tell your friends. The party has been saved.

But then it happens. A younger, less experienced, less liberal, less *everything* sort of running mate is chosen—and in a smoke-filled room to which you were not even invited! Concerning this, you are *told*, not *asked*. Your plans for going before the delegates to make a powerful oration are killed. It was bad enough when party leaders in your own state embarrassed you by keeping you off the platform committee. This is far worse. You have been ignored completely by the general and his strategists.

In the gloomy aftermath you discover faults in the general you would rather have overlooked, but candor and honesty compel you to point them out. The platform is termite-ridden, and the men who stand upon it for your party—well, you have your fingers crossed. Then they insult you by sending minor flunkies to try to placate you. You want to hear from the general. The call never comes.

Instead the call goes to Mr. Isolationist. Again you are ignored, and he is greeted like a king. He tells the general how it is going to be from here on out. The general nods approvingly. You realize instantly that your future in this party has suddenly grown exceedingly dim.

But two can play at this. When you get through, they'll be sorry. You are close enough to the President, the leader of the other party, to tell him of your disappointment. He likes you, tells you what a raw deal you have received, says you don't belong in that party anyway. You are too young at fifty-two to be content with remaining a frustrated senator in a party that no longer appreciates you. So what do you do? You can do the orthodox thing and stay in that party and go on as before, bucking the tide, never riding it. But you don't want simply to survive. You want to rise to the top. You've got to take the gamble. You bolt your party.

But the general wins. You don't worry about it. Being the outsider suits your temperament. But then both parties gang up on you in the Senate and strip you of those good committees you had. You have never been so humiliated. Nobody sticks up for you. Everyone is against you, from the phony liberals to the reactionary press.

Things move your way in your state once again. The liberals in the other party are wooing you to join them. You find that they look like awfully sound fellows, even though they audaciously tell you you can't win without joining their party. You help them select a new senator, a former student of yours. Then you help the other party take control of the Senate, and like magic, you get the prize committee assignment—Foreign Relations—which your old party always denied you. Obviously this is a party of fairness and liberality. You join this party, and in the next election you virtually transform the politics of your state. Your old party is dead. You are surely the biggest man that ever came down the pike.

Your loyal colleague recognizes this and starts boosting you for President. If only he weren't so impatient—the election is three years away, and he should know it's bad form to crest too soon.

First there is a tough job to be done. The general in the White House has his reactionary pals to tell him what to do, but nobody sees beyond that smile. He has hypnotized the people. You decide to be the one senator who is not afraid to rough him up. You'll break the hypnotic spell. That's what this country needs—outspoken, courageous, liberal leadership. That's what the country will demand when you get finished.

So you begin. You hit hard. People are shocked. But when they get over it, they'll thank you for it as they discover how right you are.

What's this? Your own colleague is disowning your leadership! No guts. Now he's saying he was wrong—you aren't qualified to be President. That amoral coward. After all you did for him. It must be a crafty plot by your enemies. You can take care of them.

Time is now short. You are no longer fifty-two, but nearly sixty. There will be no more tomorrows in which to create better circumstances. If you are ever going to be more than just a senator all your life, you must make your move now regardless of this inconvenient feud with your colleagues. You look around you in the Senate at the other contenders. None of them has been here as long as you have, or is the genuine liberal that you are. You've recognized that for years, so now you have a duty to tell the country the facts.

There are those who think you have a chance. Maybe it is a long shot, but history is full of winning long shots that shouldn't have got past the back stretch. Whom must you contend with? There's the Senator from Texas. That convention is certainly not going to nominate a Southerner who is associated with the big oil boys. Then there's the Senator from Minnesota. He thinks he can corner the liberal vote but when you get through telling the country how he runs out on liberalism, like voting for that labor bill, the party will realize you are the only true choice of liberalism. Then there is the

Senator from Massachusetts. Another phony liberal, but he won't get the nod because they still remember Al Smith, deplorable though that sort of thing is.

There is also the titular party head from Illinois. After losing the last two elections, the party isn't going to gamble on another Bryan. He's more able than the others, of course, and you tell the world he is your choice. But you know he is safely out of the race.

Now you have to stop denying you want to be President and announce your intentions. You take the plunge. The water is the iciest you've ever tried to navigate. Everyone assumes you are just in there kicking around for the fun of it. The party won't even acknowledge you as a valid entry at the ceremonial send-off dinner. The columnists snicker or scowl at your candidacy. You'll show them. They'll wake up when the prairie fire begins to catch. When you win that first primary, then they will know you are a candidate of the people. You put all you have into it. There is no turning back. It's now or never.

As the votes come in, you can't believe it. In every primary you are badly defeated. Even in your home state. They were all against you, that's why . . . You always said if the vote were light . . . The money that was poured into your opponents' campaigns . . .

You don't go to your party's national convention. You go out to the farm. It's the first time you've missed a convention. There's nothing there for you. It was this year or never.

Now you know. It's never.

Part Four

NEW FRONTIERS

20. UP FROM THE SLOUGH OF DESPOND

The Tragedy of Hubris . . . "Keep Him Busy" . . . South of the Border . . . The UN

THE election of President John Kennedy has confronted Wayne Morse with his own new frontier. For the first time since he came to Washington nearly two decades ago, Morse is serving under a President of his own party. For the first time in his political career he is shorn of the advantage of being the critical outsider, a member of the opposition who carries no burden greater than the responsibility that his constituency imposes upon him.

For the first time in his career Wayne Morse is confronted with the responsibility for being a constructive insider—a member of the President's party, carrying the burden of implementing a controversial legislative program as advanced by that President.

Is Senator Morse willing or capable of making that transition? Will he have cordial relations with Kennedy as he had with Truman and Roosevelt? Or will he defy this new President as he did Eisenhower? Is he trapped by his own Legend of maverick independence, precluded from selfless and co-operative endeavors?

Wayne Morse's performance on his new frontier will likely be decisive in determining the quality and the lasting value of his public service, not to say whether he will have a future beyond 1962, when he must once more seek the favor of Oregon voters. There are those who believe that Wayne Morse, the old maverick, the tireless campaigner, the persuasive orator, is unbeatable at the polls. That is a risky prophecy.

The question, however, is not whether Senator Morse can survive. Mere survival is too small a goal for so gifted a public man. The larger question, befitting his virtues but threatened by his faults, is whether he can serve? Whether he can creatively meet his new and greater responsibilities.

The Tragedy of Hubris

As a champion of conservation of natural resources, he has served his region and the nation in helping to block dubious policies and proposals of the past Administration. But his recent misadventures, fired by raging ambition, have burned off magnificent forests of standing good will. And, as in reforestation, the reseeding process is painfully slow. But it is imperative in the preparation for tomorrow's growth.

The condition of Wayne Morse's public estate at the time of his presidential debacle was suggested by the views of two men who have known him all of his public career. William M. Tugman, a few months before his death in May 1961, said: "Wayne Morse, perhaps more than any man I have ever known, is a figure out of Greek tragedy—a hero destroyed by a fatal fault of character, his own insatiable ambition."

Eric Allen, whose liberal Medford *Mail Tribune* was one of the last to join the chorus of critics, in 1960 offered a similar view editorially:

> Wayne Lyman Morse—brilliant, incisive, extremely able—has virtually destroyed himself as an effective force for liberal thought in the United States Senate, and as an effective representative of the state of Oregon.
>
> This is tragedy in the classic sense, for it has been wrought by the man's own character. *Hubris*, the Greek term for arrogant pride, has converted his shining virtues into the instruments of his own failure.
>
> His brilliant intellect, which has led him to the right conclusions so often, also has led him to the belief that he is always right. And he isn't always right, particularly in human relationships.
>
> His pride has led him to break with even his closest friends of the past, when they have dared to disagree with him.
>
> His arrogance has led him to castigate those who, while in general agreement with his beliefs, have dared to criticize him on one point.
>
> His "independence," his determination to place "principle above politics," are both admirable in themselves. But he has carried both to a point where he has alienated honest, sincere people of every political shade, by his implication that anyone who disagrees with him is either stupid or hypocritical.
>
> . . . .

We still think that, potentially, he has all the qualities of a great statesman—except, perhaps, humility. But we can no longer ignore the tragedy of his self-immolation on the altar of *hubris*, his arrogant pride.

Some viewed Taft as an equally tragic figure in the late years of the Truman administration. Faulted by his driving ambition to reach the presidency, Taft encouraged Joe McCarthy and resisted none of the irresponsible attacks of other Republicans, such as Jenner's assaults on General George Marshall. As William S. White puts it:

These were not only unhappy days for his admirers but, in a sense, for Taft himself. A proud and self-contained man (sometimes a haughty one), he had no talent for acknowledging personal error and once he took a position, however untenable, his habit was to press on with it in a self-generating, rising bitterness. Nearly all that he permitted himself to stand for in these days alienated him from men who wished him well, some of them almost desperately so. . . . And this was the single area in his life about which one could not question him; he drew brusquely within himself on these points. He took any criticism, even from the most solidly conservative press, as calculated attack to promote the prospects of the Democrats.

It is a strange irony that Wayne Morse and Bob Taft, such opposites in outward obvious ways, were so alike, inwardly, in their worst periods. It remains to be seen whether Morse can advance creatively, as did Taft, to better days. It would be risky to press the analogy further; but the "last, best Taft," as White sees it, was Mr. Republican rising from the shambles of his presidential misadventure to dedicate his great skill and his last strength to helping the new President of his party to succeed.

Taft, to be sure, had advantages Morse does not enjoy. He retained the leadership of a strong segment of the Republican party, notably in the Senate. Morse has no following in this sense within the Senate. Moreover Eisenhower needed Taft in a desperate way that Kennedy does not need Morse. Taft could readily pitch in for Eisenhower after the election, for he had earlier won the engagement of Morningside Heights and set the tone and shape of the Republican election campaign. Finally, Taft was Taft, basically a Cincinnati lawyer who was doing the proper thing. Morse is Morse, basically a La Follette rebel.

When Morse's presidential candidacy was obliterated in May

1960, he fell into the slough of despond. The proud warrior had been humiliated by his own people. When he returned to the Senate from his Oregon massacre, other senators found him drawing great buckets of gloom from the well of his bitterness. Nixon was going to win the presidency; the country was going reactionary again; all was lost.

Morse nearly socked the then congressman from his home district in Oregon, Charles O. Porter, who had favored Stevenson, Humphrey, and Kennedy over Morse as the presidential candidate. Porter made the mistake of trying to approach Morse on the Senate floor one afternoon. The senator turned on the intruder, doubled his fists, and dismissed him with a common oath. Others, such as Congresswoman Edith Green, kept their distance.

From this morass Wayne Morse was suddenly rescued a few weeks later. Oregon's Republican partisans, thinking Morse had all but destroyed himself politically, were aghast. The rescuer was their own leader, President Eisenhower! He had nominated Morse as a delegate to the fall session of the United Nations General Assembly.

Morse was ecstatic. He regarded it as "probably the greatest honor and opportunity for public service that has come to me since I have been in the Senate." Stimulated by this prestigious assignment, Morse began afresh.

Why, Republicans wondered, had Morse been tossed a lifesaver by the man he had most railed against for seven years? The American delegation to the UN each year includes two members of Congress, chosen alternately from the House and Senate committees on foreign relations. When the State Department advised the White House to nominate Morse and Republican George Aiken of Vermont, the President's office asked, "Why Morse?" He was next in line in order of seniority on the Foreign Relations Committee, explained State, but the President could skip over him and nominate a more temperate Democrat if he wished—but that would surely touch off an outcry by Morse against tampering with the sacred seniority system. The White House, wanting none of this grief, went through with it.

"Keep Him Busy"

"The trick is to keep him busy," a high State Department official told me as Morse prepared to go to New York. "If they do, they'll get one helluvan effective job out of Wayne. But if they don't, look out." A Republican senator added, "Wayne will do a good job at the UN. He always does a good job when they give him a good assignment. It's when they ignore him that he acts up."

Both these men are amateur analysts of Wayne Morse, having observed him at close range for many years. If they are correct, they have offered an augury of hope. Morse now has new and heavy responsibilities, and plenty of work to keep him busy. He is chairman of four Senate subcommittees, two of vast contemporary importance— education and Latin America. There is substantial evidence from Morse's conduct as chairman of the Senate's Latin America Sub-committee to offer a preliminary judgment about the soundness of the "keep him busy" theory.

South of the Border

Since the sensational stoning of Vice-president Nixon in Caracas in 1958 and the Caribbean tribulations provoked by Castro, Latin America has been a sensitive trouble area. Any imaginative politician might have grasped the potential for personal attention as chairman of the Latin Subcommittee, embarking upon a full-dress televised investigation to fix blame for America's trouble.

Chairman Morse, instead, confined his subcommittee to ordering a number of scholarly studies by expert outside organizations on Latin problems; and he confined himself to several denunciations of Castro's drumhead trials and firing-squad executions. When Castro later came to Washington in 1959 and met with the Senate Foreign Relations Committee in a closed session, Morse purposely absented himself so as not to cause any disturbance or discomfort because of his sharp criticism of Castro's shabby judicial procedures.

Later that year Morse made a quiet journey through Argentina, Bolivia, Brazil, Chile, Colombia, and Venezuela, interviewing, as he put it, "Presidents, labor leaders, foreign ministers, businessmen, majority-party leaders, opposition congressmen, missionaries, college professors, farmers, and retail-market customers." He returned convinced that there remained a "deep reservoir of good will toward the United States among the people of these countries," despite criticism of some American policies. "There is nothing wrong with U.S. policies in Latin America that could not be cured by more loan money, some additional technical assistance and human welfare

grant money, and a great deal more sympathetic understanding of
Latin American problems," he reported. "The countries of Latin
America need more capital—and they provide many opportunities
for good, sound loans. But equally they need moral and technical
assistance for their social reform movements. Specifically, they need
more evidence that the United States is on the side of the people in
Latin America."

The senator, long a critic of coddling Latin dictators just because
they claim to be anti-communist, urged greater export of "our
ideals of freedom, good neighborliness and brotherly love." He urged
that America lend assistance to democratic countries, such as Colombia, for land reform because "the most serious threat of communism
is in the rural areas, just as it proved to be in Russia and China"
due to dissatisfaction among peasants who are little more than serfs
on large estates.

In September 1960, before going to the UN, Morse went back
to Colombia for what developed into a historic conference, concluding with the Act of Bogotá. Addressing the conference attended by
diplomats from all the Western Hemisphere nations except the
Dominican Republic, the Oregon Senator emphasized the concept
of self-help. He said:

> . . . the basic, most important, factor in development is people who
> really want development and who want it badly enough not only to
> work for it but to make their own substantial economic contributions
> as well as to give up certain traditional customs in order to get it. Un-
> less this basic urge is present, no amount of outside assistance will be
> effective.
>
> Real development means adjusting the social, economic and political
> institutions of a country so that the poor do not stay poor while the
> rich get richer. The extent to which, and the manner in which, this
> is done depends of course on the decisions of each individual country.
> It is a factor, however, which will undoubtedly be taken into account
> in further congressional implementation of this program.

The United States delegation, headed by C. Douglas Dillon,
now Kennedy's Secretary of the Treasury, went to Bogotá with a
five-hundred-million-dollar blank check which Congress had granted
at President Eisenhower's request. There it was pledged for social
improvements—land reform, public health, education, housing, and
community facilities. As Dillon put it:

It is not enough only to construct modern factories, power plants, and office buildings. These things are essential to the development process. But it often takes many years for their benefits to reach down to the ordinary citizen. We must therefore broaden our efforts to help all of the people. The task is nothing less than to lift whole segments of the population into the 20th century. . . . The government of the United States is prepared to devote over the years ahead large additional resources to the inauguration and carrying forward of a broad new social development program for Latin America, dedicated to supporting the self-help efforts of the governments and people of Latin America.

Wayne Morse cannot and does not claim credit for this notable step toward improving relations in Latin America, widening the horizons of freedom and discouraging the spread of communism. But he was responsibly engaged in this co-operatively with the State Department, rather than pulling disruptively in another direction, as autocratic committee chairmen frequently do.

The State Department at this time was grateful to Morse for having helped stop what the Eisenhower administration regarded as a bad sugar bill, passed earlier by the House. Morse teamed with the G.O.P leader, Senator Everett Dirksen, when the bill came up on the last night of the 1960 session. The debate went past midnight. "Between the two of them, they turned the Senate around," a Republican official of State told me. "Morse gave a tremendous speech. That was Morse at his best."

This latter comment, like most opinion in Washington, was perhaps prejudiced because Morse on that occasion served State's interest. The same official thought Morse was "at his worst" during his tough cross-examination of another State Department official, Roy Rhubottom, about Latin American problems—a performance which struck me at the time as admirable.

Serving in the UN was something of the fulfillment of a dream for Morse, for he has cherished ideals about the utility of this organization for peaceful settlement of world disputes. In this spirit he had pressed his 1946 resolution which got the United States into the World Court. In another sense, serving in the UN under the Eisenhower administration was a frustrating experience. Although always an internationalist, Morse had been highly critical of various aspects of the Eisenhower-Dulles policies. The most relevant criticism was that Dulles bypassed the UN. As Morse put it in *The Nation* in 1958:

He seems to see himself as an Old World figure of the 19th century, a lone manipulator of world events. He roves from capital to capital, dealing and negotiating and making American policies and commitments that are often exclusively his. But the lone wolf diplomat and world-shaker of the 19th century is out of date. Nor does he have any place in the American system.

Through the Eisenhower-Dulles years, Morse was so critical of their policies that even his admirers in Washington became, as the *New Republic* put it, "his sorrowful critics" because he appeared to be against everything. Basically he found fault with giving the executive branch so much latitude in foreign-aid administration. These were his most vitriolic anti-Eisenhower days. Said the *New Republic*: "Morse has been right so often when he has stood alone that he may now be succumbing to the fallacy that to stand alone is to be right." Or as one liberal Democratic senator put it, "If Wayne found himself on the same side as the Father, the Son and the Holy Ghost, he would fear he was just going along with the crowd."

The UN

By the time Morse reached the UN, he had cast off this mood. As a member of the United States delegation, he had to follow instructions on how to vote, a new and discomfiting experience, throughout the session which began with Khrushchev banging his shoe on the table. Drew Pearson suggested that Morse, the oratorical tiger, could be America's secret weapon in the UN debating society to take on Mr. K and Castro. But the State Department had other ideas about keeping him busy. Morse was assigned to the Trusteeship Committee, which had a long agenda of colonial issues to debate.

Delegate Morse intruded into delicate affairs when he answered a reporter's question by saying that Red China's admission to the world assembly was "inevitable." Proof, he suggested, was the narrowing margin by which UN members each year have voted to reject any debate on the issue of seating Communist China. It was 42–34 in 1960. "My position on Red China has been that it cannot come in, but I think it is inevitable. We have got to be willing to have the UN negotiate conditions for the admission of Red China." Morse may have pointed the way to a neutral position. When Adlai Stevenson and Chester Bowles came before the Foreign Relations

Committee in January 1961, following their appointments in the Kennedy administration, instead of blustering manfully about the evils of Red China or sympathizing with its admission as Bowles had in the past, both took Morse's line and said the United States may not be able to prevent China's admission.

After the UN adjourned for the year, Morse filed a lengthy report of his experiences and observations. It was the old Wayne Morse who pushed a copy of his report across his desk in February 1961 and declared, "I hand you a stick of dynamite." When asked where the explosion would take place, he replied, "The State Department and the Pentagon." In the report Morse attributed to the military the insistent policy of siding with the Western European colonial powers against the emerging new nations of Africa and Asia. He wrote:

> . . . our policy makers in the Pentagon Building are not sufficiently sensitive about the policies and practices of some of the colonial powers in respect to human rights of the indigenous people whom they rule and dominate. In the name of military defense, the United States has spent huge sums of money for bases and military installations in dictator countries, resulting in great economic benefit to colonial powers and dictatorships. It is very doubtful that the over-all effect of any of these military installations has been to strengthen the security of the United States. . . . The Department of State has seemed to lack the necessary disposition either to question the military need for such requirements or to balance their importance properly against other policy objectives. Once the Joint Chiefs of Staff have spoken, that tends to end the discussion.

Morse observed that one military reason for not opposing the colonial powers in the UN has been the unwillingness to irritate America's NATO allies. He added:

> The Russians have plainly found it much easier to go around NATO than to go through it, and they are doing so by seizing on the hopes and aspirations of people in former colonies or in so-called underdeveloped countries all over the world.
> . . . .
> Historic American sympathy for and actions in support of independence movements constitute one of the strongest reasons for the leadership of the U.S. in the free world today. . . . Independence movements are

succeeding. Nothing can stop this process; people everywhere want governments of their own choosing, and the colonial powers know or should know that the end of colonialism is near.

In the Trusteeship Committee Morse was embroiled in the debates on colonial issues. The voting pattern varied only slightly, usually resulting in eighty votes for the anti-colonial proposal, cast by the Afro-Asian nations, most of Latin America, Canada, the Soviet bloc, and usually the Scandinavian countries; about five votes against, cast by Portugal, Spain, Union of South Africa, Australia, and sometimes the Dominican Republic, Belgium, and France; and about ten abstentions from the United Kingdom, New Zealand, the Netherlands, some Latin American countries, and the United States.

Morse thought the United States acted unwisely in abstaining rather than supporting a resolution expressing the opinion that Portugal's territories of Angola and Mozambique in Africa are not self-governing, as Portugal claims. It carried by nearly a 2 to 1 vote. Reported Morse:

> It is common knowledge in the UN that Portugal has threatened the United States with the loss of the use of the Azores as an airline landing base if the United States joined other nations in rejecting Portugal's claim that she does not have foreign territories but only overseas metropolitan provinces.

Before the Portuguese resolution came up, Morse made a speech in the committee siding with India and politely criticizing the legal fiction of Portugal's claim that Goa in India is not a territory but a metropolitan province of no concern to the UN. The Portuguese ambassador went to the State Department to protest Morse's remarks. In his final report Morse urged a change in policy on this issue, declaring, "Millions of indigenous people living under Portuguese reign in foreign territories cry out against such fictitious reasoning. They also cry out for independence."

Another incident which provoked Morse's ire was a resolution to send a UN subcommittee to South-West Africa to observe local conditions. Morse helped to modify this proposal offered by Guinea, and he supported its general idea. The ambassador of the Union of South Africa in Washington several times objected to the State

Department; and Morse was advised indirectly that the Union of South Africa threatened to suspend further negotiations with American military officials for establishing a missile-tracking station in that country. Morse dispatched a long telegram to Secretary of State Christian Herter which urged him to make clear that "United States support of human rights will not be traded for tracking stations." In his report he said:

> The proposal to have a committee go into South-West Africa embodied the same principle as that embodied in the Hungarian question. We have sought for several years to have the UN committee go into Hungary and make observations and report back to the UN on the charges that the Hungarian people are being denied their freedom by Russia.

The best Morse succeeded in doing was to change the United States vote from "no" to abstention. The resolution carried 65 to 0, with 15 abstainers. Morse said the abstention was "very harmful because once again we appeared to be sustaining policies of a colonial power whose policy in South-West Africa has aroused deep resentment among many African nations."

Morse found the "most glaring instance of unwise policy by the United States on the colonial question in the failure to support the resolution called the 'Declaration on the granting of independence to colonial countries and people,' which was sponsored by forty-three countries of Asia and Africa. This resolution, couched in language reminiscent of Jefferson and Madison, began by saying:

> The subjection of peoples to alien subjugation, domination and exploitation constitutes a denial of fundamental human rights, is contrary to the Charter of the UN and is an impediment to the promotion of world peace and cooperation.
>
> All people have the right of self-determination; by virtue of that right they freely determine their political status and freely pursue their economic, social and cultural development.

The resolution carried 89 to 0, with 9 abstentions. Pressure from Great Britain resulted in President Eisenhower's directing the United States delegation to abstain, in company with Belgium, France, Portugal, Spain, South Africa, England, Australia and the Dominican Republic. Morse reported that "many of our friends in the UN felt that the U.S. had let them down. Many of them stated quite frankly that our vote was grist for the Communist propaganda mills in their countries."

Wayne Morse revealed anew his basic idealism about the function and purpose of the UN. Having long maintained that the UN should be strengthened through greater usage, that any meeting of the major world powers should be conducted at the UN and under its auspices, Morse was fortified by his three months' experience to advance this theme on the New Frontier.

For example, Morse strongly opposed American assistance to the Cuban rebel invasion in April, 1961, because it constituted indirect unilateral military intervention by the United States against a neighbor state. This "colossal mistake" violated the charter of the Organization of American States, argued Morse, and threatened United States' standing throughout the hemisphere among those discontented peoples who sympathize with Castro as the agent of social reform rather than as the handmaiden of Communist penetration. "Cuba is not a dagger pointed at the heart of the United States, but is instead a thorn in our flesh. If the United States seeks to settle its differences with Cuba through the use of military might, either direct or indirect, we shall be at least a half century recovering, if we ever recover, the prestige, the understanding, the sympathy, and the confidence of one Latin American neighbor after another." A return to "Big Stick" intervention in the Caribbean "will harden and strengthen anti-American feelings in most other countries of this hemisphere, and having intervened once, we will have to intervene again and again."

The only way to deal with Castro is in concert with the other American states, acting through the OAS, urged Morse; and the way to fend off Communist expansion in the hemisphere is to eradicate the causes of unrest through social advancements, as projected by President Kennedy's "Alliance for Progress" program based on the Act of Bogotá.

It is less difficult to remain idealistic and to be a responsible senator in the foreign field, for more often than not international issues can be debated and decided strictly on the facts as they are sifted and weighed. There are few pressure groups reaching in to place a heavy thumb on the scales. There may sometimes be emotional pressures—say, the intense feeling against recognition of Red China—but economic pressures are few. The one major economic pressure comes from protective-tariff advocates; but since the advent of reciprocal trade, tariff fights have been puny as compared to La Follette's day. If there has been any hedging of his international-ism, Morse has done it periodically on trade by offering a trifling amendment to the reciprocal trade extension bill to protect Oregon cherry growers. If there is any soft spot in Morse's heart for pro-tectionism, it is for the farmers, not for manufacturers, true to the La Follette tradition.

The tougher segment of his new frontier of responsibility will be domestic affairs, where only the very strong knights fulfill their legends and fight the dragons with unremitting courage.

Labor Reform . . . The Catholic Issue . . . Post-Election Relations . . . ". . . He Has to Deal With Me."

WAYNE Morse's relations with President Kennedy are neither as convivial as those he enjoyed with Truman nor as bitterly hostile as those he had with Eisenhower. Two days before Eisenhower left office, Morse and other Northwest senators were invited to attend a treaty-signing ceremony in the President's office. The treaty provided for hydroelectric development of the Upper Columbia River in co-operation with Canada, a matter of great benefit to Morse's state. Nevertheless he shunned the invitation. His presence, he explained, would only have embarrassed everyone, including Oregon. Three days later Morse held a fund-raising reception at the Mayflower Hotel. All guests were required to pay twenty-five dollars. The object was to erase the deficit left from Morse's presidential primary campaign. Among those who showed up to pay their respects and help the cause was Harry S. Truman.

For Wayne Morse's future, however, what mattered more was his relationship with the man who that same week became President. That relationship is neither distant enough to make Morse avoid entering the White House, nor is it close enough to make John Kennedy eager to have Wayne Morse for a social companion. There passes between them, by letter and telephone conversation, a courtesy that permits ready communication. Each recognizes, a bit warily, that the other is a man to contend with.

Their past association in the Senate virtually dictates this state of affairs. As far back as 1953, Morse belittled Kennedy—in Boston, yet. When a reporter asked the Oregon maverick to identify the liberals in the Senate, the Boston *Herald* reported that he failed to mention the freshman senator from Massachusetts. Asked why, Morse replied: "Why should I? He is no liberal." This occurred during

Morse's brief, unhappy days as an Independent when he thrashed out
wildly in all directions. Kennedy, like most of his Senate colleagues,
did not support Morse's hapless committee fight of that year.

Labor Reform

When Morse became a Democrat in 1955 and was restored to
the Labor Committee, differences between the two became more apparent. For Kennedy, too, was on the Labor Committee.

The chief differences took root in events of 1956. That spring two
reporters of the *Oregonian*, Wallace Turner and William Lambert,
exposed connections between Northwest hoodlums and the highest
officials of the Teamsters' Union. In a brilliant series of articles
which won Pulitzer prizes for both men, Turner and Lambert
gave impetus to the broad-ranging investigation by the Senate's Mc-
Clellan Committee. Securing that investigation was not a routine
matter. Other investigative reporters, chiefly Clark Mollenhoff of
the Des Moines *Register and Tribune*, had dug into Teamster
scandals in the Midwest and elsewhere; but all congressional inquiries
had mysteriously proved abortive.

But this time Mollenhoff found a more willing and courageous
investigator in Robert F. Kennedy, counsel for the Senate Government Operations Committee. Kennedy took the Turner-Lambert
material, plus information developed by Ed Guthman of the Seattle
Times, and bored in. After a trip to the Pacific Northwest, the young
counsel offered evidence of wrongdoing to senators during a closed-
door session. Bob Kennedy wanted to launch a full inquiry into
labor-management racketeering with a special committee composed
of senators from the Labor Committee and from the Government
Operations Committee.

The success of this proposal depended on the attitudes of key
senators, not the least of which were two senators who served on
those committees and came from the region of suspected corruption
—Henry M. Jackson of Washington and Wayne Morse of Oregon.
Would they favor or quietly oppose the investigation? Would they
wish to serve on the investigating committee if it were created?

Turner, Lambert, and I called on Morse to sound him out. Morse
apparently had assumed that the investigation might explore Teamster
contributions to political campaigns, for obviously the union's connections and ledgers would be scrutinized. As a practical matter,

we knew the Senate would never venture to probe the sources which individual senators tap to finance their election campaigns. So when Morse offered to get together his files showing the extent of Teamster contributions to his campaigns, he was assured by his visitors that the proposed investigation was not aimed at this sensitive area. Before we left his office, Morse called in a secretary and dictated a statement supporting the intent of the rackets investigation. Senator Jackson raised no objection to the probe, and the Senate within a few weeks approved a resolution authorizing $250,000 to hire a staff of investigators and clerks.

The selection of senators to serve on this special panel, headed by Senator John McClellan of Arkansas, was another matter. Morse, as a Labor Committee member, was eligible. So was Jackson, as a member of the Government Operations Committee. Both had demonstrated ability in notable cross-examinations, Morse in the Mac-Arthur dismissal matter, Jackson in the Army-McCarthy case. This inquiry would necessarily and properly reach into the labyrinth of labor power and authority. With his long experience in labor affairs, Wayne Morse was perhaps the best qualified senator to explore the line between proper and improper use of power by labor officials. And the Morse Legend of independence, courage, brilliance, and energy pointed to Morse's participation to prevent the investigation's being scuttled by labor pressure or exploited by anti-labor forces.

But Wayne Morse, like Senator Jackson, did what any ordinary politician would have done in similar circumstances. He resisted being drawn into the vortex of the storm that broke the day that McClellan banged his gavel for order and called reporters Turner and Lambert as the opening witnesses of his penetrating probe. He shied away from having to take sides for or against a host of labor leaders and lesser figures who marched to that witness stand during the two years which the inquiry ran. He stayed clear of the klieg-lighted arena in which labor was sadly tarnished by its least respectable, its most corrupt minority. He avoided becoming entangled. Wayne Morse played it safe.

The investigation went forward with vigor and dispatch. It is altogether possible that John F. Kennedy is President today because it did so. Senator Kennedy was a member of that special committee, and his brother Bob was its hard-driving counsel, planning the moves, asking the questions—and, all the while, becoming a national figure through the devotion of television to the often sensational

proceedings. The name Kennedy made its initial household impact
during this period, 1957–58.

As chairman of the Labor Subcommittee of the Senate Labor and
Public Welfare Committee, Senator Kennedy subsequently brought
out legislation to check those abuses revealed by the McClellan
hearings. Kennedy's bill passed the Senate, 88 to 1, in 1958, but
when it was killed in the House by dissident labor and business
groups, Kennedy said acidly, "Only the Jimmy Hoffas and the
Nathan Sheffermans can find satisfaction" in its defeat. In one
important respect Hoffa had benefited by the investigation's revela-
tions about Dave Beck, for Hoffa supplanted Beck as Teamster president. Shefferman was a so-called labor-management consultant who
assisted Beck in some of his clever schemes. (Shefferman, incidentally, wrote Morse a letter during his War Labor Board days to recommend a book on how to relax, a matter of great importance because
of Morse's value to the nation, added Shefferman.)

In 1959 the labor-reform issue came to a head. The Senate again
passed a bill, sponsored by Kennedy and Morse, but the House
fought the issue on its own terms, starting in the House Labor Committee. The bills ranged from the very restrictive ideas of the big-
business organizations to the ineffective measures advanced by the
Teamsters. On the key vote, four liberal Democrats displayed the
mark of courage when they resisted the heaviest labor pressure and
voted for a moderate reform bill. One of these four courageous
representatives was Edith Green of Portland, who defied Teamster
leaders from her strong union district.

On the House floor this moderate bill lost to the more restrictive
Landrum-Griffin bill. The House-Senate conference committee, set
up to reconcile the different bills passed by either chamber, included
Kennedy and Morse in its fourteen members. The differences between the two bills had little or nothing to do with labor reform
as such, but with basic amendments to the Taft-Hartley Act concerning secondary boycotts and the jurisdiction of the National
Labor Relations Board. For two and a half weeks the conference committee met in closed session. Heated wrangling developed over the
more controversial features. At length Kennedy, as chairman, emerged
with a compromise bill which he told reporters was "the best bill
we can get—and get a bill."

Wayne Morse dissented, loud and long. In a four-hour Senate
oration he found fault with the compromise and blamed Kennedy

for yielding to House members on certain technical features rather than taking the issue back to the Senate for instructions. There, said Morse, the issue could have been debated, hopefully resulting in a more conciliatory position by the House members if the Senate stood stoutly behind its representatives on the conference. Others believed this course would have resulted in the Senate, in effect, adopting the more restrictive Landrum-Griffin bill and undermining Kennedy's position of moderation. Morse obtained only one recruit, Langer of North Dakota, to vote with him against the final version of the bill.

This, as we have seen, became the issue for Morse's presidential-campaign attacks on Kennedy and Humphrey. All those who voted for this compromise became "phony liberals." But Morse's attacks on the bill failed to mobilize strong labor support for his presidential bid. He picked up his strongest backing from the Teamsters. The AFL-CIO came out in support of Kennedy's labor compromise and ignored Morse's assaults. Even in Oregon, Morse failed to attract broad support from labor leaders other than Hoffa's underlings.

The Catholic Issue

Early in 1960, after he and Kennedy had both declared themselves as presidential aspirants, Morse suddenly raised the "Catholic issue." At that time Kennedy's chances seemed seriously handicapped by his Roman Catholic faith. This episode happened during debate on a federal aid to public schools measure. No one was in a better position than Morse to know how this side issue had plagued aid to education legislation. He and Taft had cosponsored an education bill which bogged down on this very issue more than a decade before. Even on that occasion John Kennedy was involved.

Those events began in 1949. The Senate avoided the parochial school issue by adopting Taft's suggestion that each state should determine the proper educational boundary between church and state. In adopting Taft's neutral stand, the Senate also rejected opposite amendments—one for limiting aid to public schools, the other for stipulating that federal aid could be used for private-school bus service. The bill passed 50 to 15, with Morse and Taft among its sponsors. The Senate, in effect, ducked the religious issue, leaving it to the Supreme Court to draw the line.

Emotionalism was not so neatly avoided in the House. There the bill was referred to the Committee on Education and Labor whose chairman, Lesinski of Michigan, a Catholic, delegated to Barden of North Carolina, a Protestant, the task of conducting hearings. When Barden's subcommittee acted favorably, by a 10 to 3 vote, on Barden's bill *limiting federal aid to public schools,* Lesinski accused him of drafting an "anti-Catholic bill" as a means of killing the whole proposition. This intramural Democratic sparring quickly advanced into a varsity match on the nation's front pages when Cardinal Spellman accused unidentified members of Congress of "conducting a craven crusade of religious prejudice against Catholic children and their inalienable rights." Mrs. Roosevelt, in her newspaper column, retorted, "Those who believe in the right of any human being to belong to whatever church he sees fit . . . cannot be accused of prejudice when we do not want to see public education connected with religious control of schools." Faced with this crossfire, the House committee at length decided to shelve the whole question by a 13 to 12 vote. Among those committee members who voted to pigeonhole the Taft-Morse bill were two young second-term congressmen, John F. Kennedy and Richard M. Nixon.

A decade's truce, won at the expense of deferring the aid to education question, ended in 1960 with Kennedy's presidential candidacy and the resumption of congressional consideration of this proposal. From the Senate committee this time came the McNamara bill, providing grants to the states for public-school construction. Clark of Pennsylvania, with the support of Morse and others, led a successful effort to broaden the bill to permit the states to use their federal grants for teachers' salaries. Clearly this bill excluded private schools.

Like any organized group whose interest was not here being properly served, the National Catholic Welfare Conference, headquartered in Washington, prepared an amendment providing for long-term, low-interest government loans to private schools. The Senate committee had declined to embody this proposal in the bill, so the Catholic organization dispatched a representative to Capitol Hill to find a senator who might wish to offer it during Senate debate. Senator after senator refused to touch what they reckoned to be a hot issue. Many promised to support the Catholic amendment, if only someone else sponsored it. Wayne Morse agreed to lead the way. He was not their choice, a Catholic leader told me, but he was the only senator they could find who would offer the loan proposal.

If most senators would have preferred to duck this one, Senator Kennedy was the one man in the Congress who could not possibly duck it and, I would venture, was most ready to grasp the nettle to prove an important point. For the largest political problem then facing him and his party was whether they were to risk another Al Smith type of defeat. The Gallup poll had indicated that a candidate's Catholicism was a waning consideration among most voters, but the Democratic politicians weren't so sure. Politicians do not gladly accept such uncertainties. Kennedy, it was true, had spoken out in candid detail in 1959 when he told Fletcher Knebel of *Look*:

> The First Amendment to the Constitution is an infinitely wise one. There can be no question of federal funds being used for support of parochial or private schools. It's unconstitutional under the First Amendment as interpreted by the Supreme Court. I'm opposed to the federal government's extending support to sustain any church or its schools. As for such fringe matters as buses, lunches, and other services, the issue is primarily social and economic and not religious. Each case must be judged on the merits within the law as interpreted by the courts.

What a politician says when he is seeking high office, to some citizens, is a matter for no little skepticism. Nothing seemed likely to test in any tangible way these Kennedy convictions—until Morse put before the Senate the Catholic proposal for private-school loans. When the vote came on the Morse amendment, Kennedy was out on the campaign trail where he might have ducked, as did another presidential aspirant, Symington of Missouri. But Kennedy had informed his legislative assistant, Myron (Mike) Feldman, the night before that he wanted to be recorded against the Morse rider. The Morse amendment was defeated, 49 to 37.

It is now interesting to observe that the only presidential contenders who voted against it were Kennedy and Lyndon B. Johnson. Indeed, a high Catholic official on intimate terms with the effort behind this proposal attributed its defeat to Johnson, whose support the Catholic advocates thought had been secured. When Johnson opposed it, the votes of seven Southern Democrats went with him, according to this tally, thus defeating it.

For Jack Kennedy, the Morse proposal was a fortuitous opportunity. A few months later, when embroiled in the first wave of the religious emotionalism during his West Virginia primary campaign, he repeated his convictions and pointed out that he had voted to back them up, in opposition to the wishes of officials of his church.

Morse, to be sure, had not intended doing Kennedy any favor. As an announced presidential contender, he was reviling Kennedy as a "phony liberal." One Democrat speculated that Morse had eagerly sought sponsorship of the parochial-school rider as a means of ingratiating himself with Oregon Catholics, some of whom were troubled over his treatment of Clare Boothe Luce and Kennedy. His amendment, though defeated, at least earned him prominent attention in Catholic publications.

Whatever his motivation, what of the constitutional question? Did the loan idea violate the First Amendment? "In my judgment—and I would not be a party to the amendment if I thought it to the slightest degree violated this—this amendment is completely clear of any successful challenge on the ground of violation of the principle of the separation of church and state," Morse told the Senate. Not one senator dared to debate the issue. Outside the Senate, Protestants and Other Americans United for Separation of Church and State, an organization which had commended Kennedy for his 1959 declaration in favor of separation of church and state, called the Morse amendment "dangerous." Paul Blanshard, the writer who specializes in critiques against "Catholic power," expressed confidence the Morse proposal would be held unconstitutional if ever adopted into law. Monsignor Frederick G. Hochwalt, head of the education division of the Catholic Welfare Conference, allowed that it would certainly be subject to a court challenge, and only the Supreme Court could settle the constitutional question.

In defense of his amendment, Morse contended "there are ample precedents" for it. He cited: 1. The government makes food available for school lunches in private as well as public schools; 2. housing-loans guarantees for college dormitories go to private sectarian colleges as well as state universities; 3. loans for improving science teaching facilities under the 1958 National Defense Education Act go equally to private and public high schools; 4. federal grants and loans under the Hill-Burton act go to aid construction of hospitals operated by all religious faiths as well as non-sectarian private and public agencies. Some Protestants, such as Blanshard, contend that most present programs go to aid the child's personal health and welfare, whereas the Morse loan bill would for the first time have offered subsidies in the form of low-interest loans for construction of private-school buildings.

But what did the Founders mean? The Constitution's First Amendment states simply: *Congress shall make no law respecting an establishment of religion, or prohibiting the free exercise thereof.* It was Jefferson, who belonged to no church but who was regarded as a Unitarian, who employed the popular phrase "wall of separation between church and state" in a letter to the Danbury, Connecticut, Baptist Association in 1802. Madison, an Episcopalian, in proposing the First Amendment, explained that its intent was that "Congress should not establish a religion, and enforce the legal observation of it by law, nor compel men to worship God in any manner contrary to their conscience."

Not until 1947 did the unspecific phraseology of the First Amendment come under court review. This is the famous Everson case in which a New Jersey taxpayer sued his town to prevent use of tax revenues to reimburse Catholic parents for the cost of transporting children to parochial schools. In this first Supreme Court ruling Justice Black wrote:

> The "establishment of religion" clause of the First Amendment means at least this: Neither a state nor the federal government can set up a church. Neither can pass laws which aid one religion, aid all religions or prefer one religion over another. . . . No tax in any amount, large or small, can be levied to support any religious activities or institutions, whatever they may be called, or whatever form they may adopt to teach or practice religion. Neither a state nor the federal government can, openly or secretly, participate in the affairs of any religious organization or groups and vice versa. . . .

The court in a five to four decision ruled that, notwithstanding these limitations, tax aid for transportation constituted a safety aid for the parents and their children, not an aid to the church schools themselves. From this ruling evolved the child-welfare theory which covers school-lunch and public health-examination programs.

The next year, 1948, the court ruled 8 to 1 in the McCollum case against Illinois churches' providing Protestant and Catholic religious instruction during a "released-time" period in the public schools. In 1952, in the Zorach case, the court upheld, 6 to 3, the constitutionality of a New York program for an hour of "released time" from public schools for religious classes conducted away from the public schools. Justice Douglas, speaking for the court, offered what is perhaps the most well-rounded interpretation yet advanced by the Supreme Court on this question:

There cannot be the slightest doubt that the first amendment reflects the philosophy that church and state should be separated. And so far as interference with the free exercise of religion and an establishment of religion are concerned, the separation must be complete and unequivocal. The first amendment within the scope of its coverage permits no exception; the prohibition is absolute. The first amendment, however, does not say that in every and all respects there shall be a separation of church and state. Rather, it studiously defines the manner, the specific ways, in which there shall be no concert or union or dependency one on the other. That is the common sense of the matter. Otherwise the state and religion would be aliens to each other—hostile, suspicious, and even unfriendly. Churches could not be permitted to render police or fire protection to religious groups. Policemen who helped parishioners into their places of worship would violate the Constitution. Prayers in our legislative halls; the appeals to the Almighty in the messages of the Chief Executive; the proclamations making Thanksgiving Day a holiday; "so help me God" in our courtroom oaths—these and all other references to the Almighty that run through our laws, our public rituals, our ceremonies would be flouting the first amendment. A fastidious atheist or agnostic could even object to the supplication with which the Court opens each session: "God save the United States and this Honorable Court."

We are a religious people whose institutions presuppose a supreme being. We guarantee the freedom to worship as one chooses. We make room for as wide a variety of beliefs and creeds as the spiritual needs of men deem necessary. We sponsor an attitude on the part of government that shows no partiality to any one group and that lets each flourish according to the zeal of its adherents and the appeal of its dogma. When the state encourages religious instruction or cooperates with religious authorities by adjusting the schedule of public events to sectarian needs, it follows the best of our traditions. For it then respects the religious nature of our people and accommodates the public service to their spiritual needs. To hold that it may not would be to find in the Constitution a requirement that the government show a callous indifference to religious groups. That would be preferring those who believe in no religion over those who do believe.

In declaring what government may not do, Justice Douglas added:

Government may not finance religious groups nor undertake religious instruction nor blend secular and sectarian education nor use secular institutions to force one or some religion on any person. But we find no constitutional requirement which makes it necessary for government to be hostile to religion and to throw its weight against efforts to widen the effective scope of religious influence.

Wayne Morse cited all of these cases to the Senate, quoting from the decisions at some length in the manner of an advocate very much at home amidst the pillars of legal precedent. Having done so, the senator handed down his own interpretation of what the First Amendment means. "The key to what may be done and what may not be done lies at the point where the differences between providing for the general welfare becomes 'aiding' religion." Reading the words of the Constitution to the Senate, Morse said:

We need to keep in mind the facts which existed in our country, the controversy which was waged in our country, that caused the adoption of the First Amendment. That is why it is so important that we get back to the views of our constitutional fathers. We need to remember that at the time the Constitution was adopted there were, if my recollection is correct, nine states which had state churches. In other words, the First Amendment was really the result of a controversy which was waged in this land at the time of the birth of the Republic, when there was strong opposition to the establishment by law of a state church . . . some of our forefathers left Great Britain because of the so-called state-church issue. They were in revolt against state religious authoritarianism. So it is not surprising that in the colonial days there was great controversy over the issue of whether the federal government should sanction—as some states already had done —a national church. Therefore, the founding fathers wrote this provision into the Constitution. . . . As we read the great language of Justice Douglas in the decisions to which I have just now referred, I believe it most important that we realize that he had clearly in mind the historic basis for the First Amendment.

This, of course, is not a unique interpretation of the meaning of the First Amendment. It is held by Catholic writers. Father Neil G. McCluskey, in his authoritative book *Catholic Viewpoint on Education* enhances this interpretation by noting that at the time of the Constitutional Convention in 1787 at Philadelphia, five states —New York, New Jersey, Virginia, North Carolina, and Georgia— had recently discarded their state churches; but five other states retained theirs. In Massachusetts, Connecticut, and New Hampshire the state church was Congregational, and in Maryland and South Carolina it was the Church of England. As adopted, the Bill of Rights forbade the federal government's establishing any national church. The states were left free to have state churches, until 1868 with ratification of the Fourteenth Amendment. Father McCluskey contends that there was no intent to have the federal government refrain from aiding organized religion and its various churches. He says:

> From the beginning, the federal and state government have used public funds to support religion on a nondiscriminatory basis. . . . Even the proclamation of Thanksgiving Day each year by the President is an "aid" to religion. . . . It requires money to publish the Thanksgiving Day proclamation which runs afoul of the alleged prohibition on the use of any tax, large or small, to support religious activities or institutions, whatever they may be labeled.

Morse, while taking this view of what the Constitution means, sought to avoid the issue of whether the government should "aid" religious institutions. He said he was opposed to federal grants to private schools, but his loan program did not constitute "aid" in the sense frowned upon by the Supreme Court. Rather, it offered "encouragement to the private schools of the Nation in their role of educating approximately 15 per cent of our young people." Nor would his proposal provide a "subsidy," only "co-operation with church-sponsored activities which are in furtherance of the general welfare." The High Court, needless to say, has not ruled against "encouragement" or "co-operation."

The only senator who dared to challenge Morse's proposal was the Republican floor leader, Everett Dirksen of Illinois, but only on the subsidy aspect, not the Constitutional issue. He noted that loans extended under the Morse proposal would carry an interest rate of about 2¾ per cent, but the most recent bond issues of the Treasury required the government to pay 4⅞ per cent. So even though the school loans were repaid with interest, Dirksen maintained "the Treasury would still be losing 2 per cent on every dollar which was loaned."

Morse quickly dropped his "no subsidy" argument, but pointed out that his amendment carried the same repayment formula attached to loans for college-dormitory construction. There is no constitutional difference, he contended, between lending money for sectarian colleges and sectarian elementary and high schools.

However right the senator might be constitutionally speaking, it is precisely between higher and lower education that Protestant opponents of aiding private schools have drawn their battle line. Monsignor Hochwalt recalls a vigorous discussion with the late Dr. A. Powell Davies, the Unitarian leader, on this point. "What is your reason for not objecting to aid to sectarian colleges but opposing aid for sectarian elementary and high schools?" the Catholic asked. "Do I have to have a reason?" he says the noted Unitarian retorted indignantly. "No," said the Monsignor, "but can you give me one?" Davies, he says, could not. But the Unitarian Fellowship for Social Action was not without a reason in a letter to Morse:

> The Morse Amendment violates the spirit of the Constitution because it would use the government's financial facilities to aid religious schools, at the level of compulsory school attendance. The government has never before gone so far in the direction of aid to parochial schools, and we believe that this creates a dangerous precedent. Loans can easily lead to grants, and soon the taxpayer may be asked to pay all the expenses of sectarian schools.

Catholic leaders would gladly have given up the subsidy feature, which was actually drafted by Senate Education Committee staff members. When asked what value the federal loan program would have had if the interest rate were no lower than the price of money in the open market, Monsignor Hochwalt said its value would have been to establish the principle of federal recognition of the private schools at the outset in any federal aid to education program. If the private schools were utterly excluded from the start, they would be a long time getting in on any federal aid programs. Catholic leaders, in a word, took the long-term view. With strong convictions about the sectarian necessity of the parochial school system as the only acceptable means of educating Catholic children, they would like to remove the traditional barriers against use of tax money to help finance this system.

The political irony is that this Catholic goal is more likely to be reached under the auspices of Protestant politicians seeking to demonstrate their liberality than by the action of a Catholic in the White House, especially President Kennedy, who is conscious of the inflammatory results any show of favoritism to his church would have from those Protestant citizens who were uneasy about his election on these grounds. The sponsor of this Catholic loan amendment, Morse is a Congregationalist. He was joined by another Protestant presidential contender, Hubert Humphrey, in supporting it.

When Kennedy made his declaration in *Look*, he received some criticism in Catholic publications. Significantly, he was defended by *Commonweal*, the liberal Catholic lay publication, which said:

> . . . the point is this: a President does not swear to uphold the Constitution as Catholic leaders, or any other leaders, think it should be interpreted but as the Supreme Court interprets it. He does this not because Supreme Court justices are infallible but because observance of their authority, especially by the President, is necessary to stable government.

The point here is that Kennedy, the Catholic, took his stand on what the Supreme Court has said the Constitution means in the First Amendment. Wayne Morse, the Protestant, hangs his case on what *he* thinks the Constitution means.

Post-Election Relations

After Kennedy won the election, he quickly established a working relationship with Wayne Morse, among many who were not members of the exclusive F-K-B-T-C (For Kennedy before the convention) organization. The new President showed no hostility for past slurs, such as Morse's accusation that Kennedy was trying to buy his way into the White House. Kennedy was looking for assistance for the tremendous tasks ahead, not seeking to avenge the slights of his opponents of the past.

Before the inauguration, Kennedy telephoned Morse to ask that the Senator assign a Labor Subcommittee staff expert to work on a new minimum-wage bill, a priority item on the new President's legislative program. Morse was pleased to be asked, but he told Kennedy he had no assurance that he would become chairman of that subcommittee.

They were discussing one of the numerous subcommittees of the Senate Committee on Labor and Public Welfare, whose chairman is Senator Hill of Alabama. Kennedy, as a senator, headed the Labor Subcommittee; Senator McNamara of Michigan headed the Education Subcommittee; Morse headed the lesser Railroad Subcommittee. Kennedy had assumed that Morse would be advanced to the chairmanship of the Labor Subcommittee.

But a move was already afoot to prevent Morse from securing this post. Oddly, the pressure came not from the dragons of business who distrust Morse and his labor views; it came from the dragons of labor. The AFL-CIO exerted pressure on Senator Hill to switch McNamara from Education to Labor, and to promote Senator Yarborough of Texas as chairman of Education. This plan would have prevented Morse from moving into either of these key positions.

When Kennedy's Labor Secretary, Arthur Goldberg, heard reports of this, he telephoned Morse to offer his services in interceding with AFL-CIO President George Meany. Morse would accept no aid. This was his dragon and his fight. Meany was understood to be angry still with Morse's fraternizing with the Teamsters, the union which had been expelled from the AFL-CIO. Especially galling to Meany was the film Morse made and permitted the Teamsters to distribute all over the country blasting the "Kennedy-Landrum-Griffin" labor reform bill.

Morse dug into Senate precedents on committee promotions to amass evidence supporting his right to the next vacancy as a matter of seniority. He advanced on Hill for a showdown. The gentle Alabaman said, Why, surely, he had meant no harm to Wayne. But he stalled any promises. Morse warned him that he would take the issue to the Democratic caucus and fight for his rights. Morse spread the word, especially to mild-mannered Senator Mansfield, the pipe-smoking Democratic leader, that a fight was brewing. After a war of nerves which lasted right up until the hour of the caucus, Hill backed down and designated Morse chairman of the Education Subcommittee.

By sticking up for his rights, Wayne Morse became head of the

Senate Subcommittee charged with handling one of the top proposals of the Kennedy administration—federal aid to education. The prospects for a fight seemed strong on the Catholic issue.

This time, however, Morse warned against tying the Catholic loan proposal to the education bill. He feared it would endanger chances of enacting the general aid bill. He still favored it and was confident it was constitutional, but he said he felt an obligation to the President to "bleed for his bill" because of his new job as chairman of the Education Subcommittee. He wanted to show that he could be responsible, to silence the doubting Thomases who think Morse is entirely an agent of discord.

Outside the areas of a responsibility for his education and Latin America subcommittees, Wayne Morse intends being the maverick, opposing the President when he believes Kennedy is wrong, upholding him when he agrees with him. He thought Kennedy's Inauguration and State of the Union speeches were magnificent. He thought the cabinet selections were outstanding, with the exception of Navy Secretary John Connally, whom he opposed because of his Texas oil connections.

". . . He Has to Deal With Me."

But six weeks after Kennedy took office Wayne Morse opened fire with both barrels against the new President's appointment of an Alabama politician, Charles M. Meriwether, to serve as a member of the Export-Import Bank. The Meriwether nomination received mild criticism on Capitol Hill because of the nominee's past connections with a Grand Dragon of the Ku Klux Klan and retired Rear Admiral John Crommelin, whose periodic political campaigns in Alabama had been marked by the doctrines of bigotry. Meriwether advised the Banking Committee this was all past history now, and the committee approved the nomination by a narrow margin.

The day the Senate took up the nomination, Morse became embroiled in a toe-to-toe shouting match with Senator John Sparkman of Alabama. Morse suggested that Meriwether might be or have been a drunk and that he had a police record. He offered no proof and refused to identify his anonymous source, an Alabama editor. Sparkman retorted that airing charges from anonymous tipsters raised "the ugly head of McCarthyism." The Birmingham *News* reported that Meriwether said his police record stemmed from a complaint filed by an angry employer after Meriwether drove a company car to another Alabama city against instructions. When Meriwether countered with a suit, the complaint was withdrawn, he said.

Kennedy told a news conference that before submitting Meriwether's name to the Senate, he had personally reviewed the FBI report compiled on every presidential nominee for high office. The President indicated that he was satisfied.

Morse was not. He demanded that Kennedy make the FBI report available for Senate inspection. Kennedy sent a White House aide to Morse with some notes from the FBI report, but the senator was not satisfied. "I demolished him in fifteen minutes," he later boasted to me. "I told him, 'Go back and tell the President you have wasted my time.'" Morse then moved to refer the nomination back to the Banking Committee for further study of his allegations. The Senate refused, 66–18, but deferred a vote on the nomination until the next afternoon.

The next morning, at a hearing in the Foreign Relations Committee, Morse slid into a seat next to mine at the press table and refought the Meriwether fight, blow for blow, with all the emotional intensity that whispers will allow. He was visibly riding a crest of excitement, like a high-strung boy just back from his first big hunt, still quivering from the thrill of stalking a dangerous beast. "Where were the other flaming liberals?" he hooted. "It was shameful, just shameful. In seventeen years I've never backed away from a fight, and they can't touch that."

Senator Douglas, a liberal committee member who had questioned Meriwether, had appealed for mercy and forgiveness. A man's earlier mistakes should not be held against him permanently, argued Douglas. Replied Morse, "I yield to no other member of the Senate in respect to Christian compassion, charity and forgiveness," but duty required that he oppose Meriwether for failing the character qualifications. Morse was joined by several other senators, notably Javits of New York, in opposing this appointment, but the other opponents were more temperate.

Why was Morse so intensely hostile to Meriwether? Columnist William V. Shannon of the liberal New York *Post* thought, as many did, that the Meriwether appointment commanded little respect. "But there are bad minnows and there are bad whales," observed Shannon. "Morse can't seem to tell the difference. This was just a bad minnow. Meriwether is but one of several directors of a second-class agency." Morse would say, to such a contention, that a liberal must speak out against wrong, no matter how minor, no matter where it rears its ugly head. But was that all there was to it?

As Morse reviewed the battle for my benefit that morning at the press table, he said he had been told by some Democrats that he shouldn't do this because he would get into trouble with the President. "But I tell them, *'This will show him that he has to deal with me!'*"

That afternoon, Morse "showed him" by crying indignantly that "the President owes an apology to every Jew in America and to every Negro in America for this appointment because in my judgment an investigation would show that the nominee is a racist and anti-Semitic. The President has no right to appoint such a person to a high position in his administration."

The Senate, thinking otherwise, voted 67–18 to confirm the nomination. Kennedy remarked crisply at his news conference an hour later than he was confident Meriwether would do a good job.

Is this case not a graphic illustration of the strength and weakness of Wayne Morse? He is willing and able to speak out vigorously against dubious acts; but he is unwilling or unable to confine his outspokenness to that, or to grant that others may be as righteous or well-intentioned as he.

Here, after two decades in the higher circles of national affairs, Wayne Morse was still trying to prove that he is a Big Man in Washington. Instead of moving into his new legislative responsibilities with the steadiness that comes from long accretion of tranquil power, Wayne Morse made the unsteady lunge of a man desperately seeking the recognition and respect he fears he does not have.

When Columnist Shannon collaborated with Bob Allen a decade ago in writing *Truman Merry-Go-Round*, he called Morse "a tower of strength to the liberal cause." Today, as the most liberal of the Washington columnists, he sees Morse as "a tragic figure." He puts it this way: "Wayne Morse is intellectually brilliant—superior to most all his Senate colleagues. But his egotism (granting that all senators are egotistical) has become so intensified with the passing years that it has almost destroyed his judgment. In losing his powers of judgment, he always acts as though he, alone, is the conscience of the Senate. He acts as though if he didn't speak out there would be no voice in the Senate for morality. I think he plays a useful role, but a lesser usefulness than he might have realized. It's not that what he does is bad. I would vote for him for re-election if I lived in Oregon, because he is still so far above so many other politicians. But it's that Morse has failed to realize a great potentiality. He ought to be for the Sixties what Norris and La Follette were for their times."

As Morse concluded hearings on the federal aid to education bill in the spring of 1961, other liberal observers had their fingers crossed. Columnist Doris Fleeson wondered whether he would be able to "keep his head." Conservative observers had long before written off Morse completely because of his tactics and his doctrine.

Fingers were crossed at the White House too. But Morse has not received kid-glove treatment. "We simply recognize him as our legislative leader in education, for he is head of that subcommittee," explained a top assistant to President Kennedy. The idea that Morse had to show Kennedy that "he has to deal with me" struck the White House as absurd.

In his characteristically evenhanded way, Kennedy invited Morse to the White House in mid-March, shortly after the Meriwether episode. The purpose was a strategy conference on education legislation. By chance, Morse had made a speech in the Senate several days earlier warning the Kennedy administration that he intended increasing hostilities if more attention were not given to local problems in Oregon, such as the "discrimination" in establishing expensive military installations in the adjacent states of California and Washington to Oregon's economic chagrin. Before the President received Morse, an alert assistant placed the Morse speech, clipped from the *Congressional Record*, on the Chief Executive's desk. Kennedy scanned it before Morse entered. At a party the next night, Wayne Morse was purring about "the hour and a half" he had spent with the President. "He had read my speech," glowed Morse. John Kennedy, like Harry Truman, had scratched Wayne Morse's back with salutary results.

"Some people don't seem to realize that when I am given a responsibility, I do a job," Wayne Morse said to me soon after. "I'm going to bleed for my President. I have a responsibility to him, and I'm going to carry it out."

Wayne Morse is not likely ever to regain the admiration of conservatives who once had faith in him. But perhaps he can yet regain wide respect from liberals and revise the lament of columnist Shannon. If one grants that the past decade was too placid and contented to respond to the call of constitutional liberalism, one would have to allow that the sixties may be different. The times have a way of changing. Morse's performance in steering the federal-aid-to-education bill through the Senate in May, 1961, affords substance for this prospect. The controversial education proposal divided the lawmakers in crazy quilt patterns. Neat party lines were blurred by contention between segregationists and integrationists, between states rights conservatives and federalist liberals, not to mention the hidden sectarian attitudes provoked by a revival of the Catholic issue.

As Morse conducted hearings, Kennedy came out against across-the-board loans to private schools and won Protestant plaudits for his position. Morse disagreed but cooperatively sidetracked the private school proposal. Secretary of Health, Education and Welfare Abraham Ribicoff, forewarned about Morse's temperamental nature, marveled at his down-the-line pro-Administration behavior. No maverick surprises or disruptiveness this time as Wayne Morse, for the first time, carried the burden of responsibility for a major legislative achievement. Senate leaders held their breath, for never before in his 17-years in the Senate had Wayne Morse been given the tough assignment of a legislative floor manager for a broad national proposal.

In opening debate, Morse called for support for the $2.5 billion three-year program of grants for public school buildings and teachers' salaries to "permit us as a nation to start the job of bringing full educational opportunity within the reach of every American girl or boy who can profit from it." Because the bill contained no word on whether the grants should or should not be made to states still practicing segregation, Morse caught it from both sides. He took the entirely pragmatic view that a civil rights rider "would kill the chances of the bill being passed." So, an amendment to prevent withholding of funds from segregated states, sponsored by Thurmond of South Carolina, was defeated 70 to 25; and an amendment by Republican Senator Bush of Connecticut to prevent grants to segregated schools was killed 61 to 25.

This issue persisted, however, when Ribicoff advised an inquiring senator that he doubted that the government had authority to withhold money to enforce integration. This provoked a bipartisan effort by Keating of New York and Douglas of Illinois to amend the bill to authorize a taxpayer to go into court and challenge the constitutionality of grants to states defying the Supreme Court's 1954 school decision. Senator Clifford Case, New Jersey's liberal Republican, stiffly belittled Morse's pragmatic view by saying "if in order to have this bill passed, we must 'buy' segregation with it, it comes at too high a cost."

This was the most severe test for Wayne Morse, whose Legend of uncompromising adherance to constitutional principle and liberal civil rights doctrine placed him in a difficult position to rebut this liberal assault. But the Senate's most canny debater rose to the challenge. Not only would this amendment imperil passage of the bill, but it would imperil the program by allowing suits to stop payments to any or all states, he asserted. "Neither result would further desegregation. Both results would interfere with the extremely necessary improvement of public elementary and secondary education which the bill is designed to help achieve." Morse even questioned the constitutionality of the amendment.

Sensing Morse had overstepped himself on the last point, Keating said his amendment had been modeled on a Morse proviso in the private school loan bill. "I assume that the Senator from Oregon would not propose an unconstitutional bill," mocked Keating. "Knowing of his great erudition as a lawyer, I was sure that he had studied that problem and had reached the conclusion that such a bill would be constitutional."

As Morse plunged into the deep water of legal argument, searching for precedents and decisons on which to stand, Douglas said Morse reminded him "of a German Ph.D. who could go down deeper, stay down longer, and come up muddier than anyone else." Delighting in this keen challenge to his debating skill, Morse said there was "a fundamental difference" between his proviso and the Keating-Douglas amendment. The Supreme Court had ruled against segregation only in public schools, he noted. "Unless the private school bill provided protection for the Negro taxpayer, as our bill did in several sections, such a taxpayer would have no protection whatever," argued Morse.

"The Senator from Oregon is a veritable legal Houdini in being able to escape from the bonds of logic," retorted Douglas. "Does it not all come down to saying that a lawyer can always find a reason to justify what he wants to do?"

As his foes crowded him, Morse pulled out a letter from Ribicoff designed to strengthen Kennedy supporters against the temptation to vote for this civil rights proposal. "Knowing your deep and abiding interest in the advancement of civil rights," Ribicoff wrote Morse,

"I can appreciate how difficult is your role in defending the school bill against amendments which seek to inject the civil rights issue into legislation whose sole concern should be education." Ribicoff said the Administration opposed this amendment because "to allow individual taxpayers throughout the nation to tie up this legislation with a multitude of lawsuits would be a blow to education that would not even offer the hope of a compensating gain in the field of civil rights." The amendment was defeated by a 62 to 32 vote.

When Goldwater tried to inject the Catholic issue into the debate by attaching a private school aid amendment, Majority Leader Mansfield, himself a Catholic, called for its defeat as Morse pledged later action on a private school bill. Goldwater's proposal was killed, 66 to 25. With similar dispatch and wide margins, every alteration which Morse opposed was defeated, and the Senate passed the school bill, 49 to 34.

Among the accolades that Morse received for "performing magnificently," as Mansfield put it, probably the most appropos came from liberal Senator Joseph Clark of Pennsylvania: "No one could have handled it with greater understanding or greater calm appreciation of the passions which sometimes rock this body, or with greater understanding of how well such things can be accomplished by remaining calm."

Having lost neither his head nor his temper under fire, Wayne Morse regained much of the respect which he lost in his feuds of recent years. The *Washington Post* called it "legislative statesmanship," crediting Morse with "meticulous fairness and with an unswerving sense of where to yield and where to stand adamantly firm." Robert C. Albright, the *Post's* veteran congressional reporter, was the first to report "Morse's transformation overnight from the temperamental center of recurrent Senate storms to a sort of benign statesman beaming courtesy, charm and stability."

Was this transformation a thing of the moment? Had Morse at last decided he could catch more flies with honey than with vinegar? Was he simply on good behavior because he needed a fresh record of good performance for his upcoming 1962 re-election campaign? Or was he feeling a new sense of responsibility to "bleed" for JFK, the new President who had learned to scratch Morse's back by telling him the education bill would be known as the Morse-Thompson bill? There was likely an element of each factor involved. In any event, Morse basked in the sunshine of his success. The night the bill passed the Senate, after eight days debate, he bubbled over with such good will that he praised Goldwater and Dirksen for sportsmanship and loyal opposition. Having defeated these foes at every turn, Wayne Morse that night appeared to love his enemies—or, at least, he loved the defeat he had inflicted upon them.[1]

In past years, Wayne Morse was handicapped by his subordinate positions (in either party), by the placid nature of the Fifties when maverick reformers were unfashionable, and by the tiger that roared within. Now some changes are apparent. He has gained new positions of political strength and authority, and the times, under the impact of Kennedy's New Frontier, may be changing to the advantage of liberalism once again. Morse quickly seized these fresh advantages to register an initial success. What's more, he demonstrated that in triumph he can be as magnanimous as in defeat he has been brutal.

The question that remains is whether this recent circumstantial transformation will lead to a more fundamental change that would serve Wayne Morse through good and lean political times, through the pleasing circumstances of victory but also through the anxious agonies of defeat.

[1] The Morse-Thompson bill was pigeonholed in the House Rules Committee by an 8-to-7 vote, thereby blocking its consideration by the House in 1961. Congressman James Delaney, New York Democrat and a Catholic, cast the key vote to kill the bill, apparently to please Catholic leaders who opposed the public school bill and insisted on equal aid for private schools. The Catholic bishops had belatedly asked for federal grants, instead of loans, for private schools. Morse and Kennedy agree that public grants to parochial schools would be unconstitutional. Provoked by the Catholic heirarchy's "all or nothing" attitude, Morse scored Cardinal Spellman for hampering the aid to education cause. (He took special pride in this blast because no other lawmaker had shown comparable bravery. The cardinal later asked Senator Kenneth Keating, New York Republican, to arrange a dinner for him with Morse to patch things up.)

In the administration's attempts to find a compromise acceptable to conflicting interests and Congress, Kennedy compromised his earlier stand on the Catholic issue by allowing his aides to propose loans for construction of private school classrooms used for science, mathematics, foreign languages, and physical education—all in the name of national defense, that sacred emblem under which many leaky legislative ships are launched. Morse bought this compromise; but when it, too, died in the Rules Committee, the Senate withheld action on Morse's bill. While Delaney was publicly cast as the villain, many timid congressmen privately thanked him for blocking the bill, thus permitting them to avoid taking a stand which would inevitably alienate sections of their constituencies.

22. THE FRONTIER OF THE SPIRIT

"IF MORSE could only shed some of his excess baggage, drop his feuds, not try to take on so much, he would be the most effective Senator we have." This estimate, by an eminent liberal senator who has alternately jousted and found common cause with him, largely captures the sentiment of those who hope that Wayne Morse can subdue the inner tiger of the self which threatens him far more than the outer dragons of public life.

Perhaps a compassionate fellow senator of yesterday may have said the same thing of fiery Henry Clay, of vindictive Daniel Webster, of cold John C. Calhoun, of arrogant Bob La Follette, of bullheaded Bob Taft. It is not inconceivable that all of these giants were oftimes as much the despair of their friends as they were the terror of their foes. All of them had great ambition to become President; and all of them, perhaps driven by this desperately burning drive, were intemperate lions. But the Senate a few years ago, at the recommendation of a committee led by Senator John Kennedy, ranked these five as the greatest senators of all time. History has a kind way of discounting personal shortcomings of those who render substantial public service. These senators were highly ranked for what they achieved as well as what they stood for in the times in which they served.

It is not the purpose of this final word to anticipate history's judgment of Wayne Morse. There is enough, certainly, in his record and his make-up from which to build a strong case either for or against him, depending on one's philosophical view and disposition toward the senator. Our purpose from start to finish has been to see him as he is. And he is controversial to the end.

Wayne Morse, as much as any senator, cherishes the hope of

securing history's favor. He has emulated in some remarkably consistent ways, the methods of La Follette, especially in pointing the way to the greater goal instead of settling for the smaller possibility of the moment. But in more significant ways, Morse has thus far failed to follow his leader, thereby weakening his political stature and his chance of realizing the lasting achievement which has thus far eluded him.

La Follette was the acknowledged leader of a vast reform movement that had its spiritual inspiration in the political changes which he brought to Wisconsin as its governor. He led this movement throughout his career. He started a periodical, the *Progressive*, to spread his doctrine to the people. And he held together a group of Senate mavericks who followed him through many insurrections against the majority of their day. La Follette was somewhat arrogant and hot-tempered, always outspoken, but he concentrated his fire on the conservatives with whom he greatly differed—not the other progressives with whom he did not always agree. His leadership would likely have evaporated if he had openly castigated his allies as "phony progressives" when they differed with him.

La Follette was hated, to be sure; but he was also loved. One episode reveals the intensity of these feelings. It occurred during that most famous of filibusters against Wilson's armed-ship bill in 1917. In leading this fight, the Progressive leader was convinced that giving the President authority to arm merchant vessels was a certain step to war. The country was emotionally inflamed and deeply divided. Waves of hostility broke across the shoulders of the band of isolationists whom La Follette led.

In the last tense hours before the hour of automatic adjournment, La Follette's son, Bob, Jr., sensed imminent danger as he stood watching his lionhearted father through a doorway to the Senate chamber. He had taken a revolver from his father's traveling bag, but then had not given it to him before the senator returned to the scene of the angry debate. Young Bob feared he had left him defenseless.

Then Senator Harry Lane of Oregon, a La Follette loyalist, spotted the danger. As Senator Ollie James of Kentucky lumbered across the chamber, Lane saw the glint of a revolver inside his coat. Lane moved instantly to intercept James as La Follette stood at his desk seeking recognition to speak once more. As he drew between the two men, Lane reached into his pocket and took firm hold on a long, sharp-pointed rattail file. Ollie James would never have a chance to aim that weapon, for Lane was ready for one quick fatal thrust at James' heart if he menaced La Follette.

As Lane later explained to La Follette after the tension subsided without incident, "If you slip this file inside a man's collarbone on the left side you can reach his heart with one thrust, and he will never move again."

A physician in private life, Lane was willing to use his knowledge of anatomy to kill, and perhaps be killed in return, in order to defend Fighting Bob La Follette. Even in a great cause at a moment of high emotion only a great leader of men can inspire such loyalty.

Perhaps there is no way that Wayne Morse, even in his finest hours, could hope to emulate La Follette as a recognized leader; for today there is no national or even sectional consensus on the need for a given program of reform that would unify the liberal reformers to move beyond the temperate, easy-does-it liberalism of the Kennedy administration. And, perhaps due to his preoccupation with scrapping, Morse has not revealed significant creative talent for fashioning uniquely new reforms in the La Follette tradition.

Wayne Morse might have done better on some old frontier, perhaps in the days of Clay or Calhoun when dueling was still in vogue; or even in La Follette's time when pistols were cached beneath an aggressive senator's long coattails.

But civilized conduct has evolved considerably since those days. Today a citizen's expectations of a public man compel more refined behavior—not less courage, not less willingness to fight the good fight; but greater rationality and temperance, greater tolerance and humility, greater forbearance and quiet creativity.

This may be the reason that the Senate today contains no armwaving Claghorn, a comedian's symbol of old fashioned flamboyance and bellicosity. This laughable figure has been elbowed into the past by the brisk young men of quiet action. Unlike their primitive political forebears, these men of the new Senate are more anxious to grapple calmly with the challenges of their day than to smite the air with oratorical thunderclaps.

Perhaps they are, by the La Follette-Morse code, half-a-loaf liberals. Nevertheless they must win public acceptance for that portion of the loaf they seek. Their success speaks for itself. It suggests that the sixties will require more than powerful oratory to advance new reforms.

Edmund Burke, that farsighted eighteenth-century British Parliamentarian, put it this way: "To construct is a matter of skill; to demolish, force and fury are sufficient."

Wayne Morse has been a vigorous demolition expert. But his reliance upon force and fury have limited his utility in constructing anew. Fury was common on the old frontiers, but the new frontiers severely limit its acceptance and its usefulness.

Yet his success in skillfully steering education legislation through the Senate marked a major advance in his effectiveness as an artisan in the legislative process. Perhaps this represented a discovery of lasting significance: that tough rhetoric, unsupported by legislative effectiveness, seldom moves the Senate or arouses the nation, particularly when it comes from any one whose reputation has been tarnished by intemperate affronts to contemporary codes of civility.

Perhaps it is because man now senses more keenly that he stands on the frontier of the spirit as well as the mind, that self-preservation is no longer an adequate rationalization of even intellectual or verbal brutality, that even the most liberal or idealistic ends do not justify cruel means.

Man is fearful, says theologian Paul Tillich, of losing his humanity and "of becoming a thing amongst the things he produces." Perhaps Jacqueline Kennedy's modern art will remind the politicians of this. For Tillich says, in *New Images of Man,* that "the works of art of our century are the mirrors of our predicament [in which] . . . the image of man became transformed, distorted, disrupted, and it finally disappeared."

The artists may mirror this predicament and the theologians may point the way toward the spiritual frontier. But it remains for the politicians to check rather than to fortify the "dehumanizing consequences of technical mass civilization."

Here stands the major challenge to conservatives and liberals alike. For man, caught in the clanking machinery of bigger business, bigger labor, bigger government, senses the awful puniness of his individuality. He fears he has been reduced to a series of holes in a faceless card that flashes through the gears and is gone.

If man is to retain his humanity, the new frontier of the spirit and mind will demand more, not fewer, true independents—men and women of wide-ranging thought, of creative power, with the courage to be unorthodox and the insight and humility to attain greater spiritual maturity.

Perhaps Wayne Morse, so well equipped for it in some ways, cannot or will not advance to this frontier. Certainly no man finds it easy, and many shrink from its demands.

Perhaps Wayne Morse is too threatened by the inner tiger of the self to advance, to attempt to love his enemies or even to tolerate disagreement with his friends and allies. But that is the code of the spiritual frontier.

The fundamental dilemma of Everyman plagues Everyman's senator. Can he continue to feed the tiger without ending up inside, wholly consumed by the self? Can he, dare he, face this most fearful and tireless enemy of selfless achievement?

The tiger of the old self, says Saint Paul, never dies; but he who seeks atonement with man and God is armed to drive it into the far hills of the soul. Only then is he released for selfless service.

Should Wayne Morse venture to subdue the tiger that lurks within, he challenges the toughest adversary of them all. But in this eternal struggle he would gain the good will of all who advance along the frontier of the spirit.

4